Governing after Crisis

The constant threat of crises such as disasters, riots and terrorist attacks poses a frightening challenge to western societies and governments. Although the causes and dynamics of these events have been widely studied, little is known about what happens following their containment and the restoration of stability. This volume explores "postcrisis politics", examining how crises give birth to longer-term dynamic processes of accountability and learning characterised by official investigations, blame games, political manoeuvering, media scrutiny and crisis exploitation. Drawing from a wide range of contemporary crises, including Hurricane Katrina, 9/11, the Madrid train bombings, the Walkerton water contamination, the destruction of the space shuttles *Challenger* and *Columbia* and the Boxing Day Asian tsunami, this groundbreaking volume addresses the longer-term impact of crisis-induced politics. Competing pressures for stability and change mean that policies, institutions and leaders may occasionally be uprooted but often survive largely intact. This volume explores why and under what conditions preservation trumps reform in the wake of crisis.

ARJEN BOIN is Director of the Stephenson Disaster Management and Public Administration Institute and Associate Professor of Public Administration at Louisiana State University.

ALLAN McCONNELL is Associate Professor (Public Policy) in the Department of Government and International Relations at the University of Sydney.

PAUL 't HART is Professor of Political Science, Research School of Social Sciences, Australian National University, and Professor of Public Administration, Utrecht School of Governance, Utrecht University.

Governing after Crisis

The Politics of Investigation, Accountability and Learning

Edited by

ARJEN BOIN
Louisiana State University

ALLAN McCONNELL
University of Sydney

PAUL 't HART
Australian National University and Utrecht University

CAMBRIDGE
UNIVERSITY PRESS

CAMBRIDGE UNIVERSITY PRESS
Cambridge, New York, Melbourne, Madrid, Cape Town, Singapore, São Paulo, Delhi

Cambridge University Press
The Edinburgh Building, Cambridge CB2 8RU, UK

Published in the United States of America by Cambridge University Press, New York

www.cambridge.org
Information on this title: www.cambridge.org/9780521885294

© Cambridge University Press 2008

First published 2008

Printed in the United States of America

A catalogue record for this publication is available from the British Library.

Library of Congress Cataloging in Publication Data

Governing after crisis : the politics of investigation, accountability and learning /
edited by Arjen Boin, Allan McConnell, Paul 't Hart.
        p.   cm.
    Includes bibliographical references and index.
    ISBN 978-0-521-88529-4 (hardback) — ISBN 978-0-521-71244-6 (pbk.)
  1. Crisis management in government.   2. Political leadership.   I. Boin, Arjen.
II. McConnell, Allan, 1957–.   III. Hart, Paul 't.
    JF1525.C74G68   2008
    353.9′5—dc22   2007041377

ISBN   978-0-521-88529-4 hardback
ISBN   978-0-521-71244-6 paperback

Dedicated to our children,
Charlotte, Désanne, Kim, Lalla, Naomi, Paul,
Sarah and Steven

"Too many are unprepared to handle crisis; still more are ignorant of postcrisis dynamics. This book allows us to understand the issues involved and to choose the appropriate roadmaps in the postevent phase. Do not miss these illuminating case studies: they could – tonight or tomorrow – tip the balance between fiasco and success".
– *Patrick Lagadec*
  Director of Research, École Polytechnique, Paris

"This volume laudably focuses on a relatively neglected topic, the specially political dimensions of crises and disasters. The authors also make a good case that political elites and organizations more than citizens have to be held accountable for their behavior, since they are the locus of precrisis policy decisions. Another worthwhile emphasis is on the differential effects of crisis management on politicians and public officials".
– *E. L. Quarantelli*
  Emeritus Professor of Sociology, University of Delaware

Contents

List of illustrations   page ix
List of tables   x
Contributors   xiii

Introduction

1 Governing after crisis   3
   Arjen Boin, Allan McConnell and Paul 't Hart

Part I   Crisis-induced accountability

2 Weathering the politics of responsibility and blame: the
   Bush administration and its response to Hurricane
   Katrina   33
   Thomas Preston

3 A reversal of fortune: blame games and framing contests
   after the 3/11 terrorist attacks in Madrid   62
   José A. Olmeda

4 Flood response and political survival: Gerhard Schröder
   and the 2002 Elbe flood in Germany   85
   Evelyn Bytzek

5 The politics of tsunami responses: comparing patterns of
   blame management in Scandinavia   114
   Annika Brändström, Sanneke Kuipers and Pär Daléus

6 Dutroux and dioxin: crisis investigations, elite
   accountability and institutional reform in Belgium   148
   Sofie Staelraeve and Paul 't Hart

Part II   Crisis-induced policy change and learning

7   The 1975 Stockholm embassy seizure: crisis and
    the absence of reform   183
    Dan Hansén

8   The Walkerton water tragedy and the Jerusalem banquet
    hall collapse: regulatory failure and policy change   208
    Robert Schwartz and Allan McConnell

9   Learning from crisis: NASA and the *Challenger* disaster   232
    Arjen Boin

10 September 11 and postcrisis investigation: exploring the
    role and impact of the 9/11 Commission   255
    Charles F. Parker and Sander Dekker

Conclusion

11 Conclusions: the politics of crisis exploitation   285
    Arjen Boin, Paul 't Hart and Allan McConnell

Index   317

Illustrations

3.1 Number of visits and pages of daily newspapers viewed
 on the Internet or TV/radio Web sites and day, March
 10–15, 2004   *page* 79
3.2 Symbiosis of new and old media for increasing
 oppositional frame resonance   80
3.3 Credibility – net evaluation of confidence in Prime
 Minister Aznar, 2000–2004   81
4.1 Total articles about the Elbe flood, 2002   96
4.2 Course of theme frequency   98
4.3 Framing of the Elbe flood, 2002   101
4.4 Course of government popularity during the Elbe
 flood, 2002   104
4.5 Time series analysis for western Germany   106
4.6 Time series analysis for eastern Germany   106
5.1 Constructing blame by framing political crises   120
11.1 Does blame management work? Leader behaviour and
 leaders' postcrisis fates   297

Tables

3.1 The frames of political actors   *page* 78
4.1 Crisis chronology   89
4.2 Classification scheme of the theme analysis   97
4.3 Classification scheme of the framing analysis   100
5.1 Tsunami crisis – similarities and differences in
    Scandinavian responses   124
5.2 Content analysis on the severity dimension   128
5.3 Content analysis on the agency dimension   131
5.4 Content analysis on attempts by actors to influence the
    temporal scope of accountability discussions   134
5.5 Content analysis on framing the event as incidental,
    nonrecurring or symptomatic/structural   135
5.6 Content analysis on the responsibility dimension   137
6.1 Context, process and impact of the Dutroux and dioxin
    crisis inquiries   171
7.1 Multiple streams, advocacy coalition framework
    and punctuated equilibrium in comparison   196
8.1 Strength of factors conducive to regulatory change
    in Walkerton and Jerusalem   220
8.2 Terrorism-related events in Israel during June 2001   226
11.1 Crisis outcomes: an overview   292
11.2 Crisis inquiries: a comparative overview   304

Appendices

4.1 Test statistics to augmented Dickey–Fuller and
    Phillips–Perron tests on stationarity of government
    popularity   111
4.2 Test statistics to augmented Dickey–Fuller and
    Phillips–Perron tests on stationarity of operational
    actions   112

4.3 Test statistics to augmented Dickey–Fuller and
    Phillips–Perron tests on stationarity of symbolic politics   112
4.4 Test statistics to augmented Dickey–Fuller and
    Phillips–Perron tests on stationarity of framing   113
4.5 Test statistics to augmented Dickey–Fuller and
    Phillips–Perron tests on stationarity of drama   113

Contributors

Arjen Boin Stephenson Disaster Management and Public Administration Institute, Louisiana State University

Annika Brändström Swedish Government, Office for Administrative Affairs and Department of Public Administration, Utrecht University

Evelyn Bytzek Institut für Politik und Gesellschafts Analyse

Pär Daléus CRISMART (Swedish National Defence College) and University of Stockholm

Sander Dekker Johann Wolfgang Goethe–Universität Frankfurt Hague City Council

Dan Hansén CRISMART (Swedish National Defence College), Utrecht School of Governance, Utrecht University

Paul 't Hart Research School of Social Sciences, Australian National University, and Utrecht School of Governance, Utrecht University

Sanneke Kuipers Department of Public Administration, Leiden University, and Crisisplan B.V., Leiden

Allan McConnell Department of Government and International Relations, University of Sydney

José A. Olmeda Spanish Open University, Madrid

Charles F. Parker Department of Government, Uppsala University

Thomas Preston Department of Political Science, Washington State University

Robert Schwartz Department of Public Health Sciences, University of Toronto

Sofie Staelraeve OCMW Kuurne, Belgium

Introduction

1 | Governing after crisis

ARJEN BOIN, ALLAN McCONNELL
AND PAUL 't HART

The politics of crisis management: an introduction

In all societies, life as usual is punctuated from time to time by critical episodes marked by a sense of threat and uncertainty that shatters people's understanding of the world around them. We refer to these episodes in terms of crisis.

Crises are triggered in a variety of ways; for example, by natural forces (earthquakes, hurricanes, torrential rains, ice storms, epidemics and the like) or by the deliberate acts of 'others' ('enemies') inside or outside that society (international conflict and war, terrorist attacks, large-scale disturbances). But they may also find their roots in malfunctions of a society's sociotechnical and political administrative systems (infrastructure breakdowns, industrial accidents, economic busts and political scandals).

Some crises affect communities as a whole (think of floods or volcanic eruptions), others directly threaten only a few members of the community, but their occurrence is widely publicised and evokes incomprehension, indignation or fear in many others (child pornography rings, police corruption, bombing campaigns). Yet the very occurrence of critical episodes casts doubt on the adequacy of the people, institutions and practices that are supposed to either prevent such destructive impacts from happening or mitigate the impact if they do hit.

We define 'crises' as episodic breakdowns of familiar symbolic frameworks that legitimate the pre-existing sociopolitical order ('t Hart 1993). In an anthropological sense, crises can be conceived of as bundles of real and present dangers, ills or evils that defy widely held beliefs that such things must not and cannot happen 'here'. Crises are by definition extraordinary in kind and/or scope, testing the resilience of a society and exposing the shortcomings of its leaders and public institutions (Drennan and McConnell 2007).

When a crisis pervades a community, it creates a relentless array of challenges for citizens and rulers alike. In this volume, we concentrate on the latter. Faced with a crisis, politicians and public officials have to deal with the immediate threat or damage inflicted, but they also have to come to terms with the vulnerabilities revealed and the public disaffection this may evoke. A list of recent crises – think of the 9/11 attacks, the Madrid and London bombings, the Asian tsunami and Hurricane Katrina – suggests how hard it can be to meet these challenges. Hitherto undiscovered or neglected drawbacks of existing institutions, policies and practices sometimes become painfully obvious. As a consequence, leaders and officials at all levels of government often struggle to cope.

Crises tend to cast long shadows on the polities in which they occur. Public officeholders face pressures from the media, the public, legislatures and sometimes the courts to recount how a crisis could have occurred, to account for their response, and to explain how they propose to deal with its impact. When the crisis in question is widely held to have been unforeseeable and uncontrollable, the amount of explaining and excusing they have to do is relatively limited. But when there is a widespread perception that the threat could have been foreseen and possibly avoided altogether, or that the official response after its occurrence was substandard, political leaders and officials may end up in troubled waters.

Indeed, many political leaders have seen their careers damaged if not terminated in the face of perceived failures in crisis management. Among twentieth-century UK prime ministers alone, Chamberlain, Eden and Callaghan all saw their periods in office cut short in the wake of crises they were alleged to have mismanaged. Yet crises may give birth to heroes as well as villains among public policy makers. The public reputations or political careers of some leaders have been bolstered by handling a crisis successfully (New York Mayor Rudolph Giuliani after 9/11 being the most noteworthy recent example) or deftly creating and politically exploiting one. An example of the latter is Australian Prime Minister John Howard's use of the 'children overboard crisis' during the 2001 Australian election campaign. It involved allegations by the PM and his advisors that asylum seekers headed for Australia had thrown their children from a vessel into the sea in order to force a rescue of the children and their parents. Howard's vilification of these individuals and the creation of a sense of crisis paved the way for his

Liberal Party's election victory and a tougher immigration policy (Marr and Wilkinson 2004).

The effects of crises on public policies and institutions display the same kind of variation. The events of 9/11 exacted a tragic human toll from the New York police and fire departments, but at the same time the many tales of selfless sacrifice and bravery spilled over into a strongly enhanced reputation of both agencies. By contrast, the CIA and other intelligence agencies were quickly criticised for not cooperating effectively in preventing the attacks. Some crises are followed – quite naturally it seems – by investigations and promises of reform aimed at improving policies and institutions that have proven vulnerable under pressure. The 9/11 attacks resulted in an overhaul of the U.S. intelligence sector and created a major ripple effect in security policy throughout most of the western world, which continues to this very day. Yet, as we shall see in this volume, the opposite may also occur: some crises are absorbed politically without major policy changes or reorganisations. Such cases merely confirm what many students of public administration and political science take as conventional wisdom: given the deep institutionalisation of rules, practices, budgets and communities of stakeholders, it is often extremely hard to change established policies and institutions radically – even if they fail miserably (cf. Lindblom 1959; Rose and Davies 1994; Wilsford 2001; Kuipers 2006).

How can these differences in outcome be explained? This volume inquires into precisely this issue and examines the political fates of public leaders, policies and institutions in the wake of crises. The main puzzle that occupies all its authors is that some crises have marked political consequences and trigger major policy or institutional changes, whereas others bolster the precrisis status quo. To explore these issues, the chapters in this book offer in-depth examinations of 'crisis politics' in a number of recent cases. In these cases, the political dimension of crisis management is present from the outset, but it continues to affect leaders, policies and institutions well after the operational phases of crisis management have ended.

Background and aims

Crises have been the subject of considerable academic study. Once a disjointed, segmented set of niches within the social sciences, such writings have expanded in volume and gained in coherence following major funding boosts in the wake of the 9/11 attacks.[1] By and large, comparative research has taught us how different types of crises incubate and escalate. It has identified the challenges they pose to governments and citizens and described how political-administrative elites respond to them.

The bulk of this research focuses on the managerial dimension of coping with crises: prevention and preparedness measures, critical decision making during emergency response operations, coordination of operational services, communication with the general public, and dealing with the mass media. It tends to concentrate on the functional challenges of adapting public organisations and networks to the extreme conditions that major emergencies impose. It has resulted in policy principles for risk assessment and contingency planning as well as in experiential rules and guidelines for designing and running command centres, fostering interorganisational collaboration, informing the public, and managing media relations.[2]

In contrast, the more strategic, political dimension of crisis management has received much less attention. Insofar as crisis studies deal with the broader political ramifications of crises, they tend to concentrate on the intergovernmental and interorganisational conflicts that often emerge in the course of large-scale, high-speed, high-stakes crisis response operations (Rosenthal et al. 1991; Schneider 1995). Much less research effort has been devoted in the crisis management literature to the wider impact of crises on political officeholders, governments and their policies (cf. Birkland 1997, 2004, 2006; Kurtz 2004).[3]

---

[1] A wide variety of sources exists. For a first overview of the subject, we recommend Brecher (1993); Rosenthal et al. (1989; 2001); George (1993); Farazmand (2001); Seeger et al. (2003); Boin et al. (2005) and Rodriguez et al. (2006).

[2] Most of the 'how to manage a crisis' texts are not specifically oriented to the public sector. They tend to be focused either on the private sector or are cross-sectoral. Examples include Coombs (1999); Fink (2002); Regester and Larkin (2002) and Curtin et al. (2005).

[3] Important exceptions include the social-psychological literature on collective trauma and posttraumatic stress; the sociological and development studies literatures on postdisaster reconstruction of stricken communities; urban planning literature on disaster recovery; and the emerging international relations literature on conflict termination and the implementation of peace agreements. Useful sources include Herman (1997); Pyszczynski et al. (2002); Fortna (2004); Wirth (2004); Neal (2005); Tumarkin (2005) and Vale and Campanella (2005).

This volume aims to redress this omission. It brings together a set of recent, high-profile crisis cases that in various ways directly challenged existing public policies and institutions as well as the careers of the politicians and public managers in charge of them. Each case chapter presents a particular analytical perspective on various aspects of the larger puzzle of crisis politics and probes its plausibility in applying it to the case(s) studied. Compared and synthesised in the final chapter, these various perspectives offer the beginnings of an analytical toolkit that may be used to understand the (differential) nature and impact of the politics of crisis management.

In pursuing these aims, this introductory chapter opens up the 'black box' of crisis politics. We do so by focusing on crisis-induced processes of accountability and learning. When public officeholders have to explain their actions and look toward the future in dialogue with public forums that have the capacity to significantly affect their own fortunes, they cannot help but confront, and try to shape, the political impact of a crisis. Their efforts in these venues are constrained by stakeholders and opposition forces who seek support for their definition of the causes of crisis as well as their judgements on the effectiveness of the crisis response. It is in these forums that the politics of crisis plays out in full force, determining to a considerable degree the future of leaders, policies and institutions.

We proceed in this introductory chapter as follows. First, we discuss the distinct challenges that crises pose to political – administrative elites, public policies and institutions. We then explore the characteristics of crisis-induced accountability and learning processes, particularly their permeation by investigating, politicking, blaming and manoeuvering. We also identify a range of crisis outcomes with regard to the fates of political leaders, public policies and public institutions. Third, we identify a number of situational and contextual factors that, theory suggests, shape the course and outcomes of these crisis-induced processes. We end this chapter with a brief introduction to the case study chapters and an explanation of our selection of these cases.

Crisis-induced governance challenges

When we study societal responses to crises, we must differentiate between two levels of analysis. At the *operational level*, we find the people who directly experience and respond to a critical contingency:

emergency operators, middle-level public officials, expert advisers, victims and volunteers. At the *strategic level*, we find political and administrative officeholders (both inside and outside the 'core executive') who are expected to concentrate on the larger institutional, political and social ramifications of the crisis. This level also includes people and forums who are permanently engaged in critically scrutinising and influencing elite behaviour: parliamentarians, watchdog agencies, journalists and interest/lobby groups. The focus in this volume lies exclusively on the latter.

When they are confronted with crisis, public leaders and agencies face three distinct challenges. First, there is the actual emergency response: this has to come quickly, effectively and with due consideration for the often extremely complicated logistical, institutional and psychosocial conditions that prevail. This dimension of crisis management has received the bulk of the attention in the disaster and emergency management literatures, so we shall not discuss it any further (see e.g. Rosenthal et al. 1989, 2001; Rodríguez et al. 2006).

Second, in today's age of high-speed and global mass communication, a crisis necessitates immediate and comprehensive public information and communication activities. Simply put: governments need to tell people what is going on, what might happen next and what it means to them. Failure to do so in a timely and authoritative fashion opens up a Pandora's box of journalistic and web-based speculation, rumour, suspicion and allegations that can easily inflame public opinion and sour the political climate, even as emergency operations are still under way. Several case studies in this volume demonstrate how governments may lose – and other political stakeholders may gain – control of the 'definition of the situation'.

Third, perhaps the most daunting strategic challenges for public policy makers occur well after the immediate response operations have dwindled or settled into orderly patterns.[4] In the weeks and months (and occasionally even years) after the operational crisis response has subsided, public leaders may find themselves still preoccupied with managing the 'fallout' of the crisis: searching for resources to pay for damages, fighting judicial battles, coping with the onslaught of

---

[4] For an early statement, see Rosenthal et al. (1994). For further explorations, consult 't Hart and Boin (2001).

criticism that it has evoked, but also exploiting the possibilities a crisis offers. Several case studies in this volume focus on this third set of crisis-induced governance challenges.

Crises and politics

Crises have a way of becoming politicised rather quickly. Some actors perceive a threat to their ways of working, policies and legitimacy, yet others relish the prospect of change. Political, bureaucratic, economic and other special interests do not automatically pull together and give up their self-interest just because a crisis has occurred. They engage in a struggle to produce a dominant interpretation of the implications of the crisis. The sheer intensity of these struggles tends to produce unpredictable twists and turns in the crisis-induced fates of politicians, policies and institutions alike.

As stated, this politicisation tends to evolve around two core processes. One is accountability. This relates to officeholders rendering account (in public forums) of their actions prior to and following a crisis. Where these accounts are debated, judgement is passed and possible sanctions administered (Bovens 2007). The other is learning, defined here as the evaluation and redesigning of institutions, policies and practices with a view to improving their future fungibility (Rose and Davies 1994).

Accountability is mainly about looking back and judging the performance of people; lesson drawing is more about looking forward and improving the performance of structures and arrangements. Even though learning is thus logically distinct from accountability, they may overlap in political practice. Accountability forums such as parliaments often take an explicit interest in drawing lessons for the future.

The arenas in which accountability and learning play out offer stakeholders a wide variety of opportunities to gain support for their definition of the crisis (and their envisioned solutions). The dynamics of interactions in (and between) these venues determine to a large extent the fates of leaders, public policies and public institutions.

Accountability and learning are often, if only implicitly, viewed as mechanisms for social catharsis. In liberal societies based on principles of openness and democratic control of executive power, the practices and discourses of crisis-induced scrutiny and questioning are seen as a

crucial part of a recovery and healing process. Although this is sometimes clearly the case, many crises nevertheless linger on for years –
only to erupt once again in different guises.

Catharsis can thus prove elusive. The process of looking forward is
hindered because the process of looking back turns out to be inconclu-
sive and contested. This can happen in a variety of ways. The media
may sense that there is more to the story than has come out so far and
thus continue to dig around for new revelations. Official investigations
may extend the time frame, leading to protracted political uncertainty
and sometimes breeding further investigations. Also, political stalemates and bloodletting may prompt an atmosphere of enduring bitter-
ness, while victims and other stakeholders may go public (or go to the
courts) with allegations of government negligence or wrongdoing.

Crises do have dynamic potential to prompt change. By destabilising
the veracity and legitimacy of existing policies, goals and institutions
as well as threatening the security and rewards obtained by relevant
actors and stakeholders, they provide 'windows of opportunity' for
reform (Birkland 1997; Kingdon 2003). Crisis-induced reforms may
be a matter of intelligent reflection and experimentation resulting from
the embracing of new ideas. However, things can be much more pro-
saic. Change may be the product of sheer political necessity: embattled
policy makers under critical scrutiny after an extreme event forced to
make symbolic gestures. Likewise, policy change may occur when crises
prompt a shift in the balance of power between various coalitions of
stakeholders who are engaged in ongoing struggles about particular
policies and programs (Sabatier and Jenkins-Smith 1993).

Crisis does not produce politics in a linear fashion. In particular,
processes of accountability and learning do not automatically produce
societal and political consensus on the evaluation of the past or the
way forward. In crisis politics, we tend to find a spectrum of stances
and responses. At one end, there are those who categorically advocate
a change of leaders and policies. At the other end, we find leaders and
their supporters determined to ride out the storm as well as staunch
supporters of existing policies and institutions. Therefore an initial
consensus on the need for accountability and learning in the wake of
crisis is easily fractured by argument and debate over the specific forms
that accountability and learning processes should take.

In order to pave the way for the case studies in this book, we
now introduce the concepts of accountability and learning processes

in somewhat greater detail. We will not attempt here to provide a definitive account of the complexities and contradictions of crisis and postcrisis periods. Rather, we try to identify aspects of crisis-induced accountability and lesson-drawing processes that appear to affect in a significant manner the outcomes of a crisis.

Crisis-induced accountability: leaders and blame games

The concept of public accountability is subject to considerable debate about 'ideals' of public accountability and how accountability regimes operate in practice (Mulgan 2003). In liberal democracies, accountability regimes are designed to make political decision makers answerable for their actions to public forums. These forums possess certain powers – formal and informal – to interrogate, debate with and sanction political decision makers.[5] In the emotionally charged context of crisis-induced turmoil and grief, accountability is rarely a routine, ritualistic exercise, as it sometimes is for governments that enjoy stable majorities in otherwise peaceful and prosperous democracies. Typical accountability questions in crisis-induced politics include: What happened? Who and what caused this to happen? Who is responsible? Who should be sanctioned?

Such questions and the search for answers are typically played out through an array of official inquiries, investigative journalism, political 'dirt' digging, parliamentary questions, legal investigations, victim and family campaigns, as well as lobby group interventions. Scrutiny often calls into question long-standing policies, the working of public institutions and the performance of political and bureaucratic leaders.

We picture crisis-induced accountability processes as arenas in which politicians and stakeholders struggle over causes and blame ('t Hart 1993; Boin et al. 2005). The right to question, criticise and seek responses is part of the fabric of pluralistic, liberal democratic regimes. In this context, it is almost naïve to expect some kind of societal synergy amidst crisis-induced accountability processes. Given their positions, interests and ideas, all actors involved in accountability processes will use a variety of strategies to argue their case and apportion blame. We refer to this particular and rather pervasive characteristic in terms of the 'blame game' (Brändström and Kuipers 2003).

---

[5] These forums include parliaments, auditors, courts and mass media.

Although it has never been easy for leaders to deal with this scrutiny (and manage a crisis at the same time), several often-noted trends suggest that it may be getting harder. Three trends in particular have the potential to open the accountability arena to more stakeholders and complicate the prospects for leaders to emerge as winners from these blame games.

A first trend is the transformation of the media industry. The number of media representatives and the speed with which they bring their reports to their audiences has exploded since the 1980s and especially since the advent of the Internet. Some suggest that this increased competitiveness has fueled a more aggressive approach toward public leaders (Sabato 2000). The upshot of these developments is that crisis response and crisis politics have almost become prime television events in and of themselves. This does little to prevent their politicisation in terms of a 'heroes and villains' morality tale (Wagner-Pacifici 1986).

A second trend consists of the changing attitudes of the modern citizen. Despite the array of public sector institutions and policies focused on regulating risks and promoting safety and well-being, citizens appear more fearful than ever before (Clarke 2005; Furedi 2005). The visibility in the modern media of crises and tragedy from around the globe (beamed into our living rooms and readily accessed from our PCs), coupled with the newsworthiness of the 'discourse of fear' (Altheide 2002), has heightened anxiety and feelings of vulnerability. The modern citizen has less tolerance of glitches and failure – they remind him or her that worse may be to come. Leaders engaged in the tough task of managing risk and responding to crises are less liable to be praised when they perform well and more liable to be vilified when mistakes are made (Bovens and 't Hart 1996; Beck 1999).

A third trend is the strengthened position of citizens and families affected by crises and disaster. The availability of the Internet, coupled with the newsworthiness of long-term interrogation of government, offers previously marginal citizens' groups more opportunities to keep the memory of the events and the issues they raised alive and in the public realm (Cohen 2001; Edkins 2003; Attwood 2005; Kofman–Bos et al. 2005). Victims' associations often turn out to be tenacious and resourceful lobbyists for influence over crisis-induced policy-making processes and decisions. These voices add to the general crisis-induced clamour for political accountability and fuel arguments that leaders should atone for mistakes made, change policies or, in extreme cases, relinquish political office.

Crises and the fates of political leaders

One of the most interesting and enduring features of crisis-induced accountability politics is that the line between political winners and losers is such a fine one. In this book, we seek to explore why some leaders end up on the 'good' side whereas others find their career terminated by a crisis. We may, in fact, recognise three distinct outcomes for leaders.

First, there is *elite reinvigoration*. Leaders find their electoral position and general stature enhanced after a crisis, either because they and their governments are seen to have done well prior to and during the crisis or because they accept, in a timely and graceful fashion, responsibility for mistakes made.

Second, there is *elite damage*. A crisis and its aftermath may undermine political credibility and cause a downturn in political fortunes (or even a complete downfall). Examples of political casualties are many, including French Defence Minister Charles Hernu after his role in the attack on Greenpeace's *Rainbow Warrior* and North Ossetian Interior Minister Kazbek Dzantiev after the Beslan school siege. On an even grander scale, the entire Dutch government resigned in 2002 after a report stating that the government could have done more to prevent the slaughter by Serb forces of over 7500 adults and children in the UN safe haven of Srebrenica.

A final outcome is *elite escape*, where the crisis makes little or no immediate difference, melting into a complex world of other, more salient issues. In recent years, for example, Australian Prime Minister John Howard has managed to emerge unscathed in opinion polls and electoral contests from a string of crises focused around his government's policies on refugees, immigration and detention. Whether leaders can permanently escape damage remains to be seen. In some cases, their crisis performance is later reassessed in light of new failures.

Crisis-induced learning: rhetoric, policies and institutions

The aftermath of most crises is rife with the rhetoric of learning (Drennan and McConnell 2007). Crises tend to expose political and societal shortcomings, so these episodes typically evoke a widely felt determination to do better in the future: 'we must ensure that this does not happen again'. Lessons must be formulated and implemented, most people would agree. However, both the formulation and the bureaucratic implementation of crisis lessons tend to be highly problematic.

Organisations are typically bad learners (Stern 1997), but some manage to do well. So-called high-reliability organisations (HROs) have a particularly well-developed capacity for lesson drawing. In these organisations, matters of security and safety are either the number one priority or part of the raison d'être of the organisation (LaPorte 1996; Weick and Sutcliffe 2001). Their systems and cultures are ingrained with the preemption of errors, systematic adjustments, learning in the event of tragedy and a deeper 'deuterolearning' (i.e. learning how to learn) (Argyris and Schön 1996). These organisations have both the capacity to 'puzzle' (find out what went wrong, work out what new initiatives are required) and the capacity to 'power' (bring about change) (Boin et al. 2005). Alas, most public organisations do not qualify as HROs.

Most learning prompted by crisis may actually occur outside organisational walls.[6] One would expect political learning to get to the heart of 'what went wrong' and to ensure that 'the facts' become available to inform decisions about what should be done in order to ensure that a similar crisis does not happen again (or if it does, we are better prepared and better able to manage it). The outcome should (in theory) clear up mystery and speculation surrounding the crisis, replacing them with impartiality and rigour. One would expect political investigators to draw on science and the law where relevant – epitomes of impartiality and modernity (Giddens 1990).

Some investigations and reports have been well respected and have been able to uncover credible and substantial information regarding the causes and handling of crises. They have been accompanied by sensible recommendations for improvement (e.g. the Scarman report of the 1981 Brixton riots, the McClellan inquiry into the 1998 Sydney water crisis and Lord Justice Taylor's report on the 1989 Hillsborough disaster) and various investigations into 'creeping crises', such as miscarriages of justice involving the 'Guildford Four', the 'Birmingham

---

[6] Then there are purpose-built organisations, such as the U.S. Transportation Board, which exist to examine the causes of crises in their policy domain.

Six' and aboriginal deaths in custody in Australia. One of the best examples may be the 9/11 report (Parker and Dekker, this volume).

Such celebrated investigations are, however, hardly the norm. In fact, crises rarely give rise to clear lessons that are at the same time widely supported by all relevant policy makers and stakeholders. Rather, the complex relationships between societal, organisational and individual factors that are said to have produced a crisis – whether framed as a tragedy, scandal, fiasco or a mere 'incident' – are often disputed (Bovens and 't Hart 1996; Thompson 2000; Butler and Drakeford 2003; Garrard and Newell 2006). Disputes and manoeuvring typically come to the fore in investigative forums and lesson-drawing exercises.

Complexity is added when we consider that 'more' learning is not always better learning. A surfeit of inquiries may inhibit learning because it allows competing coalitions to converge around a particular inquiry that most accords with their own views. In the *Exxon Valdez* case, for example, aspects of the disaster were investigated by fifteen Congressional committees and subcommittees (Kurtz 2004). Likewise, the garbled response to the crash of a Dutch military plane at an airport base in Eindhoven in 1996 triggered thirteen official investigations and multiple court proceedings (Rijpma and Van Duin 2001).

Whereas many stakeholders have the luxury of being outside government and can argue forthrightly for policy reforms and organisational changes, government and policy makers are rarely in the position to do so. They are typically stuck between competing imperatives in a 'mission impossible' (Boin and 't Hart 2003). On the one hand, there is the imperative to 'do something' and show willingness to learn through initiation of reforms that will make society better prepared to anticipate, mitigate and cope with crisis in the future. On the other, there is the imperative to reassure that, in essence, the system as it stands (and for which they carry responsibility) is robust.

This perennial tension between restoration and reform looms large during the aftermath of most crises. The political language of leaders tends to emphasise thorough inquiry, the need to learn lessons and the necessity of renewal. In practice, however, these same leaders lean heavily towards the status quo. After 9/11, President George W. Bush promised that every possible lesson would be learned, yet in practice he attempted to thwart the establishing of the inquiry and then the investigation itself (Parker and Dekker, this volume).

Crisis and the fates of policies and institutions

Processes of learning unleashed by crisis can have different impacts. They may lead to mere fine-tuning of current policies. They may, in contrast, produce sweeping changes to programs and organisations. Or they may alter nothing at all. Some sweeping changes announced in the wake of a crisis prove to be all rhetoric and no follow-up, while others have enduring effects on rules, practices and the commitment of public resources (March and Olsen 1975). The rhetoric of reform may dominate the limelight of media coverage and political debate while the 'real learning' takes place in the professional realm – even if it proceeds at a much slower pace than the rhetoric suggests (Van Duin 1992; Lodge and Hood 2002).

We discern three ways in which to characterise the effects of crises on pre-existing policies and institutions. Our approach is inspired by a number of typologies that disaggregate reform into degrees of change rather than conceiving it as a one-dimensional phenomenon (cf. Hall 1993; Sabatier and Jenkins-Smith 1993; Rose and Davies 1994). There is considerable commonality in these approaches, and we aim at parsimony and sharpening the focus in terms of crisis and disaster.[7] These three categories involve an element of subjectivity. A value judgement will always be required on the significance of any particular change. Nevertheless, the categories are sufficiently broad and differentiated enough to make robust judgements on where each of our cases can be located.

Fine tuning is the instrumental and incremental adaptation of policies and practices without any challenge to core political values. In this volume, we will see several cases of postcrisis change being limited essentially to modest adaptations of policy, procedures and practices (such as NASA after the *Challenger* disaster and Swedish counterterrorism preparedness after the Stockholm embassy seizure).

---

[7] We do not include here the Rose and Davies (1994) contention that symbolic gestures to change (without any procedural or policy change) can have a pacifying effect and alter people's perception of the 'problem'. Such attempts at societal reassurance are indeed an integral part of crisis management (Edelman 1977; 't Hart 1993), but our interest here is primarily on the extent to which policies, procedures and institutions become reformed in response to crisis and disaster.

Policy reform occurs when important policy principles and institutional values, which are difficult to change under normal circumstances, become subject to fundamental adaptation. In this book, an example of crisis-induced reform is the aftermath of the Dutroux crisis in Belgium, which brought structural redesign of a criminal justice sector that had long defied such efforts (Staelraeve and 't Hart, this volume).

Finally, a *paradigm shift* occurs when entire policies, organisations or even fundamental normative aspects of a political system become subject to abdication. However, such occurrences are rare. A classic example is Britain's near bankruptcy in 1976, which led to a jettisoning of long-held Keynesian beliefs and policies (commitment to full employment, public expenditures as a means of avoiding recession). The new paradigm featured 'monetarism', public sector cutbacks and the seeds of free market change (Hall 1993). A potentially classic case may be – again – the 9/11 crisis, which has brought an entirely new concept of homeland security. Ironically, the failings of FEMA in its response to Hurricane Katrina have proved a challenge to this fledgling paradigm.

Crisis politics and crisis outcomes

In this book, we view crises through the lens of politics. We explore the political dimensions of crises, which begin at the acute phase but spill over into the postcrisis aftermath. We study how crisis politics – the cogitation of competing definitions or frames on what happened prior to and during a crisis and what this means for officeholders and governance patterns alike – creates new 'futures' for a society and its leaders.

To a certain extent, *strategies* of blaming and framing play an important role in shaping the aftermath of crises (Brändström and Kuipers 2003). Actors may seek to (1) depict an event as a violation (or otherwise) of core values, (2) portray the crisis as a stand-alone disturbance or one that is symptomatic of deeper policy/systemic failure and (3) construct blame as being concentrated with certain actors or dispersed among a complex network of actors. Indeed, the growth throughout the western world of agencies positioned at 'arm's length' to national government has made the blame game somewhat easier for politicians, allowing for a structural hiving off of responsibility and blame (Flinders and Smith 1999).

Political elites can use a variety of tools and techniques to shape the debate (Elliot and McGuiness 2002; Toft and Reynolds 2005). These include:

- Avoiding a public inquiry
- Restricting the terms of reference of an inquiry
- Choosing a chairperson and members with views sympathetic to the government
- Refusing to give evidence; refusing to divulge certain information or giving evidence only under certain conditions
- Intervening to discredit an ongoing investigation
- Using official statistics to retrospectively downplay the impact of a crisis
- Utilising and strengthening existing procedures and norms in order to suppress criticism

Such strategies are not guaranteed to work in favour of the elites who deploy them. Much depends on how the nature and implications of crises become framed in public and professional debates. Much also depends on which potential lessons attract the support of powerful coalitions inside and outside government and which do not. The battle over crisis frames unfolds in the arenas in which learning and account-ability take place. In a liberal democracy, many actors can join this battle. Those who manage to gain the most support for their definition of the situation and the solutions that accompany it will have the most leverage in determining the fate of political leaders, public policies and public institutions.

Situational and contextual factors

Crisis-induced accountability and learning processes, coupled with elite strategies, do not play out in a vacuum. Crises occur in sociohistorical *situations* that can enable but more often than not limit the scope for elite manoeuvring and constrain the ability to frame the depth of the crisis, its causes, who or what should be blamed and longer-term implications.

We detect two situational factors of particular importance. First, the *scope and nature of the crisis* plays a role. Crises do not arrive in exactly the same way nor do they have the same resonance. Some types of crises may provide more room for stakeholders to forward an alternative frame than others. Each crisis may therefore be expected to cast a different shadow on the polity in which it occurs. In this book, we distinguish three crisis types (Boin et al. 2005).

Incomprehensible crises are in a class of their own and have frame-breaking qualities (such as 9/11, the Asian tsunami or the devastation of New Orleans by Hurricane Katrina). In such cases, sheer bewilderment leaves considerable political space for actors to frame the crisis in particular ways. *Mismanaged crises* are characterised by failures (actual and alleged) within governmental/bureaucratic machines. They can raise the stakes because they act as a magnet for all those media, party political and other interests who seek to capitalise on the opportunity to expose (apparent) weaknesses in the legitimacy or capacities of political elites and senior public officials. *Agenda-setting crises* 'hit a nerve' and expose wider social vulnerabilities and fears (the 1968 student riots in Paris, 1979 nuclear accident at Three Mile Island, 1981 Brixton riots in London). Typically, they lead to reflexes and reflections beyond the specific incident itself to a questioning of the vulnerability of an entire policy domain and beyond (Three Mile Island, for example, opened up a wider debate on U.S. reliance on nuclear power).

In crises where it is immediately obvious that exogenous factors play a pivotal part (e.g. volcanic eruptions, earthquakes, mudslides, floods and tsunamis; or foreign hooligans, radical demonstrators and terrorists), it is relatively easy for government actors to make authoritative statements about what happened and why. However, for crises where it appears that endogenous factors such as operator errors, political negligence, and organisational rule bending have been at work (e.g. technological accidents such as Bhopal, space shuttle *Challenger*, Chernobyl and prison riots), governments will find it harder to allay public doubts, which may create an interpretive vacuum for other, often critical voices to fill (see Staelraeve and 't Hart, this volume).

Second, the *historic record* of leaders, policies and institutions must play a role. A firm body of theoretical and empirical findings supports the claim that public policies and time-honoured institutions tend to be change-resistant. Over time, their proven worth has turned them into receptacles of resources (funding, support, trust). Even if a crisis demonstrates their 'unfitness' in the face of new threats, many stakeholders will not find it easy to divest. In a similar vein, we may assume that a proven track record can provide leaders with a 'credit line' that protects them, at least to some degree, from the impact of opposition criticism in the wake of crisis.

Contextual factors impinge upon postcrisis politics as well. Of particular importance is the *timing* of crises and the way in which they disturb ongoing patterns of governance, politics and organisational life. For example, a crisis may hit at a crucial point in the electoral cycle, such as immediately after an election, when a new leader is enjoying a 'honeymoon' period that may enable him or her to use the crisis as an opportunity to assert authority, galvanise support and appear statesmanlike. However, if a crisis appears just prior to an election (Staelraeve and 't Hart; Olmeda, this volume), the stakes are higher. Politicisation and an intensification of blame games seem increasingly likely as a result.

Timing may also be crucial in terms of the point in leadership careers or a government's wider societal and party standing when a crisis hits (Drennan and McConnell 2007). A prime minister, president or premier whose position as party leader is vulnerable because of a lack of support or even the threat of support being withdrawn, is likely to find his or her vulnerability heightened when a crisis hits. Amid questioning of causes, response and longer-term implications, a crisis allows internal party critics to challenge the leader's fitness to lead the party. Irish Taoiseach (prime minister) Charles Haughey and British Prime Minister Margaret Thatcher both lost office as a consequence of dwindling party support coupled with crisis (financial and wire tapping for Haughey and the poll tax for Thatcher), which prompted leadership challenges. Likewise, if support for a governing party is declining in opinion polls and among influential stakeholders, a crisis may accelerate the problems for leaders because it provides political space for critics to raise serious questions about fitness to govern. In 2003, when severe acute respiratory syndrome (SARS) arrived in Hong Kong, the government was already weak and the subject of popular protests. Its SARS response evoked heavy criticism in an inquiry set up by the Hong Kong Legislative Council. Only a few days after the report was published in July 2004, Health Minister Yeoh Eng-Kiong resigned – a sacrificial move intended to ease wider public discontent.

The opposite also applies. If a crisis hits at a time when a leader or government has strong support, incumbents are less liable to come under attack and may be able to exploit the crisis to their advantage. The incoming Australian Labor government led by Bob Hawke was able to exploit news about a budget deficit blowout on the eve of its election into office to dramatise the outgoing Liberal government's economic mismanagement and political untrustworthiness (by hiding the figures during the campaign) and gain political space to renege on some of its campaign promises (Goldfinch and 't Hart 2003).

The *mass media* constitutes an additional contextual factor. Apart from the changes in the media landscape (noted above), it is clear that the media are part and parcel of the crisis aftermath. They provide the venue, without which postcrisis political contestation, crisis exploitation and blame gaming could not occur (cf. Baumgartner and Jones 1993). Media reports echo and sometimes amplify or cast serious doubts upon the 'crisis frames' that political leaders, public executives and other stakeholders defend. Their neutrality is often doubted, sometimes justifiably so. Investigative reporting or editorial agendas can easily become a crisis catalyst. When public attention is squarely focused on the crisis story, media reporting can hurt and boost political and bureaucratic reputations, particularly if the various competing media organisations tell more or less the same story and voice the same opinions.

These are merely provisional conjectures. They are derived from the literature on policy and institutional reform and the voluminous body of leadership research. How these factors play out in times of crises (and their aftermaths) remains to be studied, which is exactly what we will do in the remainder of this volume – examining case studies to explore the role of these and possibly alternative factors that shape the course and outcomes of crisis politics.

This volume: design and overview

This volume seeks to enhance our understanding of crisis-induced politics in terms of leadership fates, policy change and institutional adaptation. The case studies explore how these fates play out in a variety of contexts. In this final section, we introduce the cases of this book. The case authors were free to choose which particular aspects of crisis and postcrisis politics to focus on and to employ any analytical perspective they deemed suitable as long as they explicitly addressed the core objective of this volume: to elucidate crisis-induced political processes of accountability and learning and their impact on leaders, public policies and institutions.

We introduced different logics of comparison throughout the volume. First, we explicitly selected the authors because their work entailed (pairwise or trichotomous) case comparison within the space of their own chapters. These comparisons are designed to highlight and explain analytically salient similarities and differences in crisis-induced accountability and learning processes (as explained further below). Second, we have paired various chapters to exploit the comparative potential they entailed (i.e. by addressing similar aspects of crisis politics in different national or situational contexts). In the final chapter, we shall revisit both types of comparisons set up throughout this volume, and extract their analytical yield.

Part I of this volume contains case studies of *crisis-induced accountability processes*. The case studies in this part show how public leaders have been held to account following crises, how they behave in that process and the political implications which crisis-induced accountability has had for them and their governments. It starts with three linked chapters.

Chapter 2 by Thomas Preston deals with the Bush administration's response to Hurricane Katrina. He focuses particularly on Bush's handling of the mounting criticism of the allegedly inadequate prevention, preparedness and response policies of governments at all levels, including the president himself. Preston employs his pre-existing theory (Preston 2001) about presidential leadership style to explain the nature – and weaknesses – of the management by the Bush administration of the political fallout created by this disaster.

Next are two cases where, just as in the Katrina case, the accountability process starts and intensifies not after but in parallel to the operational response to the crisis. However, in contrast to the U.S. case, in these two cases the nexus between crisis politics and electoral politics is immediate and direct, given the fact that both critical episodes occurred shortly before national parliamentary elections were held.

Chapter 3, by José Olmeda, examines the immediate aftermath of the Madrid bombings (March 2004), when Prime Minister José María Aznar's blaming of Basque terrorist group ETA backfired on his party just a few days before national elections. Amid a welter of blaming and counter-blaming, Aznar's actions helped create an opportunity for the Spanish Socialist Party opposition to score a wholly unexpected victory. Olmeda explains this remarkable outcome by conceptualising the crisis as a 'framing contest' between politically opposed groups, both seeking to shape public images of the event in ways that suited their political needs. Olmeda argues that the credibility of the government's account was effectively undermined by a combination of its own rigid insistence on its version in the face of mounting evidence from the operational level that alternative scenarios (Al-Qaeda) were getting more likely by the hour and its critics' energetic dramatisation of a 'counterframe' through the contemporary tool of 'flash mobs' (cf. Tarrow 1994).

Chapter 4, by Evelyn Bytzek, provides a neat contrast to both the Katrina and Madrid cases by examining the aftermath of the 2002 Elbe floods in Germany, where Chancellor Gerhard Schröder's Social Democratic Party was rescued from electoral defeat partly as a result of his pre-eminence in the media in relation to his role as (symbolic) leader of the national crisis response. This remarkable turnaround effect – in the midst of an acute crisis the incumbent government comes back from behind in the polls to survive an election, with the opposite occurring in Madrid – was all the more noteworthy because disaster prevention and management in Germany's federal system are largely a responsibility of the states. Bytzek argues that it was not so much the operational ability of the Schröder government to 'do the right thing' in response to the crisis that made the difference. Rather it was its 'symbolic management' of the crisis – Schröder's statesmanlike demeanour and timely on-site visits. In this lies also the main contrast with Bush's political mismanagement of the Katrina crisis. Schröder did what Bush should have done, and reaped the rewards. We may speculate that Bush escaped electoral punishment only because Katrina came after rather than just before his re-election campaign.

The next two chapters are both comparative in their own right. They were designed to probe further into factors that may account for similarities and differences in crisis-induced accountability processes and their impact on leaders and governments. In Chapter 5, Annika Brändström, Sanneke Kuipers and Pär Daléus examine the aftermath of the 2004 Boxing Day tsunami in Asia, concentrating on the experiences of Sweden, Finland and Norway. The differences between the cases are revealing. Three countries whose overall political structure and culture are highly similar and who were confronted with one and the same disaster, produced divergent outcomes. Swedish political elites got caught up in a spiral of intensive criticism from the media and citizens (this criticism has since claimed various political and bureaucratic careers), whereas their Finnish and Norwegian counterparts fared much better. The chapter documents these differences and suggests that they were due mostly to the variety of postures adopted by the responsible ministers vis-à-vis critical media and inquisitive parliaments.

In Chapter 6, Sofie Staelraeve and Paul 't Hart focus on two Belgian parliamentary crisis investigations. These investigations dealt with the dioxin contamination in foodstuffs and a failure to capture the serial paedophile and child killer Marc Dutroux. The authors examine the design, conduct and impact of the two commissions of inquiry that were set up in response to these crises. Again, the tale is one of differences between cases that could have been expected to show similarities. Therefore, by way of contrast to the chapter by Brändström et al., Staelraeve and 't Hart argue that differences can be accounted for by the political context and timing of both inquiries, and indeed the (implicit but nevertheless strong) link between them. Elite behaviour was largely predisposed by the path-dependent nature and political timing of both crises. Consequently, semantic and symbolic room for manoeuvre was far more constrained than in the Scandinavian cases.

Part II of the volume contains case studies that focus principally on *crisis-induced dynamics of policy change and learning*. As we have argued above, a common line of thought is that crises are conducive to change: policy innovation and institutional reform. The first case study in this part finds exactly the opposite: a crisis that was not followed by significant change. Chapter 7, by Dan Hansén, analyses the political aftermath of the 1975 Stockholm embassy seizure. Using contemporary theories of policy dynamics he explains the apparent anomaly his case study throws up: an unprecedented terror event in Sweden, which, nevertheless, did not result in a major push forward or significant change in its hitherto embryonic and laconic counter-terrorism policy.

In Chapter 8, the theme of understanding the selective policy impact of crises is further analysed in a cross-national comparative case study by Robert Schwartz and Allan McConnell. They contrast the 2000 Walkerton (Ontario) water contamination crisis with the Jerusalem banquet hall collapse in 2001. The common denominator in the two cases is that in both instances, regulatory failure was identified in post-crisis inquiries as being a major causal factor in the crisis.

In Ontario, however, the eventual outcome was major regulatory reform, whereas such reform remained notably absent in the Israeli case. Schwartz and McConnell contrast and discuss these outcomes, placing particular emphasis on the contextual aspects of politics and culture in Canada and Israel.

The last two chapters deal with the politics of learning in the wake of truly traumatic and paradigm-shattering crises in the United States. In Chapter 9, Arjen Boin examines the long aftermath of the 1986 space shuttle *Challenger* disaster and NASA's ability to learn while balancing engineering philosophies with intuitive judgements on risk and safety. The *Columbia* disaster in 2003 and the subsequent investigation was a tragic test of NASA's learning capacity. Boin's analysis is particularly noteworthy for its challenging of the *Challenger* investigation by the Rogers Commission and the mismatch between its findings of 'what went wrong' and the recommendations it made.

Chapter 10, by Charles Parker and Sander Dekker, examines the aftermath of 9/11, perhaps the most shocking and unexpected experience in the western world since the Second World War. Their focus on the origins, politics and investigations of the 9/11 Commission and its major contribution tells us something beyond 9/11 itself – about the factors that determine the ability of crisis commissions to perform a symbolic galvanising function that is strong enough to overcome the forces of inertia and realpolitik, highlighted in the chapters by Hansén and Schwartz and McConnell.

The final chapter of this volume revisits the findings of the various case study clusters and reveals how crises cast their shadows over political systems. It shows that crisis investigators – whether parliamentarians, ad hoc commissions or institutionalised agencies – have exceptionally difficult tasks as they seek to apportion culpability and learn lessons. They must juggle a set of logistical, methodological and philosophical problems, yet facilitate societal 'closure' of the crisis by producing an authoritative account of it. Underneath, politics as usual is omnipresent, shaping and being shaped by these very investigations as well as other accountability processes (such as criminal investigations and court proceedings). We conclude the volume by offering a number of tentative propositions about the nature and significance of crisis-induced politics for further, more systematic study. Moreover, we suggest that while political actors inside and outside government are now acutely aware of the capacity of crises to alter political careers, policy trajectories and institutional orders, political scientists would be wise to complement their traditional focus on governance and democracy 'as usual' with a rigorous probing of the politics of extreme events that 'punctuate' the normal rhythms of political life. We hope that this volume proves a modest step in this direction.

References

Altheide, D. L. 2002. Creating fear: News and the construction of crisis. Hawthorne, NY: Aldine De Gruyter.

Argyris, C., and Schön, D. A. 1996. Organisational learning II: theory, method and practice. Reading, PA: Addison-Wesley.

Attwood, B. 2005. Telling the truth about aboriginal history. Crows Nest. Sydney: Allen and Unwin.

Baumgartner, F. R. and Jones, B. D. 1993. agendas and instability in American politics. Chicago: University of Chicago Press.

Beck, U. 1999. World risk society. Cambridge, UK: Polity Press.

Birkland, T. A. 1997. After disaster: agenda setting, public policy, and focusing events. Washington, DC: Georgetown University Press.

Birkland, T. A. 2004. The world changed today: agenda-setting and policy change in the wake of the September 11 terrorist attacks. Review of Policy Research 21(2):179–200.

Birkland, T. A. 2006. Lessons of disaster: policy change after catastrophic events. Washington, DC: Georgetown University Press.

Boin, A., and 't Hart, P. 2003. Public leadership in times of crisis: mission impossible? Public Administration Review 63(5):544–53.

Boin, A., 't Hart, P., Stern, E. and Sundelius, B. 2005. The politics of crisis management: public leadership under pressure. Cambridge, UK: Cambridge University Press.

Bovens, M. 2007. Analysing and assessing accountability: a conceptual framework. European Law Journal 13(4): 447–68.

Bovens, M., and 't Hart, P. 1996. understanding policy fiascoes. New Brunswick, NJ: Transaction.

Brändström, A., and Kuipers, S. 2003. From 'normal incidents' to political crises: understanding the selective politicization of policy failures. Government and Opposition 38(3):279–305.

Brecher, M. 1993. Crises in world politics: theory and reality. Oxford, UK: Pergamon Press.

Butler, I., and Drakeford, M. 2003. Social policy, social welfare and scandal: how British public policy is made. Basingstoke, UK: Palgrave Macmillan.

Clarke, L. 2005. Worst cases: terror and catastrophe in the popular imagination. Chicago: University of Chicago Press.

Cohen, S. 2001. States of denial: knowing about atrocities and suffering. Cambridge, UK: Polity Press.

Coombs, W. T. 1999. Ongoing crisis communication: planning, managing and responding. Thousand Oaks, CA: Sage.

Curtin, T., Hayman, D. and Husein, N. 2005. Managing crisis: a practical guide. Basingstoke, UK: Palgrave Macmillan.

Drennan, L. T., and McConnell, A. 2007. Risk and crisis management in the public sector. Abingdon, UK: Routledge.

Edelman, M. 1977. Political language: words that succeed and policies that fail. New York: Academic Press.

Edkins, J. 2003. Trauma and the memory of politics. Cambridge, UK: Cambridge University Press.

Elliot, D., and McGuiness, M. 2002. Public inquiry: panacea or placebo? Journal of Contingencies and Crisis Management 10(1):14–25.

Farazmand, A. (ed.) 2001. Handbook of crisis and emergency management. New York: Marcel Dekker.

Fink, S. 2002. Crisis management: planning for the inevitable. Lincoln, NE: iUniverse.

Flinders, M. V., and Smith, M. J. (eds.) 1999. Quangos, accountability and reform. Basingstokes, UK: Palgrave Macmillan.

Fortna, V. P. 2004. Peace time: cease-fire agreements and the durability of peace. Princeton, NJ: Princeton University Press.

Furedi, F. 2005. Politics of fear: beyond left and right. London: Continuum.

Garrard, J., and Newell, J. L. (eds.) 2006. Scandals in past and contemporary politics. Manchester, UK: Manchester University Press.

George, A. L. (ed.) 1993. Avoiding war: problems of crisis management. Boulder, CO: Westview Press.

Giddens, A. 1990. The consequences of modernity. Stanford, CA: Stanford University Press.

Goldfinch, S., and 't Hart, P. 2003. Leadership and institutional reform: engineering macroeconomic policy change in Australia. Governance 16(2):235–70.

Hall, P. 1993. Policy paradigms, social learning, and the state: the case of economic policymaking in Britain. Comparative Politics 25(3):275–96.

't Hart, P. 1993. Symbols, rituals and power: the lost dimension in crisis management. Journal of Contingencies and Crisis Management 1(1):36–50.

't Hart, P., and Boin, A. 2001. Between crisis and normalcy: the long shadow of post-crisis politics. In Rosenthal, U., Boin, R. A. and Comfort, L. K.

(eds.) Managing crises: threats, dilemmas and opportunities. Springfield, IL: Charles C. Thomas, pp. 28–46.

Herman, J. 1997. Trauma and recovery: the aftermath of violence – from domestic abuse to political terror. New York: Basic Books.

Kingdon, J. 2003. Agendas, alternatives and public policies, 2nd edn. New York: Longman.

Kofman-Bos, C., Ullberg, S. and 't Hart, P. 2005. The long shadow of disaster: memory and politics in Holland and Sweden. International Journal of Mass Emergencies and Disasters 23(1):5–26.

Kuipers, S. 2006. The crisis imperative: crisis rhetoric and welfare state reform in Belgium and the Netherlands in the early 1990s. Amsterdam: Amsterdam University Press.

Kurtz, R. S. 2004. Coastal oil pollution: spills, crisis and policy change. Review of Policy Research 21(2):201–19.

LaPorte, T. 1996. High reliability organisations: unlikely, demanding and at risk. Journal of Contingencies and Crisis Management 4(2):60–71.

Lindblom, C. E. 1959. The science of 'muddling through'. Public Administration Review XIX(2):79–88.

Lodge, M., and Hood, C. 2002. Pavlovian policy responses to media feeding frenzies? Dangerous dogs regulation in comparative perspective. Journal of Contingencies and Crisis Management 10(1):1–13.

March, J. G., and Olson, J. P. 1975. The uncertainty of the past: organizational learning under ambiguity. European Journal of Political Research 3:147–71.

Marr, D., and Wilkinson, M. 2004. Dark victory. Crow's Nest, Sydney: Allen & Unwin.

Mulgan, R. 2003. Holding power to account: accountability in modern democracies. Basingstoke, UK: Palgrave Macmillan.

Neal, A. G. 2005. National trauma and collective memory: extraordinary events in the American experience, 2nd edn. Armonk, NY: Sharpe.

Preston, T. 2001. The president and his inner circle: leadership style and the advisory process in foreign affairs. New York: Columbia University Press.

Pyszczynski, T. A., Sheldon, S. and Greenberg, J. (eds.) 2002. In the wake of 9/11: The psychology of terror. Washington, DC: American Psychological Association.

Regester, M., and Larkin, J. 1997. Risk issues and crisis management: a casebook of best practice. London: Kogan Page.

Rijpma, J., and Van Duin, M. A. 2001. From accident to disaster: the response to the Hercules crash. In Rosenthal, U., Boin, R. A. and Comfort, L. K. (eds.) Managing crises: threats, dilemmas and opportunities. Springfield, IL: Charles C. Thomas, pp. 143–54.

Rodríguez, H., Quarantelli, E. L. and Dynes, R. R. (eds.) 2006. Handbook of disaster research. New York: Springer.

Rose, R., and Davies, P. L. 1994. Inheritance in public policy: change without choice in Britain. New Haven, CT: Yale University Press.

Rosenthal, U., Boin, R. A. and Comfort, L. K. (eds.) 2001. Managing crises: threats, dilemmas and opportunities. Springfield, IL: Charles C. Thomas.

Rosenthal, U., Charles, M. T. and 't Hart, P. (eds.) 1989. Coping with crises: the management of disasters, riots and terrorism. Springfield, IL: Charles C. Thomas.

Rosenthal, U., 't Hart, P., van Duin, M. J. et al. 1994. Complexity in urban crisis management: Amsterdam's response to the Bijlmer air disaster. London: James & James.

Rosenthal, U., 't Hart, P. and Kouzmin, A. 1991. The bureau-politics of crisis management. Public Administration 69(2):211–33.

Sabatier, P. A., and Jenkins-Smith, H. C. (eds.) 1993. Policy change and learning: an advocacy coalition approach. Boulder, CO: Westview Press.

Sabato, L. J. 2000. Attack journalism and American politics. Baltimore, MD: Lanahan.

Schneider, S. K. 1995. Flirting with disaster: public management in crisis situations. Armonk, NY: Sharpe.

Seeger, M. W., Sellnow, T. L. and Ulmer, R. R. 2003. Communication and organizational crisis. Westport, CT: Praeger.

Stern, E. K. 1997. Crisis and learning: A balance sheet. Journal of Contingencies and Crisis Management 5(2):69–86.

Tarrow, S. 1994. Power in movement. Cambridge, UK: Cambridge University Press.

Thompson, J. B. 2000. Political scandal: power and visibility in the modern age. Cambridge, UK: Polity Press.

Toft, B., and Reynolds, S. 2005. Learning from disasters: a management approach. 3rd edn. Leicester, UK: Perpetuity Press.

Tumarkin, M. 2005. Traumascapes: The power and fate of places transformed by tragedy. Carlton, Australia: Melbourne University Press.

Vale, L. J., and Campanella, T. J. (eds.) 2005. The resilient city: how modern cities recover from disaster. Oxford, UK: Oxford University Press.

Van Duin, M. 1992. Van rampen leren. Den Haag: Haagsche Drukkerij.

Wagner-Pacifici, R. E. 1986. The Moro morality play: terrorism as social drama. Chicago: University of Chicago Press.

Weick, K. E., and Sutcliffe, K. M. 2001. Managing the unexpected: assuring high performance in an age of complexity. San Francisco: Jossey-Bass.

Wilsford, D. 2001. Paradoxes of health care reform in France: state autonomy and policy paralysis. In Bovens, M., 't Hart, P. and Peters, B. G. (eds.) Success and failure in public governance: a comparative analysis. Cheltenham, UK: Edward Elgar, pp. 184–98.

Wirth, H. J. (ed.) 2004. 9/11 as a collective trauma and other essays on psychoanalysis and society. Mahwah, NJ: Analytic Press.

PART I

Crisis-induced accountability

2 | Weathering the politics of responsibility and blame: the Bush administration and its response to Hurricane Katrina

THOMAS PRESTON

Introduction

As forecasters and policy makers watched Katrina grow ominously in strength from a Category 4 hurricane (with sustained winds of 145 mph) into a Category 5 storm (with 160 mph winds) on 29 August 2005 (the day before its eventual landfall over Mississippi and Louisiana), the worst fears of many seemed about to be realised. For decades, planners had warned that New Orleans, with its vulnerable levee systems and bowl-shaped geography, would be at great risk of massive flooding and loss of life if struck by even a weaker Category 3 storm (120 mph winds). Indeed, emergency officials from federal, state and local jurisdictions in July 2004 had conducted a five-day training exercise at the State Emergency Operations Center in Baton Rouge in which a hypothetical Category 3 hurricane named Pam struck New Orleans. The results demonstrated not only that officials at all levels were unprepared to cope with such an event but also that only one-third of the city's population would be evacuated owing to lack of transportation, the city would likely flood and potentially tens of thousands of people would die (globalsecurity.org 2005). These results were reported to policy makers at all levels of government, including the White House. Yet only a year later, when the very real Hurricane Katrina slammed into New Orleans, government officials at all levels seemed surprised to learn that the levees had been breached (leaving 88 percent of the city submerged) and were largely unable to marshal any kind of effective emergency response after the storm had passed.

For the American public, it was an obvious *policy fiasco*, as television screens across the nation beamed increasingly gruesome images of suffering citizens, day after day, into viewers' homes – citizens seemingly abandoned by the authorities. For days, people were left out on cut-off bridges and overpasses, exposed to the baking sun without water or medical care. The bodies of the dead were moved to the side and discreetly covered over with blankets to hide them from the cameras of visiting television crews. Increasingly desperate people in the Superdome awaited rescue as supplies of food and water failed to materialise, living conditions deteriorated alarmingly and reports of violence began to emerge – again without any indication that help was on the way. Stranded people throughout the flooded city sat on rooftops or sought to wade through the water to higher ground, while many were driven by lack of food, water or medicine to break into stores in search of supplies. These powerful images shown by the media, along with reporters' increasingly incredulous tones as they reported on these events and the lack of a government response, 'framed' this event as a fiasco more completely than any kind of 'spin' or speech could later undo. The general attitude of the public shifted within those few days from one of accepting that a natural disaster had occurred to one of asking 'How could this happen in America?' The obvious failure of the authorities to respond to the disaster and their seemingly 'out of touch' expressions of confidence in the response further framed the event for the public as one of government incompetence. Although there obviously were failures at *all* levels of government, the federal response [run by the Federal Emergency Management Agency (FEMA), the Department of Homeland Security and the White House] came under increasing fire from critics as time passed, presenting President Bush with his most serious political crisis since 9/11.

The Bush administration's response to Hurricane Katrina and its aftermath provides a rich analytical case for exploring the dynamics of presidential crisis management, the impact of political accountability in the wake of crises and the nature of the political 'blame games' that take shape as a result. As noted in Chapter 1, the relationship between the postcrisis politics of accountability (or blame) and the fates of political leaders and their policies (crisis outcomes) play an important, if understudied, role in crisis management dynamics. In the case of Katrina, Bush lost the political blame games resulting from his administration's lacklustre handling of the crisis response and, as a consequence, suffered tremendous political damage. The Katrina outcome for Bush clearly fits within the category of crisis-induced 'elite damage', as per Chapter 1. In order to develop our understanding of why this was the case, the present chapter explores how Bush's blame game strategies and vulnerabilities to blame were influenced by his personality and leadership style. We also examine how leaders' personalities and styles interact with the characteristics of a given crisis to either greatly weaken or improve their ability to successfully adopt various 'blame avoidance' strategies in the wake of policy failure. For Bush, the fallout from his administration's failed management of the Katrina crisis and inability to deal effectively with the subsequent political blame game continued to do political damage long after New Orleans had been pumped dry.[1]

Katrina was also a case where the political leadership faced multiple *preexisting* 'accountability episodes' (Schönbach 1990), which had already begun to sap its resilience and credibility with the public [e.g. the increasingly unpopular war in Iraq; the absence of weapons of mass destruction (WMD); the charges of misuse of intelligence to justify the war; ongoing investigations of senior White House aides, like Scooter Libby and Karl Rove, for potential involvement in leaking a CIA operative's name to the press]. Long before Katrina began to strengthen over the Gulf, the White House was already fully involved in efforts to manage preexisting blame games on these other fronts as well, along with a sharp decline in public confidence over Bush's performance in office. As a result, missteps made by the administration during its initial response to Katrina were not judged in isolation with a fresh slate but within the context of this overall negative political climate – greatly complicating its efforts to effectively respond to the evolving blame game. Adding to this 'perfect storm' for the White House was Bush's own personality and leadership style, which significantly influenced the character of the administration's crisis management response and its efforts to deflect blame in Katrina's aftermath.

Leadership style, crisis management and the blame game

The leadership style of any national leader, whether president or prime minister, plays an important role in shaping how a given administration will respond to or manage a crisis. The mere act of setting up an advisory system to gather and analyse information, and selecting advisers

---

[1] According to a 27 February 2006 CBS News Poll, during the 6 months following the storm, those who disapproved of Bush's response to the needs of Katrina victims increased from only 48 percent in September 2005 to 64 percent by February 2006, with his overall approval rating dropping 7 points during that time, from 41 percent to 34 percent. Similarly, only 32 percent approved of his handling of Katrina, a drop of 12 points. http://www.cbsnews.com/stories/2006/02/27/opinion/polls/printable1350874.shtml.

to populate it, means that some leaders will have more complete information and diverse advice available to them than others. The need for personal control or involvement in the policy-making process also varies across leaders, so that some will be more 'hands on' and involved while others will be more delegative and dependent upon subordinates and their bureaucracies. Some will be more sensitive to context and seek out more information than others, which means that leaders will vary greatly in terms of how quickly they perceive essential elements of evolving crisis situations, how aware they are of events and how quickly they will make decisions based on the information at hand. Indeed, a growing body of research in political psychology explores the impact such individual leader characteristics have upon subsequent styles of management, use of advisers, foreign policy decision making and crisis response (Hermann and Preston 1994; Kaarbo and Hermann 1998; Preston and 't Hart 1999; Preston 2001; Preston and Hermann 2004; Dyson and Preston 2006). Below, the effects of leadership style on crisis awareness/management abilities are discussed, as are their implications for successful navigation by leaders of the treacherous waters of the blame game.[2]

The leader's need for control/involvement

How much control or involvement leaders insist upon within the policy process has been shown to be related to their individual needs for power (Winter 1973; McClelland 1975; Etheredge 1978; Hermann 1980; House 1990; Preston 2001). Leaders with high power needs tend to insist upon direct personal involvement and control over the policy-making process, actively advocate their own policy views, seek to frame issues for their followers, centralise decision making within a tight inner circle of advisers they oversee and rarely delegate important decision tasks to subordinates (Preston 2001). As a result, bureaucratic politics tends to be more muted in such administrations, with leaders

---

[2] Obviously, there are also nonleader factors, such as institutional structures, power relationships between regime actors, political context and pure luck that also impact upon how successful a given leader is in either handling a crisis or playing the blame game. Although the focus of this chapter is upon the impact of leaders and their styles upon these dynamics, the Katrina case also illustrates how such background contextual factors interact (for good or ill) with 'what the leader is like'.

avoiding the kind of delegation that could spark bureau-political conflict at lower levels (Preston and 't Hart 1999). In contrast, those with lower power needs tend to require limited personal involvement/control over policy, advocate their own personal views less and actively delegate policy formulation and implementation tasks to subordinates – whose roles are greatly enhanced. As a result, bureau-political conflict is often increased, greatly complicating decision tasks (Preston and 't Hart 1999).

For crisis management purposes (and dealing with the blame game), these style differences have potentially important consequences. Leaders who insist upon personal involvement and control are probably more likely to remain engaged during a crisis, tend to insert themselves into all key policy decisions and are unlikely to be 'left out of the loop' on any decision or policy adopted. Moreover, the appearance of a highly visible, directive and engaged leadership style often translates into a more positive view of the leader being formed on the part of the observing public and media. Obviously this can be a positive thing if the crisis response is a good one or perceived to be effective and successful by the public (which craves strong, decisive leadership in such times). Unfortunately, it also makes it much harder to avoid accountability or blame if the response comes to be perceived as a failure. In contrast, for less controlling leaders, there is the danger of *either* not receiving full credit for good crisis management (since a hands-off style was assumed to be in play) or (and far worse) getting a large measure of the resulting blame for any policy failure (because of their perceived lack of involvement or engagement on such a critical matter). Moreover, bureau-political conflict is far more likely with this kind of style, which could greatly complicate effective and efficient governmental response to a crisis, lead to visible in-fighting between various agencies/departments and reflect poorly upon the leadership. Such outcomes make it even more difficult to deflect blame, since the lack of coordination and bureau-politics would be seen as a consequence of the leader's less engaged style.

The leader's sensitivity to context

Another critical dimension relevant to crisis management and response is the leader's general sensitivity to context and need for information in making decisions. Within the American presidential literature, scholars have routinely noted profound differences across presidents in their 'cognitive need' for information in making decisions, in how broadly they cast their advisory nets to gather relevant information and whether they value diverse advice or collect only that which is broadly consistent with their own views (George 1980; Hess 1988; Burke and Greenstein 1991; Preston 2001). Such differences have also been observed in world leaders more generally (Hermann 1980, 1984, 1987; Kaarbo and Hermann 1998; Taysi and Preston 2001; Hermann et al. 2001) and builds upon a much larger body of psychological research linking the complexity of individual leaders to their subsequent styles of leadership, assessments of risk, decision-making patterns and quality of information-processing within decision groups (Schroder et al. 1967; Nydegger 1975; Driver 1977; Tetlock 1985; Wallace and Suedfeld 1988; Vertzberger 1990; Boettcher 2005). Such differences in a leader's sensitivity to context and need for information have a tremendous impact not only upon the speed of executive decision making, but also upon its quality and connectedness to the realities of the surrounding policy environment – factors absolutely critical to effective crisis management.

Leaders more sensitive to context (who possess greater cognitive needs for information) tend to be those who score high in complexity, while low scores on this trait generally translate into less sensitivity to context.[3] Across U.S. presidents, Preston (2001) found that those scoring high in complexity, as opposed to those scoring low, preferred more open advisory systems. Moreover, high-complexity presidents tended to be far more sensitive than others to the external policy context and the existence of multiple policy dimensions or perspectives on issues. During policy deliberations, they engaged in broad information-search routines emphasising the presentation of alternative viewpoints, discrepant information and multiple policy options by advisers. Such leaders focused upon future policy contingencies and the likely views or reactions of other policy actors in the environment. They were also less likely to employ simplistic analogies,

---

[3] The coding technique used to obtain scores for leaders' needs for power and complexity is the Leader Trait Assessment (LTA) content analytic technique developed by Margaret Hermann. For a full explanation of this approach, how coding is conducted, and how scores are interpreted, see Hermann (2003), Preston (2001) or the Social Science Automation website at http://www.socialscience.net/.

ERRATUM

Please note that the contributor list on page xiii should read:

Contributors

Arjen Boin Stephenson Disaster Management Institute and Public Administration Institute, Louisiana State University

Annika Brändström Swedish Government, Office for Administrative Affairs and Department of Public Administration, Utrecht University

Evelyn Bytzek Institut für Gesellschafts und Politikanalyse, Johann Wolfgang Goethe Universität, Frankfurt

Pär Daléus CRISMART (Swedish National Defence College) and University of Stockholm

Sander Dekker Hague City Council, Netherlands

Dan Hansén CRISMART (Swedish National Defence College)

Paul 't Hart Research School of Social Sciences, Australian National University, and Utrecht School of Governance, Utrecht University

Sanneke Kuipers Department of Public Administration, Leiden University, and Crisisplan B.V., Leiden

Allan McConnell Department of Government and International Relations, University of Sydney

José Olmeda Department of Political Science and Public Administration, Spanish Open University, Madrid

Charles F. Parker Department of Government, Uppsala University

Thomas Preston Department of Political Science, Washington State University

Robert Schwartz Department of Public Health Sciences, University of Toronto

Sofie Staelraeve Department of Political Sciences, University of Ghent, Belgium

'black-and-white' problem representations or stereotypical images of opponents during policy deliberations. However, complex leaders also had far less decisive, more deliberative (and time-consuming) decision-making styles – a finding consistent with their heavy emphasis upon extensive policy debate and information search. Less complex presidents – with their lower cognitive need for information – were far less sensitive to both information and the external policy environment. This reduced sensitivity manifests itself in limited information search and little emphasis upon alternative viewpoints, discrepant information or multiple policy options. Such leaders are more likely to rely upon simplistic analogies, 'black-and-white' problem representations or stereotypical images of opponents during policy deliberations. Further, given their limited interest in extensive policy debate or broad information search, low-complexity leaders were found to have very decisive, less deliberative decision-making styles.

Obviously, such differences in leader sensitivity can have important consequences for crisis management and can increase leaders' vulnerability to the blame game – and this holds equally true for *both* sensitive and insensitive leaders. For example, sensitive leaders who are high in complexity tend to be much more deliberative and slow in their decision making (compared to their less complex counterparts). Although this deliberative approach may produce more considered and generally higher-quality decisions under normal circumstances, it opens up sensitive leaders politically to blame from a public and media that expect immediate, decisive responses to crises. Particularly in the case of catastrophic crises involving high societal costs, such delays also provide political opponents with ample ammunition to attack the leader's slow response. In contrast, less sensitive leaders tend to react (in some form or another) much more quickly to crises contexts than their complex counterparts and will more rapidly develop a 'frame' of the situation (and the needed response) that is consistent with their preexisting beliefs and limited information search.

Unfortunately, although this may provide the rapid reaction desired by the public to a crisis and be deemed quite successful if the initial diagnosis of the situation proves accurate, it can be disastrous if that diagnosis is inaccurate. The reason is simple: insensitive leaders are not generally attentive to context, nor do they gather broad and diverse information – so their monitoring of the situation and response to feedback is far less effective than that of more sensitive leaders. Whereas sensitive leaders are quick to adjust their approach to changing circumstances or negative feedback, less sensitive leaders tend towards rigidity and are slow to alter policy to reflect a changing situation. As a result, if they either (1) get the initial diagnosis of the situation wrong or (2) find themselves in a rapidly evolving, changing crisis environment, insensitive leaders quickly find themselves creating a 'target-rich environment' for later blame games. Thus, the more complicated and nuanced the nature of the crisis itself becomes, the more effective sensitive leaders will be in the long run, especially if that sensitivity is coupled with a high need to be involved. Such leaders, because of their attentiveness to feedback, tend to be far more adaptive to changing contexts and much less rigid regarding changing policy course if circumstances require it. Complex types of crises are much less suited to insensitive leaders, who are far more effective in dealing with fairly straightforward crises requiring not only a rapid response but also possessing limited ambiguity and providing generally clear lines of policy response (e.g., G. W. Bush immediately after 9/11).

Finally, sensitive leaders (with more open advisory systems) not only gather more information but are more willing to hear (and accept) bad news from advisers without it being viewed as disloyalty. Less complex, insensitive leaders tend to be more ideologically rigid and to view the world more in absolute, black-and-white terms. This results in a tendency to surround themselves with 'like-minded' advisers who share similar views (along with a tendency to view policy disagreement by advisers as disloyalty). This can lead to policy advisers being unwilling to provide 'bad news' or to disagree on policy matters, resulting in various group decision pathologies and malfunctions (Janis 1972; 't Hart 1994; 't Hart et al. 1997; Preston and 't Hart 1999). In terms of crisis management or later blame games, this can have the consequence of creating a 'disconnect' between how leaders and their inner circles perceive the crisis/policy environment and its true realities on the ground. Such disconnect can lead the public, media or rival politicians to charge the leadership with being 'out of touch' with reality, 'uncaring' towards the victims or incompetent. It can also lead to misperception regarding the effectiveness of the emergency or crisis response policies adopted and an unwillingness to accept their ineffectiveness until a virtual tidal wave of criticism (or consequences) breaks through their closed advisory systems.

Compatibility of the current 'type' of crisis with the leader's style

Leadership styles also vary in their suitability for dealing with differing types of crises. In laying out their typology of crisis development and termination patterns, 't Hart and Boin (2001: 32) suggest that crises can be distinguished along two basic dimensions: (1) the speed of their development (fast/instant vs. slow/creeping) and (2) the speed of their termination (fast/abrupt vs. slow/gradual). The resulting four types of crises are the *fast-burning* crisis (instant development/abrupt termination), the *cathartic* crisis (creeping development/abrupt termination), the *long-shadow* crisis (instant development/gradual termination) and the *slow-burning* crisis (creeping development/gradual termination). These different types of crises place some styles at either a distinct advantage or disadvantage in terms of both crisis management and efforts to avoid blame.

For example, leaders with high needs for control/involvement in policy are at an advantage when a crisis has a rapid onset (*fast-burning* or *long-shadow* crises) because they are less likely to be 'out of the loop' regarding initial responses to the event. However, while instant involvement has its advantages, if the handling of the crisis (or its outcome) becomes problematic, it becomes very difficult for leaders to avoid accountability. Even so, the image of strong, decisive leadership goes a long way towards allowing engaged leaders to make the claim (even in a policy failure or fiasco) that they made a good-faith effort to manage the crisis effectively. In contrast, less controlling or involved leaders often take quite some time to become more personally engaged in dealing with a crisis and often do so only after subordinates have either been unable to cope or the scope of the event obviously necessitates leader involvement. Such leaders tend to delegate substantial authority over policy (both formulation and implementation) to subordinates, often leading to bureau-political conflict that hampers effective governmental response to crises. In cases where substantial delegation exists, it is more difficult to rapidly coordinate a response from diverse agencies and departments (who are often competing with one another). This further lengthens the less engaged leader's response time to an event – and to be seen as slow to respond can be enormously damaging to leaders politically and create the perception among observers of 'detachment'.

Coupled with these leader control needs are varying sensitivities to context. Once again, differing style types vary greatly in terms of their strengths and weaknesses depending upon the 'type' of crisis. For example, insensitive leaders tend to respond to crises based more upon their own internal beliefs regarding the external policy or political environments involved and less upon detailed assessments of current information from the surrounding environment. In other words, they are inattentive to context and approach policy in an idiosyncratic fashion. Given their lack of emphasis upon information search, less sensitive leaders react in a far more decisive and rapid fashion than their sensitive counterparts. This may take the form of quickly issued statements of confidence in the emergency/crisis response, promises to help victims or vows to punish perpetrators. The greatest danger for such leaders in the later blame game is this initial response, based on limited information search, may be ill suited to a nuanced crisis event or unrealistic given the facts on the ground. This is especially true when rapid-onset crises involve a high degree of ambiguity (regarding either the nature of the situation itself or the appropriate policy response). The less sensitive leader's limited information search, especially if coupled with a less engaged style, increases the odds that the situation may be misread. Moreover, such leaders are also highly vulnerable to even slowly developing crises (i.e. *cathartic* or *slow-burning*) because their general inattentiveness to the policy environment and limited information search increases the likelihood that they will be caught unawares or unprepared by slowly evolving threats.

In contrast, sensitive leaders have almost the reverse problem. They are most effective at dealing with slowly developing crises, since these provide adequate time for the kind of broad information search and policy debate preferred by such styles. Their attentiveness to the policy environment also increases the odds that slowly building crises will be noticed. And since time is less critical, they are more likely to adapt to feedback and effectively modify their policy approach as needed. On the other hand, sensitive leaders are at their greatest disadvantage during fast-burning crises and will be vulnerable to blame afterwards, given their inevitably slow, tentative response to rapid-onset events. Such crises take sensitive leaders out of their 'comfort zones' (where information can be gathered, debated and weighed) and forces them into making decisions with far less information/deliberation than normal. This accounts for the often awkward, choppy response of sensitive leaders to the initial stages of a crisis. With *fast-burning* crises that begin and end rapidly, sensitive leaders may never have time to adequately catch up with events, leading to opponents charging them with 'indecisiveness' or 'waffling' in the face of the crisis (especially if the outcome was a bad one). Yet, when there is more time, sensitive leaders have the advantage of being flexible and adaptable to changing circumstances. So while they are at an initial disadvantage in instantly developing crises of the *long-shadow* type, their slow termination allows time for such leaders to engage in information search and to modify policy to better reflect the realities of the crisis environment.

The preexisting style of George W. Bush

The leadership style of George W. Bush couples a low need for personal control and involvement in the policy process with a low general sensitivity to context and a limited need for information in making decisions (Preston and Hermann 2004).[4] As a result, the *preexisting* advisory arrangements and style of decision making within the administration prior to Katrina were of a sort where a substantial degree of policy formulation and implementation tasks were delegated to loyal subordinates throughout the government, with little direct presidential oversight (Milbank 2000; Kahn 2000; Berke 2001; Bruni 2002). A high degree of bureau-political conflict between departments and agencies became quite routine as subordinates competed with one another for policy influence (Duffy 2002; Sanger 2002). This was most visible in the struggles between the Pentagon, National Security Council (NSC), State Department and Central Intelligence Agency (CIA) over Iraq policy (Sipress 2002; Zakaria 2002). Consistent with the general pattern of advisory arrangements seen among less sensitive leaders, both Bush's inner circle of advisers and his political appointees throughout Washington were largely composed of like-minded individuals whose personal loyalty was paramount over professional qualifications (Preston 2001; Tumulty et al. 2005). The closed nature of the resulting advisory system, where information tended to be gathered mostly from quarters where policy agreement was assured and dissonant views avoided, greatly reduced its ability to actively (or accurately)

---

[4] President Bush scores low on LTA measures for need for power and cognitive complexity when compared to a general population of over 140 world leaders.

monitor the policy or political environments for feedback or relevant information (Allen 2005). This led to a high degree of selective processing of information and a tendency to gather only such information and advice as was supportive of preexisting views or policies and an increased likelihood of closing off access channels to negative feedback or warnings coming from nonadministration sources. When coupled with the president's own low sensitivity to context and limited need for personal engagement, this increased not only the chances of important signals being missed or policy decisions being made in the absence of critical information/advice but also magnified Bush's vulnerability to blame in the face of policy reversals. Overall, one would expect this type of style to result in policy being driven more by idiosyncratic factors or ideological beliefs than by a monitoring of the existing political context. The importance of this preexisting presidential style becomes obvious in the administration's handling of Katrina and its aftermath.

The evolving politics of responsibility and blame over Katrina

Although an analysis of the 'politics of blame' surrounding Katrina could quite easily focus upon any number of different levels of the government (federal, state, local), or follow the specific actions of those singled out initially for the most blame [such as Michael D. Brown, director of the Federal Emergency Management Agency (FEMA)], the focus of this chapter is upon the national leader – in this case, President Bush.[5] From the standpoint of presidential crisis management, Katrina posed stark challenges to an administration already losing credibility with the public over its handling of the war in Iraq, a leak enquiry and its truthfulness regarding its use of intelligence surrounding WMDs. This *preexisting political context* meant that the administration could ill afford to appear unprepared, ineffectual or purposefully misleading over Katrina – primarily because this would serve to immediately

---

[5] The sources of data for this case must, of necessity, rely upon purely journalistic accounts and congressional testimonies of participants. Obviously, there is the potential for bias in such data and it is undoubtedly not a complete record of the decision-making processes within the Bush administration surrounding Katrina. However, these still represent (in the absence of official records becoming available after 30 years and publication of participant memoirs) the best available data on the case at present and every effort has been made to find multiple corroboration of accounts described in this case study.

activate preexisting political frames in the public's mind that could all too readily link this event with other perceived policy failings. For leaders, this preexisting political context is critical, since it means the difference between operating with a relatively clean slate politically (where blame can be more easily deflected) to one in which the leader becomes a political magnet attracting blame. During the initial response to Katrina, the overly optimistic views expressed by Bush and White House spokesmen about the federal response and the situation on the ground in New Orleans were immediately refuted by media coverage of the situation and rescue workers on the scene (Stevenson 2005; Thomas 2005). This caused immense political damage to the president, who was seen by detractors as being either out of touch with events (at best) or downright duplicitous (at worst) – neither of which helped the administration to deflect blame.

Past political decisions by leaders also increase their vulnerability to blame. In the case of Katrina, the deployment of Louisiana's National Guard to Iraq meant that it was short-handed (or could be perceived as such) in its response to the storm, immediately linking any failure in its response to the unpopular war in Iraq (Sanger 2005a). Similarly, the administration had substantially cut (by more than half) the Army Corps of Engineers' budgets for levee repairs and improvements around New Orleans in the years preceding Katrina (despite repeated warnings about the threat posed by major storms), providing obvious ammunition to later critics (Ripley 2005; Blumenthal 2005). Bush's own style of substantial delegation to subordinates, limited active involvement and emphasis on loyalty over expertise in appointments served to *preset* the roles of many of the policy actors prior to Katrina – actors whose performances would later be criticised as lacking (such as FEMA director Brown, Department of Homeland Security Secretary Michael Chertoff and others). Media investigations of the backgrounds of Bush's political appointees afterwards further opened the administration up to charges of cronyism and the placing of officials (like Brown) into positions for which they were not qualified (Tumulty et al. 2005). This was an especially damaging charge, given the obvious importance (and failure) of federal emergency managers during Katrina.

Closely related to past political decisions is the problem of *dueling divergent perceptions regarding the 'type' of crisis* just experienced. In the case of Katrina and its aftermath, two differing 'types' of crises were perceived by participants and observers. For those who had long worried about and modeled the impact of a major hurricane on New Orleans (and lobbied for the matter to be given higher priority), the crisis was perceived to be a *slow-burning* one, where a long-standing vulnerability and growing danger had existed for many years and now continued to exist even after Katrina. By the Bush administration, Katrina was generally perceived (or argued) to be a *long-shadow* crisis (rapid onset/slow termination) that was difficult to anticipate fully ahead of time (see 't Hart and Boin 2001). This 'perception gap' serves as one of the main battlefields for the blame game. Obviously, in crises with long run-ups (providing ample warning or time to react had policy makers been more vigilant and competent), it is much easier to assign blame than it is in crises that could have legitimately arrived as a *bolt from the blue* (Parker and Stern 2005). For example, Bush's statement on 1 September that 'no one could have foreseen the levees being breached' can be seen as an attempt to define the crisis one way, while a competing definition would note that Bush was told 56 hours before landfall by the National Weather Service and the National Hurricane Center that there was an 'extremely high probability' New Orleans would be flooded (Hsu 2006). Successfully 'defining' the type of crisis to the public often determines the winner of the blame game.

Leaders must also calculate the *contestability* of existing perceptual frames held by the public, the media or the political system regarding their allotment of responsibility (or blame) for an event. As long as policy makers believe that the final image (or perceptual frame) of the crisis and its aftermath remains contestable – or malleable enough to be shaped by either denial of responsibility, deflection of blame to others or positive spin (showing themselves or their management of events in a positive light) – leaders will continue to adopt various tactics of blame avoidance to protect themselves (Bovens et al. 1999; Brändström and Kuipers 2003; Boin et al. 2005). Only when this image is no longer contestable do policy makers tend to publicly accept blame, issue mea culpas, or seek out damage-limitation strategies to minimise the political fallout of events on their futures. Therefore the longer it takes for policy makers to perceive a 'lack of contestability' in how a given crisis is being framed, the longer they will continue to claim that their policies/responses are effective, refuse to accept responsibility, and damage themselves politically.

Obviously, less sensitive leaders (like Bush), who employ closed advisory systems gathering limited information from the surrounding political environment are far more likely to miscalculate such 'contesta-bility' than are more sensitive leaders (who monitor that environment closely). Further, given their general rigidity towards changing adopted policy positions, insensitive leaders tend to 'contest' the public frame for as long as possible – often long past the point where political dam-age is avoidable. Indeed, the Bush administration, which has made a hallmark of never admitting to policy mistakes or reverses publicly, has followed this general pattern on Iraq, WMDs and Katrina – con-testing frames long after public opinion on these topics shifted away from the image the White House continued to try to present. In the case of Katrina, the administration's efforts to contest the developing public perceptual frame of the crisis and divert blame away from itself dealt with three basic sets of postcrisis dilemmas (Boin et al. 2006). These reflect the cross-cutting tensions that inevitably exist after a crisis occurs along the spectrum of either 'conserving existing polit-ical structures/relationships' (stability) on the one hand versus 'adopt-ing reform measures' on the other. Essentially, the postcrisis tensions between conservation and reform processes provide the battlefield on which leaders contest the 'war of blame,' with fighting occurring along two main fronts involving the processes of *meaning making* and *inquiry and investigation*.

Meaning making (strategic agenda setting)

The meaning-making stage of a crisis (Boin et al. 2005) is where the central leadership task involves creating a 'definition of the situation' for the public or the political system that provides a particular meaning to the crisis, what solutions/sacrifices are required to resolve it, and a story line that shows leaders to be competent, in command and empa-thetic. In other words, it is the time for policy makers to define the situation in a positive light politically and to influence how others per-ceive (and frame) the crisis and their response. Unfortunately for Bush, Katrina was a perfect example of the *long-shadow* crisis (fast onset, slow termination) that tends to place less engaged/insensitive leaders at a disadvantage (at least in the beginning) owing to their general lack of attentiveness to context (meaning that they are often caught unawares or unprepared by events).

Consistent with his delegative, less engaged style, Bush histori-cally has taken lengthy vacations on his ranch in Crawford, Texas, during the summers, leaving most policy tasks to trusted subordinates in Washington. Such delegation, especially given his closed advisory system and tight inner circle, makes it critical for trusted advisers to be on hand to adequately monitor the policy environment. Unfortunately, as Katrina formed, not only was Bush on vacation but so were other senior members of the administration, with Vice President Cheney in Wyoming, Condoleezza Rice in Manhattan, White House Chief of Staff Andy Card in Maine, and both White House Communications Director Nicolle Devenish and Senior Media Adviser Mark McKinnon in Greece (Cooper 2005: 51). This served to impede the flow of advice and information to the president, thus magnifying the seeming 'disconnect' between Bush's actions/statements and developing events. During this critical meaning-making stage, it was fully 24 hours after Katrina hit (on 30 August) before senior aides finally decided Bush should cut his 5-week vacation short to return to Washington, where he could meet top advisers the next day (Thomas 2005: 30–1).

   That Bush remained on vacation (and did not immediately return to Washington) during such a catastrophe was broadly criticised by the media, and the lack of strong presidential statements regarding the situation aggravated this public perception of detachment. Although he often boasted that he did not read newspapers or watch the media, in the case of Katrina, Bush seemed surprisingly uninformed throughout the crisis about events that were being covered live by most U.S. news networks. For example, observers noted that 4 days after Katrina, during a briefing for his father and Bill Clinton, Bush's own rosy perception of the progress being made in New Orleans 'bore no resemblance to what was actually happening' (Allen 2005: 44). Indeed, White House staffers, who had been watching the increasingly dire reports coming out of New Orleans, made up a DVD of the newscasts so Bush could watch them (and presumably catch up with events) as he flew over the Gulf Coast the morning of 31 August (Thomas 2005: 32). Although photos taken of Bush aboard Air Force One, peering intently out of his window at the devastation below, were intended by the White House to show the president's engagement and concern, their impact on public opinion and how they were covered by the media (especially when coupled with the lack of significant federal assistance to the region and his perceived slowness to end his vacation) conveyed an entirely unintended image of detachment. Later that day, in a Rose Garden speech, Bush sought to demonstrate he was engaged, reciting statistics on the number of meals-ready-to-eat delivered and of people rescued or in shelters (Sanger 2005a). But significant political damage had already occurred, as the photos aboard Air Force Once became the first visual images of the president's response to Katrina.

As days passed and the situation in New Orleans continued to deteriorate in the absence of effective relief efforts, the administration faced a growing need to reverse the political damage being inflicted upon it due to the growing public perception that it was out of touch or incompetent. Competing with the president during this critical meaning-making phase, where he sought to show his engagement and an effective federal response, was the constant, largely negative media coverage coming out of New Orleans. This coverage was uncomfortably juxtaposed against Bush's 1 September Oval Office statement expressing 'sympathy' for the victims, his belief the federal government had an important role to play and his expressed desire 'to make sure I fully understand the relief efforts' (Stevenson 2005: A8). This response again fell short of what the public expected and was roundly criticised in the media. Seeking to avoid blame using the *explaining behavior* of *ignorance* (Bovens et al. 1999: 143), Bush argued in an ABC interview that same day that no one had expected the levees in New Orleans to be breached. However, the intensity and salience of the media images continued to overwhelm the White House explanations. On 2 September, Bush acknowledged on the South Lawn of the White House (as he left for his first, highly visible tour of the Gulf Coast and New Orleans) that the results of the federal relief efforts were 'not acceptable' thus far – with the symbolism of his trip intended to convey a more engaged, active leadership role on his part (Stevenson 2005: A8).

Although his visits to Alabama, Mississippi and Louisiana were timed to coincide with the arrival of relief supplies and National Guard troops in some of the areas, a series of well-publicised statements by Bush weakened these efforts. For example, during his visit to Mobile, Alabama, Bush touched only briefly on the hundreds of thousands of displaced people in the region and focused instead upon wealthy Senator Trent Lott's intentions to rebuild his upscale home and his own desire to sit on Lott's porch when it was done (Stevenson 2005: A8). This public identification with his wealthy friend's plight, which hardly compared to the situation facing poorer evacuees or those still stranded in New Orleans, was immensely damaging politically and widely criticised. Even more damaging politically was Bush's infamous public congratulations on camera to FEMA director Michael Brown ('You're doing a heck of a job Brownie!'), during a meeting with government officials in Mississippi (Stevenson 2005: A8), while tens of thousands still remained stranded and without aid days after the storm. Again, these administration efforts at making meaning were easily overwhelmed and instantly rebutted by the readily available media imagery contradicting such statements. In fact, after Bush's televised address to the nation from New Orleans, polls showed that the number who thought he was doing a good job in handling Katrina had decreased to 35 percent (from 39 percent prior to the speech), and those who gave him poor marks handling the crisis increased from 37 to 41 percent (Rasmussen Reports 2005). With charges that race played a role in the slow governmental response and lack of White House interest in the crisis (since a large proportion of evacuees were poorer blacks), Secretary of State Rice was sent to her native Alabama on 4 September to observe the recovery efforts and help deflect the charge (Stevenson 2005: A8).

As Boin et al. (2006) observe, tactics to ameliorate the public mood can portray a crisis as an unavoidable act of nature, a 'fluke' or the product of a rogue individual (or group) as opposed to any procedural, institutional or societal failings; hence Bush's 1 September contention that no one could have foreseen the levees being breached (Hsu 2006). If one cannot effectively improve the public mood (which, given Katrina's media coverage, was clearly impossible), playing the blame game (and controlling the *processes of inquiry and investigation*) became a preferred solution for the administration (Hood 2002; Brändström and Kuipers 2003). But, unlike 9/11, the Katrina crisis did not provide the administration with a politically advantageous crisis that it could prolong and capitalise on. Indeed, the longer this crisis continued, the more political damage was inflicted on the president.

Processes of inquiry and investigation

The second major dilemma described in Chapter 1 is that surrounding the character of the *processes of inquiry and investigation* in the postcrisis period. As Bovens and 't Hart (1996: 130) observe,

The politics of blaming start at the very selection and instruction of investigative officials and committees, but it is highlighted especially by the behavior of many stakeholders during the 'postmortem period.' Many of the officials and agencies involved in an alleged fiasco will engage in impression management, blame shifting, and bureau-political maneuvering. Their reputations are at stake. The odium of failure can ruin their careers and weaken their institutional position.

This postcrisis period represents an extremely dangerous one for policy makers because inquiries and investigations not only ask what went wrong (whether it could have been avoided or handled better) but also assign responsibility or blame to policy makers for mistakes or mishandling of the crisis, thereby undercutting their legitimacy and providing political ammunition to opponents. For the Bush administration, the nature of the various inquiries into the Katrina response posed the following three basic dilemmas (Boin et al. 2006):

1. Maintain a tight grip on inquiries vs. allowing genuine independence
2. Blaming others vs. accepting responsibility
3. Hiding failings vs. exposing failings

Maintaining a tight grip on inquires vs. allowing genuine independence

Like its pattern after 9/11, the Bush administration strongly opposed calls to establish an independent commission to investigate the federal response. And while the political context (and the pressure being placed on Congress by the public and media) required some form of inquiry, the White House was the beneficiary of a clear political reality – namely, if the administration (or the president) were held directly accountable, the Republican Party itself would find it impossible to escape blame. As a result, there was a clear effort by Republicans to maintain a tight grip on the Katrina inquiries (and the blame game) and to limit their scope. These efforts were greatly assisted by GOP control over Congress, allowing them to defeat repeated calls by Democrats for an independent commission and to establish two separate GOP-dominated congressional commissions in the House and Senate. In fact, the House 'bipartisan' committee, which issued its Katrina report, *A Failure of Initiative*, in February 2006, was composed solely of Republican members (after a boycott by Democrats).

That same month, the White House issued its own Katrina report, emphasising the theme of 'lessons learned' while predictably accepting only limited blame for the outcome (see The White House 2006). Although these inquiries resulted in some embarrassing revelations, this strategy proved largely successful at insulating the White House from the lion's share of the blame, which settled (as so often happens in Washington) upon lower-ranking officials (like Brown and Chertoff) and a wide range of state and local officials. Still, the clear public perception that the Katrina response had been a fiasco led even the GOP-dominated reports to lay some blame upon the White House directly (although from the presidential perspective, it was Bush's staff who were blamed for not making use of information, not engaging the president, etc., with Bush himself largely avoiding any significant criticism). Later, a nonpartisan investigation by the Government Accountability Office (GAO) placed primary blame for the failed federal response on Homeland Security Secretary Chertoff rather than lower-level officials (Neuman 2006: A1; GAO February 2006).

What the White House could not control, however, were inquiries by journalists in the media, who began investigations into the apparent cronyism surrounding many Bush administration appointments after FEMA director Brown's qualifications for the job proved lacking. As noted earlier, Bush's style (less sensitive/closed) emphasised subordinate *loyalty* over expertise. Predictably, when *Time* magazine published its own investigation of cronyism in the administration (Tumulty et al. 2005), it found numerous examples similar to Brown (where appointees had no relevant professional experience to qualify for their posts beyond being Bush loyalists). Such charges and continued publicity about Brown's (and Chertoff's) qualifications served to undercut White House efforts to avoid blame.

Blaming others vs. accepting responsibility

Along with its efforts to maintain a tight grip over the Katrina inquiries, the White House was also forced to decide between two conflicting blame avoiding or mitigating tactics: (1) *blaming others* (or allowing others to be blamed) for the bad outcomes or (2) *accepting responsibility and blame* (in some form or other) for the events. The first tactic, blaming others, holds out the hope of deflecting direct blame away from oneself and is obviously the preferred tactic for policy makers. It can take the form of subordinates playing the role of 'lightning rods' (purposefully deflecting blame away from the leaders and onto them-selves). It can also involve such subordinates becoming inadvertent lightning rods, or scapegoats, due to their official positions in the government – especially if their portfolios include responsibility for the arena in which the fiasco occurred. It can take the form of blaming the opposition political party for 'playing the blame game' and living in the past rather than looking ahead to the future – thereby creating a public frame that political motivations are driving criticism rather than more legitimate concerns. In other cases, it can be a foreign enemy (e.g., Al-Qaeda and the 9/11 attacks) that can be blamed as being *more* culpable for the event than any lack of foresight or planning on the part of government officials. All of these strategies seek to either avoid or at least reduce the political damage caused by blame upon policy makers.

In his landmark study of American presidential use of subordinates as lightning rods to deflect blame, Ellis (1994: 8) notes that the term suggests 'not merely the attraction of criticism but the deflection of criticism away from someone or something'. For the strategy to be successful, it requires presidents to 'keep their intentions ambiguous', allowing opponents to believe that if the president had paid closer attention or been more involved, he would have behaved differently (and better) than the subordinate (Ellis 1994: 22). Of course, this tactic works only when such ambiguity of intentions does not come across as being out of touch with a hugely significant event. Ellis (1994: 34) notes that 'avoiding blame on a policy gone awry was bound to be easier for a president who was widely reported to be inattentive to and uninformed about the details of policy' – with Reagan being used as the example; but again, when it is a serious crisis, that leadership style attracts blame for being disengaged. Indeed, as Ellis (1994: 169) observes, 'the success of a lightning rod strategy is contingent on the degree to which people expect a president to be in command of a policy area. The greater the expectation of presidential involvement and control, the less likely a president will be able to deflect blame for administration actions onto subordinates'.

For Bush, the traditional 'lightning rod' use of advisers was compli-cated by two factors. First, given that the dominant public frame the White House was seeking to counter was one of presidential detach-ment, a strategy of keeping his intentions ambiguous would have only reinforced the damaging image already developing. Second, the successful use of subordinates as lightning rods can be affected by varying leadership styles. For leaders like Bush, whose less complex, insensitive style emphasises loyalty over expertise, a 'two-way street' regarding loyalty is often created – with such leaders being less willing to 'throw followers to the wolves' and show disloyalty themselves. Thus, even when it became patently obvious that Brownie had not done 'a heck of a job' handling the crisis, Bush still defended his subordinate until a tidal wave of bipartisan criticism eventually forced Brown to be removed from oversight of the Katrina efforts, reassigned to Washington and eventually to resign. So, while Brown was certainly attracting the majority of the initial criticism over Katrina (and did serve, for a time, to deflect it away from the White House), Bush's style prevented him from distancing himself and releasing his grip upon the metal rod. More sensitive leaders, attuned to the political context, are far more likely to recognise the need to distance themselves from such subordinates (Ellis 1994; Preston 2001). Indeed, this 'lightning rod' relationship was explicitly understood in advance between Eisenhower (a complex/sensitive leader) and his White House Chief of Staff Sherman Adams (Ambrose 1990; Preston 2001).

In contrast, there is no evidence that Bush explicitly sought to use subordinates as lightning rods during the Katrina case. However, subordinates did serve as inadvertent lightning rods owing to their official responsibilities, with first FEMA director Brown taking most of the blame, followed by Secretary of Homeland Security Chertoff during later congressional inquiries. But crises are not like thunderstorms, and in the case of Katrina, these political lightning rods received a cascade of strikes – and, as the fiasco worsened, the stronger and more persistent became the bolts. In such cases, the deflection ability of the rods is undermined, especially when the blame game logically turns to the question of how such officials were in charge in the first place! Thus, when Brown's lack of specialist background for the FEMA job became known, not only was he a good source to blame, but these very characteristics spread blame to President Bush for appointing cronies to posts – in other words, he was no longer deflecting blame but channeling it towards the White House. But some inadvertent rods still worked. During his February 2006 testimony before the Senate, Chertoff acknowledged and accepted substantial blame for the response, especially regarding his misplaced confidence in Brown (Lipton 2006b). With his mea culpa, Chertoff avoided having the committee call for his resignation, and White House Press Secretary Scott McClellan provided further support by stating that 'Secretary Chertoff is doing a great job' (Lipton 2006c).

Though he was notoriously unwilling to publicly admit mistakes or policy shortcomings, the unrelenting political pressure led Bush, during a 13 September press conference, to acknowledge that while Katrina exposed problems at all levels of government, 'to the extent that the federal government didn't fully do its job right, I take responsibility' (Bumiller and Stevenson 2005: A1). But while Bush accepted a limited measure of blame, the White House immediately embarked on the blame-avoidance tactic of impugning the political motives of opponents. Press Secretary McClellan used the blame-game phrase fifteen times over the course of just two White House press briefings in reference to any criticism of the administration's response (Krugman 2005). Similarly, White House spokesman Duffy, responding to continued criticism, noted that it was

shocking to hear yet more and more blame-gaming and finger-pointing from Democrats, but at least they've finally found something to be good at. The president, his staff and thousands of men and women did all they could to help save lives and property from the worst disaster to ever hit the U.S. President Bush was also the first to stand up and take personal responsibility for any real or perceived shortcomings associated with the effort. (Hosenball 2006).

Another tactic the White House employed was to demonstrate a few weeks later, when Hurricane Rita formed and began moving towards the Gulf Coast, that *lessons had been learned* from Katrina, and the media was briefed in depth about how deeply Bush was involved in calling governors and federal officials to ensure that relief efforts would be carefully coordinated (Sanger 2005b). The February 2006 White House Katrina report included 'lessons learned' in its title, touted 125 specific recommendations, and emphasised the president's view 'that we must do better in the future'. As White House spokesman Duffy stated after the House report, 'the president is less interested in yesterday, and more interested with today and tomorrow ... so that we can be better prepared for next time' (Hsu 2006: A01).

Hiding failings vs. exposing them

Finally, even with the tightly controlled nature of the congressional inquiries, the White House also sought to deflect blame by refusing to fully cooperate with the committees, supply key documents or allow testimony by top administration officials (citing executive confidentiality privileges). These tactics led Joseph Lieberman, the ranking Democrat on the Senate Governmental Affairs Committee, to complain that 'there has been a near total lack of cooperation that has made it impossible, in my opinion, for us to do the thorough investigation we have a responsibility to do' (Lipton 2006a).

Conclusion

As this brief case study of Katrina illustrates, leaders and their management styles play a critical role in shaping not only how they approach the task of crisis management, but also how vulnerable to blame they will be across differing types of crises and how effective they are likely to be at playing the blame game in the face of policy reversals. The personalities of leaders not only shape their strategies for dealing with blame but also create (through the development of various types of advisory systems) decision-making and management processes that either strengthen or greatly reduce their ability to cope with (and deflect blame arising) from crises. During Katrina, as expected for a less controlling, insensitive leader, Bush's lack of personal engagement and substantial delegation to subordinates, coupled with his lack of attention to the surrounding policy environment, greatly slowed his personal response to the crisis. Moreover, given the insular, closed nature of the White House advisory system, where information tended to flow in primarily from loyal insiders, it is hardly surprising that Bush's political response to the crisis was often out of step with the views (and perceptions) of those outside of his inner circle. This led to the clear disconnect observed during the Katrina response between those events being widely covered by the media (and viewed by the public) and White House pronouncements on the subject. Given the normal policy rigidity associated with such styles, it was to be expected that Bush would be slow to either adapt his policy approach once it had been adopted or accept blame. This rigidity was particularly damaging given the immense emotive power of the imagery coming out of New Orleans, which easily overpowered the White House's clumsy attempts at positive spin. Not only was Bush's own leadership style ill fitted to the nature of the crisis in which he found himself, serving to greatly exacerbate his administration's vulnerabilities to blame (through appointment of loyalists rather than experts to critical positions, etc.), it also led to the selection of blame-avoidance strategies that were poorly suited to the situation for both *meaning making* and the *processes of inquiry and investigation* following the crisis. Katrina is a clear case of crisis-induced 'elite damage' (as per Chapter 1 of this volume) – an outcome influenced significantly by the leadership style of George W. Bush.

References

Allen, M. 2005. Living too much in the bubble? A bungled initial response to Katrina exposed the perils of a rigid, insular White House. Time, 19 September.

Ambrose, S. E. 1990. Eisenhower: soldier and president. New York: Simon and Schuster.

Berke, R. L. 2001. Jokes remain, but many say Bush is showing signs of war's burden. New York Times, 9 December.

Blumenthal, S. 2005. Katrina comes home to roost. Guardian, 4 September.

Boettcher, W. A. 2005. Presidential risk behavior in foreign policy: prudence or peril? New York: Palgrave Macmillan.

Boin, A., 't Hart, P., Stern, E. and Sundelius, B. 2005. The politics of crisis management: public leadership under pressure. Cambridge, UK: Cambridge University Press.

Boin, A., McConnell, A. and 't Hart, P. 2006. Inertia or change? Political leadership dilemmas in the aftermath of crisis. Refereed paper presented to the Australasian Political Studies Association Conference, University of Newcastle, Australia, 25–27 September, http://www.newcastle.edu.au/school/ept/politics/apsa/abs.publicpolicy.html

Bovens, M., and 't Hart, P. 1996. Understanding policy fiascoes. New Brunswick: Transaction.

Bovens, M., 't Hart, P., Dekker, S. and Verheuvel, G. 1999. The politics of blame avoidance: defensive tactics in a Dutch crime-fighting fiasco. In Anheier, H. K. (ed.) When things go wrong: Organizational failures and breakdowns. London: Sage, pp. 123–47.

Brändström, A., and Kuipers, S. 2003. From 'normal accidents' to political crises: understanding the selective politicization of policy failures. Government and Opposition 38:279–305.

Bruni, F. 2002. Ambling into history: the unlikely odyssey of George W. Bush. New York: Harper Collins Publishers.

Bumiller, E., and Stevenson, R. W. 2005. President says he's responsible in storm lapses. New York Times, 14 September.

Burke, J. P., and Greenstein, F. I. 1991. How presidents test reality: decisions on Vietnam, 1954 and 1965. New York: Russell Sage Foundation.

Cooper, M. 2005. Dipping his toe into disaster. Time, 12 September.

Driver, M. J. 1977. Individual differences as determinants of aggression in the inter-nation simulation. In Hermann, M. G. (ed.) A psychological examination of political leaders. New York: The Free Press, pp. 337–53.

Duffy, M. 2002. Trapped by his own instincts. Time, 6 May.

Dyson, S. B., and Preston, T. 2006. Individual characteristics of leaders and the use of analogy in foreign policy decision making. Political Psychology 27:265–88.

Ellis, R. J. 1994. Presidential lightning rods: the politics of blame avoidance. Lawrence, KS: University Press of Kansas.

Etheredge, L. S. 1978. A world of men: the private sources of American foreign policy. Cambridge, MA: MIT Press.

George, A. L. 1980. Presidential decision-making in foreign policy: the effective use of information and advice. Boulder, CO: Westview Press.

globalsecurity.org 2005. Hurricane Pam. www.globalsecurity.org/security/ops/hurricane-pam.htm.

't Hart, P. 1994. Groupthink in government: a study of small groups and policy failure. Baltimore: John Hopkins University Press.

't Hart, P., and Boin, R. A. 2001. Between crisis and normalcy: the long shadow of post-crisis politics. In Rosenthal, U., Boin, R. A. and Comfort, L. K. (eds.) Managing crises: threats, dilemmas, opportunities. Springfield, IL: Charles C. Thomas, pp. 28–46.

't Hart, P., Stern, E. and Sundelius, B. (eds.) 1997. Beyond groupthink: political group dynamics and foreign policymaking. Ann Arbor: University of Michigan Press.

Hermann, M. G. 1980. Explaining foreign policy behavior using personal characteristics of political leaders. International Studies Quarterly 24:7–46.

Hermann, M. G. 1984. Personality and foreign policy decision making: a study of 53 heads of government. In Sylvan, D. A. and Chan, S. (eds.) Foreign policy decision-making: perceptions, cognition, and artificial intelligence. New York: Praeger Press, pp. 53–80.

Hermann, M. G. 1987. Assessing the foreign policy role orientations of subsaharan African leaders. In Walker, S. (ed.) Role theory and foreign policy analysis. Durham, NC: Duke University Press, pp. 161–98.

Hermann, M. G. 2003. Assessing leadership style: trait analysis. In Post, J.M. (ed.), The psychological assessment of political leaders. Ann Arbor: University of Michigan Press, pp. 178–212.

Hermann, M. G., and Preston, T. 1994. Presidents, advisers, and foreign policy: the effect of leadership style on executive arrangements. Political Psychology 15:75–96.

Hermann, M. G., Preston, T., Korany, B. and Shaw, T. M. 2001. Who leads matters: The effects of powerful individuals. In Hagan, J. and Hermann, M.G. (eds.) Leaders, groups, and coalitions: understanding the people and processes in foreign policymaking. Boston: Blackwell Publishers, pp. 83–131.

Hess, S. 1988. Organizing the presidency. Washington, DC: Brookings Institution.

Hood, C. C. 2002. The risk game and the blame game. Government and Opposition 37:15–37.

Hosenball, M. 2006. Katrina's paper trail. Newsweek, 1 February. http://www.msnbc.msn.com/id/11103206/site/newsweek/.

House, R. J. 1990. Power and personality in complex organizations. In Staw, B. M. and Cummings, L. L. (eds.) Personality and organizational influence. Greenwich, CT: JAI Press, pp. 181–233.

Hsu, S. 2006. Katrina report spreads blame: homeland security, Chertoff singled out. Washington Post, 12 February.

Janis, I. L. 1972. Victims of groupthink. Boston: Houghton Mifflin.

Kaarbo, J., and Hermann M. G. 1998. Leadership styles of prime ministers: how individual differences affect the foreign policy process. Leadership Quarterly 9:243–63.

Kahn, J. 2000. Bush filling cabinet with team of power-seasoned executives. New York Times, 31 December.

Krugman, P. 2005. Point those fingers. International Herald Tribune, 9 September.

Lipton, E. 2006a. White House declines to provide storm papers. New York Times, 25 January.

Lipton, E. 2006b. White House knew of levee's failure on night of storm. New York Times, 10 February.

Lipton, E. 2006c. Senators assail Chertoff's job handling storm: lawmakers from both parties cite failures. New York Times, 16 February.

McClelland, D. C. 1975. Power: the inner experience. New York: Irvington.

Milbank, D. 2000. The chairman and the CEO: in incoming corporate White House, Bush is seen running board, Cheney effecting policy. Washington Post, 24 December.

Neuman, J. 2006. GAO puts blame on Chertoff for Katrina fiasco. Baltimore Sun, 2 February.

Nydegger, R. V. 1975. Information processing complexity and leadership status. Journal of Experimental Social Psychology 11:317–28.

Parker, C. F., and Stern, E. K. 2005. Bolt from the blue or avoidable failure? Revisiting September 11 and the origins of strategic surprise. Foreign Policy Analysis 1:301–31

Preston, T. 2001. The president and his inner circle: Leadership style and the advisory process in foreign affairs. New York: Columbia University Press.

Preston, T., and 't Hart, P. 1999. Understanding and evaluating bureaucratic politics: the nexus between political leaders and advisory systems. Political Psychology 20:49–98.

Preston, T., and Hermann, M. G. 2004. Presidential leadership style and the foreign policy advisory process. In Wittkopf, E. R. and McCormick, J. M. (eds.) The domestic sources of American foreign policy: insights and evidence, 4th edn. New York: Roman & Littlefield, pp. 363–80.

Rasmussen Reports 2005. Bush Katrina ratings fall after speech. http://www.rasmussenreports.com/2005/Katrina_September%2018.htm.

Ripley, A. 2005. An American tragedy: how did this happen? Time, 12 September.

Sanger, D. E. 2002. War was easy. The rest of the world is a mess. New York Times, 21 April.

Sanger, D. E. 2005a. Hard new test for president: disaster at home adds to challenges of Iraq. New York Times, 1 September.

Sanger, D. E. 2005b. Bush compares responses to hurricane and terrorism. New York Times, 22 September.

Schönbach, P. 1990. Account episodes: the management and escalation of conflict. Cambridge, UK: Cambridge University Press.

Schroder, H., Driver, M. and Streufert, S. 1967. Human information processing. New York: Holt, Rinehart, and Winston.

Sipress, A. 2001. Policy divide thwarts Powell in mideast effort: defense department's influence frustrates state department. Washington Post, 26 April.

Stevenson, R. W. 2005. In first response to crisis, Bush strikes off-key notes. New York Times, 3 September.

Taysi, T., and Preston, T. 2001. The personality and leadership style of President Khatami: implications for the future of Iranian political reform. In Feldman, O. and Valenty, L. O. (eds.) Profiling political leaders: a cross-cultural study of personality and behavior. Westport, CT: Praeger, pp. 57–77.

Tetlock, P. 1985. Integrative complexity of American and Soviet foreign policy rhetorics: a time-series analysis. Journal of Personality and Social Psychology 49:565–85.

Thomas, E. 2005. How Bush blew it. Newsweek, 19 September.

Tumulty, K., Thompson, M. and Allen, M. 2005. 'How many more Mike Browns are out there?' Time, 3 October.

US Government Accountability Office. 2006. Statement by Comptroller General David M. Walker on GAO's preliminary observations regarding preparedness and response to hurricanes Katrina and Rita. GAO-06–365R. Washington, DC: US Government Printing Office, 1 February.

Vertzberger, Y. 1990. The world in their minds: information processing, cognition, and perception in foreign policy decision making. Stanford, CA: Stanford University Press.

Wallace, M. D., and Suedfeld, P. 1988. Leadership performance in crisis: the longevity-complexity link. International Studies Quarterly 32:439–52.

The White House. 2006. The Federal response to hurricane Katrina: lessons learned. The White House: Washington, DC: US Government Printing Office.

Winter, D. G. 1973. The power motive. New York: Free Press.

Zakaria, F. 2002. Colin Powell's humiliation: Bush should clearly support his secretary of state – otherwise he should get a new one. Newsweek, 29 April.

3 | A reversal of fortune: blame games and framing contests after the 3/11 terrorist attacks in Madrid[1]

JOSÉ A. OLMEDA

Introduction

With only 3 days to go, Prime Minister José María Aznar and his ruling Popular Party (PP) appeared certain of victory in the general elections to be held on 14 March 2004. Pushing a firm antiterrorist agenda – read: anti-ETA (Euskadi Ta Askatasuna)[2] – and conservative fiscal policies, Aznar's PP held a comfortable 5 percent lead in the polls over the socialist contenders. Aznar's designated successor (Aznar had announced his retirement), former Interior Minister and Vice Prime Minister Mariano Rajoy, thus seemed a near certainty to continue the 8-year-old PP government.

The attacks of 11 March 2004 in Madrid changed all that. A series of bomb explosions on four trains heading to one of Madrid's main stations killed 192 persons and wounded 1,430. In addition to the horror and grief caused by the onslaught, Spain witnessed a stunning political shift. The socialist opposition led by José Luis Rodríguez Zapatero won the elections just three days later.

Crises are often thought to foster solidarity, a phenomenon commonly known as the 'rally-'round-the-flag' effect. Following the 9/11

[1] I thank Fermín Bouza and Josep Ramoneda for the opportunity to participate in the Symposium 'Comparing the Impacts of 11 September 2001 and 11 March 2004', in New York, 8–9 April 2005. A first version was delivered as a paper in the Workshop entitled 'Crisis and Politics: Investigation, Accountability and Learning', in the Joint Sessions of the ECPR, in Granada, 14–19 April 2005. I thank the comments of all participants, and especially those from Paul 't Hart, Arjen Boin, Stefan Olsson, Evelyn Bytzek and Lina Svedin, as well as the helpful criticisms provided by César Colino, Juan Jesús González, José Luis Dader and Angustias Hombrados. Without 'beyond the call of duty' editorial help from Paul and Arjen, this chapter would not have achieved its final form. The flaws that remain are mine alone. The ECPR paper with minor corrections and a Spanish version with some more information are available online, thanks to Real Instituto Elcano.
[2] ETA is the acronym for the Basque separatist movement Euskadi Ta Askatasuna.

attacks in the United States, President George W. Bush's hitherto meagre job approval rating shot up 35 to 40 percentage points.[3] Likewise, the public's appreciation for Tony Blair's leadership as prime minister rose (on a ten-point scale) from 5.07 to 5.55 after the terrorist attacks in London on 7 July 2005. The fate of the Spanish government thus sharply contrasts with the fates of its western partners.

This chapter analyses a remarkable shift in political fortune. It asks why there was no rally-'round-the-flag effect in Spain, catapulting the sitting government to electoral victory. What happened in the hours and days after the attack that made so many people hold Prime Minister Aznar and his government accountable for the attacks?

The political parties offered radically different interpretations of the attacks. The PP explicitly suggested ETA authorship of the attacks, trying to mobilise Spanish society behind its antiterrorism agenda (Prime Minister Aznar had been a victim of an ETA attack in 1995). The opposition offered a different story line, which framed the attacks as 'punishment' for Spanish participation in the occupation of Iraq. In the hours and days after the attack, the opposition managed to replace the initial and official story line with one of its own. This chapter seeks to explain how the 3/11 crisis created new venues for 'meaning making', which were more skillfully exploited by the opposition than by the ruling PP.

The chapter begins by outlining a theoretical perspective, focusing on framing and counterframing, to help in exploring the PP's reversal of electoral fortune. After sketching the context of vulnerability in which the ruling PP approached the elections, the chapter provides a detailed account of the immediate reactions to the Madrid bombings of 2004. The empirical section is followed by an analytical section in which the stunning reversal of fortune is explored by applying the theoretical framework.

Framing contests in the wake of crises: A theoretical perspective

In the introduction to this book, we were reminded that the fate of crisis leaders hangs in the balance. Leaders may enjoy a lift in popularity and even gain a degree of respect they may have never known in the absence of crisis. But a crisis can also become the prism through

---

[3] It reached as high as 90 percent a few weeks after the attacks and hovered in the upper 80s in the months that followed.

which the electorate reviews earlier performances. It may then escalate a latent process of eroding trust, culminating in a sudden and seemingly unexpected fall from grace. This latter scenario unfolded in the wake of the 3/11 bombings.

This chapter investigates accountability processes in terms of framing contests. The introductory chapter explained that crises are characterised by deep uncertainty and conflicting interpretations of what is happening, why and what ought to be done. Apart from the operational response (coordinating the emergency services), the performance of crisis leaders depends to a considerable degree on the political process by which the various participants – political actors, media, victims and citizen bystanders – make sense of the emerging threat and the proposed means of dealing with it (Boin et al. 2005).

Framing is a pivotal instrument of crisis management by governments and other political actors alike ('t Hart 1993). Framing is defined here as 'selecting and highlighting some facets of events or issues, and making connections among them so as to promote a particular interpretation, evaluation, and/or solution' (Entman 2004: 5). Frames offer 'meaning' to what many experience as bewildering and frightening events. A crisis frame, in other words, forwards particular causes, consequences, culprits and cures. A crisis frame that becomes widely accepted as a true account can thus settle – in informal and unforeseen ways – the question of who is to blame.

Why is the crisis frame that absolves government from any blame (a frame that typically originates within that same government) embraced during one crisis and scorned during the other? The conveyers of a crisis frame need to be seen as accurate and trustworthy (Druckman 2001). The single most important factor that determines the effectiveness of governmental crisis communication efforts is the degree of credibility that governments possess. In this regard, their past performance in these domains is heavily influential. A track record of lies and deception may well undermine the credibility of the framing agent.

It appears that rally-'round-the-flag frames have effect only when opposition leaders do not criticise the government's policies. If the public receives primarily positive messages about governmental actions and interpretations and no legitimate counternarratives emerge, it may easily (and sometimes eagerly) accept the official explanation of adverse events (Brody and Shapiro 1989a, b). The absence of negative elite

evaluations indirectly leads to the absence of negative public evaluations, facilitating surges in the popularity of incumbent leaders.

Apart from any trust deficits, there are political hurdles that crisis framers must overcome. The acceptance of a crisis frame follows a
stratified path. A frame must make its way through various levels (governmental elites, oppositional elites, old and new media, news frames,
public). Some actors have more power or are more adept than others in pushing their crisis narratives in particular venues, such as the
media or parliament. Each venue, in turn, makes its own contribution
to the mix and flow of ideas (Entman 2004: 9–11). If a prime minister
mismanages relationships with oppositional elites and journalists and
fails to offer a compelling explanation for the impending emergency,
he or she may lose control of the meaning-making process. Despite all
the communications resources typically at the disposal of governments,
it is possible for elite opponents and oppositional journalists to take
control of the meaning-making process (Tarrow 1994; Entman 2004).

A crisis provides a good moment for political entrepreneurs and
groups seeking to turn latent discontent into effective political action
by proposing and dramatising 'counterframes' that challenge those put
forward by authorities (Tarrow 1994; Kingdon 1995). A seemingly
stable and dominant interpretation of (crisis) events may suddenly give
rise to an alternative frame that radically alters the shared perception
of problems, causes, heroes, villains and solutions. The more attention
the public pays to a crisis, the easier it will be for a government's
political opponents to make their case in the event of a perceived failure
(Baum 2004). Crisis should, in fact, be viewed as a 'tipping point' in a
longer process of declining legitimacy of government leaders and their
narratives (cf. Baumgartner and Jones 1993).

Media reporting remains indispensable for such tipping points to
occur. The media spotlight validates the relevance of both the frame
and its sponsor. The sponsor of an alternative frame needs the media to
broaden the scope of conflict. Where the scope is narrow, the weaker
party has much to gain and little to lose by broadening the scope, drawing third parties into the conflict as partisans (Gamson and Wolsfeld
1993: 116).

The rise of the Internet and digital media has facilitated loosely structured networks, weak identity ties and patterns of organising (around
issues and demonstrations) that define a new global protest politics

(Bennett 2003). Digital network configurations facilitate permanent political campaigns, the growth of broad networks (despite relatively weak social identities and ideological ties among the participants) and the rapid elevation of messages from desktops to television screens. In other words, new media can alter public images of issues through the old mass media. The creation of a public sphere based in *micro media* (e-mail, lists) and *middle media* Internet channels (blogs, organisation sites, e-zines) offers activists an important zone for framing information independent from, but potentially influential with, the traditional mass media. This introduces new dynamics in traditional postcrisis blame games.

These theoretical notions help explain why in some cases, a crisis can generate a stunning reversal of fortune. When the dominant party fails to communicate a convincing frame for major political adventures, it becomes vulnerable to negative feedback. When a new problem emerges, it is hard to explain away. Rigid adherence to existing frames only reinforces the emerging impression that the incumbents are vulnerable. This process of 'runaway meaning making' may lead to a tipping point: suddenly the majority no longer accepts the official position. This is, of course, a well-known process. The Spanish case shows us that it may happen very quickly and in situations where it is least expected.

The context: creeping vulnerability

Back in his days as opposition leader, Aznar had always been conscious of the need to win over public opinion for his strong Atlantic defence policy (Aznar 1994: 159). After years in power, however, he seemed to have forgotten his own lesson. The Spanish prime minister positioned himself as a loyal partner to Bush and Blair (meeting with them at the Azores conference in the Spring of 2003), and single-handedly pledged Spanish troops to the operation in Iraq. After announcing his decision to the Spanish Congress on 18 March 2003, the Spanish humanitarian mission arrived in Iraq on 9 April 2003.

Spanish public opinion had been critical of Saddam Hussein long before Bush and Blair started their public campaign. Surveys showed that 60 percent of Spaniards considered Saddam a danger to international security, 54 percent believed he was linked to international terrorism and 80 percent agreed with the UN resolutions that ordered

Iraq to disarm. Moreover, 58 percent believed Iraq possessed weapons of mass destruction. At the same time, 62 percent of Spaniards opposed the American policy on Iraq. The great majority (91 percent) of the public opposed military intervention, with 67 percent preferring Spain to remain neutral (Centro de Investigaciones Sociológicas 2003). Tellingly, only 11 percent supported Aznar's line on Iraq, with 35 percent favoring the socialist opposition's policy.

A large demonstration in Madrid against the looming war on 15 February and a smaller one on 23 February 2003, provided a tell-tale sign that significant segments of the public would not support Spanish participation in the Iraqi war. Even though the Spanish troops were sent on a peacekeeping mission with very strict rules of engagement, the socialist and postcommunist opposition framed the Spanish engagement in terms of a war mission, which proved rather effective in mobilising both their followers and uncommitted voters against the PP government.

Aznar pushed ahead on his Iraq policy without popular and political backing.[4] This created a latent vulnerability. He failed to formulate a frame that interpreted and defended Spanish involvement in an increasingly unpopular war. As Lamo (2004: 198) observed, 'the government of Aznar did not know how to carry out that campaign [to legitimise the use of force in Iraq] or did not want to do it. The Iraq war could have been illegal but legitimate, like Kosovo. But it was not to be'. This vulnerability would play a major role in the hours and days after the 3/11 attacks.

During the election campaign, Aznar and his ministers did not try to convince the Spanish electorate of the merits of their position. The Aznar government could boast a strong economy, which it had already made a main campaign subject. It could not boast much success on its second main theme: the antiterrorism agenda. A recent scandal (January 2004) involving secret negotiations between the socialist-secessionist government coalition in Catalonia and ETA contrasted with the antiterrorist platform of the PP. When ETA announced a unilateral cease fire (only in Catalonia) on 18 February 2004, the Ministry of the Interior declared a 'maximum alert' and warned that a terrorist 'attack or at least an attempt' would be very likely before the 14 March election (a favourite moment for ETA attacks).

---

[4] Aznar later implicitly acknowledged his mistake (Aznar 2004:150–151).

The March attacks: initial responses

On Thursday 11 March at 7:35 a.m., ten bombs exploded on four inbound trains at Madrid's Atocha Station. The carnage caused 192 deaths and 1,400 injuries. In the context of preelection claims and counterclaims about Basque terrorism, most Spaniards immediately suspected an ETA attack, despite the partial cease-fire declaration and the momentary weakness of the terrorist organisation.[5]

The government's response: blaming ETA

Around 9:55 a.m., Prime Minister Aznar contacted the king, his 'heir apparent' Rajoy, and the opposition leader to tell them he was going to call for a demonstration under the slogan '*With the victims, with the Constitution, for defeating terrorism*' to be held the next day. No one objected. In keeping with his personal leadership style, Aznar did not mobilise the government's official crisis management group. Instead, he summoned an informal crisis cabinet of his most trusted lieutenants. The minister of defence and the director of the National Centre for Intelligence were absent in this informal crisis management group.

The attacks placed the minister of the interior in the media spotlight. He asked everyone to remain calm and to care for the victims. He said there had been no previous warning (a difference with respect to the majority of ETA attacks) and announced that emergency and security forces had been deployed (*Cadena Ser* 11 March 2004: 11–12).[6]

Several senior officials of the police and the Civil Guard met at noon. ETA authorship seemed clear. In December 2003, ETA had planted two bombs made of titadyne, a commercial brand of dynamite stolen in France, in backpacks on a train from Irún to Madrid. The bomb was programmed to explode after the arrival of the train at Chamartín Station in Madrid. In February 2004, a civil guard stopped a van loaded with explosives. ETA had planned to explode the van near the same spot where the March 2004 bombs were planted. Around 12:45 p.m.,

---

[5] The front page of the daily newspaper *ABC* on this same morning had reported on the special deployment of security forces in order to prevent an ETA attack during the upcoming election weekend.

[6] Cadena Ser 2004/03/11 (Date): 11–12 (hour of broadcasting), http://www.cadenaser.com/static/especiales/2005/sonidos11_14/.

a senior police official called the police deputy director[7] from the scene of the attacks, informing him that the explosive was titadyne with a fuse. The National Center for Intelligence released a report stating that 'it is believed to be nearly certain that the terrorist organization ETA is the perpetrator of these attacks', pointing to the various antecedents listed above.

The minister of the interior immediately politicised this internal assessment. He put forward this 'ETA authorship frame' at his first press conference, stating that 'ETA was looking for a massacre; you have heard me say that in recent days'. He reminded his audience that ETA's plans had been thwarted four times by security forces, and that now they were keener than ever to commit an attack with many victims. The new event had demonstrated that ETA was unbroken by the police's recent successes against them and that the terrorist organisation was prepared to create massive psychopolitical disruption.

The minister then answered a reporter's question about the possible involvement of Al-Qaeda. He replied that there was no doubt about ETA authorship, and that the spokesperson for the political branch of ETA had been cheap and treacherous by denying ETA involvement. When asked what type of explosive was used, he said that this was being investigated, but that the general modus operandi of the attack had been vintage ETA: bombs in trains, bombs in backpacks. Answering a question about the way in which ETA usually acknowledges its attacks, he said that nobody had claimed authorship yet, and that ETA did not always immediately claim responsibility. He concluded by promising that 'with no change in our strategy, we will win' (*Cadena Ser* 11 March 2004: 11–12, 13–14).

Aznar's press appearance around 2:00 p.m. reconfirmed the ETA authorship frame. The prime minister did not mention ETA by name, referring to the 'terrorist band'. He implicitly condemned both ETA's political and terrorist branches, justifying his own counter-terrorism policy as the appropriate remedy. He used pep talk: 'Everybody knows that it is not their first try, several attempts have been stopped by security forces [but] we will defeat them; we will finish off the terrorist band with the force of the rule of law and Spaniards' unity. With strong laws, the work of security forces, justice tribunals firmly backed and decided to enforce the law, these criminals will be arrested and judged under

---

[7] The chief police official under political authority.

the rule of law'. And then he announced his plan for a public march: 'to defend these objectives, the government calls a civic demonstration under the slogan: With the victims, with the Constitution, for defeating terrorism' (*Cadena Ser* 11 March 2004: 14–15).

In the meantime, new evidence emerged. Near the Alcalá de Henares railway station, a van had been found. A tape with verses of the Koran in Arabic and seven fuses made in Spain were found in it, with traces of a dynamite type called Goma 2-ECO (which ETA had used before, but not in recent years). A meeting of senior police officials was called at 5:00 p.m. Confusion reigned and the meaning of the new clue remained unclear. A new line of inquiry was opened, but the original line of inquiry that presumed ETA authorship was not questioned.

At his second press conference, the minister of the interior announced the new development: 'The terrorist organisation ETA is the first line of police inquiry, its priority, but a second line has been opened. I am telling you everything with transparency'. Nevertheless, he argued that explosives and antecedents pointed to ETA. The attacks had a modus operandi similar to the ETA attack of 24 December 2003 (backpacks in a train) (*Cadena Ser* 11 March 2004: 20–1) and the new information did not alter the official frame.

The opposition did not offer an alternative frame on the day of the attacks. At 8:45 a.m., opposition leader Rodríguez Zapatero had been the first political leader to attribute authorship of the Madrid attacks to ETA (in an interview on *Cadena COPE*). Later he declared his support for Aznar and his call for a demonstration. The Basque nationalist head of the Basque regional government denounced ETA, taking for granted its authorship of the attack. The spokesperson from ETA's political branch was the only deviant voice that morning, but the Intelligence Service dismissed his denial.

A counterframe emerges in the media

The mass media supported the ETA authorship frame well into the first night. It was only when the largest radio station in Spain, the prosocialist *Cadena Ser*, began to report rumors undermining the ETA frame that an alternative account – a counterframe – began to emerge.[8]

---

[8] *El País*, *Cadena Ser* and CNN+ all belong to the powerful prosocialist mass media group PRISA.

Three different sources reported the discovery of a suicide bomber among the corpses. The minister of the interior denied the story but the station broadcast it around 10:00 p.m. (*Cadena Ser* 11 March 2004: 20–1, 22–3). This new information coincided with an alleged Al-Qaeda statement in the London daily *Al-Quds Al-Arabi*, which claimed responsibility for the Madrid bombings. If the suicide bomber rumour was correct, the ETA authorship frame would fall flat; and it would be the only missing element for the attacks to meet the Al-Qaeda modus operandi.[9]

This new 'evidence' enabled the opposition to develop a counter-frame in accordance with their electoral platform. To understand the speed with which the government frame lost credibility, it is important to note how this relatively complete and coherent counterframe emerged. Such framing does not just happen; it requires work. Below we document how this work evolved and who performed it.

A framing contest develops

The counterframe began to be developed at the elite level by the daily paper *El País* and at the mass level by the *Cadena Ser*. After discovering a backpack with a nondetonated bomb, a police fuse setter was able to disassemble it around 5:15 a.m. (12 March). This finding proved a breakthrough in the investigation: the explosive and mechanism were now known (Goma 2-ECO dynamite and copper fuses of Spanish origin). In addition, a cellular phone and its connection card were found. This new evidence undermined the dominant idea that ETA was responsible for the attacks.

Chief government figures had great difficulty in coping with the emerging challenge to their reading of the situation and indeed to their personal credibility. Aznar gave a press conference at 11:00 a.m. He expressed his commitment to transparency and promised that no line of inquiry would be discarded. Aznar insisted on the ETA authorship frame: after 30 years of terrorism, ETA remained the logical culprit. The star journalist of the *Cadena Ser*, Gabilondo, criticised Aznar and suggested that the Azores agreement (among Bush, Blair and Aznar for the Iraq war) might have turned the Islamist terrorist weapon against Spain (*Cadena Ser* 12 March 2004: 11–12).

---

[9] Islamist terrorism expert Yigal Carmon (2004) denied the authenticity of the Al-Qaeda document.

At a different press conference, the minister of the interior described the newly discovered evidence. He insisted on the similarities of the modus operandi with ETA attacks. He confirmed that the dynamite and fuses were identical to those found in the van on 11 March. Police inquiries would pursue all clues, but the minister argued that circumstantial evidence still made ETA the most likely suspect (*Cadena Ser* 12 March 2004: 18–19).

Meanwhile, the socialist opposition adopted a familiar Janus-faced political communication tactic: its leader and prime-ministerial candidate, Zapatero, would ask for unity and solidarity, while his party secretary attacked the government for hiding information. The latter pointed out that the political response to the attacks would have to depend on the source of the attack (Al-Qaeda or ETA). He 'urged the government to inform with diligence', as if it were not doing so, and criticised the government for not calling a meeting with all parliamentary groups to share information in a direct dialogue (*Cadena Ser* 12 March 2004: 9–10, 13–14).

The framing contest had begun and it was being waged in different media. Aznar and the minister of the interior, confident in their control of government media (especially public television) did not seem to realise that their frame was being disputed. We can only speculate why they did not address the emerging counterframe.

The daily newspaper *ABC* accepted the ETA authorship frame. *El Mundo* was more critical. Its editorial mentioned that the BBC had spoken of the possibility of a 'joint venture' between ETA and Al-Qaeda. It further criticised the hastiness of the minister of the interior. *La Vanguardia* agreed that authorship of the attack was still open. It added that if it were Al-Qaeda, it would be a 'punishment for supporting the Iraq war'. *El País* questioned, not very subtly, the ETA authorship frame: first, pointing to 'the eventuality of it being a job by Al-Qaeda and that had to do with the role played by Aznar's government in the Iraq War', and, second, stating 'one can only hope that there has not been concealment or manipulation by the government'. If Al-Qaeda did turn out to be the perpetrator, the attacks would be 'an attempt at extending the Iraq war on Spanish territory'. If the bombing was the product of a joint venture between Al-Qaeda and ETA, Aznar would be to blame for pulling them together by his repeated assertions that 'all terrorisms are the same' (editorials, *ABC*, *El Mundo*, *La Vanguardia*, *El País*, 12 March 2004).

The 'day after' ended with mass demonstrations. More than 11 million persons, out of a population of 42 million, demonstrated in the cities of Spain. But this climate of unity was already dissolving. On the eve of the demonstration, the Catalan regional government had declared its disagreement with the demonstration's slogan. Several PP politicians were attacked in the Barcelona demonstration. In the Madrid demonstration, small groups of activists shouted at the front of the march: '¿*Quién ha sido?*' (Who did it?). In other parts of the demonstration, people shouted against ETA. In hindsight, it is clear that the demonstrations provided a venue at which opposition forces could spread the budding counter-frame.

Flash mobs and high politics

The elections were set to take place on Sunday 14 March. During the 'day of reflection' on Saturday, any kind of electioneering was prohibited. Despite this regulation, the framing contest reached its climax through the frame alignment of oppositional media and flash mobs surrounding PP locales that Saturday afternoon.

Late Friday night, 12 March, the police inquiry had produced its first concrete results. The phone card led the police to a group of Moroccans. The suspects' nationalities were not revealed by the police information service except to the judge who was going to sign the arrest order.

At his Saturday press conference (his fourth), the minister of the interior doggedly kept with the ETA narrative, citing antecedents, logic and common sense. While he told the media that there had been no suicide bombings, the minister did not rule out a possible cooperation among different terrorist organisations. He reiterated that he had informed with honesty and transparency about the new clues as soon as he had been briefed by the security forces, but he did not mention the imminent arrest of the suspects.

Outside, it was clear that perceptions had shifted. At 3:00 p.m., the *Cadena Ser* radio station reported that the Intelligence Service was dedicating 99 percent of its resources to the Islamic terrorism hypothesis. This report was denied by the Service at 4:50 p.m. *Cadena Ser* began to broadcast from PP headquarters in Génova Street at 6:30 p.m., covering a demonstration that was organised through Internet and SMS

(Short Messaging Service) messages.[10] The websites, in turn, announced that *Cadena Ser* and *CNN+* were going to broadcast the demonstration.

At 8:10 p.m., the minister of the interior announced the arrest in Madrid of two Indians and three Moroccans. Several house searches were being carried out. The minister still did not abandon the official frame, insisting it was too early to trace connections with previous Islamist attacks or extremist Moroccan groups (*Cadena Ser* 13 March 2004: 14–15, 20–1).

At 8:55 p.m., the radio station gave information about 'flash mobs' rallying against the government that were spreading in different cities throughout the country. At 9:14 p.m., the ruling PP candidate, Rajoy, issued a statement denouncing the flash mobs surrounding the PP headquarters in Madrid and in other cities during the day. He also tried to take credit for the arrests:

I appear before public opinion to stop this illegal demonstration; different political parties have created the climate for this call. I have presented a complaint to the Central Electoral Board. I ask all citizens not to demonstrate against other PP locales. These are intolerable pressures, repeating the attacks on PP locales during local and regional elections. Finally I congratulate the security forces on the arrests, and ask you to vote for the best defense against terrorism. (*Cadena Ser* 13 March 2004: 21–2)

It took only 15 minutes for the socialist spokesperson, intervening on behalf of opposition leader Zapatero, to claim vindication of the emerging counterframe:

Spanish citizens deserve a government that does not lie to them, that always tells them the truth. We have been silent when the government has made disqualifications or affirmations that did not always fit with the truth; we will never, never, use terrorism as a political weapon. Tomorrow we have the opportunity to participate in the elections as homage to the victims, to reinforce our common convictions of peace and freedom. Citizens want to know the whole truth about the terrible events; the truth, the whole truth will be known at last, that is our commitment to the victims. (*Cadena Ser* 13 March 2004: 21–2)

At 11:20 p.m., a journalist asked for the creation of a research commission in the Parliament, which was to ascertain if the minister of

---

[10] Main sites included plataformaculturacontralaguerra.org, noalaguerra.com, nodo50.com and lahaine.org.

the interior and the government had manipulated, withheld and conditioned information about the terrorist attacks with the aim of avoiding electoral defeat. Later the same journalist spoke of 'a governmental temptation to declare a state of emergency' (*Cadena Ser* 13 March 2004: 15–16, 18–19, 19–20, 20–1, 23–4).

The mainstream media were cautious and sometimes openly critical of the government's policy. *ABC* said that the government had acted with realism and a caution consistent with the timing of the data, coupled with an information policy and sufficient appearances of Aznar (two times), and the minister of the interior (three times), in 36 hours. *El Mundo* wrote that its view would depend upon the perpetrator of the attacks. It nevertheless urged its readers to vote for the PP, while publishing an interview with its candidate. *La Vanguardia* guardedly criticised the minister of the interior but professed understanding because of the special circumstances. *El País* criticised the emphasis of the minister on ETA authorship and highlighted the political nature of his stance. It admonished the government and the prime minister 'to be prudent and not convert a hypothesis into a certainty' (editorial, *El País*, 13 March 2004).

Apotheosis: the election

Voting began Sunday morning at 9:00 a.m., while the last remaining flash mobs strolled through the center of Madrid and shouted their anti-PP slogans. The final turnout was 75.7 percent, 6.9 percentage points more than in the 2000 general elections.

As Spain voted, the major dailies and electronic media passed their provisional verdicts on the behaviour of various parties during the preceding hours and days. *ABC* criticised the anti-PP flash mobs. The left had accused the PP government of covering up information, but *ABC* denied the charge: 'Those who said that ETA could not condition political agendas, that terrorism could not be used as an electoral weapon. . . . For them, Islamic terrorism does serve to attack a democratic government'. *El Mundo* observed that the fundamental lack of knowledge about authorship still existed: 'The government has been in shock since Thursday, and this is influencing crisis management'. The newspaper attributed this state of paralysis to the emotional impact that the bombings had on Aznar – previously a victim of terrorism himself. The paper did note that the government had behaved in an honest and transparent way. It mentioned the connection between the demonstrators and PRISA's media, which were closely associated with the socialists (editorials, *ABC, El Mundo*, 14 March 2004).

La Vanguardia asked whether it is 'relevant to know who was responsible for the massacre in Madrid? Is it plausible, even feasible, to know [who did] it in three days? We are afraid that it is not'. The editorialist compared 3/11 with the 9/11 attacks, noting that two and a half years after the fact, many details of that other attack were still unknown. *El País* found 'no justification for blaming the government for the attacks'. At the same time, this newspaper confessed to having 'new and grave doubts' about information management by the government: 'At the last moment, finally, Spanish citizens began to receive concrete data about the inquiry' (editorials, *La Vanguardia, El País*, 14 March 2004).

The night of the election marked the end of the framing contest: Islamist authorship was now certain, and a new and more elaborate blame game was about to begin. The PP had lost the election: 43.27 percent of the vote went to the opposition party PSOE; the PP only received 38.31 percent. Prime Minister Aznar and his party had become the scapegoat of Spain's deep crisis.

Analysis: the selective politicisation of a security crisis

The 3/11 bombings in Madrid caused a turning point in the electoral fortunes of the ruling PP party. With the government only a few days removed from an easy reelection, the Spanish voters suddenly decided to vote the opposition party into power. Whereas deep crises usually cause a rally-'round-the-flag effect, which easily carries the ruling party to the electoral finish, this case is clearly different.

The majority of the Spanish electorate did not buy into the crisis narrative forwarded by Aznar and his colleagues. More importantly, they accepted the counterframe formulated by the opposition, which suggested that the prime minister had sought to capitalise on the crisis for electoral gains. Clearly, the opposition did not win this framing contest because their frame was 'true' and the official story was 'false'. The incumbent party lost because the prime minister and his trusted inner circle did not handle the framing contest particularly well. The opposition proved a more adept player at the postcrisis blame game.

The post-3/11 framing battle played out in the context of a highly publicised and controversial electoral campaign, which had reached its emotional culmination in the last days before the election. The PP government had increased polarisation among the electorate. In this setting, the terrorist attacks were the necessary condition for: (1) increasing the turnout on voting day, (2) a transformation of the originally 'expressive' vote for the postcommunist party into a pragmatic vote for the Socialist Party, (3) an increase of the antigovernment electorate, especially in the social strata mobilised by the flash mobs and (4) the constitution of the populist antiwar frame in the master frame to attract younger, new voters nurtured by the cycle of protest against the PP and its policies in different sectors. The 'fear' effect of the bombings thus helped to create a climate in which the government rather than the terrorists were blamed. Let us revisit the process to analyse how this happened.

Immediately after the attacks, most Spaniards suspected ETA. The Spanish government fell back on its default position with regard to ETA attacks. It reacted in the very same manner as in the kidnapping and murder of Miguel Ángel Blanco by ETA in July 1997 which triggered an intense mobilisation against Basque terrorism, denouncing ETA in the strongest possible terms and staging mass protests against it (Sádaba 2004).

In the days following the attacks, an alternative frame – the Al-Qaeda hypothesis – emerged and gradually gained strength. The dominant conception of terrorism within the Spanish administration did not allow it to construct an all-encompassing frame that included both ETA and Al-Qaeda. It was rigidly attached to the ETA authorship frame – perhaps because Aznar himself had been victim of an ETA attack in 1995. The administration responded in a rigid and inflexible manner to the attacks without properly weighing the new information. It concentrated power in the hands of the prime minister, reinforcing the process of rigidification (Staw et al. 1981). This inflexible response provided an opening to the socialist opposition, which it seized upon with speed and effectiveness. The opposition framed the rigid response of the administration as an indicator of governmental failure and unethical behavior. The opposing frames, using Entman's analytical categories, are summarised in Table 3.1.

By calling for large demonstrations on 12 March, the administration appealed to widespread feelings of allegiance to the Spanish democratic political system and solidarity with the victims and their families. Following the handbook of political psychology, the administration thus

Table 3.1. *The frames of political actors*

	PP Government: 'the ETA authorship' frame	PSOE and oppositional media: 'the government's lies' frame
Problem	ETA	Al-Qaeda
Evaluation	Known evil	Unknown evil
Cause	Basque nationalism	Spanish government support for the Iraq war (framed by opposition as participation)
Remedy	PP counterterrorism policy (Vote PP)	Peace (Iraq troop withdrawal) (Vote PSOE)

began to produce a classic rally effect. But this process was quickly disrupted by the emerging frame contest.

The very demonstrations convoked by the government created an opportunity to quickly spread rumours and nurture suspicions against the ETA authorship frame amongst a great number of people. Aznar's participation in the Iraq coalition and his refusal to generate a 'master frame' that explained the Spanish partnership with Bush and Blair rendered the ETA hypothesis vulnerable to doubt and suspicion. Such feelings were quickly bolstered by each new forthcoming piece of evidence suggesting Al-Qaeda authorship.

Opposition politicians and journalists used the old media, whereas extremist social movements used the new media. Together, they fed a master frame that unified opposition forces and symbolic messages which assigned the blame to government. This movement was strengthened by the government's rigid defence of its frame and its recent track record of inadequate crisis communication. As a result, the government rapidly lost credibility, the framing contest and the elections.

Of pivotal importance in explaining the sheer speed and force of this political change of fortunes was the role played by several 'hub' organisations and websites of very different ideological persuasions (socialist, communist, ecopacifist, ecologist, anticapitalist, anarchist, antiglobalisation). These are Internet umbrella organisations created to initiate and coordinate issue campaigns. Demonstrations often take on distinctive network forms based on how they allow users to access and communicate through the site. Many of these organising networks have survived beyond the action that originally drew them together,

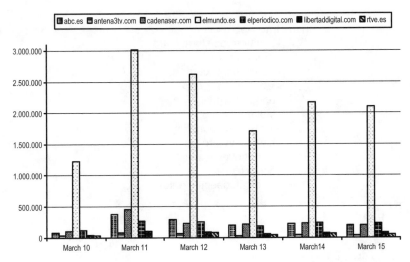

Figure 3.1. Number of visits and pages of daily newspapers viewed on Internet or TV/radio Web sites and day, 10–15 March 2004. (*Source:* www.ojd.es.)

because they generally offer networking services and calendars that become useful for future communication and planning. In some cases, these secondary planning features of Internet-only mobilising networks help to create successor organisations to mobilise future events. This is what transpired in Spain in the spring of 2004. Following the Madrid bombings there was also an increase in Internet use, as can be seen in Figure 3.1.

In fact, the flash mobs against the PP headquarters were convoked from these sites,[11] through SMS on cellular phones and allegedly from socialist and postcommunist automatic calling centres.[12] These sites recommended listening to the *Cadena Ser* and watching *CNN+*.

---

[11] The process started around 5:00 p.m. on 13 March, in Plataformaculturacontralaguerra.com created at the moment of the demonstrations against the Iraq war. This site recommended listening to the *Cadena Ser* and watching *CNN+*.

[12] These demonstrations were called spontaneous but were carefully planned by the above-mentioned networks of activists. The question is: Did socialist and/or postcommunist parties have a role in the calling? I think the answer could be yes, because some activists declared having received 'robotic voice' multimedia messages [Sampedro (ed.) 2005:70] – i.e. a multimedia message that costs four times as much as a written SMS message. The majority of youngsters use cellular phones with a prepaid card, and multimedia messages are beyond personal budgets.

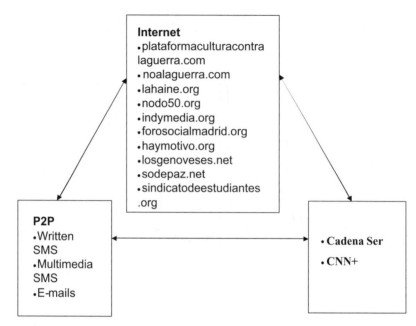

Figure 3.2. Symbiosis of new and old media for increasing oppositional frame resonance.

As Cañada (2004) points out, the cellular phones broadcast action, and the transistors offered context. The diagram of this symbiotic networking can be seen in Figure 3.2. There was a continuous feedback among the nodes, amplifying the diffusion of the oppositional frame of blaming the government and in itself constituting an authentic master frame. This provided the interpretive medium through which collective actors associated with different movements within the cycle of anti-PP protest assigned blame to the PP government.

Overall, the process of blaming and framing followed the pattern so aptly described by Brändström and Kuipers (2003). The opposition elites and oppositional media accused the government of having violated core values: at first it was just manipulation; near the end it was constructed as the political sin of lying. The opposition shifted blame from the national security apparatus to the foreign policy of the incumbent government. The opposition took the issue of Madrid and connected it directly to the decision to go to war in Iraq, and highlighted the responsibility of the prime minister and his party for what it portrayed as the root cause of the crisis. Moreover, the opposition

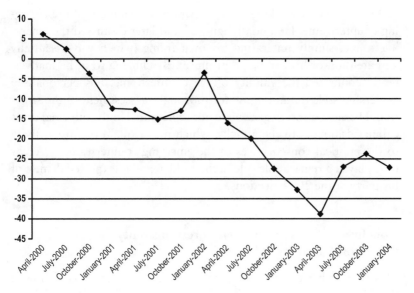

Figure 3.3. Credibility – net evaluation of confidence in Prime Minister Aznar, 2000–2004. (*Source:* CIS 2000–2004.)

concentrated the blame on the prime minister and his party for both the ill-fated Iraq adventure and the current misinformation regarding the Madrid attacks.

Aznar did not offer a solid defence to any of these charges. In fact, his vulnerabilities weakened his credibility in the framing contest. He was a political lame duck as well as the condensed symbol of the left's aversion to years of conservative policy.

When the Spanish people looked for an all-encompassing frame, Aznar could not deliver one because he had not built it when he supported the Iraq war. In addition he had several image problems. He had lost credibility due to the implementation of popular reform during 2000–2004 (see Fig. 3.3). Also, he failed to perform the ritual of solidarity ('t Hart 1993: 43), visiting the families of the victims and the wounded,[13] whereas the royal family, different members of PP government and the socialist leader did.

[13] Juan Luis Cebrián, Founder-Director of *El País*, said in the New York Symposium that Aznar was beaten by a victim's relative. A member of 11-M Victims Association said this was a lie. Cebrián said he had the name of the hospital and the doctor, but the member of 11-M Victims Association said again that it was a lie.

Aznar's biggest weakness, however, was his handling of the emerging counterframe. He initially ignored and later dismissed the emerging frame, simply reiterating his own frame (which was essentially an extension of his campaign promise). By clinging to it, he inadvertently confirmed the validity of the counterframe. His personalised leadership style did not allow for thorough reassessment of the situation. His election strategists were not represented in the informal crisis cabinet dealing with the attacks, which may explain the insensitivity to the political consequences of the emerging counterframe.[14] Aznar thus played a remarkable role in the sudden and unexpected demise of his party at the 2004 elections.

Conclusion: from governmental responsibility to electoral accountability

This chapter has considered the meaning-making battle that followed the 3/11 attacks in Madrid. It asked why the incumbent political party did not experience the benefits of a rally-'round-the-flag reaction, which so often helps to boost sitting powers. The chapter offers a plausible yet untested explanation to this question: the incumbent party did not understand or play the postcrisis framing contest particularly well. More fine-grained data and comparative research is, of course, needed before this explanation can be elevated to the status of tested theory. Yet the explanation forwarded in this chapter helps us understand one of the most stunning political shifts in recent European history.

The story is easy to recapture. The Socialist Party and other opposition parties had constantly framed Aznar's political support for the Iraq war as belligerence. The PP government never really countered that allegation effectively. This left a vacuum in the public sphere, opening up space for antigovernment social movements of different ideological persuasions. The government did not fight to win the public opinion battle because it expected the Iraq war to be a relatively painless *blitzkrieg*. But the war turned sour and finally produced devastating terrorist attacks abroad and eventually at home.

Because the government had not built a frame that convincingly explained Spain's role in the Iraq war, it was not able to counterframe

---

[14] Rajoy, the governmental specialist in crisis management, had left the government to wage the PP campaign.

the oppositional discourse that blamed the government instead of the assassins. The government panicked because of electoral fear and rigidly insisted on the ETA authorship frame, pushing it beyond the boundaries of reasonable evidence. That it did pursue alternative scenarios in the actual investigation paled in comparison. The oppositional forces framed the government's communication of the Madrid security crisis as an act of deceit and managed to displace public crisis perceptions onto voting intentions. As a result, the PP government took the blame and lost the elections – a clear example, as outlined in Chapter 1, of crisis-induced 'elite damage'.

This chapter illustrates how a crisis can create a window of opportunity for political entrepreneurs to advance a radically different frame and reap the political spoils of winning such a framing contest. It underlines the notion that such windows can be skillfully exploited, not only by media-savvy commanders in chief but also by opposition figures who come from behind. The ultimate lesson may be a deceptively simple one: it ain't over till it's over ('t Hart and Boin, 2001).

References

Aznar, J. M. 1994. España: La segunda transición. Madrid: Espasa Calpe.
Aznar, J. M. 2004. Ocho años de gobierno: una visión personal de España. Barcelona: Planeta.
Baum, M. A. 2002. The constituent foundations of the rally-'round-the-flag phenomenon. International Studies Quarterly 46:263–98.
Baum, M. A. 2004. How public opinion constrains the use of force: the case of Operation Restore Hope. Presidential Studies Quarterly 34:187–226.
Baumgartner, F. R., and Jones, B. D. 1993. Agendas and instability in American politics. Chicago: University of Chicago Press.
Bennett, W. L. 2003. Communicating global activism: strengths and vulnerabilities of networked politics. Information, Communication & Society 6:143–68.
Boin, A., 't Hart, P., Stern, E. and Sundelius, B. 2005. The politics of crisis management: public leadership under pressure. Cambridge, UK: Cambridge University Press.
Brändström, A., and Kuipers, S. L. 2003. From 'normal incidents' to political crises: understanding the selective politicization of policy failures. Government and Opposition 38:279–305.
Brody, R. A., and Shapiro, C. R. 1989a. A reconsideration of the rally phenomenon in public opinion. In Long, S. (ed.) Political Behavior Annual, vol. 2. Boulder, CO: Westview Press, pp. 77–102.

Brody, R. A., and Shapiro, C. R. 1989b. Policy failure and public support: the Iran-Contra affair and public assessment of President Reagan. Political Behavior II 4:353–69.

Cañada, J. 2004. Pásalo: redes y dispositivos en la víspera electoral. http://www.terremoto.net/x/archivos/000080.html.

Centro de Investigaciones Sociológicas (CIS). 2003. Estudio No. 2,481, Barómetro de febrero.

Druckman, J. N. 2001. On the limits of framing effects: who can frame? Journal of Politics 63:1041–66.

Entman, R. M. 2004. Projections of power: framing news, public opinion, and U.S. foreign policy. Chicago: University of Chicago Press.

Gamson, W. A., and Wolfsfeld, G. 1993. Movements and media as interacting systems. Annals of the American Academy of Political and Social Science 528:114–25.

González, J. J. 2004. Voto y control democrático: las elecciones del 14-M. CPA Estudios/Working Papers 7/2004. http://www.uned.es/dcpa/estudios.html.

't Hart, P. 1993. Symbols, rituals and power: the lost dimensions of crisis management. Journal of Contingencies and Crisis Management 1(1):36–50.

Kingdon, J. W. 1995. Agendas, alternatives, and public policies, 2nd edn. New York: Harper Collins.

Lamo de Espinosa, E. 2004. Bajo puertas de fuego: el nuevo desorden internacional. Madrid: Taurus.

Long, S. (ed.) 1989. Political behavior annual, vol. 2. Boulder, CO: Westview Press.

Morris, A. D., and Mueller, C. M. (eds.) 1992. Frontiers in social movement theory. New Haven, CT: Yale University Press.

Sádaba Garraza, T. 2004. Enfoques periodísticos y marcos de participación política. Una aproximación conjunta a la teoría del encuadre. Política y Sociedad 41(1):65–76.

Sampedro, V. (ed.) 2005. 13-M: Multitudes on line. Madrid: la Catarata.

Scheufele, D. A. 1999. Framing as a theory of media effects. Journal of Communication 49:103–22.

Staw, B. M., Sandelands, L. E. and Dutton, J. E. 1981. Threat-rigidity effects in organizational behavior: a multilevel analysis. Administrative Science Quarterly 26:501–24.

Tarrow, S. 1994. Power in movement: social movements, collective action and politics. Cambridge, UK: Cambridge University Press.

4 Flood response and political survival: Gerhard Schröder and the 2002 Elbe flood in Germany

EVELYN BYTZEK

Introduction: floods and political tides

In August 2002, six weeks before the German federal election on 22 September and right before the flash flood in eastern Germany, only 44 percent of voters would have chosen the incumbent government coalition of Social Democrats and the Green Party. A majority of 51 percent favoured a coalition of conservatives and liberals. After the flood, the picture had changed dramatically: 53 percent would have voted for the incumbent government and only 43 percent for the CDU opposition.[1] The timing of this remarkable shift suggests that the crisis must have had some positive influence on the government's or the chancellor's popularity. This view is supported by the possible elite enhancement features of crisis, especially of incomprehensible ones, which give political leaders considerable space for political action and framing efforts, as already spelled out in the introduction to this volume. Hence, if we assume this to be the case, the question is: What made this happen? What did Schröder and his government do about the crisis to cause this reversal in their electoral fortune? What made a significant segment of the German voters abandon their prior predispositions? What made them change their evaluation of the government's record?

German researchers have taken up this question and explained the positive impact of the Elbe flash flood on government popularity as a consequence of the effective crisis management performance of Chancellor Schröder and his party (Roth and Jung 2002: 7; Jung 2003: 24; Hilmer 2003: 194). This explanation has two shortcomings: first, it does not explicitly state *why* voters include the government's crisis management performance when making up their minds in the polling booth. Even though the evaluation of the governing parties on the

[1] Politbarometer Flash 08/2002, interviews conducted from 5 to 8 August 2002, and Politbarometer 09/2002, interviews conducted from 9 to 12 September 2002.

basis of their crisis effectiveness seems to be evident, this assumption does not fit into common approaches towards individual voting behaviour. These are dominated by sociopsychological attitude theories and political science models emphasising the ideological distances between parties and voters on major, ongoing policy issues. Second, recent research assumes a priori that the crisis management response was effective *because* it led to an increase in government popularity. This turns the relationship between crisis management and government popularity upside down and produces a tautological explanation. In order to tackle these problems, this study will take a closer look at the relations between the Elbe flood, the crisis management response and its influence on government popularity.

In the first section, I will introduce the case of the Elbe flood and the German federal election of 2002, followed by a discussion about why and how crises and their management by governments affect voters' evaluations. I argue that the main reason for the impact of the government's crisis management performance lies in voters' expectations which every government has to fulfil, independent of its political colour. Crises can have a negative impact on these expectations, and the onus is upon the government to do something about them: 'manage' them operationally but also reassure the public (by symbolic means). A key factor mediating the link between crises and government popularity is the way a crisis is presented in the mass media, since the bulk of the voters experience crises and government responses to crisis through the media. Therefore 'priming' and 'framing' effects must be considered. This is done here by a content analysis of the two most important German daily newspapers, the *Frankfurter Allgemeine Zeitung* (FAZ) and the *Sueddeutsche Zeitung* (SZ). Finally, the hypotheses derived from the theoretical discussion will be tested by means of aggregated daily polled data and time-series analysis. The concluding section summarises the results and puts them in theoretical and practical perspective.

The 2002 Elbe floods: civil emergency as political opportunity

The German federal election of 1998 signalled the end of the long-standing coalition of Helmut Kohl's Christian Democrats and the Liberal Democratic Party. It brought to power a coalition of Social Democrats and Green Party headed by Gerhard Schröder. The new government had generated public expectations concerning its ability to achieve much-needed labour market and social security reforms. This was not to be: although the new government experienced peaks in its popularity (due to a major financial scandal involving the Christian Democrats as well as the terrorist attacks of 11 September 2001 in the United States), it was seen by many to fall short of these expectations. Its popularity fluctuated several times from these highs to severe lows (Roth and Jung 2002: 4).

When the 2002 elections came near, the impact of the events favouring the government had mostly vanished, and the focus of voters had shifted to the tenuous economic situation in Germany. Schröder's government had been unable to deliver on his 1998 promise to reduce the number of unemployed to under 3.5 million. The coalition's economic management capability was widely criticised and the polls gave the conservative opposition a lead of up to 15 percent (Hilmer 2003: 193). Even though opposition candidate Edmund Stoiber's personal popularity could never match Schröder's, in the summer of 2002 a solid majority of Germans seemed convinced that the conservative opposition was the better choice at the upcoming election (Roth and Jung 2002: 7). Then the rains started.

The flash flood of the river Elbe in summer 2002 is a typical example of a fast-burning crisis that '... suddenly arrives and visits only briefly' (Boin et al. 2005: 97). It was caused by heavy rainfalls in the catchment area of Elbe, Donau, Moldau and Mulde. On 12 August 2002 the seriousness of the situation became evident with the overflowing of several dams in nearby mountains. First the situation on the Donau and Mulde escalated, flooding the historic centre of the town of Grimma on 13 August. Soon after, the river Elbe was out of control, flooding the old town of Dresden, including many of its famous heritage sites. On 17 August the Elbe flood reached its peak in Dresden, with downstream regions in danger of being flooded as a result of dike bursts. A large part of the town of Bitterfeld, home to several chemical firms, was evacuated. On 19 August the flood wave reached northern Germany, but caused much less damage there. In all, the 'flood of a century' caused damage worth 9 billion euros and generated disaster relief operations involving more than 128,000 helpers (Schuett 2003: 136–7).

In cases of natural disasters in Germany, the German federal government is not in charge of operational crisis management. Disaster prevention and management is assigned by law to the states (Bundesländer, cf. Dombrowsky and Ohlendieck 1998: 153). Central government can only provide financial aid to disaster victims, offer military assistance and assume a coordinating role in case of a crisis involving multiple Länder. Media coverage of the government's role in the 2002 flood mainly focused on the first two options. The army had previously been deployed during floods (the river Oder, in 1997), and now people expected this same kind of support. This did not apply to the allocation of financial aid. Promising such aid gave the government the opportunity to demonstrate compassion and commitment towards the victims. And it did. It promised financial aid at a very early stage of the disaster. Moreover, it also announced the delay of a planned tax reform in order to pay for the crisis aid package.

The state of emergency eased the pressure on the Schröder government to manage the existing high budget deficit: money spent on helping flood victims was money well spent as far as public opinion was concerned. The Christian-Democratic opposition criticised these moves as being opportunistic and irresponsible. But they misread the public mood: its bickering about the budget was now seen not as a sign of fiscal responsibility but as a lack of empathy with the plight of the flood victims. Moreover, Schröder seized upon another set of opportunities offered by the flood to the incumbent government: to work in close cooperation with the country's major television channels to raise donations (and thus raise one's visibility and profile); and to make well-publicised early field visits in the hardest hit regions in the main electoral battleground of eastern Germany. This made an interesting contrast to opposition leader and Bavarian premier Stoiber, who prioritised visits to flooded regions in the much less hit, less mediagenic and electorally already secure Bavaria. Table 4.1 provides a summary of polling results and government actions during the Elbe flash flood.

The 2002 floods constituted a major emergency by any yardstick. They threatened and damaged vital cultural and industrial locations. They set back the already tenuous economic upswing in eastern Germany. They rendered thousands of people homeless and caused a lot of psychological damage. Given these stakes and their timing in relation to the upcoming elections, the floods were surely a major test case for the government and to some extent also the opposition. The question is: How can we factor people's evaluations of government (and opposition) crisis responses into existing models of voting behaviour? These models do not address popular expectations of crisis management capacities at all. In the following section, I attempt to develop

Table 4.1. *Crisis chronology*

Date	Events and actions
5–8 August 2002	Polling results: SPD/Green Party 44%, CDU/CSU/ FDP 51%
13 August 2002	Chancellor Schröder announces a program for immediate aid
	Bavarian Premier Stoiber visits flooded Passau/ Bavaria
14 August 2002	Schröder visits Grimma/Saxony
	The federal cabinet decides to give 100 million euros
15 August 2002	Stoiber announces financial aid for eastern Germany
20 August 2002	Minister of the Interior Schily visits Wittenberge/ Brandenburg
22 August 2002	Minister of Defence Struck visits the armed forces helping in flooded areas
9–12 September 2002	Polling results: SPD/Green Party 53%, CDU/CSU/ FDP 43%
22 September 2002	Election result: SPD/Green Party 47.1%, CDU/ CSU/FDP 45.9%

Sources: Polling and election results from Politbarometer Newsletters of Forschungsgruppe Wahlen eV, Mannheim. Government actions from articles about the Elbe flood in the FAZ.

an approach that will allow us to conceptualise crisis management in terms of voting behaviour.

Crisis management and voter expectations

Besides evaluating the government on partisan grounds (e.g., the ideological distance of the parties or their long-term commitment towards a party), citizens have more general expectations of government. There are responsibilities that every government, independent of its partisan composition, must live up to simply because of its function as federal executive (Ostrom and Simon 1985: 337–45). These expectations differ slightly between countries and can be deduced from the assignments of the state as laid down in the law. In Germany these include maintaining peaceful relations with other countries (both politically and economically); maintaining adequate national defence; protecting the life, health and property of citizens; maintaining and developing the legal and economic order; stimulating the economy; maintaining public order and stimulating civic culture (Reineck 2003: 19–20). It is assumed that every German government regardless of its party-political composition needs to fulfil these assignments to be evaluated positively by voters. Civil emergencies fit into this picture because they constitute an acute threat to the life, health and property of citizens and can destabilise entire communities and regions. Citizens expect governments to act vigorously when these contingencies occur, and to restore the status quo ante as much as possible.

The salience of meeting these expectations is increased because civil emergencies and other types of crises are intensively reported in the mass media. Accordingly, voters are informed about the threat that a current crisis poses and are able to monitor the government's reaction to it in considerable detail. Evaluating the government on the basis of its crisis management performance thus becomes both a relevant and feasible task for them. Moreover, so-called priming effects are likely to occur: crises are issues that rise to the top of the public agenda because of their massive media coverage. Therefore the government's crisis management performance becomes a chief criterion for voters' evaluations of their politicians and parties (Iyengar and Kinder 1987: 63–5).

Crises, therefore, can have a positive impact on the government's popularity if its crisis management performance strikes a sympathetic chord with voters. But what exactly constitutes voters' expectations regarding the government's crisis behaviour? What, electorally speaking, is 'good' crisis management? I presuppose here that crisis management can be conceptualised in terms of two domains: operational response (e.g., the deployment of resources, coordination efforts, and planning and accomplishing evacuations) and psychological reassurance ('the situation is serious, but the government can bring it under control'; see, e.g. Edelman 1977).

As stated, operational crisis response in Germany is dealt with mostly by the Bundesländer. In so far as the federal government gets involved, when it coordinates responses across Länder, these activities largely take place 'off screen' as far as mass media interest is concerned. The political opportunity (and threat) structure that crises harbour for incumbent governments is therefore located mainly in the second domain. I hypothesise that voters seek reassurance by convincing themselves that the government takes charge during a crisis, provides strategic direction to crisis management operations and demonstrates tangible compassion towards victims (Boin and 't Hart 2003: 546–8). Since its operational mileage in Germany is limited, the federal government will have to excel in the symbolic domain.

This accords with classic arguments by writers such as Edelman that symbolic politics involves compensatory actions to 'real policy' (cf. Sarcinelli 1998: 729). According to Edelman, symbolic politics stands in contrast to political actions by which the government allocates resources to social groups (Edelman 1977: 12). It aims at the reassurance of people who feel threatened by some contingency or political action (Edelman 1977: 12–15). Therefore symbolic politics becomes especially important during times of crises characterised by widespread public feelings of threat and uncertainty (Boin and 't Hart 2003: 544). The scope and indeed the need for symbolic politics is further supported by the conditions which the modern mass media system places on politics. Symbolic actions are easier to show to people (by using media imagery) than showing the daily and difficult grind of allocating resources (Sarcinelli 1998: 729). One of the most important means of symbolic politics is rituals. Edelman (1977: 16) defines these as 'motor activity that involves its participants symbolically in a common enterprise'. By means of rituals, politicians can show their relatedness to the people. During natural disasters, for example, site visits by government leaders are an important ritual, which shows that the government takes seriously the crisis and the hardships of victims ('t Hart 1993: 43).

In times of crisis, the very speed of government response gains a symbolic value too (see Brändström et al., this book, on the tsunami response case, which was all about the perceived sluggishness of government responses to the disaster). One area where speed matters is the timing of government announcements of aid packages to victims. Governments that defer announcements about aid until the full extent of the damage is known generally do not fare as well symbolically as governments that jump ahead and commit themselves right in the thick of things. Besides speed, effective symbolic management of crisis aid also involves using code words like 'comprehensive', 'generous', 'straightforward' and 'unbureaucratic' when it comes to describing the kind of aid given and the mode of its delivery.

An additional component of symbolic crisis management is manipulation of the definition of the situation ('t Hart 1993: 41). This effort can have an impact on the frames used by the mass media to depict the crisis, and therefore on the evaluation of the government's crisis behaviour. Media framing is a process by which (1) certain objects and relations between these objects (and thereby certain details of reality) are emphasised and (2) certain benchmarks and attributes that can be applied to objects become salient (Scheufele 2003: 46). The media emphasise certain aspects by reporting a crisis in such a way that can be positive or negative for the government. Implicitly and at times explicitly, therefore, it is suggesting to voters a certain type of evaluation with regard to government's handling of the crisis. Especially with unknown events and topics like natural disasters, a particular evaluation of the government can effectively be forced upon voters by the media through its use of framing.

As always in politics, both governments and oppositions will try to define crisis episodes in terms that make them look good (and/or damage their opponents). But in crisis the stakes of this ongoing 'framing contest' are raised dramatically (see Olmeda, this volume). Moreover, since crises tend to generate a veritable explosion of media interest, it becomes harder for any party to frame the public perception of a crisis. Crises, being unstructured and low-frequency events by definition, present ample opportunities for journalists to create their own story lines. When the bulk of the mass media's crisis representations produce criticism of the government, this may generate calls for investigations, a search for culprits, and more generally force office holders to account for the alleged shortcomings in the government's crisis preparedness and response. Simply put, media reports to the effect that government negligence helped cause the crisis to begin with or that government indifference and disorganisation have complicated crisis response operations are bad news politically for any government.

We need to dissect the precise nature of the presumed relations between operational and symbolic governmental crisis management as well as media crisis reporting more generally. Obviously the intensity, emphasis and tone of media reporting by itself reflects journalistic proclivities and editorial policies. Media can choose to ignore or highlight the operational as opposed to the symbolic component of a government's crisis response; they can applaud or criticise either or both. To gain insight into these relationships, I will treat media reporting separately from media commentary.

I have shown above that in the German federal system, central government has limited possibilities to play a major role in operational crisis management. When some major disturbance occurs, central government actors will nevertheless be under pressure to respond and therefore are likely to engage in various forms of symbolic action. I argue that if central government actors are successful in performing symbolic crisis-response functions (displaying control and coordination, demonstrating commitment and, particularly, imposing a definition of the situation on the wider public discourse about the crisis – while managing to avoid the impression that their behaviour is self-serving), then an increase in government popularity is likely – even if its de facto contribution to the operational crisis response remains largely invisible. The impact on popularity is achieved in this case on the wings of a priming effect: the government manages to influence the way in which voters evaluate its performance. Therefore, the argument is synthesised in the following hypotheses on the relationship between crisis and government popularity:

> *Hypothesis I: German federal government responses to crises have an effect on the government's postcrisis popularity; this effect is mainly produced by the symbolic component of governmental crisis management and to a lesser extent by the operational component.*
>
> *Hypothesis II: Government popularity following crises will increase to the extent that media reporting follows the definition of the situation espoused by government actors; it will decrease to the extent that media divert from the government storyline and articulate critical opinions about government performance.*

The crucial variable mediating between government crisis behaviour and government popularity is media reporting. In the section that follows, I will present the results of the media content analysis for the 2002 flood crisis. The dependent variable, government popularity, will be constructed by aggregating daily polled data.

From papers to polls: media crisis reporting and its consequences

I have chosen two papers as sources, the *Frankfurter Allgemeine Zeitung* (FAZ) and the *Sueddeutsche Zeitung* (SZ). Equating 'the media' with two newspapers is a serious limitation of this study, especially considering the current predominance of television. Nevertheless, in Germany, daily newspapers have 77 percent of contact proximity (Bloedorn and Gerhards 2004: 2). Moreover, the reason for relying on newspapers is their greater information density. In comparison to the few minutes of daily television news bulletins devoted to any given issue, newspapers give more detailed information and, even more importantly, articulate explicit opinions about the government's and other actors' crisis responses. Finally, relying on newspapers and not on television news should be a harder test of the hypotheses, since television news is biased towards showing symbolic actions – which, after all, are partly designed to look good on TV – while newspapers also offer elaborate coverage of the operational domain and thus present a richer, more balanced picture. The main reason for the choice of these particular newspapers is that among the nontabloid press, they are Germany's media system opinion leaders. Other media will follow them with subjects and tenor of reporting; hence it is reasonable to assume that they represent the main thrust of German media's reporting and opinionating (Kepplinger et al. 1986: 267). These two newspapers will therefore reach many voters: first, directly, for being nationally distributed and having a considerable print run (FAZ: more than 370 000, SZ: more than 450 000) and, second, indirectly, by influencing other media's reporting of events. Therefore it is quite common in German political and communication research to rely on these two newspapers in assessing the picture of the political world, or crisis in particular, transported by the media (e.g. Brosius and Eps 1993; Gerhards 1996; Scherer et al. 2005).

The content analysis covers the first to the last day, when articles about the crisis were published. The thematic search for articles in Lexis/Nexis was abandoned after the first full week without any articles about the crisis. Only articles on the political pages of the newspapers were chosen because they pertained to the political dimension of crisis management – our main interest here.

The hypotheses presented above produce three main questions to be answered by the content analysis: (1) How prominently did both newspapers cover the floods over time (i.e. when are priming effects most likely to have occurred)? (2) Which aspect of governmental crisis management dominated newspaper coverage at any given time – operational crisis responses or symbolic management efforts? (3) How did the media frame the crisis, particularly with regard to evaluating the government's crisis management performance? In a nutshell, the content analysis needs to contain a priming, theme and framing analysis.

Intensity

To answer the first question, all articles have been coded on a day-by-day basis. Figure 4.1 shows the total number of articles per day and by newspaper as well as the grand totals. It reveals that media attention for the Elbe flash flood was high from the outset, starting with four articles on 13 August and jumping to fifteen articles on 17 August. After the continuous decline of reporting between 31 August and 3 September, the media briefly abandoned the flood story. Between 4 and 7 September, reporting fell back to low levels with just two articles a day. The core of the reporting therefore lies between 13 August and 7 September. In this short time span, media attention was very intense, raising the likelihood that priming effects may have occurred during this time.

Thematic content

The thematic and framing analyses are more complicated. The unit of analysis changes from articles as such to paragraphs within articles, classified by their contents. Analysing paragraphs instead of sentences is easier to do without much risk of information getting lost, since separate themes and statements are usually presented in separate paragraphs. Some articles clearly dealt with just a single theme and were classified as such.

The coding scheme for the thematic analysis included four categories. In addition to the theoretically relevant categories of operational acts and symbolic crisis management, I also used the categories of information (facts and figures about the event as such) and drama (human interest) in order to produce a comprehensive coding. Every paragraph was coded according to this scheme (see Table 4.2).

In addition to coding the four themes, the author of the information, actions or promises cited in the articles was recorded whenever this information was available. The actor scheme first distinguishes federal actors from those at other levels of government. Among those actors coded as federal, the scheme then differentiates between the federal

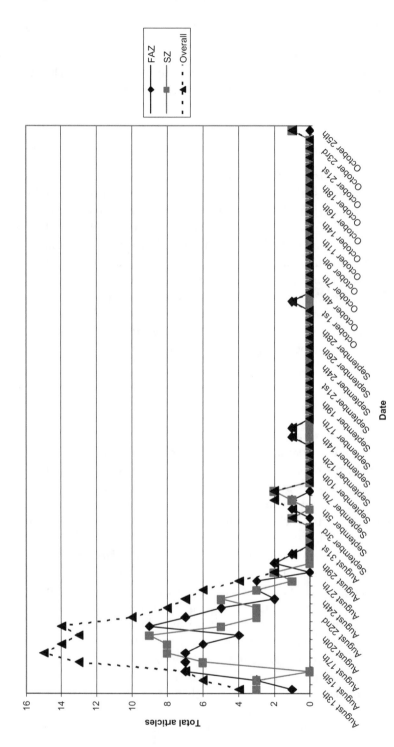

Figure 4.1. Total articles about the Elbe flood, 2002.

Table 4.2. *Classification scheme of the theme analysis*

Code	Category	Content
1	Facts and background information about the floods	Water levels, flooded areas, forecasts, causes of the floods, background information about flood abatement, affected regions and rivers
2	Operational matters	Building provisional dikes, making and treating sandbags, evacuations, coordination efforts, suggestions for avoidance of future floods, concrete financial aid, no promises
3	Symbolic politics	Presence of politicians in concerned regions, appeal for solidarity and aid, promises for financial aid and steps for crisis prevention
4	Drama	Presentation of individual fates and situations which show more than mere information and aim to hit recipients emotionally

government as a whole and/or its constituent agencies (e.g. operations of the German Federal Armed Forces); the major (Social Democratic Party) and minor (Green Party) coalition parties; and the federal opposition. At the subnational level, the Bundesländer and the municipalities are important actors in crisis management because of their operational responsibilities, and therefore part of the actor scheme.

The presentation of the evolution of theme frequencies over time has been organised according to the main variables mentioned above. Hence the figures that follow contain the counts for the thematic categories of frequencies of information, operational actions of the federal government (e.g. counts for the government as a whole as well as for its two constituent parties), symbolic management efforts and drama. I have omitted days when no reporting of the crisis took place and concentrated on the core reporting period where priming effects are likely (i.e. 13 August to 7 September 2002) (see Fig. 4.2).

The figures show that media reporting was clearly dominated by the government's operational actions, followed by the government's symbolic politics. Perhaps surprisingly, given the 'high end of the media

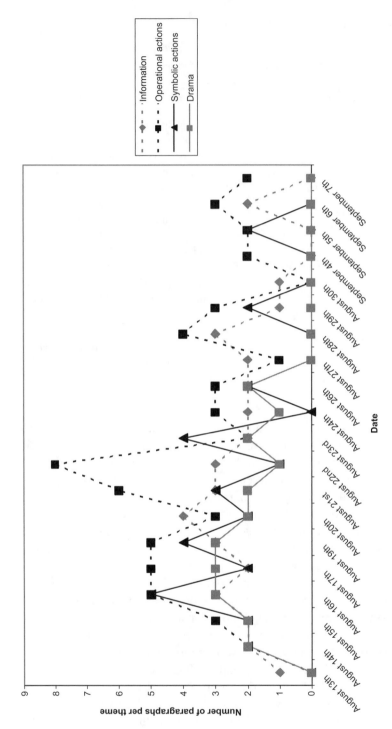

Figure 4.2. Course of theme frequency.

spectrum' sources used, personal drama was still a quite important theme in the two newspapers' coverage during the Elbe flood, but not as important as operational and symbolic actions. The reporting of basic information and human drama all but ceased at the beginning of September, whilst operational and symbolic crisis management responses remained newsworthy, partly due to the political postmortems conducted after the water had receded.

Other than expected, the government's operational responses were also intensely covered by the mass media. The high frequency of reporting about crisis operations was partly due to the mobilisation of the armed forces, whose massive effort to support weakened dikes was depicted as decisive in preventing further flood damage. Although the armed forces story was constantly in the news, symbolic actions of the government were covered in short, sharp jolts of much higher intensity. Hence, whereas operational crisis management matters, it seems safe to assume that the coverage of symbolic acts has the greatest impact on the voters' minds, since media coverage of it is so intense.

Framing

The popularity of the government during a crisis depends not only on media reports about its operational and symbolic crisis management but also on the general picture of the crisis conveyed by the media. How the media frame a crisis (e.g. selectively highlighting certain aspects of its causes or consequences) can also have an impact on voters' evaluations of the government's crisis behaviour. Hence I coded for situation reports and assessments that were positively or negatively related to the government. For example, a flood that is portrayed as having been triggered by bad weather but allowed to escalate into a major crisis by regulatory oversight will hurt the government's standing. By contrast, one that is solely attributed to a tragic coincidence of circumstances beyond government control will not. Second, I coded for statements about the government's crisis management performance. Table 4.3 shows the classification scheme used for the framing analysis. This scheme is also related to the actor scheme shown above.

For the sake of clarity, the frequency of all ten categories is not presented. Positive categories are allocated +1, negative categories –1, and the ten categories are summed up to come to a framing balance.

Table 4.3. *Classification scheme of the framing analysis*

Code	Evaluation	Content
1	Positive	The flood is not caused by human defaults.
2	Positive	Symbolic politics is useful.
3	Positive	There is control over the situation.
4	Positive	Everything is done to prevent further damage and to help victims.
5	Positive	Direct positive evaluation
6	Negative	The flood is caused by human defaults.
7	Negative	Symbolic politics is self-interested and debilitating.
8	Negative	There is no control over the situation.
9	Negative	Shortfalls at crisis management
10	Negative	Direct negative evaluation

The framing balance shown in Figure 4.3 distinguishes only between the federal government and other actors, since this is the main concern of this chapter. This figure also focuses on the core reporting period, 13 August to 7 September.

The framing balance of the government during the Elbe flood was overwhelmingly negative, as was the framing balance of other actors, mainly due to direct negative evaluations of their behaviour during the crisis. The high number of direct negative evaluations for all actors can be ascribed to the discussion about the financing of crisis aid packages, which led both government and opposition to blame one another as well as to criticism from journalists about the inappropriateness of having such a politicised discussion at that point in time, when urgent needs remained to be met. Only once, on 23 August, was the framing positive for the government. When reporting about the crisis decreased in September, the framing became more neutral towards the government as well as the other actors. So in this case the government was not at all successful in defining the situation on its own terms.

Analysis

What do the findings of the media coverage of the Elbe flood tell us about expected changes in government popularity? First, the Elbe flood was subject to massive reporting between 13 August and 7 September,

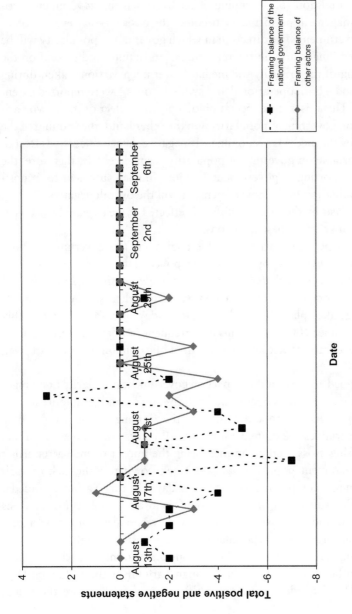

Figure 4.3. Framing of the Elbe flood, 2002.

a key condition for a priming effect by which the government's crisis management performance becomes the basis of voter evaluation of the government. The direction in which government popularity will be affected hinges first on the reporting of its actions and second on the framing of the crisis by the media. Government actions taken during the flood – both operational and symbolic ones – were reported extensively. This raises the expectation of a positive effect of these two variables on government popularity. On the other hand, the framing of the crisis by the media is predominantly negative, hence a negative effect of this variable on government popularity seems likely. Is, therefore, the heavy reporting of governmental actions in itself sufficient for a positive evaluation of the government, or will the overall negative framing of the crisis by the media nullify this effect? Let me explain how I went about answering these questions.

The dependent variable in this analysis is the government's popularity, constructed by aggregating polled data from the 2002 surveys of the *Gesellschaft für Sozialforschung und statistische Analysen*.[2] The advantage of this data compared to other surveys is that its polling takes place from Monday to Friday instead of just monthly (see Guellner 2000: 568). This high frequency of data gathering allows us to accurately trace any changes in public opinion due to short-lived events.

I argued above that the impact on government popularity first hinges on the government's operational actions and second (and more importantly) on its symbolic actions and the framing of the crisis. These three variables are quite common for all voters but change over time. Analysing cross sections in measuring the impact of media reporting on government popularity does not help, owing to the lack of variance in media reporting for voters per day. The time variance of media reporting suggests a time series analysis instead. The unit of analysis is a day, and the answers of the survey respondents must be aggregated accordingly. The popularity of the government will be measured by using the question for the respondents' voting intention if there was to be an election to the German parliament the following Sunday. The dependent variable of this analysis is therefore the ruling

---

[2] The data set is available at the Central Archive for Empirical Social Research, University of Cologne, named ZA3909.

coalition's share of the vote as it appears from this survey question. Given the well-documented differences between voters in eastern and western Germany and the fact that the flood hit eastern but not western Germany, the time series analyses must be performed for eastern and western Germany separately.

One problem caused by the data structure is the fact that the newspapers used for the content analysis do not appear on Sundays and that no surveys were administered during weekends. To correct for missing data, the Friday and Saturday media reporting has been cumulated and branded as Friday's media reporting. The reason for this procedure lies in the following analysis of the data, where the media reporting at time *t* will not affect voters' minds at time *t* but only a few days later. Saturdays and Sundays are thus excluded from the data set. The analysis covers the time span between 1 August and 30 September, thereby adding days without media reporting of the crisis. It is possible that a common rise in government popularity might occur before the national election, which would also show up before and after the crisis. Therefore, by adding extra days, this rise will not be totally ascribed to the crisis. The rise in government popularity due to the crisis must be higher than the overall trend or be very strongly connected to government actions to show up in this analysis design. By looking at government popularity in August and September 2002 and omitting Saturdays and Sundays, the analysis comprises 43 days.

Figure 4.4 presents the scores for the main dependent variable, the share of the governing parties in relation to the vote intention question in eastern and western Germany. The government's popularity shows an upward trend both in eastern and western Germany, beginning before the crisis and lasting until the federal election on 22 September. Against this overall trend, government popularity decreases slightly in mid-August, rising afterwards until the end of the crisis reporting period and remaining almost at this high level. The fluctuations in eastern Germany are partly due to the lower number of respondents (about 100 compared to about 400 in western Germany). Notwithstanding the slight upward trend, both series are essentially stationary, as shown by an augmented Dickey–Fuller and a Phillips–Perron Test (see test statistics in the appendices to this chapter).

The independent variables are the media reporting about the government's operational and symbolic actions as well as the media's general

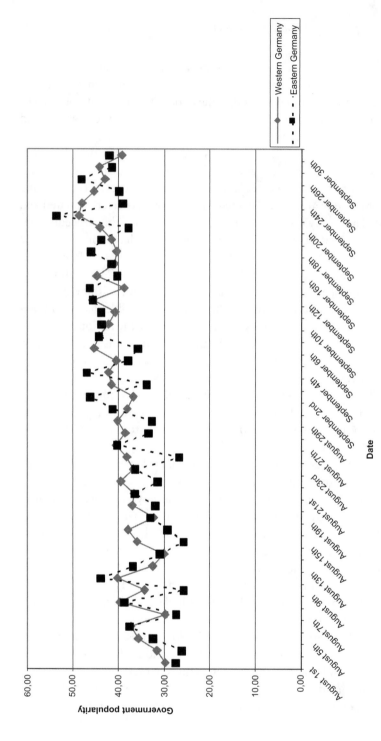

Figure 4.4. Course of government popularity during the Elbe flood, 2002.

framing of the crisis in regard to the government. In addition, the number of instances of reporting which are classified as 'drama' (human interest stories related to the flood) has been included. All time series of the independent variables are essentially stationary.

Although there are considerable changes in government popularity from one day to another, it is unrealistic for it to move from 0 to 100 percent. A certain number of people always support one party regardless of the incidents of the day. Hence there is a strong relation between government popularity yesterday and today, because only relatively few people within the mass of supporters will change their minds on any given day. To take account of this fact, the analysis contains a further independent variable, a so-called lagged dependent variable with one lag. This variable measures the government's popularity the day before. Also, it does not make sense to assume that the reporting of 'today' will have an immediate impact on the minds of voters that same day. There is a time delay between reporting and government popularity, but how long is this delay? Other priming studies show that voters react quite fast to changes of the media agenda by using the new top issues as a basis for their evaluation (cf. Peter 2002). The delay between reporting and government popularity therefore seems to be quite short. Here it will be assumed that voters need 2 days to build new information into their government evaluation. Put in the form of a regression equation, the model looks like this:

Government popularity$_t$

$$= \alpha + \beta_1 \text{ government popularity}_{t-1} + \beta_2 \text{ operational actions}_{t-2}$$
$$+ \beta_3 \text{ symbolic actions}_{t-2} + \beta_4 \text{ framing}_{t-2} + \beta_5 \text{ drama}_{t-2} + \varepsilon_t$$

After discussing the data structure and the design of the model at length, the results can now be presented, starting with western Germany (Fig. 4.5). In essence, the model works poorly for western Germany. None of the variables measuring the media coverage of the crisis has a significant effect on government popularity. There is an upward trend in government popularity, displayed in the significant positive effect of yesterday's on today's popularity. But this trend does not depend on media coverage of the crisis. In contrast, the model works quite well with eastern Germany, as shown in Figure 4.6.

The lower R^2 of 13 percent seems to be due to the insignificant effect of the lagged dependent variable, which is caused by the great

Source	SS	df	MS	Number of obs	= 41
				$F(5, 35)$	= 3.79
Model	270.604832	5	54.1209663	Prob > F	= 0.0075
Residual	499.450011	35	14.2700003	R-squared	= 0.3514
				Adj	= 0.2588
				R-squared	
Total	770.054843	40	19.2513711	Root MSE	= 3.7776
Popularity t	Coef.	Std. Err.	t	P>|t\}	[95% Conf. Interval]
Popularity t−1}	5390186	.1391304	3.87	0.000	.2565689	.8214682
Operat A. t−2}	−.0206493	.4330171	−0.05	0.962	−.8997208	.8584222
Symbolic A. t−2}	.0174437	1.338324	0.01	0.990	−2.699499	2.734386
Framing t−2}	.2933002	.4749176	0.62	0.541	−.6708337	1.257434
Drama t−2}	−.0467457	1.5818	−0.03	0.977	−3.257971	3.164479
Constant	18.5769	5.60568	3.31	0.002	7.196762	29.95703

Figure 4.5. Time series analysis for western Germany.

fluctuations in government popularity in eastern Germany. Contrary to expectations, the government's operational actions and the framing of the flood by the media do *not* have a significant impact on government popularity, but – as expected – the government's symbolic actions have a strong positive and significant impact. The issue is whether, despite a negative framing of the crisis, the heavy reporting of government actions is in itself sufficient for a positive evaluation of the government. This, in fact, is the case, at least for symbolic actions. The significant and highly negative effect of drama shows that the heavy reporting of

Source	SS	df	MS	Number of obs	= 41
$F(5, 35)$	=	2.19			
Model	426.305241	5	85.2610482	Prob > F	= 0.0771
Residual	1360.31774	35	38.8662211	R-squared	= 0.2386
				Adj	= 0.1298
				R-squared	
Total	1786.62298	40	44.6655745	Root MSE	= 6.2343
Popularity t	Coef.	Std. Err.	t	P>|t	[95% Conf. Interval]
Popularity t−1	.2308875	.1551815	1.49	0.146	−.0841478	.5459228
Operat A. t−2	−.2587144	.71315	−0.36	0.719	−1.706486	1.189057
Symbolic A. t−2	4.625279	2.201617	2.10	0.043	.1557586	9.094799
Framing t−2	.4587059	.7828679	0.59	0.562	−1.1306	2.048012
Drama t−2	−5.871737	2.561557	−2.29	0.028	−11.07197	−.6714997
Constant	29.86905	6.185449	4.83	0.000	17.31192	42.42618

Figure 4.6. Time series analysis for eastern Germany.

personal hardships of crisis victims hurts the government's popularity. This may be because voters get the impression that the government is not able to prevent these hardships. In sum, the Elbe flash flood of 2002 had a positive impact on government popularity, generated during the short period when the mass media devoted intensive attention to it. However, the effect occurred only in eastern Germany. The strong positive effect of the lagged dependent variable in western Germany leads to the conclusion that there certainly was an upward trend in government popularity. Nevertheless, this was not due to the Elbe flash flood. This difference in the electoral impact of crisis between eastern and western Germany, though not addressed in the theoretical argument, is intuitively comprehensible: the crisis hit mainly eastern Germany, and other research has shown that these two constituent parts of the German polity are wont to behave in different ways (e.g. Hartenstein and Mueller-Hilmer 2002: 18). The positive impact of the crisis in eastern Germany was not caused by the government's operational actions, although they were the subject of intense reporting. Contrary to expectations, the overall media framing of the crisis had no significant impact on government popularity. That the government is shown to demonstrate commitment to the victims of the crisis seems to be more important to voters than the media's own evaluation of the situation. Apparently the framing of a crisis in positive or negative terms for the government is not as powerful a shaper of public opinion as the sheer force of the images of a statesman like Chancellor Schröder visiting the flooded areas and promising the full force of the government's power to help them.

Conclusions

The positive impact of a crisis on government popularity is often ascribed to its effective crisis management performance. In this chapter I have distinguished two components (or kinds) of crisis management: operational and symbolic. I argued that the operational aspect of governmental crisis management is hardly visible to voters, and that voters harbor certain expectations about governmental crisis behaviour. These expectations relate to the need for government to reduce the collective stress generated by the emergency: governments are likely to engage in symbolic actions to fulfill these expectations and to try and define the crisis in their terms. Both were taken to be preconditions for governments to benefit politically from crises.

Contrary to these theoretical considerations, a content analysis of two German newspapers revealed that in the 2002 Elbe flood crisis, the operational actions of the government were reported intensively and thus were highly visible to voters. Despite this visibility, the operational actions of the government turned out to have had little impact on the government's popularity. By contrast, its symbolic actions did have a strong and positive effect on its popularity. This effect occurred despite the fact that the newspapers tended to frame the overall story of the flood in terms that were mainly negative for the government. Occurring right before the federal election in September 2002, the flood-related reporting seems to have been decisive in the election that saw the Social Democratic-Green coalition government led by Schröder retain its majority. I have demonstrated that the upswing that did occur was mainly due to the coalition's symbolic crisis management activities. The effect was, however, dampened by the lack of positive impact that the flood stories had on public opinion in the western part of Germany. Also, the actual polling day came a little late for the Schröder government. As the last preelection polling results indicate, the positive effects of the flood on its share of the vote would probably have been bigger had the election taken place in early September. Crisis effects on voter intentions may, in other words, be short-lived.

It has been argued that before a national election the incumbent parties often experience upswings because the electorate is more sensitised to the 'governmental mood' (Hilmer 2003: 191). This chapter suggests that crises occurring in immediate preelection periods may affect this upswing or serve as a rationale for voters to support the government – but only when the government and its main public 'faces' are seen to do well in symbolic communication via the mass media.

References

Bloedorn, S., and Gerhards, M. 2004. Informationsverhalten der Deutschen. Media Perspektiven 1/2004:2–14.

Boin, A., 't Hart, P., Stern, E. K. and Sundelius, B. 2005. The politics of crisis management: public leadership under pressure. Cambridge, UK: Cambridge University Press.

Boin, A., and 't Hart, P. 2003. Public leadership in times of crisis: mission impossible? Public Administration Review 63:544–54.

Brosius, H.-B., and Eps, P. 1993. Veraendern Schluesselereignisse journalistische Selektionskriterien? Framing am Beispiel der Berichterstattung ueber Anschlaege gegen Auslaender und Asylanten. Rundfunk und Fernsehen 41:512–30.

Dombrowsky, W. R., and Ohlendieck, L. 1998. Flood management in Germany. In Rosenthal, U. and 't Hart, P. (eds.) Flood response in western Europe: A comparative analysis. Berlin: Springer Verlag, pp. 153–87.

Edelman, M. 1977. The symbolic uses of politics. Urbana, IL: University of Illinois Press.

Gerhards, J. 1996. Soziale Positionierung und politische Kommunikation am Beispiel der oeffentlichen Debatte ueber Abtreibung. WZB-Jahrbuch 1996:83–102.

Guellner, M. 2000. Methodische Entwicklungen in der empirischen Wahlforschung. In Klein, M., Jagodzinski, W., Mochmann, E. and Orr, D. (eds.) 50 Jahre Empirische Wahlforschung in Deutschland. Entwicklung, Befunde, Perspektiven, Daten. Wiesbaden: Westdeutscher Verlag, pp. 564–83.

't Hart, P. 1993. Symbols, rituals and power: the lost dimensions of crisis management. Journal of Contingencies and Crisis Management 1(1):36–50.

Hartenstein, W., and Müller-Hilmer, R. 2002. Die Bundestagswahl 2002: Neue Themen – neue Allianzen. Aus Politik und Zeitgeschichte B49–50/2002:18–26.

Hilmer, R. 2003. Bundestagswahl 2002: Eine zweite Chance für Rot-Grün. Zeitschrift für Parlamentsfragen 34:186–219.

Iyengar, S., and Kinder, D. R. 1987. News that matters. Chicago: University of Chicago Press.

Jung, H. 2003. Analyse der Bundestagswahl 2002. Politische Studien 54:21–33.

Kepplinger, H. M., Donsbach, W., Brosius, H.-B. and Staab, J. F. 1986. Medientenor und Bevoelkerungsmeinung. Eine empirische Studie zum Image Helmut Kohls. Koelner Zeitschrift für Soziologie und Sozialpsychologie 38:247–79.

Ostrom, C. W., and Simon, D. M. 1985. Promise and performance: a dynamic model of presidential popularity. American Political Science Review 79:334–58.

Peter, J. 2002. Medien-Priming – Grundlagen, Befunde und Forschungstendenzen. Publizistik 47:21–44.

Reineck, K.-M. 2003. Allgemeine Staatslehre und deutsches Staatsrecht. Hamburg: Maximilian-Verlag.

Rosenthal, U., and 't Hart, P. 1998. Flood response and crisis management in western Europe: a comparative analysis. Berlin: Springer Verlag.

Roth, D., and Jung, M. 2002. Abloesung der Regierung vertagt: Eine Analyse der Bundestagswahl 2002. Aus Politik und Zeitgeschichte B49–50/2002:3–17.

Sarcinelli, U. 1998. Symbolische Politik. In Jarren, O., Imhoff, K. and Blum, R., Zerfall der Öffentlichkeit? Opladen: Westdeutscher Verlag, pp. 729–30.

Scherer, H., Froehlich, R., Scheufele, B., Dammert, S. and Thomas, N. 2005. Bundeswehr, Buendnispolitik und Auslandseinsaetze. Die Berichterstattung deutscher Qualitaetszeitungen zur Sicherheits- und Verteidigungspolitik 1989 bis 2000. Medien & Kommunikationswissenschaft 53:277–97.

Scheufele, B. 2003. Frames – Framing – Framing-Effekte: Theoretische und methodische Grundlegung des Framing-Ansatzes sowie empirische Befunde zur Nachrichtenproduktion. Wiesbaden: Westdeutscher Verlag.

Schuett, E. C. 2003. Chronik 2002. Tag für Tag in Wort und Bild. Guetersloh: Chronik Verlag.

Appendix 4.1. *Test statistics to augmented Dickey–Fuller and Phillips–Perron tests on stationarity of government popularity*

Government popularity in western Germany:

Dickey–Fuller test for unit root

Number of obs = 42

| | Test Statistic | Interpolated Dickey–Fuller | | |
		1% Critical Value	5% Critical Value	10% Critical Value
Z(t)	−3.500	−3.634	−2.952	−2.610

MacKinnon approximate *P* value for Z(t) = 0.0080

Phillips–Perron test for unit root

Number of obs = 42
Newey–West lags = 3

| | Test Statistic | Interpolated Dickey–Fuller | | |
		1% Critical Value	5% Critical Value	10% Critical Value
Z(rho)	−15.640	−18.356	−13.044	−10.540
Z(t)	−3.406	−3.634	−2.952	−2.610

MacKinnon approximate *P* value for Z(t) = 0.0108

Government popularity in eastern Germany:

Dickey–Fuller test for unit root

Number of obs = 42

| | Test Statistic | Interpolated Dickey–Fuller | | |
		1% Critical Value	5% Critical Value	10% Critical Value
Z(t)	−4.530	−3.634	−2.952	−2.610

MacKinnon approximate *P* value for Z(t) = 0.0002

Phillips–Perron test for unit root

Number of obs = 42
Newey–West lags = 3

| | Test Statistic | Interpolated Dickey–Fuller | | |
		1% Critical Value	5% Critical Value	10% Critical Value
Z(rho)	−29.672	−18.356	−13.044	−10.540
Z(t)	−4.619	−3.634	−2.952	−2.610

MacKinnon approximate *P* value for Z(t) = 0.0001

Appendix 4.2. *Test statistics to augmented Dickey–Fuller and Phillips–Perron tests on stationarity of operational actions*

Dickey–Fuller test for unit root

Number of obs = 40

	Test Statistic	1% Critical Value	5% Critical Value	10% Critical Value
		Interpolated Dickey–Fuller		
Z(t)	−2.883	−3.648	−2.958	−2.612

MacKinnon approximate *P* value for Z(t) = 0.0474

Phillips–Perron test for unit root

Number of obs = 40
Newey–West lags = 3

	Test Statistic	1% Critical Value	5% Critical Value	10% Critical Value
		Interpolated Dickey–Fuller		
Z(rho)	−12.920	−18.220	−12.980	−10.500
Z(t)	−2.761	−3.648	−2.958	−2.612

MacKinnon approximate *P* value for Z(t) = 0.0641

Appendix 4.3. *Test statistics to augmented Dickey–Fuller and Phillips–Perron tests on stationarity of symbolic politics*

Dickey–Fuller test for unit root

Number of obs = 40

	Test Statistic	1% Critical Value	5% Critical Value	10% Critical Value
		Interpolated Dickey–Fuller		
Z(t)	−3.272	−3.648	−2.958	−2.612

MacKinnon approximate *P* value for Z(t) = 0.0162

Phillips–Perron test for unit root

Number of obs = 40
Newey–West lags = 3

	Test Statistic	1% Critical Value	5% Critical Value	10% Critical Value
		Interpolated Dickey–Fuller		
Z(rho)	−17.523	−18.220	−12.980	−10.500
Z(t)	−3.268	−3.648	−2.958	−2.612

MacKinnon approximate *P* value for Z(t) = 0.0164

Appendix 4.4. *Test statistics to augmented Dickey–Fuller and Phillips–Perron tests on stationarity of framing*

Dickey–Fuller test for unit root

Number of obs = 40

	Test Statistic	1% Critical Value	5% Critical Value	10% Critical Value
		Interpolated Dickey–Fuller		
Z(t)	−5.418	−3.648	−2.958	−2.612

MacKinnon approximate *P* value for Z(t) = 0.0000

Phillips–Perron test for unit root

Number of obs = 40
Newey–West lags = 3

	Test Statistic	1% Critical Value	5% Critical Value	10% Critical Value
		Interpolated Dickey–Fuller		
Z(rho)	−38.445	−18.220	−12.980	−10.500
Z(t)	−5.509	−3.648	−2.958	−2.612

MacKinnon approximate *P* value for Z(t) = 0.0000

Appendix 4.5. *Test statistics to augmented Dickey–Fuller and Phillips–Perron tests on stationarity of drama*

Dickey–Fuller test for unit root

Number of obs = 40

	Test Statistic	1% Critical Value	5% Critical Value	10% Critical Value
		Interpolated Dickey–Fuller		
Z(t)	−2.709	−3.648	−2.958	−2.612

MacKinnon approximate *P* value for Z(t) = 0.0725

Phillips–Perron test for unit root

Number of obs = 40
Newey–West lags = 3

	Test Statistic	1% Critical Value	5% Critical Value	10% Critical Value
		Interpolated Dickey–Fuller		
Z(rho)	−12.999	−18.220	−12.980	−10.500
Z(t)	−2.714	−3.648	−2.958	−2.612

MacKinnon approximate *P* value for Z(t) = 0.0717

5 | The politics of tsunami responses: comparing patterns of blame management in Scandinavia

ANNIKA BRÄNDSTRÖM, SANNEKE KUIPERS
AND PÄR DALÉUS

Introduction

On Boxing day 2004, an earthquake in the Bay of Bengal triggered tsunamis that flooded the coasts of India, Indonesia, Burma, Sri Lanka and Thailand, killing hundreds of thousands and leaving millions homeless and destitute. The involvement of citizens from other continents gave this crisis a truly global dimension. Governments in Europe and Australia slowly but surely realised that this catastrophe far from home required a response beyond simply expressing sympathy, collecting money and sending relief.

Thailand has long been a popular tourist resort for Scandinavians, especially during Christmas. Approximately 30 000 Swedes and thousands of Norwegians and Finns were on holiday in the disaster area in the last weeks of December. Soon after the waves hit the beaches, it became clear that many Scandinavian tourists were missing, making this the worst peacetime disaster ever in all three countries. Even so, it took the three governments more than 24 hours to react to the crisis and several days to initiate rescue attempts, triggering media and political criticism at home. Interestingly, despite the similarities in context and government responses to crisis, the tsunami disaster triggered markedly different political processes in the three most affected Scandinavian countries.

Some political leaders in Sweden, Finland and Norway found themselves to be the targets of intensely critical media scrutiny and political criticism left, right and centre, whereas others managed to escape this media onslaught. Why? This study focuses on different blaming processes – an inevitable and to some degree necessary part of societal responses to crisis (cf. Douglas 1992). Blaming theory provides a basis for intelligent speculation about why the criticism of the three

114

Scandinavian governments varied so widely. It probes into the accountability processes that evolve as part of the politics of crisis management. Accountability judgements depend to a large extent on how extreme events are framed politically: the dominant definition of the crisis includes an implicit reference to responsibility. Accountability and framing – the story of crisis management that is woven in the wake of the crisis events themselves – determine the fine line between heroes and villains, between fame and blame. As Boin et al. (2005: 92) argue: 'Crises have winners and losers. The political dynamics of the accountability process determines which crisis actors end up where'.

As the introductory chapter pointed out, accountability debates are hardly models of truth-finding dialogue. Here we substantiate the claim that these debates can rather be more like 'blame games', particularly when influential actors succeed in publicly framing the events and government actions in relation to these events as blameworthy violations of crucial public values. Blaming generates efforts by the accused to defend themselves, attack their opponents or to 'pass the buck' to others, setting in motion a spiral of reactions that can prolong or aggravate the crisis considerably.

News media play an important role in the blame game, in offering a public stage for framing strategies and by reporting and commenting on the events and actions. Media can frame actors as either heroes or villains during a crisis, as the supporting media coverage of President Bush after 9/11 and the critical media attack on the president after Hurricane Katrina might very well illustrate.[1]

Blaming theory assumes that the allocation of responsibility regarding crises, and thus the fate of key politicians, officials and organisations involved is determined by three factors: the institutional and political conditions under which blame games occur; the blame management strategies that actors choose to employ; and the skill with which they apply these strategies in the public arena. These factors can help to explain the puzzle of the tsunami blame games in Scandinavia: one crisis triggers highly similar polities and administrations; highly similar government responses; yet markedly different political consequences.

In order to explain these differences, we begin by presenting a model of how blame games evolve. We then apply it to the political process during the tsunami crisis in Sweden, Norway and Finland. We further

[1] See Preston as well as Parker and Dekker, this volume.

elaborate the model by inducing specific institutional and individual factors that help explain why the distribution of blame took different turns in the three countries. We conclude by formulating hypotheses that specify the conditions under which crisis-induced blame games take shape.

Playing hardball: blaming strategies in crisis management

When things are perceived to have gone wrong in government, policy makers sometimes willingly accept responsibility. However, ceteris paribus, most policy makers will try to avoid being linked to the problem, which is exactly what opposition spokespersons, media critics and others may try to do. Under criticism for alleged failures and wrongdoing, policy makers resort to rhetorical strategies to escape blame, including moves to deflect it to others. The latter are then prompted to do likewise. And so a 'blame game' develops: a verbal struggle between protagonists inside and outside of government about the allocation of responsibility for negative events.[2] They struggle about the framing of the situation and the role that policy makers (should have) played in bringing critical incidents about or failing to prevent them. The literature suggests that there are three core components of framing strategies in blame games:

1. *Constructing severity*: depicting events as violations of specific core public values
2. *Constructing agency*: depicting events as operational incidents or as symptoms of endemic problems
3. *Constructing responsibility*: depicting the events as caused by a single actor or by 'many hands'[3]

These strategies are the same for defenders and attackers, because the essence of a blame game is that initial defenders to outside criticism engage in the game by becoming attackers themselves. We argue that

---

[2] A 'frame' is a shared construction of reality (see Goffman 1974) and 'framing' activities can relate to both the *use* and the *impact* of frames (see for instance: Edelman 1988; Schön and Rein 1994; Kingdon 1995; Iyngar 1996; D'Angelo 2002; DeVreese 2003; Hurst 2004; Eriksson 2004). In this chapter a 'framing' move can be interpreted according to the definition of Boin et al. (2005: 88) as 'the production of facts, images and spectacles aimed at manipulating the perception and reaction to a crisis'.

[3] The problem of 'many hands' was first coined by Thompson (1980).

a blame game is a staged process: it involves deliberate choices with regard to the way one frames a particular failure and its causality. The selective adoption of these framing strategies by political elites will lead to different outcomes of political blaming (Brändström and Kuipers 2003). Let us examine these strategies in turn.

Constructing severity

The degree to which an event is framed as a violation of core public values (security, integrity, social justice, etc.) determines the extent to which that event becomes the subject of political and societal debate about blame. Different interpretations of the event put forward by different actors will struggle for domination. Personal, political and organisational gains and losses are at stake in this process (Edelman 1964, 1977, 1988, 1995; 't Hart 1993; Kingdon 1995; Anheier 1999; Boin et al. 2005). Media are explicitly biased towards negative events (good news is no news). An additional explanation of this focus on failure and the consequent efforts to avoid blame in this process is the negativity bias of the electorate. Voters are more likely to withdraw their electoral support when something negative occurs (cutbacks, scandals, austerity measures) than they are to express support when political behaviour is beneficial to them (Bloom and Price 1975; Kernell 1977; Lau 1985). The negativity bias in electoral behaviour instructs politicians to duck accountability whenever possible. Highlighting governmental failures is a powerful weapon in the hands of political opponents – one that government actors wish to deprive them of as much as possible by denying or reframing failure or by passing the buck to others (Brändström and Kuipers 2003).

Following McGraw (1991), we distinguish blame avoidance from blame management.[4] Blame avoidance refers to the construction of 'severity': it implies that public actors seek to frame incidents as inconsequential, not negative in their social implications or as lacking political ramifications.[5] More political actors have a stake in the political debate if issues can be linked to substantive values that touch on sweeping social and political themes such as justice, democracy, liberty (Nelkin 1975) or national security (Edelman 1977; Bostdorff 1994; Buzan et al. 1998). Framing an issue in terms that are salient to

---

[4] See also Sulitzeanu-Kenan and Hood (forthcoming).
[5] That is, beyond the realm of political affairs, such as 'the free market, the private sphere or matters for expert decision' (Buzan et al. 1998: 29).

ongoing political themes is the key to capturing political and public attention (Rochefort and Cobb 1994). Timing and substance are also important reasons why attention focuses on certain issues. As Kingdon (1995: 104) notes, momentum is essential: when an issue fails to catch on, 'participants quickly cease to invest in it'. When a story about a negative event does 'catch on' and is publicly perceived as falling within the realm of politics and government, attempts at blame avoidance have run their course and give way to blame management strategies, which accountable actors employ to avoid being pinpointed as culpable and/or responsible for the problems that have been identified (McGraw 1991: 1135).

Constructing agency

Once journalists or oppositional political entrepreneurs have 'discovered' a potential fiasco or scandal, they will put questions about responsibility and blame squarely on the table. Whilst government actors will be driven to depict the events as having been caused by incidental, ad hoc factors in an otherwise sound system, their critics will attempt to portray the event as an embedded incident, epitomising a much larger systemic failure.

Likewise, in temporal terms, incumbent elites trying to avoid blame will emphasise the immediate causes of a crisis – such as 'pilot error' or 'rule violations' to explain a plane crash. The search for causes then stops at the technical, operational, subordinate level. By contrast, their political opponents tend to place the incident in a broader time perspective in order to shift focus to powerful underlying causes – such as the nature of the relevant laws and regulations, government cutbacks or reforms, management decisions with consequences for safety practices, embedded organisational routines and cultures tolerant of rule violation.[6] Going back in time often means going up the hierarchy, from street-level implementing actors to top-level strategic policy makers (Bovens and 't Hart 1996). Top-level policy makers facing a crisis are therefore usually keen to define the scope of investigation and debate narrowly while their critics will want to broaden the time horizon and deepen the scope of postmortems. The latter might receive support from operators and middle managers who feel that their superiors are

---

[6] See an overview of such factors in Vaughan (1999).

trying to frame them as scapegoats (Brändström and Kuipers 2003). These operators and middle managers will feed the debate by leaking implicating information about their superiors to media or opposition critics.

The core assertion here is that framing a failure in narrow technical terms decreases the likelihood of escalating blame games. Only if the problem becomes perceived in wider systemic terms and solutions to it become harder to agree upon will blame games affect political fates.

Constructing responsibility

Even if there is a widespread presumption that the unwanted events were not just operational incidents but were in fact linked to earlier decisions of top-level officials or embedded in organisational culture, the question remains who precisely should be punished. Incumbent policy makers are likely to argue that the incident is the result of what we might call a 'network' failure: a complex interplay of structures, actors, decisions and actions. If this causal story sticks, responsibility for failures becomes a matter of the proverbial 'many hands'. If causality is 'dispersed', then any blame will have to be too; and since blaming everyone for something to which they arguably contributed only in small measure often seems unfair, sanctions are not administered to anyone – an agreeable outcome for the top brass (Thompson 1980).

By contrast, pinning down the root of failure to individuals or parts of organisations will facilitate scapegoat solutions (Ellis 1994; Jones 2000). When incumbent politicians succeed in constricting the diagnosis of a critical event, they can relieve pressure on themselves by signalling that they are ready to take steps: firing subordinates and implementing additional measures to deal with the problem (Rochefort and Cobb 1994). Having a scapegoat at hand is obviously convenient for policy makers. For that reason, some argue, providing for this blame-absorption device has become an important consideration in the design of public institutions, particularly in the more politically risky areas of government policy (Hood 2002).[7]

---

[7] Hood argues that ex ante blame avoidance strategies influence the selection of institutional arrangements for policy implementation – e.g., the choice for delegation instead of direct control.

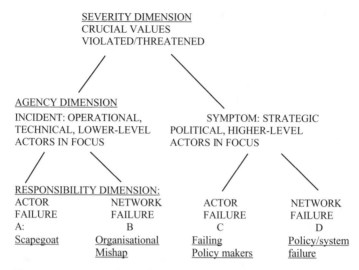

Figure 5.1. Constructing blame by framing political crises. [*Source:* Bränd-ström and Kuipers (2003: 302).]

Synthesis: the blaming tree

A blame game can develop in different directions, depicted in Fig-ure 5.1 as a decision tree. For each dimension, two alternative options that influence the final outcome of the blaming process are presented. The evolving blame game can result in four different outcomes. Firstly, the event can be framed as either ad hoc or endemic, depending on the time perspective that becomes the dominant reference frame in the debates. Subsequently, both stand-alone incidents and systemic failures can be attributed to either complex networks or single actors. The resultant locus of blame of these alternate strategies is (1) the scape-goat, an isolated single-actor failure; (2) the organisational mishap, an incident produced by 'many hands'; (3) the policy maker(s), responsible for shaping flawed policies and/or tolerating deficient implementation strategies and organisational malpractices; and (4) the endemic sys-tem failure, a structural problem implicating many actors in a range of organisations.

Now why and how do some accountability processes turn into blame games with any of these outcomes? Comparative research will reveal under which conditions actors employing certain framing strategies are likely to be successful in (re)directing the postcrisis media onslaught – to avoid being blamed or to focus blame on others. This is not as easy as it might seem. Boin et al. (2005) argue that blame strategies have a reflexive quality. A strategy can become self-defeating – for example, when actors at the operational level who find themselves scapegoated by skillful blame-managing superiors react by feeding media or government opponents with the necessary evidence to shift blame back to the upper echelons. Our analysis may have to follow different strategies by actors involved up and down the tree initially, but in the end we aim to assess the strategies employed and the resulting outcome for each case.

The framing tree serves as an analytical model to dissect the cases and understand how the blame games evolved. The comparative design of this study allows us to delve deeper into these cases in order to develop hypotheses in the end about the specific factors that influenced the blaming process and consequently its outcomes. Our assumption here is that both the scope of the crisis and the behavior of accountable actors in the end define the public perception of the crisis (as either a single-actor deficiency, organisational mishap, failing governance or system failure). The behavior of accountable actors is in turn influenced by a mix of situational, individual and institutional factors.

An Asian disaster making waves in Scandinavia

This study compares Scandinavian public debates following the tsunami disaster: a crisis that could be characterized as an *incomprehensible crisis* according to the typology presented in the introduction of this book. We study the framing strategies employed at the strategic level by policy makers in Sweden, Norway and Finland when confronted with criticism of their performance as crisis managers. We also examine which factors – individual, institutional, cultural, situational – may account for the differential outcomes of these debates. The controlled variation produced by this 'natural experiment' allows us to analyse whether the obviously bigger human and material impact of the tsunami in Sweden provided more room for stakeholders to present alternative frames and has influenced the course and outcomes of the accountability process as compared to the other two countries (see Chapter 1). It seems intuitively appealing to expect that the more severe the material and personal damage, the more likely it is for political blame games to occur and escalate (see also Chapter 1).

Research on the politics of policy evaluation suggests that the relation between actual government performance and its public evaluation is low (Bovens and 't Hart 1996; Bovens et al. 1999; Kofman-Bos et al. 2005). The government performance of the three countries is comparable but Swedish losses (number of victims) were much bigger. We hypothesise that not so much government performance but the scope and depth of the crisis (in terms of losses) affected the nature of the accountability process and the gravity of the outcome. Simply put: the bigger the 'bang', the bigger the political fallout, regardless of actual government performance. The scope of the crisis would explain why the Swedish government was blamed more severely for its handling of the crisis than the two neighbouring governments, even though their operational crisis responses did not differ all that much.

We have performed a content analysis of national newspaper articles to reveal if, when and how often political actors use blaming strategies, evaluate government behaviour, (re)allocate responsibility, or attribute blame to specific culprits. We have coded all articles published on the tsunami disaster in two daily newspapers in each country published between 2 January 2005 and 22 January 2005.[8] Each article was coded according to a codebook.[9] We chose to start the survey one week after the tsunami since our reading of the press coverage revealed that in this case – unlike Bytzek's flood coverage in Germany reported elsewhere in this volume – the media coverage of the first 7 days focused virtually exclusively on depicting the human drama and the course of disaster operations. It was not until the initial shock was over that media coverage shifted towards accountability issues.[10]

[8] Complete reference lists with official sources, daily newspapers, news agencies and articles coded in the three cases can be obtained, upon request, from any of the authors.

[9] The codebook and codebook instructions based on Verheuvel (2002) with detailed information on the method applied can be provided as an appendix by the authors upon request.

[10] The selection of newspapers was based on their status as national newspapers with a potentially large number of readers and thus potential influence on the key actors. The newspapers chosen (Svenska Dagbladet, Dagens Nyheter, Aftenposten, VG Nett, Helsingin Sanomat and Hufvudstadsbladet) are all among the most widespread newspapers in each country. Swedish and Norwegian newspapers were read in original language. The international edition (in English) of the largest newspapers in Finland (Helsingin Sanomat) was chosen as well as the dominating newspaper in Swedish (Hufvudstadsbladet) in Finland. Finland is constitutionally bilingual and its

Table 5.1 summarises the similarities and differences of the crisis response in the three Scandinavian countries. We use the dimensions of the blaming tree developed above to analyse how the accountability process evolved in the media, and which blame avoidance and blame management strategies were used by the chief protagonists.

Constructing severity

'Norway is the best country to live in. But not the best country to belong to when a disaster hits you on vacation.' Thus wrote a journalist on the Norwegian government's response to the tsunami disaster.[11] This comment reflected the sentiments in the media in Norway's neighbouring countries in the weeks after Christmas 2004. The Swedish king concluded in an unprecedented and constitutionally controversial interview when asked if the government had done its job: 'I have a feeling that we have been very busy, but at the same time it is hard to see that we have done anything at all'.[12] In Finland criticism was hard on the failing emergency number at the Ministry of Foreign Affairs: 'In Nokia-land where there are millions of telephones, the Ministry of Foreign Affairs has only five!'[13]

The content analysis revealed that in Norway and somewhat later in Sweden both opposition leaders and experts participating in the debate (such as government agency directors, political scientists, writers, etc.) were fast to claim that the disaster response left much to be desired, and that it had compounded the victims' plight instead of relieving it. In interviews with opposition leaders and experts, the Swedish and Norwegian governments were severely criticised for their inadequate handling of the crisis (see Table 5.2). In response, government figures in both countries framed the tsunami disaster as an 'unimaginable' surprise that had simply been 'too big to handle'. For example, the foreign affairs ministers asserted in almost identical terms that they

main newspaper in Swedish is widely read. Newspapers and Internet editions were carefully scanned every day during 3 weeks. Articles were coded if the headlines contained references to key political actors, responsibility or accountability. A complete reference list of the articles coded can be provided upon request by the authors.

[11] Dagsavisen, 30 December 2004 (Norwegian daily newspaper).
[12] Dagens Nyheter, 10 January 2005.
[13] http://www.dn.se/DNet/jsp/polopoly.jsp?d=148&a = 360198

Table 5.1. *Tsunami crisis – similarities and differences in Scandinavian responses*[1]

	Finland	Norway	Sweden
Number of people potentially affected	2500 in southern Thailand[2]	3000 in Thailand or other parts of Asia[3]	10 000–15 000[4] in Thailand
Number of people initially missing	200–300[5]	700–800	More than 2000.
First government reaction	The PM held his first press conference on 27 December.[6]	PM arrived in Oslo after 2 days. PM and MFA had no contact until Monday. First press release from the FM on 26 December.[7] First press conference by the MFA on 27 December.[8] First press conference by the PM on 30 December.[9]	PM arrived in Stockholm next day. MFA arrived at the office 31.5 hours after the floods. She was later criticised for going to a theatre on Sunday night, 26 December. First press conference with PM and MFA on Monday, 27 December.[10]
Operation of information channels	The hotline established at the FM after 9/11 jammed quickly on Sunday 26 December. Less than 10% of the people calling the FM got through.[11]	Emergency team established at the FM operating six different telephone numbers on Sunday.[12] Emergency telephone number was activated 2 days later. No one knew how to operate it. Only 50% of the incoming phone calls were answered.	The FM encouraged relatives to call switchboard at the FM, which jammed immediately. On 10 January, the PM appointed a new committee to be the contact point for victims and relatives.[13] A call centre was set up to take all phone calls from victims and families.

Responsible actors	An ad hoc emergency team was created. The FM became responsible.	At the FM, a crisis staff was established on the 26th to get an overview of the catastrophe.[14]	The FM led the operative crisis management. The PM led the press conferences. A coordination group was established in the cabinet office.
Handling the lists of missing persons	Decision by the FM not to publish the list. National Criminal Police took over, lists were published and the number of missing reduced.[15] Officials spoke of 250 Finns missing, the police updated the list to 260 missing on 30 December. On 1 January the list dropped to 193.[16]	New numbers every day. Police blamed the FM for poor handling of registration and ignoring police task and capacity in this regard. The government blamed travel agencies for handling unregistered tourists.	After the first week, 2,000 Swedes were still reported missing. After the third week, national police took over registration of missing persons (1,600). The names of the missing were published on 9 February and the numbers dropped by more than half.[17]
Crisis management preparedness and training	The Ministry of Interior had a well-prepared crisis management response system, but in this case it was the responsibility of the FM.	A 2-year-old crisis management coordination plan had not yet been implemented.	The government cancelled regular crisis management exercises for civil servants when the incumbent PM came to office.[18] Recommendations of prior crisis inquiries and evaluations had not been implemented.

(cont.)

Table 5.1 (cont.)

	Finland	Norway	Sweden
Authorisation of evacuation and assistance by rescue services	The first airplane that arrived in Phuket carried insurance staff. Finnair was sent to Thailand to evacuate Finns on Monday 27 December. On 2 January the last Finns were evacuated. The Finnish rescue team was not authorised to go. Red Cross representatives argued their aid was sufficient.[19]	On 29 December, Scandinavian Airlines planes were made ready to repatriate citizens. A team of seven rescue workers went to Aceh province on New Year's Eve under the UN flag.[20] A military plane with doctors and nurses took off on 29 December.	On 29 December, the first government-ordered plane left to evacuate victims. Offers by the Swedish Rescue Service Agency to assist had been declined by government on 26 December.[21] First medical teams were authorised to go by the end of first week.
Visits to affected area	On 16 January, the PMs of the Scandinavian countries visited Thailand together to express their sympathy.	Idem. The MFA went to the area on 5 January.[22]	Idem. The MFA visited the affected area 27 December.[23] The king and queen visited Phuket on 17 February.
Inquiries and commissions	High-profile commission of former top politicians assigned by the government on 13 January to investigate government response; report delivered in June 2005.[24] Also, an internal investigation started on 10 January within the FM and was presented on 27 January.[25]	Parliament and government agreed on 13 January on an expert committee to evaluate responsible agencies.[26] Report delivered April 2005.[27] An internal investigation of the FM was also initiated.	On 13 January a commission was assigned by the PM after parliamentary approval to investigate the government response. The commission members were mainly high-level experts. Report was delivered December 2005.

[1] FM = Foreign Ministry, MFA = Minister of Foreign Affairs, PM = Prime Minister

[2] Helsingin Sanomat, 30 December 2004 (Finnish daily newspaper).

[3] Aftenposten, 27 December 2004 (Norwegian daily newspaper).

[4] Dagens Nyheter, 13 January 2005.

[5] Helsingin Sanomat, 29 December 2004.

[6] Aftonbladet, 2 January 2005 (Swedish daily newspaper).

[7] Pressemedling (Press release), nr 174/04, 26 December 2004.

[8] Pressemedling (Press release), nr Unr./04m, 27 December 2004.

[9] Aftonbladet, 2 January 2005.

[10] Aftonbladet, 2 January 2005.

[11] Svenska Dagbladet, 8 January 2005 (Swedish daily newspaper).

[12] Press release Norwegian FM, nr 173/04, 26 December 2004.

[13] Committee directive, 2005:1.

[14] Press release Norwegian FM nr 174/04, 26 December 2004.

[15] Svenska Dagbladet, 8 January 2005.

[16] Helsingin Sanoma, 30 December 2004 (& updated article on 30 December), 1 January 2005.

[17] Dagens Nyheter, 9 February 2005.

[18] Dagens Nyheter, 16 January 2005.

[19] YLE 24, 4 January 2005 (Finnish News Agency).

[20] Direktoratet for Samfunnssikkerhet og Beredskap, 2 January 2005.

[21] TV4, Kalla Fakta, 14 February 2005.

[22] The Norwegian government's website for information on the disaster.

[23] Sydsvenskan, 29 January 2005 (Swedish daily newspaper).

[24] Helsingin Sanomat, 12 January 2005.

[25] Internal review of the measures taken by the Ministry for Foreign Affairs in connection with the tsunami disaster in Southeast Asia.

[26] Aftenposten, 14 January 2005.

[27] Commission website.

Table 5.2. *Content analysis on the severity dimension*

	Week 2				Week 3				Week 4				Total			
	Deny	Frame	Neu	T	Deny	Frame	Neu	T	Deny	Frame	Neu	T	Deny	Frame	Neu	T
Progovt.																
Norway	8	1	2	11	3	1	2	6	0	0	1	1	11	2	5	18
Sweden	2	3	1	6	4	2	0	6	3	1	1	5	9	6	2	17
Finland	–	–	–	–	6	0	4	10	1	0	0	1	7	0	4	11
Antigovt.																
Norway	0	7	0	7	0	3	0	3	–	–	–	–	0	10	0	10
Sweden	0	8	0	8	0	16	0	16	0	6	0	6	0	30	0	30
Finland	–	–	–	–	1	3	1	5	1	–	–	–	1	3	1	5

Note: This table indicates whether progovernment actors on the one hand (Progovt.) and opposition and critics on the other hand (Antigovt.) deny that crucial values were violated (Deny), frame the event as a violation of crucial values (Frame) or stay neutral (Neu). T means total, the hyphens indicate an absence of articles on the event in that week.

Brief Explanation: The government actors in Norway and Finland predominantly denied any blameworthiness in their accounts of the events. In Sweden government actors admitted in the first week that crucial values had been violated but later on increasingly denied the blameworthiness of their actions. As for the opponents, the Swedish and the Norwegian oppositions exclusively and undoubtedly framed events as blameworthy. Finnish media analysis only yielded articles and quotes in the third week after the disaster, but in those quotes government actors were all in denial, whereas the opinions among opposition actors were divided on the topic of blameworthiness.

were 'simply unprepared for the scope of the disaster', 'this was of a magnitude that could not have been predicted', and 'the extent of the disaster surprised us'.[14] The media compared their governments' performance with the response of other European countries, which soon rendered these arguments unacceptable. The comparisons revealed that the national rescue teams could have been sent to the affected areas much quicker. By not doing so, it was argued, the Swedish and Norwegian governments had failed to help their citizens. For instance, Italy had commandeered all Italian flights bound for Thailand the first day after the disaster, to fly down and bring Italians home.

At first sight, Finland was the odd case out. It had quickly sent national airline Finnair to evacuate Finns. Like their Norwegian and Swedish counterparts, Finnish authorities were nevertheless criticised, mainly by journalists and disaster experts, for their slow and inadequate handling of information and for the indecisive government reaction. In fact, Finnish parliamentary investigators later credited the speedy evacuation by Finnair to prompt decisions by travel insurance companies rather than to government intervention.[15]

Initially, the governments did not consider themselves primarily responsible for their citizens abroad in the case of such a disaster overseas. The first response was to plan for humanitarian aid to the affected areas. Meanwhile, citizens witnessed increasingly alarming media reports on television of the devastating situation in the coastal areas, where many had gone missing and were desperately calling for help from national authorities. The Swedish and Finnish governments repeatedly denied that their failure to respond was blameworthy, whereas the Norwegians only denied this initially (see Table 5.2). In all three countries, the prime ministers assigned the responsibility for handling the crisis to the foreign ministries. Even though the disaster was no one's fault, the media uniformly and increasingly portrayed the government response in Sweden and Norway as falling short of meeting the state's responsibility to protect its citizens. By mid-January, the Swedish foreign minister felt forced to admit that the government should be better able to protect its citizens abroad.[16]

---

[14] Aftenposten, 30 December 2004; Svenska Dagbladet, 27 December 2004; Helsingin Sanomat, 29 December.

[15] Hufvudstadsbladet, 19 January 2005 (Finnish daily newspaper).

[16] Dagens Nyheter, 16 January 2005; MFA speech at the Conference of Society and Defence, 16 January 2005.

Constructing agency

In the three Scandinavian countries the initial criticism by media, public and experts focused on the technical problems, such as overloaded telephone lines at the ministries of foreign affairs, and on the slow dissemination of information to the respective cabinets. In Sweden and Finland especially, special emergency phone numbers had jammed within hours and only a slight percentage of callers had gotten through. Likewise, it was reported in Norway that existing 'crisis hot lines' had proved dysfunctional and that improvisation to fix them had taken many hours.

Once it was established that pivotal parts of the operational response in all three countries appeared to have failed, the public spotlight turned to the top decision makers. The Swedish prime minister argued that his slow response was due to a lack of information. He complained that incoming fax messages had not been sent up the hierarchy: 'The information we got was not forwarded to the decision makers. The problem is not the organisation as such but the fact that someone has not performed his or her duties' (SR, Ekot 12 January 2005). The other two Nordic governments attributed their belated response to similar technical problems. Both the Swedish and the Norwegian ministries of foreign affairs also blamed the travel agencies who had said they would manage to evacuate the victims themselves and did not need governmental aid.[17] As Table 5.3 shows, Norwegian and Swedish policy makers tried to frame the failures as operational mishaps whereas their critics highlighted the political responsibility for the mishaps that occurred.

The management of victims' lists became a delicate issue in all three countries.[18] The prospect of potentially minimising the number of missing by publishing their names was sacrificed to protect the privacy of the victims and their families. When the three governments chose different approaches to this dilemma, critics compared their actions to one another, which elicited critical scrutiny by the media. Swedish and Norwegian police officials blamed their foreign ministries for their

---

[17] Nettavisen, 31 December 2004 (Norwegian daily newspaper).
[18] Similar problems occurred during other crises, see for instance the account by Kofman-Bos et al. (2005) of the Bijlmer air crash and the Estonia Ferry disaster.

Table 5.3. *Content analysis on the agency dimension*

	Week 2				Week 3				Week 4				Total			
	Techn	Pol	Neu	T	Techn	Pol	Neu	T	Techn	Pol	Neu	T	Techn	Pol	Neu	T
Progovt.																
Norway	7	0	4	11	6	0	0	6	1	0	0	1	14	0	4	18
Sweden	4	1	1	6	6	0	0	6	4	0	1	5	14	1	2	17
Finland	–	–	–	–	8	0	2	10	1	0	0	1	9	0	2	11
Antigovt.																
Norway	0	7	0	7	0	0	3	3	–	–	–	–	0	7	3	10
Sweden	0	8	0	8	1	14	1	16	0	6	0	6	1	28	1	30
Finland	–	–	–	–	1	0	4	5	–	–	–	–	1	0	4	5

Note: This table indicates whether progovernment actors on the one hand (Progovt.) and opposition and critics on the other hand (Antigovt.) frame the event as operational, technical (Techn), frame the event as strategic, political (Pol) or stay neutral (Neu). T means total, the hyphens indicate an absence of articles on the event in that week.

Brief Explanation: Government actors in all three countries almost exclusively framed the events as technical, operational, indicating that blame should rest on the shoulders of lower-level officials, instead of on themselves. The Swedish opposition fiercely contested this interpretation of events by their government, whereas their Norwegian counterparts commented in a more neutral manner in the third week and the Finns practically agreed with their government.

failure to release the names promptly like other countries, as for example Finland and Denmark had done.[19] The rescue services in all three countries were similarly critical of the slow organisation of evacuation flights and their governments' failure to utilise assistance offered by public agencies.[20]

In each country, the foreign ministers played down any organisational shortcomings but did admit that their response had been too slow. They promised internal evaluations of their ministries' crisis management capacities.[21] Framing the problem as mainly a lack of resources, they sought to absorb responsibility in a politically 'safe' way, and at the same time move the debate towards possible solutions to the problem – e.g. additional resources and organisational improvements.

This appeared to work in Finland and Norway, where critics framed the causes of the problems mainly in technical-organisational terms, but not in Sweden where they persistently emphasised the strategic and political factors at work (see Table 5.3). Correspondingly, Finnish and Norwegian government actors continued to concentrate public discussion on issues such as the lack of information, technical malfunctions and slow reactions by civil servants and agencies, whereas their Swedish counterparts could not.

In Sweden the blame game escalated when the political leadership was unable to field the criticism. Swedish Prime Minister Persson declared early after the occurrence of the tsunami that all other matters should rest, and that it was time for national solidarity. The parliamentary opposition honoured this call, but only temporarily. In a number of interviews, Persson unsuccessfully continued to focus on failures by lower-level officials, arguing that he had trusted the ministry to do their job: 'I contacted my state secretary, and asked him to inform me about the situation. He contacted the Foreign Ministry, which replied that the situation was being monitored and was under control'.[22] The media and opposition criticised the Swedish PM's attempt to blame

---

[19] Aftenposten, 3 January 2005; Dagbladet, 3 January 2005 (Norwegian daily newspaper); Swedish SvD, 8 January 2005

[20] Aftonbladet, 13 January 2005; Aftenposten, 30 December 2004; YLE24, 4 January 2005.

[21] More telephone lines, on-call teams, better information systems and computer support. Finnish Prime Minister's Office, Press Release, 10 January 2005.

[22] Swedish Television (SVT), interview with the PM, 12 January 2005.

individuals at the Ministry of Foreign Affairs as unjust and as another attempt to pass the buck. It left him open to even more intense scrutiny of his own and his government's actions dating back a long time before the tsunami. Table 5.4 documents the attempts to influence the temporal scope of accountability discussions.

In response to Persson's accusations, civil servants leaked compromising information about a long-term neglect of crisis management preparedness and systemic disregard of evaluations of earlier crises. Table 5.4 shows that in week 3, opposition speakers and independent experts seized their chance to widen the time frame. This new perspective fuelled the Swedish debate and the tsunami response became symptomatic of an endemic vulnerability: an institutional lack of preparedness and thus an organisational incapacity to handle crises.[23]

By contrast, Norwegian political actors admitted their part in the slow response together with the lower levels in the government hierarchy. Although it became clear that the Norwegian government had failed to implement a 2-year-old plan to enhance crisis management capacity, this did not arouse much criticism. In Norway, even opposition leaders and critical experts labelled the tsunami an incident.

In sum, government leaders in each country attempted to focus debates about the causes of crisis management shortcomings on technical, situational malfunctions and lower-level organisational mishaps. Their success varied, partly because of the aforementioned reflexive nature of blame games: at a certain point the blamed (in this case at the operational level) may react by broadening the time frame to include the responsibility of others (their superiors). This happened in Sweden, where ministers were least successful in making blame stick to lower levels only (see Table 5.5).

Constructing responsibility

Finnish Prime Minister Matti Vanhanen stated in his New Year's message that 'Under conditions such as these, government action alone is

---

[23] A Swedish media study recognised that the national media coverage soon got a political element and stated that the criticism of the social democratic government was unprecedented. Fifty percent of the media (TV, radio and newspapers) reports commenting on the prime minister were negative, and for the Foreign Minister the number was 75 percent (DN, 11 March 2005, 'Kritiken lyfte Göran Persson', media study by Observer).

Table 5.4. *Content analysis on attempts by actors to influence the temporal scope of accountability discussions*

	Week 2				Week 3				Week 4				Total			
	Nar	Exp	Neu	T	Nar	Exp	Neu	T	Nar	Exp	Neu	T	Nar	Exp	Neu	T
Progovt.																
Norway	3	0	8	11	1	1	4	6	0	0	1	1	4	1	13	18
Sweden	3	1	2	6	4	0	2	6	3	0	2	5	10	1	6	17
Finland	–	–	–	–	6	0	4	10	0	0	1	1	4	6	5	11
Antigovt.																
Norway	0	3	4	7	0	2	1	3	–	–	–	–	0	5	5	10
Sweden	0	6	2	8	0	11	5	16	0	4	2	6	0	21	10	30
Finland	–	–	–	–	6	0	5	5	–	–	–	–	0	0	5	5

Note: This table refers to articles where government actors (Progovt.) and opposition and critical experts (Antigovt.) narrow the time frame (Nar), expand the time frame (Exp) or stay neutral (Neu).

Table 5.5. *Content analysis on framing the event as incidental, nonrecurring or symptomatic/structural*

	Week 2				Week 3				Week 4				Total			
	Inc	Sym	Neu	T	Inc	Sym	Neu	T	Inc	Sym	Neu	T	Inc	Sym	Neu	T
Progovt.																
Norway	3	0	8	11	0	0	6	6	0	0	1	1	3	0	15	18
Sweden	4	1	1	6	4	0	2	6	2	0	3	5	10	1	6	17
Finland	–	–	–	–	0	0	10	10	0	0	1	1	0	0	11	11
Antigovt.																
Norway	0	5	2	7	0	3	0	3	–	–	–	–	0	8	2	10
Sweden	0	8	0	8	0	11	5	16	0	5	1	6	0	24	6	30
Finland	–	–	–	–	0	0	5	5	–	–	–	–	0	0	5	5

Note: This table refers to articles where government actors (Progovt.) and opposition and critical experts (Antigovt.) frame the event as incidental and nonrecurring (Inc), as symptomatic and structural (Sym) or stay neutral (Neu).

never enough'.[24] Political leaders of all three Scandinavian countries conveyed the same message: this was not just their responsibility. A broad range of actors, both private and public, had been unprepared for the scope of the crisis and the coordination and actions required. According to the third dimension of the blaming tree, policy makers can choose to either attribute responsibility to one specific actor or disperse responsibility across a complex network of actors, with varying consequences for the intensity of criticism this provokes.

Government actors handled criticism differently in the three countries. In Finland, the government chose to quickly admit shortcomings such as lack of preparedness and inadequate resources. It also signalled its awareness of the importance of the events through Prime Minister Vanhanen's early decision to assign a high-level investigation committee. Finnish opposition parties refrained from criticising the government, for which Prime Minister Vanhanen expressed his gratitude in a hearing on 2 February 2005.[25] His predecessor, Ahtisaari, the chair of the Finnish Investigation Committee, stated in a press conference on 11 January 2005 that the aim of his committee was not to assign blame, but to evaluate in order to improve future operations.[26] In a parliamentary hearing the prime minister claimed that the organisation at large had functioned well.[27] As a consequence, no specific actor was blamed.[28] Ahtisaari effectively dispersed blame across 'many hands': various government agencies for lack of information, the Ministry of Foreign Affairs for insufficient emergency hotlines and staff capacity, the EU for lack of cooperation between EU countries, and media for not correctly reporting the crisis.[29]

The Norwegian government also chose to accept blame when initial attempts at blame avoidance backfired. The minister of foreign affairs initially defended his ministry stating that 'everything worked automatically'.[30] Top civil servants at the Foreign Ministry pointed out that the travel agencies had overestimated their own capacity to evacuate victims during the first week.[31] In response, the director of

[24] Prime Minister's Office, 30 December 2004.
[25] Hufvudstadsbladet, 4 February 2005.
[26] Helsingin Sanomat, 12 January 2005.
[27] Hufvudstadsbladet, 4 February 2005.
[28] YLE24, 12 January 2005.
[29] Dagens Nyheter, 13 January 2005.
[30] VG NETT, 7 January 2005 (Norwegian daily newspaper).
[31] Nettavisen, 31 December 2004.

Table 5.6. Content analysis on the responsibility dimension

	Week 2				Week 3				Week 4				Total			
	Dis	Con	Neu	T	Dis	Con	Neu	T	Dis	Con	Neu	T	Dis	Con	Neu	T
Progovt.																
Norway	7	1	3	11	5	1	0	6	1	0	0	1	13	3	2	18
Sweden	5	1	0	6	2	4	0	6	3	0	2	5	10	5	2	17
Finland	–	–	–	–	9	0	1	10	1	0	0	1	10	0	1	11
Antigovt.																
Norway	0	7	0	7	1	0	2	3	–	–	–	–	1	7	2	10
Sweden	1	7	0	8	6	7	3	16	1	5	0	6	8	19	3	30
Finland	–	–	–	–	0	3	2	5	–	–	–	–	0	3	2	5

Note: This table refers to the number of articles where government actors (Progovt.) and opposition and critical experts (Antigovt.) disperse (Dis), concentrate responsibility (Con) for perceived crisis response failures or stay neutral (Neu).

the travel industry federation did admit that their emergency plan had failed.[32] Still, criticism of the government did not abate. Then, during a web chat, the Norwegian minister of foreign affairs went a step further. He stated that 'the responsibility [for the belated response] is mine'.[33] Likewise, the Norwegian prime minister eventually admitted that the government reaction had been too slow and that more aid should have been sent to the disaster area immediately.[34] The opposition welcomed the government's acknowledgements of its responsibility, and – like in Finland – the debate ended there and then.[35]

In Sweden, the government did not manage to placate the increasingly vociferous criticism. Its leaders initially denied that it had reacted too tardily; when this became untenable, they emphasised that the slow response was not due to any blameworthy behaviour on its part. They pointed at mistakes made by lower-level civil servants in processing the incoming information. These attempts at blame deflection opened a political Pandora's box. The opposition seized the opportunity: 'I think it is a sign of weak leadership if political leaders don't take responsibility in this situation', one opposition leader said, deriding the prime minister's attempts to scapegoat civil servants.[36] In a joint article in a daily newspaper, the Swedish opposition parties blamed Prime Minister Persson for being weak and blinded by his long hold on power. The Norwegian Social-Democratic Party leader came to his neighbour's aid and criticised the Swedish opposition for playing 'party politics' and politically abusing a tragedy.[37] Meanwhile, stories about the prime minister's lack of concern for government crisis management capacities started to leak from ministry sources. This information exposed the extent of the government's failures and shifted attention to the prime minister. Political opponents joined forces in accusing Persson of having cancelled crisis management exercises and holding him personally accountable for not implementing recommendations of previous crisis management audits.[38]

In response to opposition critique, the Social Democratic Party secretary charged the Swedish king – who had made a speech on the

---

[32] Dagbladet, 1 January 2005.
[33] Dagbladet, 3 January 2005.
[34] Dagens Nyheter, 8 January 2005.
[35] VG NETT, 10 January 2005.
[36] Expressen, 12 January 2005 (Swedish daily newspaper).
[37] Dagens Nyheter, 24 January 2005.
[38] Dagens Nyheter, 16 January 2005.

tsunami crisis which contained thinly veiled criticism of the government's response – of overstepping his constitutional mandate as the nonpolitical head of state.[39] Commentators duly retorted that the prime minister had sent in his party secretary as a 'kamikaze pilot' to attack the king whose emotional speech during a memorial ceremony for the victims had struck a chord with the entire nation.[40] When Prime Minister Persson criticised the Thai government for failing to react to a warning it had received two hours before the tsunami, the opposition called this yet another ill-chosen attempt to pass the buck: 'Göran Persson seems to be very eager to disperse blame and avoid responsibility'.[41] The more the prime minister defended his government by explaining the late response in terms of other people's failures, the more scathing his opponents and the media became of his own performance.

After considerable debate, on 13 January 2005, the PM had to accede to an independent investigation led by the chief justice of appeal.[42] The commission delivered its report in late 2005, blasting the government as a whole and the foreign minister in particular for what it depicted as institutionalised negligence and a failure to learn from prior experiences and investigations. Given the reality of his personal dominance over his party, and his party's dominance within parliament, the report had no immediate political consequences, but it remained an awkward sting in the government's side in the run-up to the September 2006 elections. In spring 2006, after weeks of hearings of the top political elite in the committee of the constitution, the minister of foreign affairs resigned. Formally her resignation was not linked to the tsunami crisis but the media and public saw her stepping down as a direct result of the massive critique and the damaged reputation of the government and the minister herself.[43]

In May 2006, the prime minister's state secretary and right-hand, Lars Danielsson, took a 'time out' as media started probing into his actions during the tsunami. Danielsson had been under severe media attention since the tsunami commission's report because he could not give a clear account of what he did, whom he called and what he

[39] Swedish Radio, Ekot, 14 January 2005.
[40] Dagens Nyheter, 14 January 2005; Dagens Nyheter, 15 January 2000; Svenska Dagbladet, 11 January 2005.
[41] Debate in Parliament, 19 January 2005 & Swedish Television, (SVT) 17 January 2005.
[42] http://www.regeringen.se/content/1/c6/03/68/53/b7d6be2c.pdf
[43] Svenska Dagbladet, 21 March, 2006.

had said to the prime minister to alert him on the 26th of December 2004. His presence in the cabinet became untenable after several critical media reports, implying that he had lied to the tsunami commission and to the standing committee on the constitution.[44]

In August 2006 the justice ombudsman criticised the government for the handling of the tsunami crisis and especially the actions of Danielsson.[45] The Social Democratic government lost the elections in September 2006 to the center right coalition of opposition parties. But postcrisis investigations continued by intensified media scrutiny. Media accounts revealed that phone records as well as tapes containing information on the e-mail communication in the government offices in the days following the tsunami had been erased. Critics claimed the previous cabinet had orchestrated an elaborate coverup. Within a few days, the new prime minister announced in a press conference that the tapes containing e-mail traffic had been found.[46] On 8 February, the commission of 2005 was reinstated to analyse the new information and its implications for the actors involved in the tsunami. The Commission presented its conclusions on 25 April 2007. The head of the commission stated that he wanted to present the 'truth' about the actions of the top civil servants close to the prime minister and their involvement in a potential coverup.[47]

Conclusions

The aim of this study was to employ a framing and accountability model to conduct a comparative analysis of three Scandinavian cases. We were especially interested in what factors influenced the different outcomes of the blaming process. Why did the three cases yield such diverging outcomes in terms of blame assignment, and under what conditions are these different outcomes likely to emerge? Given the methodological constraints of this study – only two newspapers were studied per country; no electronic media – this comparative case study offers a rather coarse cut of crisis-induced accountability processes in

[44] Svenska Dagbladet, 19 May, 2006.
[45] Svenska Dagbladet, 28 August, 2006.
[46] DN, September 2006 (www.dn.se/DNet/jsp/polypoly.
 jsp?d=1042&a=578247), Svenska Dagbladet 12 October
[47] Svenska Dagbladet, 31 January, February 7 and 15, 2007, Committé directive 2007:15, Ministry of Finance (http:www.regeringen.se/sb/d/8735/a/76597)

the three countries. Its empirical findings can only provide provisional hypotheses of the corollaries of crisis-induced blame games that remain to be tested in a more rigorous fashion.

The comparative analysis shows that in all three cases, media, public and experts needed little convincing that a terrible thing had happened and that their victimised countrymen had a right to expect more and quicker support than they actually received. The first attempts by government officials to avoid blame by framing the flood disaster as an 'act of god' failed. As the governments were increasingly seen as responsible and dissatisfaction was growing, accusations were made against them. In terms of constructing severity of government failure, we can conclude that all three countries initially denied that their flawed response had aggravated the crisis. Later, the public apologies by the Finnish and Norwegian governments seemed to have had a cushioning effect on the blaming process and the political elite could escape further damage (compare the fate of leaders in Chapter 1). The Swedish government's reaction stands in sharp contrast to this apologetic approach.

In Finland and Norway, the prime ministers had been delegating crisis management duties to their agencies to a much greater extent than the Swedish prime minister had done. Consequently, in the Finnish and Norwegian case many hands were implicated and responsibility was shared between multiple actors, mainly the ministries of foreign affairs and government agencies. The representation of what caused the slow response concurs with outcome B, *organisational mishap*. Moreover in Norway, the travel industry was implicated alongside public authorities. It accepted its culpability, as opposed to the Finnish and Swedish travel industry which could demonstrate that they had been pushing for the government to take action, to no avail.

The framing strategies used to assign agency played out differently in the three cases, partly because Finland and Norway had crisis management delegation structures in place. Consequently, media and public criticism focused on operational, technical failure at the level of government agencies (cf. Hood 2002). In Sweden there was no explicit delegation for crisis management capacities in place and agency responsibilities were unclear. Persson had informally centralised crisis management authority during previous extreme events in Sweden, therefore criticism and blame shifted automatically up the hierarchy.

In Sweden the government continued to deny responsibility. The political opposition accused it of a long-standing neglect of crisis

management capacity-building at the very core of the state apparatus. The mandates and responsibilities of the government agencies in
coping with crises were still under consideration and remained unresolved. The fact that the Swedish prime minister had assumed a more
direct, informal symbolic role as the 'father of the nation' during other
crises that had taken place in the recent past rapidly turned the tsunami
response into a matter of high politics: where was he now? This finding supports the notion that the *historic record* of leaders matters for
the blame game (Chapter 1). The government's attempts to widen the
frame of responsibility, and cast blame towards unlikely culprits such as
the Swedish king and the Thai government were, if anything, counterproductive. The reflexive quality of this framing strategy is illustrated
by these attempts. When Persson made implausible and unsubstanti-
ated allegations against others, a boomerang effect kicked in, aggra-
vating critique on the prime minister himself.

The Swedish blame game kept fuelling itself: the more the government denied having acted inappropriately, the more fault-finding took
place at the hands of the governments' political opponents and the mass
media. In response, the Swedish prime minister finally proposed a number of improvements to crisis management capacities, although initially
none of these pertained directly to his own cabinet office (Debate in
Parliament, 19 January 2005, Rixlex. SvD, 20 January 2005).

One explanation for the severity of the critique of the political elite
in Sweden was the lack of a synchronised political response to the
media and public that encompassed both recommended improvements
(a solution) and acceptance of responsibility on a high level. The unresolved institutional issue of who should be responsible for coping
with a national crisis provided a rich background for critical media.
Whereas the public blame focused on failing policy makers (outcome
C), these policy makers' response aimed at repairing organisational
mishaps (outcome B). This clash in these two interpretations intensified rather than tempered the criticism. Similar to the findings in the
Madrid bombing case (see Olmeda, this volume) the credibility of the
government and the prime minister in particular was undermined by
their continued rejection that they got it wrong. The Swedish prime
minister and the minister of foreign affairs became the personification
of the failure, and bore the brunt of the inadequacies of the entire
Swedish crisis management system.

In December 2005, the Swedish commission investigating the response concluded that: 'Prime Minister Göran Persson has the overall responsibility for the shortcomings in the government offices' response to the consequences of the tsunami', and that the lack of crisis management capacities in the government offices during Persson's incumbency was due to a conscious choice on his part.[48] Sweden was hit worse in terms of affected victims than Finland or Norway and the drive to assign responsibility and blame seems to have been stronger in Sweden. This finding confirms our initial claim that the size of the crisis matters in accountability processes. Also, uncertainty increased the impact of the event. The fact that Sweden did not substantially bring down the number of missing persons in the first month made every political move delicate and fixed the eyes of the entire nation on the way government was handling the crisis. Because no one knew precisely who was missing, many more people were potentially involved as relatives and acquaintances, and the crisis thus had a direct impact on a larger part of the population. The Swedish government had a bigger crisis to deal with, but the perceived failures in managing the crisis aggravated the public perception and political criticism to a greater extent than in their neighbouring countries.

The road ahead

From this analysis, we infer three hypotheses that explain why different patterns of blaming emerged in the cases, and might do so in others as well. The first conditional factor stems from an important difference between the cases. The formal or informal concentration of power negatively influenced the possibilities for incumbent elites to deflect blame in the Swedish case. During his incumbency, Swedish Prime Minister Persson had deliberately centralised informal power within his Cabinet and had been accused of assigning weak ministers under a tight rein.[49] There was no agency at 'arm's length' that would allow for a blame shift to a delegated agency. When the crisis hit Sweden, all

---

[48] SOU 2005:104 (2005) *Sverige och tsunamin – granskning och förslag.* Fritzes Offentliga Publikationer.

[49] Ögren, M. (2005); Dagens Nyheter, 7 January 2004, 11 January 2005, 14 January 2005; Svenska Dagbladet, 31 December 2004, 7 January 2005.

attention automatically turned to the prime minister, much more so than in the Finnish and Norwegian cases. In future comparisons, we would therefore like to test the following hypothesis: *The higher the degree of formal and perceived centralisation of executive power, the more likely the blame will go up the governmental hierarchy.*

The second factor we detected is the importance of decisive action to launch a heavy weight inquiry. In fact, our hypothesis for future research would be that *the sooner policy makers announce a fully independent inquiry by a prominent commission or institution, the less likely that blaming will escalate for the time pending the inquiry.* Contingent upon the assignments and conclusions of the inquiry commission, a blame game can still spark off when the inquiry report holds government actors responsible (see Brändström and Kuipers 2003). Timely assigning of investigations to prominent (but nonincumbent) politicians made political escalation less likely in Finland than in Sweden and Norway. Also, the Finnish inquiry committee specifically focused on improving the existing crisis management preparedness and communication structures rather than on accountability for failures made. The timing and form of inquiry certainly served to depoliticise the crisis in Finland. In Sweden, the delay in assigning an inquiry was compared to the swift action in Finland and it was therefore met with more impatience by critics than might otherwise have been the case.

The third factor of importance is the mitigating effect of manipulating political opposition. We learned from the Finnish case in particular that generous public apologies by the incumbent government and recognition of their own failure may have a cushioning effect on the subsequent debate. We therefore hypothesise for further research that *the sooner the government acknowledges mistakes of its own, the less room for intense criticism by the opposition.* Proactive, unforced government self-criticism robs the opposition of the opportunity to lash out at it. It leaves opponents no option but to agree with the government's own statements, and support its intention to remedy the errors made. However, government actors need to strike a balance in proactively taking on responsibilities and encouraging other actors to also take their share of responsibility.

It is necessary to further test the relation between political escalation and personal and material damage. In this study the link between escalation of blame and the size of the damage was fairly straightforward (in contrast to Bovens and 't Hart 1996; Bovens et al. 1999): the hardest-hit country also manifested the toughest accountability process. Nevertheless, the comparison also brought to the surface striking differences in actor behaviour during the accountability processes in the three countries. Blame games turn out to be short-lived when generous public apologies are made early on by a country's political leaders and when timely investigations are started. Some strategies that were successfully employed in one country were less successful in another, because of institutional factors such as centralisation of authority and the lack of designated agencies to take responsibility (see Chapter 1). This chapter has shed some light on explanations for diverging blame games in similar situations. When political leaders fail to manage blame in a crisis characterised by considerable damage or threat, they create for themselves a crisis after the crisis.

References

Anheier, H. (ed.) 1999. When things go wrong. London: Sage.

Bloom, H., and Price, H. D. 1975. Voter response to short-run economic conditions: the asymmetric effect of prosperity and recession. American Political Science Review 69(4):1240–54.

Boin, A., 't Hart, P., Stern, E. K. and Sundelius, B. 2005. The politics of crisis management: public leadership under pressure. Cambridge, UK: Cambridge University Press.

Bovens, M. and 't Hart, P. 1996. Understanding policy fiascoes. New Brunswick, NJ: Transaction Publishers.

Bovens, M., 't Hart, P. and Peters, B. G. 1999. Success and failure in public governance. Aldershot, UK: Edward Elgar.

Bostdorff, D. M. 1994. The presidency and the rhetoric of foreign crisis. Columbia, SC: University of South Carolina Press.

Brändström, A., and Kuipers, S. 2003. From normal incidents to political crises: understanding the selective politicization of policy failures. Government and Opposition 38(3):279–305.

Buzan, B., Waever, O. and De Wilde, J. 1998. Security: a new framework for analysis. Boulder, CO: Lynne Rienner Publishers.

D'Angelo, P. 2002. News framing as a multi-paradigmatic research program: a response to Entman. Journal of Communication 52(4):870–88.

DeVreese, C. H. 2003. Framing Europe: television news and European integration. Amsterdam: Aksant Academic Publishers.

Douglas, M. 1992. Risk and blame. London: Routledge.

Edelman, M. 1964. The symbolic uses of politics. Urbana, IL: University of Illinois Press.

Edelman, M. 1977. Political language: words that succeed and policies that fail. New York: Academic Press.

Edelman, M. 1988. Constructing the political spectacle. Chicago: University of Chicago Press.

Edelman, M. 1995. From art to politics: how artistic creations shape political conceptions. Chicago: University of Chicago Press.

Ellis, R. 1994. Presidential lightning rods – the politics of blame avoidance. Lawrence, KS: University Press of Kansas.

Eriksson, J. 2004. Kampen om hotbilde: Rutin och drama i svensk säkerhetspolitik. Stockholm: Santérus Förlag.

Goffman, E. 1975. Frame analysis: an essay on the organization of experience. Harmondsworth, UK: Penguin Books.

't Hart, P. 1993. Symbols, rituals and power: the lost dimension of crisis management. Journal of Contingencies and Crisis Management 1(1):36–50.

Hood, C. 2002. The risk game and the blame game. Government and Opposition 37(1):15–37.

Hurst, S. 2004. The rhetorical strategy of George H. W. Bush during the Persian Gulf crisis 1990–91: how to help lose a war you won. Political Studies 52(2):376–92.

Iyengar, S. 1996. Framing responsibility for political issues. Annals of the American Academy of Political and Social Science 546(12):59–70.

Jones, D. 2000. Sultans of spin: the media and the new labour government. London: Orion Books.

Kernell, S. 1977. Presidential popularity and negative voting: an alternative explanation of the midterm congressional decline of the president's party. American Political Science Review 71(1):44–46.

Kingdon, J. 1995. Agendas, alternatives and public policies, 2nd edn. New York: HarperCollins.

Kofman-Bos, C., Ullberg, S. and 't Hart, P. 2005. The long shadow of disaster: memory and politics in Holland and Sweden. International Journal of Mass Emergencies and Disasters 23(1):5–26.

Lau, R. 1985. Two explanations for negativity effects in political behavior. American Journal of Political Science 29(1):119–38.

McGraw, K. M. 1991. Managing blame: an experimental test of the effects of political accounts. American Political Science Review 85(4):1133–57.

Nelkin, D. 1975. The political impact of technical expertise. Social Studies of Science 5:35–54.

Ögren, M. 2005. Makten framför allt. Stockholm: Wahlström & Widstrand.

Rochefort, D., and Cobb R. 1994. The politics of problem definition: shaping the policy agenda. Lawrence, KS: University Press of Kansas.

Schön, D. A., and Rein, M. 1994. Frame reflection: toward the resolution of intractable policy controversies. New York: Basic Books.

Thompson, D. F. 1980. Moral responsibility of public officials: the problem of many hands. American Political Science Review 74(3):905–16.

Vaughan, D. 1999. The dark side of organizations: mistake, misconduct, and disaster. Annual Review of Sociology 25:271–305.

6 | Dutroux and dioxin: crisis investigations, elite accountability and institutional reform in Belgium

SOFIE STAELRAEVE AND PAUL 't HART

Introduction: catalytic crises in the Belgian polity

On 13 August 1996, the Belgian police arrested Marc Dutroux, his wife Michèle Martin and their associate Michel Lelièvre. In the following weeks, these three individuals led the authorities to two kidnapped girls and the dead bodies of four others. It was a gruesome end to what had been a long search for a series of missing children. The fate of the children shocked the nation, and shock turned into anger when it subsequently transpired that a range of mistakes had been made during the investigation. Communications between police and the judiciary had been poor. Judicial authorities in different parts of the country did not cooperate with one another. Families of the victims had been treated disrespectfully, and previous clues leading to Dutroux and his associates had not been checked thoroughly.

The revelations unleashed a storm of public indignation. Suspicions were aired that political and judicial authorities were aiding and abetting paedophile and other criminal networks. In the end, no political casualties ensued from the inquiry that was undertaken, nor could the parties agree on the wide-ranging reform package proposed by the inquiry. With no catharsis resulting from the initial inquiry, the sense of crisis unleashed by the Dutroux affair deepened into an institutional crisis challenging the foundations of not only the justice system and to some extent even the entire Belgian political order (Deweerdt 1997: 497; Barrez 1997: 172–81; Maesschalck 2002; Van den Bossche 2004).

Almost 3 years later, on 26 May 1999, Belgian television news reported incidences of dioxin contamination in poultry and eggs. The cabinet's crisis response was beset by problems. The European Union (EU) banned Belgian exports, accusing the Belgian government of negligence (Larsson et al. 2005). Because it occurred during a parliamentary election campaign, the dioxin crisis ignited heated political controversy.

In stark contrast with the Dutroux crisis, two ministers resigned instantly. Moreover, the major coalition parties took a severe beating at the election, which brought a new, liberal-led government to power.

In this chapter we compare the political management of both crises. Both were powerful agenda setters, bringing to the fore deep and hitherto latent societal disaffection with the political system and major public institutions. Coming on the wings of two decades of similar crises in the justice system (scandals, interagency conflicts, unresolved armed gang murders and other shocking crimes), the Dutroux crisis unleashed unprecedented grass-roots pressure for purification and change, and forced the government into all-party talks. Although the dioxin crisis stirred up less collective stress, it acted as a final blow to the outgoing coalition government, which had already been weakened by the Dutroux affair and two major party finance scandals (Rihoux 2000: 341–4).

Both cases were remarkable exercises in political blame management; in combination, they are even more puzzling. The Dutroux crisis brought hundreds of thousands onto the streets in protest, it yielded a highly publicised and rigorous parliamentary inquiry, yet it initially failed to make a dent in the bulwark of elite complacency. A system whose long-faltering performance claim was shattered by the symbolism of avoidable child murders proved nevertheless resilient enough to withstand an unprecedented wave of grass-roots disaffection with it. Its resilience did not crumble until mass disaffection with the system was revived dramatically a year later, when Marc Dutroux managed to escape from prison (albeit only briefly). It was then and only then that political heads started rolling and political stalemates regarding institutional reform were broken definitively. In contrast, in the much more 'ordinary' dioxin contamination crisis, ministerial resignations were immediate and political change was deep. The odd twist here was that all these consequences had already occurred before the parliamentary inquiry started. When it got under way, the dioxin inquiry had all the hallmarks of a political ritual.

Hence the puzzle of this chapter. The Dutroux crisis was deep and its inquiry had teeth and enjoyed staunch public support, yet it took protracted negotiations, a second inquiry and, most of all, a freak event (the Dutroux escape) to claim scalps and make its criminal justice reform agenda really stick; in contrast, the dioxin crisis triggered major political consequences despite an ineffectual inquiry. The question is why? Both crises occurred in the same polity led by the same government. The obvious explanation – the bigger the crisis, the more likely incumbent elites have to pay and policy changes will be made – clearly cannot account for this pattern. Nor can another obvious explanation: inquiries with political teeth and social legitimacy are more likely to have political and policy consequences than those that do not. As discussed above, the Belgian pattern was actually the reverse.

So how do we explain what happened here, and what can this teach us about the role of inquiries in crisis-induced processes of political blame management? Partly inspired by the literature on political scandal and its investigation, we argue that the role and impact of crisis inquiries is the product of the interplay between two types of forces: the political *context* in which they occur (cf. Markovits and Silverstein 1988; Lowi 2004; Garrard and Newell 2006), and the political management of the inquiry *process* (see, e.g., Parker and Dekker, this volume). We have articulated a tentative proposition for each factor. Specifically, key contextual factors examined here include:

1. *The nature of the crisis trigger*: the more visible and dramatic the revelation and the more salient the violation or threat a critical incident entails, the more likely it is that its inquiry will have a tangible impact on incumbent elites and existing policies.
2. *The 'fit' in ongoing political narratives and struggles*: the more a crisis or scandal is constructed in leading media outlets as a new manifestation of personal and/or systemic flaws that have been on the political agenda before, the more likely it is that its inquiry will have a tangible impact.
3. *The placement in political time*: the closer to an upcoming election a crisis or scandal occurs, the more likely it is that its inquiry will have a tangible impact, particularly in claiming political 'victims'.
4. *The relative strength of the government at the time of the crisis*: the less internally coherent an incumbent government and the smaller the size of its parliamentary majority at the time of a crisis or scandal, the more likely it is that its inquiry will have a tangible impact.
5. *Media and societal responses to the crisis and the crisis inquiry*: the more constantly key media outlets report on the crisis, the bigger the public criticism of the government's role in the crisis, and the more positive the public image of the inquiry body, the more likely it is that its inquiry will have a tangible impact.

The factors concerning the actual management of the inquiry process examined in this chapter are the following:

1. *The composition, mandate and staffing of the inquiry*: the more prestigious the membership, the bigger its investigative powers and its staff support, the more likely it is that a crisis inquiry will have a tangible impact.
2. *The modus operandi of the inquiring body and particularly its leading figures*: the more the inquiry – as personified by its chairperson – acquires a reputation of vigour and tenacity, the more likely it is that the inquiry will have a tangible impact.
3. *The framing of inquiry findings*: (a) unanimous inquiry reports are more likely to have a political impact than nonunanimous ones; (b) the more an inquiry report focuses blame on a limited number of high-level actors, the more likely it is to generate political fatalities; (c) the more specific and 'technical' an inquiry's policy recommendations are, the more likely they are to be implemented.

Depending on their configuration in any given crisis inquiry episode, these various context and process factors can amplify or extinguish one another in shaping the course and outcomes of inquiries and, by implication, the resilience of incumbent elites and policy systems to the delegitimising effects of crisis politics. Our comparative examination of two Belgian crisis inquiries offers not more than a first plausibility probe of these propositions. More rigorous testing requires a much more comprehensive research effort than is possible here.

This chapter begins by outlining the evolution of both crises. It then briefly describes Belgian parliamentary investigation rules and practices. The bulk of the paper is devoted to describing, first, the process factors and then the context factors as they played out in both crisis inquiries. In the final section we compare and contrast the impact of these factors in view of this chapter's main puzzle, and we conclude by offering suggestions for future research.

One government, sequential crises

The Belgian political system has often been characterised as 'consociational' and 'neocorporatist' (Lijphart 1994; Witte et al. 2005: 477). Political decision making is a product of complex bargains and often informal arrangements. Belgium's multiple social and political fault lines – linguistic, cultural, regional, socioeconomic, religious – make it an extraordinary polity. Its constitutional architecture has been a constant source of debate and has been subject to a series of changes in recent decades, resulting in a unique five-tiered system of government whose complexity regularly baffles Belgians and outsiders alike.

It is in this complex system that the federal parliament is embedded. Like any other parliament, its main tasks are to colegislate and control the executive; but since the Belgian executive is split into many different parts, the federal parliament operates alongside other representative bodies having similar competencies. Although parliamentary investigations at the national (federal) level may be part of the consultative and information-gathering stages of 'routine' lawmaking and oversight, the main triggers prompting ad hoc parliamentary inquiries have tended to be crisis situations of some sort or other (23 out of 25 inquiries, see Staelraeve 2003: 28). Each of the two chambers in the federal parliament has a constitutional right of investigation.

At the time of the two crises, Belgium had been governed for decades by a swirl of coalition governments consisting of Christelijke Volkspartij (CVP) and Parti Social Chrétien (PSC) (Flemish- and French-speaking Christian-democratic parties) and Parti Socialiste (PS) and Socialistische Partij (SP) (Flemish- and French-speaking socialists). These parties dominated the country's political and administrative landscape. The crises presented major challenges to the legitimacy of the latest incarnation of that political cartel – the second coalition government led by Jean-Luc Dehaene. The Dutroux case first emerged early in its period of office but continued to dog it for years, whilst the dioxin crisis occurred at the very end of its term in office.

The Dutroux affair: from sex crimes to institutional crisis (1996–1998 and after)

Marc Dutroux, his wife Michèle Martin and Michèl Lelièvre had kidnapped, sexually abused and imprisoned six Belgian girls. The kidnappings happened in the Walloon as well as in the Flemish part of Belgium. The girls (who were between 9 and 19 years of age) were kidnapped between June 1995 and the beginning of August 1996. On 12 August 1996, the police arrested Dutroux, Martin and Lelièvre after a witness to the last kidnapping remembered some numbers from Dutroux's license plate. Three days later, police released two girls from a purpose-built hidden cellar in one of Dutroux's houses. A few days later, two bodies were found buried in the garden of another house, and two more in the backyard of one of Dutroux's accomplices.

Soon, charges appeared in the press that police, public prosecutors and judges had made crucial mistakes during their search for the missing girls, which probably had cost the lives of two of them. Media and opposition commentary began to interpret the crisis in light of a story line that had been pursuing the Belgian criminal justice system for over a decade, namely that institutional fragmentation and endemic internecine conflict had severely compromised the performance of the police and the judiciary. This interpretation fell on fertile ground with the overwhelming majority of the Belgian public: the Dutroux case took community anger with the political elite's apparent inability or unwillingness to reform the justice system to new heights, most likely because of the gruesome nature of the crimes involved, which highlighted as never before the terrible consequences that the organised ineptness of police and judiciary could have. For example, Dutroux and Martin had been convicted in 1989 for the rape of under-age girls. They had received sentences of 13 and 5 years respectively but were released on parole in 1992. The Belgian public could not understand how this could have been possible; neither did it understand why Dutroux received social benefits and how he could own three houses even though he was unemployed. Dutroux was questioned when the first two girls were reported missing, and police had searched his house twice. The fact that the girls were not found during these searches only strengthened the public conviction that something was seriously wrong (De Mulder and Morren 1998).

The Dehaene II coalition government saw its poll ratings slump to unprecedented lows. Suddenly it seemed to exemplify all the ills of the Belgian political culture – that of a self-sustaining but ill-governing 'particracy'. Public sentiment deepened further when the immensely popular Judge Connerotte, who had been given the lead in the Dutroux investigation and who had pursued it with zeal and integrity, was forced to resign by a Supreme Court ruling. The ruling followed an appeal of Dutroux's lawyers that Connerotte had displayed bias by agreeing to attend a dinner in honour of the victims (Ponsaers and De Kimpe 2001: 48–9). The Court's decision fuelled a variety of conspiracy theories, the most persistent of which was that Dutroux and his gang enjoyed protection from paedophile networks that included high-level politicians, judges and police officers. An unprecedented wave of street protest followed: the 'white march' on 20 October 1996 attracted more than 300 000 people in Brussels, was replicated in other cities and gave rise to a grass-roots movement demanding a wholesale political cleanup. The Belgian king took the dramatic step of publicly demanding a thorough investigation into the matter (foreshadowing the equally remarkable intervention by his Swedish counterpart in the 2004–2005 tsunami crisis; see Brändström et al., this volume).

Initially, the Dehaene government's blame management strategy was to do nothing. It remained aloof and did little more than offer compassion to the victims, treating the case as a criminal investigation currently being *sub judice* and thus not amenable to political management. This did little to calm public outrage; it merely reinforced the story line: the government was inept at best, and at worst senior political figures were somehow implicated in the whole affair.

Bowing to public pressures 2 weeks after Dutroux was arrested, the minister of justice set up an internal inquiry into police and judicial handling of the kidnapping of two of the murdered girls. This belated move failed to contain the cascading sense of crisis. For its part, the Belgian parliament struggled to find an appropriate answer. Several debates took place but no firm conclusions were reached – parliamentarians were seemingly paralysed by the sheer scope and depth of the crisis. Politicians from both 'left' and 'right' were literally at a loss for words (Furedi 2005).

The politicisation of the crisis gained momentum when coalition parties disagreed who was to blame most for the botched-up kidnapping investigation: police or magistrates. The trade unions representing state police and judicial police exchanged criticism. The blaming process peaked after the investigating judge, Connerotte, was discharged by the Supreme Court on 14 October 1996. The liberal opposition parties Vlaamse Liberalen en Democraten (VLD) and Mouvement Réformateur (MR), in parliament, demanded a special committee of inquiry 'to offer a fast answer to the questions of the citizens' and the government parties felt that in the given opinion climate they could no longer resist this call (Reynders et al. 1996). The parliamentary inquiry started on 17 October 1996 and lasted until 14 April of the following year. Its first report gave birth to a second parliamentary inquiry, leading subsequently to a series of reforms – notably the creation of an integrated police force.

The crisis mood was deepened when 'the unthinkable became reality' (Fijnaut 2001: 237): Dutroux escaped from custody. Although he was arrested within hours, the political fallout of yet another painful mishap in the criminal justice system was huge. On the wings of the renewed public outcry that followed the escape, the justice minister resigned and a political breakthrough was forged in the hitherto stalemated discussions about the commission's initial recommendations for police and judicial reform.

The dioxin contamination: from electoral dynamite to political obscurity (1999–2000)

The dioxin crisis, 3 years later, took a different course. On 26 May 1999 it was announced on Belgian television that chickens and eggs were contaminated with dioxin (Deweerdt 2000: 177–8). The minister of agriculture (Karel Pinxten) and minister of public health (Marcel Colla) initially denied the severity of the contamination, but 2 days later all chickens and eggs were taken off the market. The ministers explained that at first they had known only about a contamination of feed – *not* in animals or food products. They argued that it had been necessary to wait for test results to see if dioxin was also in chickens and eggs (Van der Donckt 2000: 29).

On 31 May 1999, the two ministers reported on the dioxin contamination to Prime Minister Dehaene. In an official press release after the meeting, the prime minister declared that 'based on currently available information, my ministers took their responsibility from the moment they had all necessary information about the dioxin contamination' (Van der Donckt 2000: 34). At this point, Dehaene still trusted his ministers and accepted their explanation. Later that day, the ministers organised a press conference and repeated their contention that they could not have acted before 26 May because they were uncertain about the scope of the dioxin contamination. Colla added: 'Resignation is out of the question' (Van der Donckt 2000: 35). Neither minister felt he should accept responsibility for the crisis and located blame outside the political domain altogether: the contamination was an industry problem, not a regulatory failure.

In the meantime, liberal opposition leader Verhofstadt struck political gold when he obtained a document showing that both ministers had in fact known about the contamination a month before it became public. On 1 June, he took it straight to the prime minister, who had no alternative but to force Colla and Pinxten to resign immediately. Pinxten continued to defend himself, claiming he had never seen the document, adding that the only thing he had been guilty of was 'faulty communication' – an argument he would later repeat during the subsequent parliamentary inquiry. Colla, in turn, was bitter and commented publicly that he was sick and tired of being blamed (Van der Donckt 2000: 38–40). Clearly, neither had resigned of his own accord. They had been sacrificed by Prime Minister Dehaene in the run up to the parliamentary elections, due in 2 weeks.

The government attempted to contain the crisis with a series of seemingly disjointed and often unclear decisions in the face of compensation claims from various stakeholders. It also had to cope with criticism from European Commissioner Franz Fischler, who suggested that Belgium had not been fast enough in informing the EU about the contamination, which might have devastating economic consequences for meat and meat product exports throughout Europe (the EU is a fully integrated agricultural market). The commission proceeded to ban all Belgian poultry and egg exports (Larsson et al. 2005). Duped Belgian farmers then protested against the government, blocking border crossings. The cabinet eventually managed to produce a list of 'safe' farms and companies (Deweerdt 2000: 180).

The ministerial resignations did not provide a political catharsis. The dioxin crisis continued to consume the media as well as the political debate during the remainder of the election campaign. All political parties tried to exploit the crisis for their own purposes. The prime minister tried depoliticising the issue. He sought to project himself as a statesman, announcing that he would stop all campaign activities to handle the crisis: 'I don't care about my image right now. I have to get in control of the situation. We'll worry about everything else after 13 June 1999. At this very moment, my personal future is not my main concern' (*Het Belang van Limburg*, 7 June 1999). Moreover, he sought to avoid being typecast as the leader of a government eschewing its responsibility by announcing that a parliamentary inquiry into the crisis would be held after the elections. His political message to the voting public was that his government was in control and would be best placed to oversee a postelection inquiry and lesson-drawing operation. His attempt to present the government as a unified front was compromised when the Flemish socialist coalition partner duly reminded Dehaene's Christian Democrats of their earlier refusal to merge the regulation of food production (a responsibility of the Ministry of Agriculture) and distribution (handled by the Ministry of Public Health) in one department.

These manoeuvres on the government side were all but nullified by the clamour of opposition parties left, right and centre to portray the dioxin crisis as symptomatic of a deeper weakness – Dehaene's 'chaotic' style of governance (Deweerdt 2000: 181). The Green Party saw one of its main platforms, food production and safety, reach the top of the political agenda and capitalised on it at the polls. On 13 June 1999, the coalition parties received a battering. The victorious Liberal and Green parties established a parliamentary committee of inquiry. It commenced its work on 16 July 1999 and presented its report in early March 2000. Its low-key, mostly technical recommendations were accepted in parliament without difficulties.

Parliamentary investigations in Belgium

Whenever certain events become labelled as crises, scandals or fiascoes, the parliamentary opposition usually leads the calls for an inquiry. Every individual member of parliament (MP) and every party in the Chamber or the Senate has a right to submit a proposal for the establishment of an investigation committee. This happens often, and hence the number of proposals to begin inquiries far exceeds the number actually held. This is in large measure due to the fact that a parliamentary majority is required to instigate an inquiry. Obtaining such a majority presupposes the support of at least one of the governing parties, who often have few incentives to lend this support – delicate multiparty coalitions are easily destabilized by such 'defections' to the opposition. Hence, it is only when negative publicity and public pressures to take action are so overwhelming that inquiries become politically feasible.

Technically, parliamentary investigations are fully independent. Their scope of inquiry can be limited only when it interferes with a judicial inquiry. The political reality is different. By the time an inquiry committee meets for the first time, the parties have already selected their committee member(s), and they will have selected the chairperson. Such agreements are informal and can be the product of intense political maneuvering within parties and between them (Staelraeve 2004: 17). The number of committee members varies from ten to fifteen. Crucially, the balance of membership among the parties is proportional to the number of their parliamentary seats. This rule guarantees the governing coalition a majority on every committee, which effectively limits its scope and political potential – unless, as we shall see, extraordinary circumstances arise. Just as the selection of committee members is a party's political decision, the time horizon of the inquiry can be politically controversial. Some interests are keen simply to have sufficient time for investigation, whilst others may advocate what amounts to a 'freezer scenario' – extending and delaying an inquiry until the media and the public forget about the whole thing (Staelraeve 2004: 18–19).

Committees possess procedural powers that are quite similar to those of an examining magistrate in court. The committee can hear witnesses, hold domiciliary visits, appoint experts and interrogate key persons. A committee would typically spend much of its time in preparing and conducting hearings with sworn-in witnesses. Most hearings are open to the public and the press, and hearings are only closed on the request of witnesses. The internal dynamics of committee meetings are confidential. Ultimately, the committee produces a final report, which must be approved by a parliamentary majority. Often, therefore, political anticipation and bargaining takes place not only within committees but also between committees and their wider parliamentary environment.

The Belgian parliamentary inquiry process is thus based on a relatively fixed legal framework of investigation, responsibilities and recommendations. Whatever the formal rules under which they operate, crisis and/or scandal inquiries are part and parcel of the broader social and political 'meaning-making' process that necessarily follows surprising, disturbing or otherwise extraordinary events and revelations (Boin et al. 2005: 116). As we have argued in the introduction, such inquiries are therefore shaped by the political and temporal context in which they occur as well as by the political 'management' of the inquiry process by the investigators, the investigated, parliament as a whole, external stakeholders, mass media and the active public alike. It is to these clusters of factors that we now turn, beginning with the latter.

The investigation process: exploiting the moment

The Dutroux inquiry (and its aftermath)

In the Dutroux case, the broad message of both the press and public was that the victims, their families and the Belgian people had been let down by failures in the political, criminal justice and police systems.

Such a high degree of scrutiny was focused on the responsibilities of key actors, accompanied by a lack of trust in institutional processes, that a full-blown crisis emerged, challenging the legitimacy of key public institutions. The sense of shock, typical of what Boin et al. (2005: 100) call 'the incomprehensible crisis', limited interelite blame games and produced an unusually thorough search for the causes of the crisis. From this point of view, a parliamentary inquiry seemed an obvious route for processes of investigation and accountability. This was strengthened because not only was there strong human interest in the kidnapping and murder of the girls but it tapped into core values in society – justice, democracy and national security. The revelation of multiple crimes and failures, accompanied by massive media attention, made the crisis even more severe (Manssens and Walgraeve 1998: 16–17).

Even in these circumstances, the necessity of a parliamentary inquiry was not evident to all political players. The governing Christian-Democratic CVP wanted a different type of investigation – enlarging the remit of an existing committee of inquiry on the so-called Bende van Nijvel (an extremely violent gang that had spawned bloodshed in supermarkets), with its own MP Tony Van Parys as its chairman. This general committee should then be split into two subcommittees, one investigating the gang as well as the murder of French socialist politician André Cools, the other tackling the Dutroux crisis. It is not clear whether this preference betrayed a desire to bury the entire case into a political 'freezer' or whether CVP simply wanted to retain firm control of all justice-related inquiries, if only to make sure that these would not compromise the political future of its own Minister of Justice Stefaan De Clerck, who was seen as a rising star within the party. The other parties accused the Christian Democrats of playing a political game and ganged up on it. Buckling under the combined pressure of the other parties and an increasingly irate public opinion, the CVP finally agreed with a special committee of inquiry on the Dutroux case, which started its work on 17 October 1996.

Time pressures were important in the Dutroux inquiry because public opinion demanded swift action. Opposition parties were of a similar mind. The committee initially got only 3 months to hold its investigation, although some parties had argued for 6 months (Reynders et al. 1996: 4). However, it is likely that the shorter deadline was part of a compromise with the CVP, whose proposed 'comprehensive inquiry' was to last only 3 months. Time was also important for another reason. The Dutroux crisis had laid bare the widely divergent views of political elites, judiciary, public, media and citizens' groups on the quality and integrity of the justice system. The very act of instigating an investigation would signal a commitment by the political elite to respect public opinion on this highly emotional issue. Furthermore, a thorough inquiry with a sufficient time allocation would be more liable to produce a settled operational and political closure on the case.

The remit of the Dutroux committee was broad. It included not just an investigation of the circumstances and facts pertaining to the case but also involved making appropriate recommendations for reform of the police and the judiciary. Chairing the Dutroux investigation was Marc Verwilghen, a Flemish liberal MP. Verwilghen obtained that vital position more or less by 'accident'. The right to lead the Dutroux committee had in fact belonged to the largest opposition party, the French-speaking Parti Réformateur Libéral (PRL). However, the PRL had close affiliations with the officers of one of the judicial districts under scrutiny, and so they refused committee leadership. The floor leader of the VLD, Patrick Dewael, wanted to 'keep his hands free to criticise the government', and so the hitherto unknown Marc Verwilghen took leadership of the Dutroux committee (De Mulder and Morren 1998: 167).

All parties took interest in the investigation and were keen to influence committee decision making. Chairman Verwilghen surrounded himself with vice presidents and a large team, with all political parties being represented (Landuyt and De 't Serclaes 1997: 9). In turn, the two 'rapporteurs' for the investigation belonged to government parties. Typically, another key division within Belgian society was also respected: one rapporteur was Flemish; the other, Walloon.

The media swiftly transformed the energetic and determined inquiry chairman Verwilghen into a national hero (Ponsaers and De Kimpe 2001: 55–9). Verwilghen had been a backbencher but was one of the three MPs who had introduced the proposal for a parliamentary investigation. Once the inquiry got under way, Verwilghen kept a tight grip on how the committee operated. He led the hearings and displayed empathy for the families of victims but was tough with other witnesses. He tried to convince other committee members to work in the public interest – and, for once, to put their parties' interest in second place. His image of a sound and neutral politician was firmly established in several confrontations with witnesses, and particularly his statement that 'nobody will leave the room before we know which one of you is lying'. Verwilghen did well after the Dutroux committee. In 1999, he was one of the most popular Belgian politicians and became minister of justice in the new Liberal-Green coalition.

More than half of the Dutroux committee meetings were open to the public. Nevertheless, it was necessary for some very sensitive information to be discussed behind closed doors. But as always, the committee suffered from leaks to the press. This was no surprise. The focal point for the investigations of the inquiry was in Wallonia, and its ruling elite had much to fear from the inquiry. To cope with press leaks, the Dutroux committee strengthened its standing orders about public statements (Landuyt and De 't Serclaes 1997: 26–7), making it possible to punish committee members who broke the code. This in turn reinforced Verwilghen's leadership and helped him mitigate, though not fully stem, the tide of leaks from the commission.

The Dutroux investigation gave central stage to the parents of the victims – their questions, complaints and worries. It did so by hearing them first and then again at the end of the inquiry. The committee also kept close contact with the victims. The investigation was, in part, the result of a request of the 'Committee Julie and Melissa', named after two of the Dutroux victims (Landuyt and De 't Serclaes 1997: 12). It was the first time in Belgian history that 'ordinary', nonorganised citizens had formed a political action group with such an immense influence on public opinion. Pressure groups in the field of criminal justice barely existed (Van Outrive 1998: 35). Whenever they were challenged about deficiencies in the justice system, magistrates normally insisted on the importance of the separation of powers and asked for 'more of the same': more money, more personnel and so on. Their interest was in strengthening the status quo rather than reform of the judiciary.

Other stakeholders played a role in the Dutroux crisis. The king, for example, held an audience with the parents of the missing children. Afterwards, he organised a roundtable conference on child abuse and missing children, making a remarkable statement which criticised magistrates, ministers and government. He demanded a thorough investigation into the matter and presented a list of questions and comments to the minister of justice (Van Outrive 1998: 24; Fijnaut 2001: 237). These actions and declarations were exceptional (and constitutionally debatable). The moral force of the king's intervention was great: parliament

and the government were urged to act by the last remaining symbol of national unity whose public authority at the time far exceeded
theirs. The trade unions also played an unusual role in the aftermath
of the crisis. After the examining judge, Connerotte, was taken off the
Dutroux case, masses of people spontaneously ceased working, and
many schools closed their doors. Trade unions supported their rank
and file in these actions (Ponsaers and De Kimpe 2001: 49–50).

The Dutroux Commission dominated Belgian newspapers throughout its life span. An average of 30 percent of all news in that period
was about the Dutroux case (Manssens and Walgraeve 1998: 16–17).
Almost every day the headlines were devoted to the case. At the outset
of the investigation, some media tried to tease out tensions between
political factions within the committee. Some committee members
reportedly felt that reform would come faster without the fanfare of an
investigation; others believed the investigation was vital regardless, as
a platform for enacting public accountability for what had happened
(Ponsaers and De Kimpe 2001: 53). As the investigation progressed,
media ceaselessly reported on its quarrels with various stakeholders,
internal tension and dissent, accusations against individual committee
members, and a steady stream of leaks. Polls taken at the time suggested the commission by and large managed to gain and retain the
respect of a large majority of the Belgian public regardless.

The inquiry report found fault in the entire policing and criminal
justice systems. It recommended two structural reforms: integration of
all police services in a two-level structure and changes to the organisation and functioning of the Public Prosecution Service (Fijnaut 2001:
241–2). Similar proposals had been discussed by the government and
several committees prior to the Dutroux crisis, but had not produced
major reforms. And the Dutroux commission's product did not bide
well either. Despite its judiciously maintained veneer of consensus, disagreements within the commission were never far below the surface.
Under pressure for a consensus from public and press opinion, the
committee could only agree on very general recommendations, sufficiently ambiguously worded so as to allow much room for interpretation (Ponsaers and De Kimpe 2001: 64–8). The report was adopted
unanimously in committee and in parliament. But this hardly mattered,
as in subsequent debates the parties disagreed profoundly on the meaning of phrases like 'the integration of police services.' Magistrates and
judicial services were highly critical of the reform proposals. Although

they stated that they were 'willing to contribute to measures which guarantee a better functioning of judicial institutions', they deplored the 'public executions' of witnesses in the committee and in the report. The National Committee of Magistrates was of the opinion that 'the committee's resolutions are a threat to the independence of the judiciary' (*De Tijd*, 18 April 1997).

The Dutroux report identified general and individual failings: forty people from police and judicial services were judged to have made mistakes during the search for the missing children. In this context, the government was under great pressure to act. Blame was focused primarily on judicial and police forces, making it easier for ministers to survive if they took collective and considered action. The cabinet endorsed the report, accepted responsibility and announced that it would work out a reform plan. The government also began disciplinary investigations against all the individuals cited in the report.

A few months after the report, debate on police reform was still fierce and Dehaene's coalition government was unable to reach agreement on the way forward. As a consequence, it turned to a committee of experts to devise a new police structure, but these efforts also failed (Ponsaers and De Kimpe 2001: 70–1; Fijnaut 2001: 244). The big bang of the Dutroux crisis seemed to end in an institutional whimper – until Marc Dutroux made a sensational escape from the Palace of Justice in Neufchâteau on 23 April 1998. Dutroux was arrested a few hours later, but the damage was done. Journalists chided that Belgium's most important criminal could 'go for a walk in the woods' and make politicians, magistrates and the police look like fools.

News of the escape became public while Prime Minister Dehaene was debating in parliament. The opposition promptly submitted a motion of no-confidence. Dehaene needed to protect the government from the public firestorm that broke out, and two ministers resigned the same day: the Minister of Home Affairs Vande Lanotte and Minister of Justice De Clerck. One week later, the commander of the national police also resigned (Ponsaers and De Kimpe 2001: 223–4; Fijnaut 2001: 244). This time, swift action by the government helped to restore some of its legitimacy – a vital move, given that parliamentary elections were only one year away.

Crisis-induced political sacrifices paved the way for institutional reform (Eppink and Verhoest 1998). Joint talks between government and opposition parties were initiated about the reorganisation of police and reform of the judiciary. These talks became known as the 'Octopus talks' and culminated a month later in an agreement on wholesale reforms in the entire criminal justice system. This ended a deep political and institutional crisis that had started almost two years before, when Dutroux was arrested.

The dioxin inquiry (and its political pre-emption)

News of the contamination broke during the middle of an election campaign. Public opinion, stakeholders and press saw the dioxin crisis as not just an operational and personal failure of the two sacked Christian democratic ministers and their party, but as a political failure on the part of all other governing parties. The Christian Democrats tried to contain the crisis by proposing a parliamentary inquiry after the elections, which all major political parties agreed to. Throughout the acute crisis period, the cabinet did not give the impression of being in charge (Van der Donckt 2000: 45–9). It proved unable to put crisis operations on a firm footing before the elections took place.

This combination of perceived incompetence and electoral inducements gave the dioxin crisis the hallmarks of an 'agenda setting crisis' (Boin et al. 2005). It came to symbolise hitherto neglected risks and vulnerabilities, providing a major rhetorical opportunity for the Green Party AGALEV-Ecolo to frame the underlying problem as one of 'food safety'. Two weeks after the crisis broke, the Christian Democrats lost the parliamentary elections and their hold on federal government power, which they have not regained since.

The short-term issue of blame assignment had to a large extent been dealt with through the resignations of the two ministers. As a result, the inquiry – held after the elections – faced the danger of a lack of media and public interest – potentially undermining its role as a vehicle for policy learning and an accountability forum. The new Liberal–Socialist–Green coalition parties nevertheless wanted to keep their pre-electoral promise and proceeded to start the dioxin inquiry while their negotiations for a new government were still going on (Landuyt et al. 1999). The inquiry lasted 9 months, but all parties were keen to move forward and put the crisis behind them as quickly as possible (Van der Donckt 2000: 161). The Christian Democrats wanted to minimise any further political damage from the issue; the socialists were preoccupied with finding their way into a very different type of coalition environment; the other parties gave priority to the operational aspects of the crisis. This made it more difficult for the committee to formulate 'hard' conclusions and make clear judgements about administrative responsibilities and underlying institutional questions.

The remit of the dioxin committee of inquiry was to document all facts that led to the dioxin contamination; describe the entire production chain of eggs, dairy and meat in Belgium; document all existing control services and mechanisms; investigate all current rules about the production of eggs, dairy and meat and make suggestions to improve them; and identify responsibilities (Vanhoutte and Paque 2000: 6). Prior to the election, the opposition parties had wanted the scope of the inquiry to be as large as possible, but when in government they sought to narrow it. A liberal MP commented: 'It would be stupid to complicate things for the government. This is not the Dutroux inquiry. There is no interest of the state at stake' (*De Morgen*, 28 August 1999) – a clear manifestation of the political about-faces of parties who were in opposition before the crisis and in government after it.

Charles Janssens, a member of the Walloon socialist government party PS, chaired the dioxin inquiry. His appointment was remarkable, since the scandal was set in Flanders and his ability to understand and speak Dutch was known to be limited. This odd choice had to do with the fact that almost all Flemish parties had been implicated in the dioxin crisis one way or another, either before or after the elections of 13 June 1999. Furthermore, the dioxin committee differed from the Dutroux committee in other respects. It counted only five members, and there was no clear division between opposition and government parties or between representatives of the Dutch- and French-speaking communities in Belgium (Vanhoutte and Paque 2000: 5).

The media framed Janssens' leadership of the inquiry in terms that differed markedly from their depiction of Verwilghen as chairman of the Dutroux inquiry. Verwilghen was made a hero, Janssens was ridiculed. He was depicted as a clumsy, inept politician unfit for the task assigned to him. Moreover, he had not signed the proposal for a parliamentary investigation in the dioxin case. Unlike Verwilghen, therefore, his early track record on the issue did not display an unequivocal commitment to an inquiry. In combination with his linguistic handicap and low standing within his own party, these factors limited his capacity to exercise strong leadership during the investigation – often delegating important tasks to other members. This, in turn, made it difficult to present the media with images of a strong and forceful investigation. A self-fulfilling prophecy took hold: the committee was plagued incessantly by political allegations and press leakages, impairing the accountability process.

The dioxin crisis attracted considerable media attention, although not at the same level as the Dutroux case. Press articles about dioxin were mostly on pages two, three or four. Throughout the investigation, the press was largely critical of the committee's work.[1] It focused initially on the limited capabilities of chairman Janssens and the political squabbles concerning the appointment of committee members. It then highlighted several disagreements between committee members as well as insinuations about a cover up by the political elite (Van der Donckt 2000: 171). Some newspapers pointed out that the committee did not really get up to speed until two months into its investigation, and that even then internal conflicts and allegations continued. In the months that followed, the inquiry focused on the ambivalent role played by the civil servant who had fed the key documents to liberal leader Verhofstadt, veterinarian Dr. Destickere. Besides being an inspector in the Institute for Veterinarian Control, Destickere had been employed as an insurance specialist for the feed production company that discovered the dioxin contamination. Destickere's minister, Colla, had refused permission for Destickere to combine both jobs. After the dioxin contamination became public, it was Destickere who gave Verhofstadt proof Colla had known about the contamination earlier than he had stated publicly. The press wondered aloud if Destickere was a genuine whistleblower who had acted in the public interest or simply a self-serving, disgruntled employee misusing confidential information.

The dioxin committee presented its report in March 2000. Press, parliament and government showed relatively little interest in the parliamentary presentation and subsequent debate (Van der Donckt 2000: 160–1). Opposition parties did not approve the report because no reference to the role of the new Verhofstadt government was made in it (Deweerdt 2001: 290–1). Although a list of conclusions, recommendations and responsibilities was formulated, the report did

---

[1] The paragraphs that follow are based on a content analysis of four Belgian newspapers during the investigation period. Detailed referencing has been omitted given this book's international readership, but original sources can be requested from Sophie Staelraeve at: sofie.staelraeve@sociaalhuiskuurne.be.

not create a big splash in the food sector or in Belgian politics at large. It recommended some useful government actions; for example, the establishment of the Federal Food Safety Agency, but this had been under way anyway. The committee's report appeared when political closure on the crisis had already come about: two ministers had resigned and a new coalition was voted in. The operational response to the contamination was ongoing but was handled by the new government and not covered in the report (Deweerdt 2001: 292). The dioxin crisis and investigation did put the broader issue of food safety higher on the political agenda, partly aided by the fact that around the time of the publication of the commission report Belgium was experiencing a number of Bovine Spongiform Encephalopathy (BSE) cases – further alerting citizens to the need to take food chain management seriously. The commission report's recommendations were partly targeted at making it possible to detect indications of food chain contaminations and react more effectively to them – an unspectacular but welcome thrust in a BSE-affected country needing to regain standing with the European Commission (Deweerdt 2001: 294; Rihoux et al. 2001: 259). However, compared to the Dutroux inquiry, the dioxin committee's wider institutional and symbolic impact was limited.

The upshot of this brief examination of the inquiries process in the two cases reveals some important differences between them, which, contrary to some of the propositions, did not always prove to be very consequential for the inquiries' outcomes. For one, although both commissions operated under the same set of parliamentary investigation rules, which set their investigative powers and staffing and the like, the Dutroux commission was clearly the weightier of the two. Its chairman was a rising political star who seized the opportunity to act as a moral entrepreneur and an advocate of institutional reform, whereas his counterpart in the Dioxin inquiry was weak and quite possibly selected for that very reason. Secondly, the two commissions' modi operandi differed much less than their respective public images would have it. Both, for example, failed to keep a united front throughout the full duration of their investigations and were plagued by leaks and well-publicised rivalries. Yet the public profile of the Dutroux inquiry was high and mostly favourable, whereas the dioxin inquiry struggled to make headline news and to offset the impression of being a mere 'after the event' ritual. Finally, in framing its findings the Dutroux commission's report paired a system-wide allocation of responsibility with the naming and shaming of forty-four individuals and sweeping albeit vague reform proposals, whereas the dioxin inquiry went more down the technical, specific and incremental route in its recommendations, partly because the need to allocate blame had been obviated by the prior resignation of the two key cabinet ministers. No compelling explanation for their differential significance and impact emerges from this review of process factors. Let us therefore turn to the other key factor in inquiry politics: the social and political context in which crises, scandals and inquiries are set.

The inquiry context: a polity scarred by scandals

The peculiar Belgian blend of a highly segmented state structure, intense multiparty competition, deeply rooted corporatism and the widespread politicisation of public service appointments went hand in hand with a political culture characterised by informal, nontransparent cooptation and osmosis between social, political and bureaucratic elites. Informal networks of patronage and loyalty both along and across party lines created a system that harboured many veto players standing in the way of policy and institutional reforms even after the biggest of crises (Kuipers 2005). Crises by their very nature require some sort of political response. Yet because its very structure makes it very difficult to adopt and enact substantive policy change, the Belgian system thrives on symbolic crisis management. Following Brunsson (1989), it can be characterised as a system of 'organised hypocrisy': much talk, few clear decisions and surreptitious action.

Against this backdrop it is perhaps less surprising that a series of outrages occurring during the 1980s and 1990s, particularly in the field of criminal justice and public order, duly led to the establishment of numerous inquiries. These produced sometimes searching analysis of the institutional weaknesses of the system and made detailed reform recommendations. But they tended to result in modest 'modernisations' at best, which remained mostly confined to uncontroversial domains such as staffing, training, equipment, communications and so on. The spiral of crisis > inquiry > stalemate/symbolism > crisis went through several iterations during this era. Major inquiry triggers in the period included: a long spate of extremely violent (twenty-eight killed, many more wounded) attacks on supermarkets perpetrated by the mysterious 'Nijvel Gang'; a European Cup Final stadium riot killing thirty-nine and wounding hundreds; the unsolved murder of a prominent French socialist politician often linked to corruption and mafia practices; the unsolved murder of a veterinary inspector on the trail of widespread illicit hormone trade in the Belgian meat industry; and a defence helicopter procurement bribery scandal involving long-time minister and former NATO Secretary-General Willy Claes.

Hence, as Fijnaut (2001: 235) observes, 'the Dutroux scandal was therefore by no means unique. In fact, it represented yet another climax in a perpetual cycle of crises. The proportions assumed by the Dutroux crisis would be difficult to grasp if it were not for all the crises that had preceded it and that had gradually eroded the legitimacy of the criminal justice system'. He could have added 'and in the political institutions and elites in general' (cf. Huyse 1996; Elchardus and Smits 2002).

The essence of a contextual explanation of the different course and outcomes of the two crises and their inquiries can now be presented. It is twofold. First, although the two crises inevitably shared this historical context of repeated cycles of scandalisation and stabilisation, the key difference between them was the cumulative effect that occurred: the Dutroux crisis and its legacy of popular distrust of the government and disgust with 'old-style' politics became part of the immediate context of the dioxin inquiry. It was the most conspicuous evidence of what Pujas (2006: 33) calls a 'breakdown of key political bargains' upon which the dominant position of the ruling political cartel in Belgium rested. It not merely added another of these cycles, it created an unprecedented 'market for scandal' (Lowi 2004) by weakening and disorientating the government and demonstrating that concerted opposition aided by popular outrage could force elites to accept far-reaching institutional reforms. The Dutroux crisis demonstrated that the cumulative effect of these scandal–stabilisation cycles had been to push down the legitimacy of public elites and institutions. Its 'added value' in this ongoing trend was that it pushed public disaffection with government below a critical threshold, triggering a unique type and level of mass mobilisation in the form of the White Marches.

The whole experience of the Dutroux crisis harboured two mobilising lessons for the government's critics. One was negative: our system is in even worse shape than we thought. The other was positive: massive and sustained popular protest triggered by extraordinary events can force the ruling caste to abandon its complacency. These lessons were part of the mental space that all players in the system occupied by the time the dioxin crisis occurred. During the late 1990s and beyond, the spectre of Dutroux hung over everything that smacked of governmental 'mismanagement' and 'scandal' in the Belgian polity – a scare source of historical analogy, available for rhetorical use by every public actor that chose to muster it (cf. Brändström et al. 2004). Its impact was to shrink the political space available to the governing coalition to engage in denial, delay and deflection in case another crisis event occurred.

The second contextual factor is more obvious but at least as important in explaining the difference between the cases: the dioxin case burst into the open during the immediate preelection period, whereas the Dutroux crisis did not. The political logic of electoral survival played out differently in both cases. Whereas in late 1996 the Dehaene government could still afford to take a calculated risk of trying to ride out the Dutroux crisis without getting itself into the federal, political and bureaucratic minefield of reforming the criminal justice system – there was enough time for popular discontent about this lack of vigour to blow over and be nullified by the government's intended achievements in other policy domains – this was clearly impossible in 1999. The dioxin issue fed right into the election campaign and there was no way in which any of the parties could afford not to be associated with a 'safety first' and 'hard-line' approach to containing health risks, both present and future ones. Hence instead of reluctantly agreeing to an inquiry as in the Dutroux case, the government now proposed one itself. Moreover, the prime minister had no choice but to project himself as a devoted crisis manager and forego electoral politicking during a time when his opponents were free to hack away at the government for its presumed neglect of food safety.

Crisis investigations in Belgium: beyond ritual?

This chapter has analysed the course and outcomes of two crises and crisis-induced parliamentary inquiries facing the Dehaene II government in Belgium (1995–1999). As explained in the introduction, our analysis is focused on explaining the significant differences in their course and outcomes; but before we evaluate our main findings (see Table 6.1), we should reemphasise the considerable similarities that also exist between them. As far as elite survival is concerned, the Dehaene government managed to outrun the long and deep shadows

Table 6.1. *Context, process and impact of the Dutroux and dioxin crisis inquiries*

	Dutroux crisis	Dioxin crisis
Context factors		
The nature/scope of the crisis trigger	Highly emotional: abused and murdered children, bungled investigations, conspiracy theories.	Potentially emotional: a 'victimless' food scare, a bungled coverup attempt.
Crisis framing in relation to ongoing political narratives	'Another dramatic indication of organised incompetence (and possibly rot) in the criminal justice system'.	'Yet another example of a government that cannot or will not put the safety of its citizens first, and that has learned nothing from "Dutroux"'.
Placement of crisis/inquiry in political time	Crisis occurs in government's midterm period. Inquiry and postinquiry process drags on for 18 months.	Crisis occurs during election campaign; inquiry promised during campaign, but not started until after the election.
The prevailing balance of political forces at the time of the inquiry	Parliament: ascendant coalition, neutralised opposition. External: vocal, powerful and deeply critical judicial and bureaucratic 'players'.	Parliament: embattled coalition, aggressive opposition. External: deeply discredited agro-food sector; weak resistance from relevant ministries.
Media and societal responses to the crisis and the crisis inquiry	Immediate, deep and lasting public indignation and trauma. Enduring saturation of media coverage of the 'moral panic' kind. Media heroification of inquiry chairman.	Momentary public uncertainty followed by disinterest. Sharp but comparatively short burst of media coverage. When inquiry began, the public had largely lost interest. Media consistently critical of inquiry and its chairman.

(*cont.*)

Table 6.1 *(cont.)*

	Dutroux crisis	Dioxin crisis
Process factors		
The politics of the inquiry's composition, powers and staffing	Major struggle about scope of inquiry: focused versus 'diluted' mandate. Tussle for the chairmanship, gained by ambitious 'outsider' candidate.	Postcathartic inquiry: ministerial resignations had already occurred. No political heavyweights involved.
The modi operandi of the inquiry and its leading figures during the investigation process	Leadership selection by default: ambitious, independent-minded and tenacious chairman acting as moral entrepreneur in advocating reform. Victim-centred inquiry process. High-profile support from the king. Initial internal cohesion of commission broke down eventually.	Leadership by government design: French-speaking chairman in a largely Flemish sector. Chairman had low standing in own party. No victims to be mobilised in inquiry process. Few allies in the extraparliamentary arena. Commission fraught by internal conflict and dissent from the outset.
The framing of inquiry findings and recommen-dations	Report faulted entire police and criminal justice system; ministers largely exculpated. Forty officials singled out for individual failures. Unanimous but ambiguously worded recommendations.	Technical, politically unspectacular diagnosis and recommendations.

cast by the Dutroux affair, but ended up having to sacrifice two ministers more than a year into the crisis process, long past the end of the initial inquiry. In the dioxin case, the ministerial sacrifices were made early into the crisis, but the voters punished the government out of office nevertheless. They were able to do so by virtue of the fact, coincidental or not, that the dioxin crisis broke out 2 weeks before parliamentary elections were to take place. In both cases, therefore, the dismissal of ministers was not a case of political accountability being enacted by a parliamentary forum. The parliamentary inquiries as such had little to do with both sets of resignations. In fact, parliamentary inquiries have never caused resignations in Belgium, and the Dutroux and dioxin crises did not break with this tradition. Belgian ministers do not quit unless their resignation is politically necessary to save a governing coalition. Decisions about ministerial exits are made by prime ministers and party barons, not by parliamentarians in their role as controllers of the executive.

Still, there is little doubt that both inquiries did play an important role in the accountability process relating to both crises. They both reached deep into the often complex political and bureaucratic constellations and interactions that had allowed both crises to develop. And, importantly, they did most of their work in full public view. Although they uncovered alarming facts about the efficacy and resilience of the policy systems they investigated, both committees took pains to restore public confidence in the checks and balances of parliamentary democracy by trying as much as possible to conduct their investigations coherently and professionally. Although itself all but flawless, the Dutroux commission did succeed somewhat better at this than the dioxin commission – also by organising public hearings with several stakeholders so as to enable the voices from the grass roots to be heard in the otherwise rather secluded chambers of Belgian federal politics. To the extent that both crises at least partly revolved around citizens' chronic distrust of government, the inquiries by and large assisted in 'working through' both crises in a fashion befitting a liberal democracy.

In political and policy terms, there were important differences between both inquiries, as pointed out at the outset of this chapter. In the middle part of the chapter we examined both contextual and process factors that may account for these differences. At the end of the day, these can be summed up as follows. First, the Dutroux commission went to work prior to any political catharsis taking place – it was a brainchild of the opposition parties designed to force the government's hand, and because of huge public pressure for decisive action, the government could not use its regular majority hold on inquiry politics to stave off a serious, probing investigation. The government had to go along with a firm and high-profile inquiry; any other course of action might have triggered severe popular unrest. The dioxin commission began as an electoral damage-limitation ploy by Prime Minister Dehaene, and ended up largely as a postcathartic ritual after two ministers had already been forced out and the voters had already inflicted political punishment by bringing about an unprecedented liberal-led coalition without Christian Democratic participation. The new coalition had little use for a commission whose birth they had supported during the campaign, and did what it could to marginalise it. Notwithstanding that, and perhaps in response to it, the commission's main impact was within the policy sector it investigated, providing it with an agenda for adapting its practices that met with little opposition and was largely implemented.

Second, time and timing were important factors explaining the course of events. The Dutroux crisis was situated at the beginning of the Dehaene government, giving a relatively young and coherent government room to manoeuvre and diffuse tension by adopting familiar methods: painstaking multiparty negotiation and consensus formation in response to the inquiry's highly sensitive reform recommendations. In contrast, the dioxin contamination became public only two weeks before an election. As predicted by the propositions, the lack of time before election day, the 'heated up' political climate and the decreased coherence of the government prevented it from successfully controlling the political fallout of the crisis.

Third, the investigative scope of the Dutroux inquiry was broad and allowed it to examine underlying institutional constellations. Although fact finding and allocation of responsibility were integral to its mission, its key ambition (certainly of its chairman) was to achieve a breakthrough in the institutional stalemate surrounding criminal justice policy. Its main handicap was just that: the existence of that stalemate. It divided the commission. The price of unanimity was a watering down of the specificity of its proposals. And it looked as though the commission's recommendations would suffer the same fate as those of its various precursors. As it happened, fate intervened: the game was changed entirely by the Dutroux escape and the political firestorm this generated. Making major changes and making them fast had become a matter of elementary political and institutional survival for the main veto players in the criminal justice policy game. Hence, in the end, it was not the commission as such but the events on the ground that forged the political breakthrough (cf. Maesschalk 2002).

The dioxin investigation was much narrower and technical in scope. The commission could not use the political lever of a still due accountability debate (including the shadow of possible sanctions against key ministers and officials) to gain momentum for any broader reform objectives. Moreover, the new government had already committed itself to some of the institutional innovations and policy changes that the dioxin commission proposed. Also, elections seemed to deal with the accountability issue, and so the inquiry lost what otherwise might have been an important driving force.

Fourth, committee leadership was important. Public and press pressure to produce results were much higher during the Dutroux investigation. Dutroux commission chairman Verwilghen rose to the occasion. He exerted a form of situational leadership that at times seemed to border on the charismatic – considering the undiluted public admiration and 'heroification' surrounding him for some time. Given the depth of the crisis the Dutroux revelations had triggered – the entire institutional make up of the justice system and indeed the political culture in Belgium at large was targeted by unprecedented and symbolically powerful forms of grass-roots political mobilisation – and the incessant media coverage of the affair along a villains–heroes story line, the potential for charismatic relationships developing around a new, untainted, tough-talking political figure was clearly there (Van Dooren 1994). Verwilghen jumped into that window – earning the jealousy, hatred and obstructionist intrigue of many establishment actors in the process, even within the commission itself (Brouwer 1997). Cause and effect are not so easy to disentangle, however. One may also argue persuasively that the strong public support for the Dutroux inquiry and for Verwilghen in particular was the product of a successful though fleeting coalition between the parents of the victims and other citizens' groups. They instinctively realised that Verwilghen and his commission were their best if not their only bet in forging the government to render account and to make significant policy changes instead of the kind of symbolic patchwork it had done in the past. In contrast, the dioxin inquiry was lacking such bottom-up wind in the back and its hapless chairman was never likely to elicit momentum either.

Fifth, as predicted, media representations of crises and crisis inquiries proved a weighty factor. The press in the two cases examined tended to converge on storylines about the 'real' nature of the crisis, the stature of the inquiry and the performance of its chairman. In doing so, media coverage 'made' the Dutroux inquiry and 'broke' the dioxin inquiry. To be sure, the Dutroux committee was also exposed to considerable media pressure about its internal workings, but by and large the media's tone enhanced the popularity of Verwilghen and other committee members and gave the commission status as an 'interpretive authority' (see Parker and Dekker, this volume) of the Dutroux crisis.

When confronted with severe crises, political leaders will be tempted or feel forced to propose or condone an official inquiry. In Belgium, such inquiries tend to be conducted by parliament. Compared to practices in other countries such as the UK and other Western democracies, where there is frequent reliance on expert-led 'blue ribbon' inquiries, the Belgian mode of political crisis management tends to politicise the very conduct of the inquiry itself. In the Dutroux case, this served to augment its stature and potential impact, whereas in the dioxin case it served to detract from it. This chapter has demonstrated the unique blend of factors that enabled the Dutroux commission to temporarily escape the seemingly inevitable marginalisation of Belgian crisis inquiries – although its policy impact was delayed and disappointing to many. Another combination of contextual factors ensured that a much smaller crisis had more immediate and enduring political consequences, but at the same time preempted the ensuing inquiry of much of its clout. These circumstances were indeed unique, and despite the much vaunted 'new political culture' that is said to have emerged in Belgium in recent years following the face lifts and generational changes in most of the traditional parties, significant parts of the populace and plenty of sceptical observers feel that the 'Belgian system' of old is alive and well under the surface of relabelled party names and the rhetoric of political innovation (cf. Elchardus and Smits 2002).

The propositional framework used here provided a parsimonious yet versatile torchlight for both selecting the material and interpreting the findings. Whilst some of the individual propositions may border on the obvious to political science cognoscenti, in combination they seem to 'work', particularly through the juxtaposition of context and process factors in crisis inquiries they enable. As stated in the introduction, we make no pretence of having conducted a rigorous test of this analytical framework, nor do we claim it exhausts all possible factors impinging upon crisis inquiries. But taking it as a starting point in further, more ambitious controlled comparison research designs seems as good an analytical strategy as any in the ongoing endeavour to comprehend the dynamics of crisis inquiry politics.

References

Barrez, D. 1997. Het land van de 1000 schandalen. Encyclopedie van een kwarteeuw Belgische affaires. Groot-Bijgaarden: Globe.

Boin, A., 't Hart, P., Stern, E. and Sundelius, B. 2005. The politics of crisis management: public leadership under pressure. Cambridge, UK: Cambridge University Press.

Van den Bossche, G. 2004. Political renewal, citizenship and identity: the 'new political culture' in Belgium. Acta Politica 39(1):59–78.

Brändström, A., Bynander, F. and 't Hart, P. 2004. Governing by looking back: historical analogies and crisis management. Public Administration 82(1):191–210.

Brouwer, A. 1997. Bitter België. De Groene Amsterdammer, 8 October.

Brunsson, N. 1989. The organization of hypocrisy: talk, decisions and action in organization. Chichester, UK: Wiley.

Van der Donckt, S. 2000. Vet drijft altijd boven. De verzwegen dioxinecrisis. Gent: Globe.

Deweerdt, M. 1997. Overzicht van het Belgische politiek gebeuren in 1996. Res Publica 4:468–521.

Deweerdt, M. 2000. Overzicht van het Belgische politiek gebeuren in 1999. Res Publica 2/3:166–246.

Deweerdt, M. 2001. Overzicht van het Belgische politiek gebeuren in 2000. Res Publica 2/3:369–96.

Van Dooren, R. 1994. Messengers from the promised land: an interactive theory of political charisma. Leiden: DSWO Press.

Elchardus, M., and Smits, W. 2002. Anatomie en oorzaken van het wantrouwen. Brussel: VUB-Press.

Eppink, D. J., and Verhoest, F. 1998. Het diskrediet van België. De Standaard, 23 April.

Fijnaut, C. 2001. Crisis and reform in Belgium: the Dutroux affair and the criminal justice system. In Rosenthal, U., Boin, A. and Comfort, L.

(eds.) Managing crises. Threats, dilemmas, opportunities. Springfield, IL: Charles C Thomas, pp. 235–47.

Furedi, F. 2005. Politics of fear: beyond left and right. London: Continuum.

Garrard, J., and Newel, J. (eds.) 2006. Scandals in past and contemporary politics. Manchester, UK: Manchester University Press.

Huyse, L. 1996. De lange weg naar Neufchâteau. Leuven: Van Halewyck.

Kuipers, S. 2005. The crisis imperative: crisis rhetoric and welfare state reform in Belgium and the Netherlands in the early 1990s. Amsterdam: Amsterdam University Press.

Landuyt, R., Bourgeois, G., Eerdekens, C. et al. 1999. Voorstel tot oprichting van een parlementaire onderzoekscommissie belast met een onderzoek van de Belgische vlees-, zuivel- en eierproduktie en naar de politieke verant-woordelijkheden in het licht van de zogenaamde 'dioxinecrisis'. Brussel: Kamer van Volksvertegenwoordigers (K 18/1–1999).

Landuyt, R., and De 't Serclaes, N. 1997. Verslag namens de onderzoekscom-missie van het parlementair onderzoek naar de wijze waarop het onder-zoek door politie en gerecht werd gevoerd in de zaak Dutroux-Nihoul en consorten. Brussel: Kamer van Volksvertegenwoordigers (K 713/6–1996/97).

Larsson, S., Olsson, E.-K. and Ramberg, B. 2005. Crisis decision making in the European Union. Stockholm: Crismart/Swedish Defence College.

Lijphart, A. 1994. Democracies: forms, performance and constitutional engi-neering. European Journal of Political Research 33(1):1–17.

Lowi, T. J. 2004. Power and corruption: political competition and the scandal market. In Apostolidis, P. and Williams, J. (eds.) Public affairs: politics in the age of sex scandals. Durham, NC: Duke University Press, pp. 69–100.

Maesschalck, J. 2002. When do scandals have an impact on policy making? A case study of the police reform following the Dutroux scandal in Belgium. International Public Management Journal 5(2):169–93.

Manssens, J., and Walgraeve, S. 1998. Populair en/of kwaliteit? De Vlaamse pers over de zaak-Dutroux, PSW-papers 10:1–35.

Markovits, A., and Silverstein, M. (eds.) 1988. The politics of scandal: power and process in liberal democracies. New York: Holmes and Meier.

De Mulder, M., and Morren, M. 1998. De zaak-Dutroux van A tot Z. Antwerpen: Icarus.

Van Outrive, L. 1998. The disastrous justice system in Belgium. a crisis of democracy? In Gray, P. and 't Hart, P. (eds.) Public policy disasters in western Europe. London: Routledge.

Ponsaers, P., and De Kimpe, S. 2001. Consensusmania. Over de achtergron-den van de politiehervorming. Leuven: Acco.

Pujas, V. 2006. Understanding the wave of scandal in contemporary western Europe. In Garrard, J., and Newel, J. (eds.) Scandals in past and contemporary politics. Manchester, UK: Manchester University Press, pp. 30–45.

Reynders, D., Dewael, P. and Verwilghen, M. 1996. Voorstel tot instelling van een parlementaire onderzoekscommissie belast met het onderzoek naar de wijze waarop het onderzoek door politie en gerecht werd gevoerd in de zaak Dutroux-Nihoul en consorten. Brussel: Kamer van Volksvertegenwoordigers (K 713/1–96/97).

Rihoux, B. 2000. Belgium. European Journal of Political Research (Political Data Yearbook 1999) 39(7–8):338–47.

Rihoux, B., Dumont, P. and Dandoy, R. 2001. Belgium. European Journal of Political Research (Political Data Yearbook 2000) 40(5–6):254–62.

Rosenthal, U., Boin, A. and Comfort, L. (eds.) 2001. Managing crises. Threats, dilemmas, opportunities. Springfield, IL: Charles C. Thomas.

Staelraeve, S. 2003. Parlementaire onderzoekscommissies: zin en onzin. Gent: Academia Press.

Staelraeve, S. 2004. Committees of inquiry and other instruments of oversight in Belgian federal parliament. Unpublished paper for the workshop National parliaments and the European Union. Limerick, UK: University of Limerick.

Vanhoutte, P., and Paque, L. 2000. Verslag namens de onderzoekscommissie over het parlementair onderzoek naar de Belgische vlees-, zuivel- en eierproductie en naar de politieke verantwoordelijkheden in het licht van de zogenaamde dioxinecrisis. Brussel: Kamer van Volksvertegenwoordigers (K 0018/7–2000).

Witte, E., Craeybeckx, J. and Meynen, A. 2005. Politieke geschiedenis van België. Van 1830 tot heden. Antwerpen: Standaard Uitgeverij.

PART II

Crisis-induced policy change and learning

7 | The 1975 Stockholm embassy seizure: crisis and the absence of reform

DAN HANSÉN

Introduction

This chapter focuses on one of the most dramatic days in Swedish contemporary history and the subsequent Swedish counterterrorism policy process. The day in question is 24 April 1975, when the West German Stockholm embassy was attacked and occupied by West German Red Army Faction (RAF) terrorists. For all involved, it was obvious that the Swedish police did not have the capacity to act professionally in a terrorist situation. Yet the decade that followed was marked by stasis in the realms of Swedish counterterrorism policy making. This development is puzzling, not least from the perspective that acts of terrorism typically put a spin on counterterrorism policymaking. For example, the West German antiterrorist force GSG 9 was set up as a direct consequence of the 1972 Munich massacre (Tophoven 1984); even in Norway, a similar force was installed in 1975 after the Stockholm experience (Flyghed 2000). More recently, the events of 9/11 led to an overhaul of domestic security measures in the United States (see Parker and Dekker, this volume).

Crises are often viewed as catalysts for policy change, but such change is not inevitable. The aftermath of the Stockholm embassy seizure is an example of policy stasis; the focus of this chapter is to explore the reasons for this. In doing so, we utilise multiple-streams theory (MS) (Kingdon 1984, 2003), the advocacy coalition framework (ACF) (Sabatier and Jenkins-Smith 1993; Sabatier 1999) and punctuated equilibrium theory (PE) (Baumgartner and Jones 1993, 2002). Unlike some cases where the link between crisis and swift, radical policy change is relatively easy to ascertain, the link between crisis and policy stasis is less easy to determine. Nevertheless, the application of contemporary conceptual perspectives on policy change (and its absence) makes our task much more feasible.

In the next section we become acquainted with the Stockholm embassy seizure and the aftermath of initiatives, discussions and decisions. Thereafter, we explore state-of-the-art theoretical perspectives on policy change and its absence. We then revisit the Stockholm case in the light of theoretical discussions. The concluding section reflects further on both the case study and the relevance of theoretical perspectives on policy change.

One dramatic day and an inconclusive decade

Thursday 24 April 1975 developed into one of the most dramatic days in Swedish contemporary history. Six West German RAF terrorists occupied the West German Stockholm embassy for 12 hours. During the siege, two diplomats were shot dead by the terrorists, who demanded that the West German government release no less than twenty-six RAF members from West German prisons. At 14 minutes to midnight, the terrorists accidentally caused their TNT to explode and the premises caught fire. The remaining hostages escaped and the terrorists were captured.[1]

The day was marked by chaos, bewilderment and decisional paralysis on behalf of the Swedish police and the crisis cabinet that gathered around Prime Minister Olof Palme. Several units of the Stockholm police and Säpo (the national security service) gathered at the embassy without any clear operational leadership. There existed no purposefully trained and equipped antiterrorist police unit. As a result, a small group of neighbourhood police resorted to practicing for a break-in outside the premises during the day. The West German government declared that they would not meet the terrorists' demands. They handed over the seizure response entirely to the Swedish government. This information was devastating to the Swedish crisis cabinet. Prime Minister Palme shouted to the director general of the Swedish police, Carl Persson: 'You have to do something!' Persson hesitated; he knew that a rescue operation would be a suicide mission; therefore the accidental explosion came as a relief to everyone.

The embassy drama put the police and Sweden's political leadership under extreme pressure. The police had risked their lives with deficient equipment and a lack of training, while the government had risked

[1] For a detailed description of the case, see Hansén and Nordqvist (2005).

losing face internationally for not meeting conventions on diplomatic safety and security. And this was not the first time that Sweden had become the theatre for international terrorism. In 1971, the Yugoslavian ambassador was killed at the Stockholm embassy by Croatian separatists and, in 1972, yet another group of Croatians skyjacked a domestic flight in order to get the assassins released from prison – a demand that succeeded. These events called for action and the Swedish Terrorist Act was instituted, which made it possible to deport foreigners on suspicion that they might commit politically motivated violence. The fact that RAF terrorists had entered the country and also managed to occupy the West German embassy demonstrated that the Terrorist Act was a blunt and largely ineffectual instrument.

In the aftermath of the Stockholm embassy seizure, police reform investigations (both external and internal) became entwined with wider issues regarding the safety of nuclear power plants and changes in the wider climate of democratic governance. Below, each of these strands is considered in detail.

Police reform

On 26 June 1975, the government set up a commission of experts to scrutinise the police. In giving direction to this commission, the government stressed that the world of 1975 was not the same as that of 1965 (when the police were nationalised). Dramatic changes had taken place and there was a need for the police to adjust (SOU 1979 Vol. 6: 33–7). However, when Justice Minister Geijer presented the Police Commission with its directives, he did not mention the recent seizure of the West German embassy. Rather, he focused attention on other problem areas. The main challenge was identified as the need to strengthen public confidence in the police. A service-minded police, working preventively and close to the local communities, was considered the best way forward.

In late December 1978 the Police Commission presented its report (SOU 1979 Vol. 6), called *Polisen* [the Police], which contained a comprehensive revision of organisational, functional and principal aspects of the Swedish police. The commission produced a wide range of suggestions and recommendations with two recurring and strong themes throughout: decentralisation and legitimisation. The former theme implied changes in the chain of command as well as delegation of power on a more structural level. The latter stressed the need for a higher degree of transparency, implying both codetermination and stronger public accountability for police work. The commission also brought topical interest to the need for a police act. At this time, no such act existed in Sweden. Room for manoeuvre on the part of the police was decided by regulations. This did not balance the coercive powers of the police with the civil rights of individuals (as formulated in the 1974 Constitution).

The Stockholm police special-response units and special events

Meanwhile, in the aftermath of the embassy seizure, an internal inquiry into the performance of Stockholm police by the Stockholm Police Board produced harsh self-criticism. Lack of appropriate equipment coupled with poor handling and weak tactics led many officers to be wounded unnecessarily. Also, police leadership at the embassy was conflictual and disorganised (Stockholm police 1975b). The Stockholm police wanted to reform their special-response units to be better pre-pared for policing severe situations, such as the embassy drama. Among other things, they wanted the two response units in Stockholm to be merged into one and an increase in personnel from 80 to 124 officers – all requiring special training. On 25 January 1976, the National Police Board submitted its request to the government. However, the govern-ment passed the issue to the Police Commission on 13 May 1976. The objects to be scrutinised more closely were the special-response units and the Stockholm subway police.

The Police Commission felt that the type of incidents referred to it by the Stockholm police affected all aspects of the police organisation at local, regional and national levels. Therefore the commission oper-ated on two levels. Organisational matters were referred to and dealt with by the main inquiry, while a special investigation was undertaken that dealt only with educational matters (Ds 1977 Vol. 2).[2] In January 1977, therefore, the Police Commission presented the results of its spe-cial assignment (Ds 1977 Vol. 2), where a defensive attitude towards reforming police capacity was visible. It did not touch organisational

---

[2] For this reason, the suggestions by the Stockholm Police Board related to the subway police were also referred to the main inquiry, since the suggestions were only of organisational character (Ds 1977: 2).

matters or suggest any changes to its tasks or command structures. In terms of training, the commission stressed the importance of correct behaviour, psychology and psychiatry. It was deemed that additional training for the flying squads should not be provided at the expense of the training of other units within the police district. In addition, the commission recommended that the two existing flying squads be enlarged by twenty staff (from forty plus forty to fifty plus fifty) in order to be operable 24 hours a day (Ds 1977 Vol. 2).

To the expert advisers of the commission, the proposals appeared meagre and even disappointing. In a separate memorandum, they expressed the view that the commission's suggestions only partially fulfilled their requirements for a secure working situation for the police, as well as meeting public demands and expectations (Ds 1977 Vol. 2). In the government budget proposition (Prop. 1977/78 No. 100, appendix 5), the justice minister concurred with the commission's special assignment report, which was implemented in February 1979 (Protocol 1978/79 No. 57 § 13).

Nuclear safety and the 'atom police'

Police counterterrorism measures had another dimension. Nuclear power plants had become targets for environmentally concerned protesters after the mid-1970s. Therefore the Swedish police started to develop suggestions for enhancing security at nuclear reactors (Nylén 2004). In March 1979 a working group within the National Police Board began to examine police needs in relation to recapturing occupied space in power plants (Svensk Polis 1980 No. 5). In May 1980 the project team presented its results and recommendations. These were:

- A special force for dealing with security breaches should be organised within Stockholm police special-response units
- The staff of the special response units should be increased by 100 percent
- The organisational leadership of this special force should be strengthened
- More and specialised equipment should be procured
- Airborne transportation should be organised for the flying squads
- The education for this team should be extended and specialised (Svensk Polis 1980 No. 5).

In August 1980, the government's response was to lay down guiding principles for reform of the police (Prop. 1980/81 No. 13). However, the National Police Board and its advocates were to be severely disappointed. Counterterrorism concerns were swept over with a referral back to what the 1975 Police Commission had stated and what the government and Parliament had decided a few years earlier (Ds 1977 Vol. 2). There was only brief discussion of the proposals the National Police Board made regarding the Stockholm police Special Response Units and the potential threat of a terrorist attack on nuclear power plants. Indeed, in a subsequent budget proposition (Prop. 1980/81 No. 100 appendix 5), the Justice Minister stated that he was not prepared to have a special response unit solely for dealing with security breaches. Instead, it was proposed that the government should let the National Police Board further investigate how police preparedness for serious criminal assaults could be organised in Stockholm, Gothenburg and Malmö – the three largest cities in Sweden. The outcome was that on 15 March 1982, the National Police Board presented its report (RPS 1982), which was far less ambitious than the original suggestions. For example, proposed manpower increases in the Stockholm police Special Response Units were limited to an extra 35 police, compared to the initial proposition to increase it by 100 percent (i.e. by 120 police). However, even these 'meagre' reform proposals were to be thwarted. In the general elections of September 1982, the Social Democratic Labour party regained power. In their first budget proposition, Justice Minister Ove Rainer rejected the suggestions provided by the National Police Board on the grounds that economic conditions were not favourable (Prop. 1982/83 No. 100, appendix 4).

Macropolitical preconditions: conducive to change?

In addition to specific counterterrorism policy issues, the decade after the embassy drama produced wider changes on the political and administrative scenes. In some respects, these developments (as detailed below) *could* have acted as catalysts for policy change. For a large part of the Swedish population, the events of 19 September 1976 came as a complete surprise. For the first time in 44 years, the Social Democratic Labour Party lost governmental power. The ramifications of this cannot be underestimated. For the Social Democrats, the experience was bewildering (Peterson 2002: 248; Leijon 1991: 169). The three nonsocialist parties formed a coalition government. Within circles involved in justice politics, it came as a surprise that the Moderate Party's (conservative) chair of the Parliament justice committee, Astrid Kristensson, was not given the justice minister's post. She had profiled herself as a police politician and was allegedly quite disappointed (Falkenstam 1983; Welander 2003).

The nonsocialist parties retained governmental power until 1982, but the 6 years were turbulent. The first government broke in 1978 due to the issue of nuclear power and the second broke in 1981 when the Moderate Party left due to controversies over tax issues. The period saw three justice ministers, but only one with a political affiliation: conservative MP Håkan Winberg, 1979–1981. In 1983, Social Democratic Justice Minister Ove Rainer had to resign over a tax affair.

Amid this wider upheaval, Carl Persson resigned in 1978 as director general of the National Police Board after 14 years in the post. Holger Romander, the former chief prosecutor, replaced him. The demise of Persson marked a new epoch at the National Police Board. Some welcomed the peace and quiet, while others missed the dynamics that had characterised the Persson era (Falkenstam 1983).

This turbulence on the political and administrative scenes, which indeed affected the criminal justice sector, did not have much impact on counterterrorism policies or police politics. The changes suggested by the 1975 Police Commission (SOU 1979, Vol. 6) remained low on the political radar and in keeping with the Labour Party's intentions when setting up the 1975 Police Commission (Falkenstam 1983). More generally, political and/or administrative turnovers are normally seen to be conducive to policy change, and not to policy stability (Sabatier and Jenkins-Smith 1993). In this case, wider upheaval and changes in the governance of Sweden proved conducive to the issue of police counterterrorism reform, remaining an issue of low political saliency.

Crisis and perspectives on policy change: beliefs and attention

Having outlined the years subsequent to the 1975 embassy seizure as a mix of multiple inquiries, organisational and policy complexities, high politics and limited policy reform, we can now turn our attention to a number of theoretical tools which will help provide an explanation for this limited postcrisis policy change.

Multiple streams theory (Kingdon 1984, 2003), the advocacy coalition framework (Sabatier and Jenkins-Smith 1993; Sabatier 1999), and punctuated equilibrium theory (Baumgartner and Jones 1993, 2002; True et al. 1999) have spearheaded recent thinking about policy dynamics. Kingdon's 'window of opportunity' metaphor, Baumgartner and Jones's 'positive feedback processes' and Sabatier and Jenkins-Smith's notion of 'policy oriented learning' are typically evoked and referred to when explaining instances of policy change. To a certain extent they have fostered separate research communities, although efforts to explore commonalities have also been carried out.[3]

These approaches do not explicitly focus on policy processes after crises, yet crises do play a role in their accounts of policy change and stability. Here we compare the frameworks with the specific task of understanding the relationship between crisis and policy change/stability, focusing particularly on the link between individual perceptions and collective action formation.

Why these three frameworks? Other perspectives might seem to be equally fruitful. For example, path dependency and policy inheritance (Rose and Davies 1994; Pierson 2000) deal with similar issues when explaining policy stability. Both, for instance, rely on assumptions of 'increasing returns to scale' when accounting for collective behaviour (Kuipers 2004). However, as Jones and Baumgartner (2005: 50) maintain: '[p]olicy inheritances must be understood as organizational phenomena'. Path dependency and policy inheritance are eminently suitable for explaining why policy structures – often translated into bureaucratic organisations – remain in place for very long periods once they have been established. But the policy-making processes presented in the previous section tell us that Swedish counterterrorism experiences to a large extent have revolved around establishing new policy structures. Theories that focus on agenda attainment and opportunities and restrictions for an issue to move from the policy agenda to policy decision-making hold a better promise to actually shed light on the processes at work.

---

[3] Baumgartner and Jones (2002) and Sabatier (1999) account for an abundance of researchers who have pursued studies under their auspices or solicited by them. Some initiated onlookers have compared and contrasted them, such as John (1998), Mintrom and Vergari (1996), Schlager (1999), etc.

MS, ACF and PE are commonly treated together – at least two or three of them, or even sometimes together with a fourth framework such as epistemic communities (Parsons 1995; Dudley and Richardson 1996; Mintrom and Vergari 1996; John 1998; Schlager 1999; Meijerink 2005). The most obvious reason for grouping these frameworks together is that they all focus on policy stability and change. Moreover, they depart from assumptions of the individual as being boundedly rational, albeit in different ways (Schlager 1999). Therefore, in light of the patterns of policy change with regard to the crisis presented above, MS, ACF and PE are not only a random selection of interesting theoretical frameworks, they are very promising.

MS, PE and ACF: concealed similarities and apparent differences

The criteria for this comparison are: (1) a model of the individual, (2) collective action and institutional settings and (3) policy change. These points of comparison, derived from Schlager (1999),[4] capture the basic elements of the policy process in relation to crises. Criteria 1 and 2 represent the key mechanisms promoting and/or inhibiting policy change. It should be clear, however, that none of the three theories presume a clear-cut causal chain reaction from crisis to policy change.

Individuals: ideas, beliefs and preferences

When it comes to how individuals experience and act upon new information and situations, the three theories rely on bounded rationality. Individuals are assumed to be goal-oriented and act in ways they believe are good for them. Yet reality is complex and ambiguous. The three theories' notions of the boundedly rational individual take this complex and ambiguous policy making context into account in trying to understand individual choice: 'Choice becomes less an exercise in solving problems and more an attempt to make sense of a partially comprehensible world' (Zahariadis 1999: 75). Therefore, in all three perspectives, there is recognition that contextual matters place boundaries on rationality. However, despite these commonalities, Schlager (1999: 241–4) points out that on close examination, each perspective

---

[4] Besides these points of comparison, Schlager (1999) includes the 'boundaries and scope of inquiry'.

holds different assumptions about the individual. In MS the individual is a 'satisficer', in ACF a 'belief-er' and in PE a 'selective attender'. Let us briefly consider each.

In MS theory, bounded rationality means that the logic of rationality has grown into a logic of time. The streams metaphor reflects a time-dependent flow of problems, solutions and contextual prerequisites which act as major constraints on policy makers:

> The multiple-streams perspective translates into a process in which individuals are viewed as less capable of choosing the issues they would like to solve and more concerned about addressing the multitude of problems that are thrust upon them, largely by factors beyond their control. (Zahariadis 1999: 75)

In an environment marked by constant time constraints in combination with a multitude of solutions, the best solution (allowed by the politics stream) is likely to remain in the primeval soup of ideas. Therefore, the policy maker is principally a *satisficer* (Schlager 1999: 244), with independence in ideas, beliefs and preferences left to the margins.

ACF explores the cognitive world and takes a foothold in the individual's belief systems. Belief systems determine individual choices and actions, forming the basis for coalition creation. When confronted with new information or a new situation, the individual interprets that impetus with the belief system as a benchmark. Depending on the type of belief system affected (deep core, policy core or secondary aspects), the individual's tendency to refute or be persuaded is more or less likely. He or she will also use information to persuade others of the rightness of his or her own belief.

In PE, attributes of the situation, rather than the belief system, characterise the boundaries of individual choice. Since the individual is limited when it comes to processing large amounts of information, he or she can pay attention only to selective parts of the complex reality. Therefore behaviour may change faster than preferences, because the individual has been presented with a new and different dimension to the problem. For the selective attender, the decision-making setting is crucial, since its characteristics affect what aspect of a given problem will have salience.

In sum: MS, ACF and PE give different perspectives on individual choice, but is there some common ground? The MS satisficer shared traits with the PE selective attender, in that the situation determines the choice rather than being determined by the conviction of the individual. However, all three support the view that ideas, preferences and beliefs are robust and hard to change. The ACF beliefer is just a little less easily influenced by situational information overload or situational impression management.

Further commonality can be found in the fact that choices made by the satisficer and the selective attender are arguably not essentially different from their ideas and preferences. The PE selective attender can arrive at different choices at different times, due to the decisional situation, but most likely not at choices that run counter to the individual's policy core beliefs. PE does not deal in any significant way with different degrees of beliefs and preferences. If it did, it is likely that the selective attender would be flexible about different secondary aspects within the parameters of a given policy core realm. At the least, such an interpretation does not shake PE to its foundations. Hence, the different concepts of the boundedly rational individual are largely overlapping and complementing.

Collective action and institutional settings

Based on models of the individual, the three theories provide different accounts on how individuals come together and produce policy change or stability. The context that sets the boundaries of individual rationality consists to a large extent of institutional settings. To various degrees these institutional arrangements are accounted for as venues for collective action formation.

MS pays scant attention to collective action as a means for individuals to achieve policy stability or change. Focus is rather directed towards influential entrepreneurs. Movements in the politics stream form the preconditions and the contextual basis for collective action: 'Policy entrepreneurs do not control events or structures, but they can anticipate them and bend them to their purposes to some degree' (Kingdon 2003: 225). Entrepreneurs hence have to be sensitive to national moods or other broadly supported currents that work in favour of their ends. Within this perspective, institutional settings play only an indirect role. In MS reasoning, the institutional position of policy entrepreneurs affects their ability to influence the policy-making process. Different venues produce different accession points. This in turn creates varying conditions for access to these points in order that policy entrepreneurs can attempt to 'couple streams'.

Collective action is paramount to ACF. The issue of how coalitions actually take shape and are kept together has become a key concern for ACF scholars. The existence of advocacy coalitions has never been taken for granted, but has always been a matter for empirical scrutiny. Coalition participation is empirically verified by tangible manifestations of shared belief systems. However, it is not always clear how tightly or loosely the coalitions are tied together. Implicitly, institutional arrangements provide relatively fixed harbours for beliefs and thereby important coalition pillars. Institutional settings therefore also appear in ACF as more or less susceptible venues for a certain coalition's intentions.

Similar to MS, policy entrepreneurs play a crucial role in PE. Unlike MS, PE counts on the entrepreneur not only as a spearhead of policy change, but also as a gatekeeper against change. However, PE pays attention to collective action, where entrepreneurs act in groups, but also where interest groups and a more broad-based public mobilise for their cause. To achieve policy change, entrepreneurs and interest groups need to break through institutional rigidity. But once under way, unclear jurisdictional boundaries between institutional arrangements may allow players from various settings to participate in the policy-making process. In fact, evoking interest for an issue among the previously disinterested is an entrepreneurial strategy to break institutional deadlock and achieve collective action.

The three theories focus on different dynamics to account for collective action and how institutional settings affect such processes. MS and PE share the notion of clever entrepreneurship as a driver for collective action. MS and PE also share a view on macrosocietal movements, events and structures as contextual preconditions for entrepreneurial manoeuvring. ACF largely ignores the impact of entrepreneurs as motors of collective action, just as MS for the most part ignores institutional arrangements and collective action when accounting for policy change. ACF and PE, on the other hand, share an analysis of institutional settings as being, to various degrees, susceptible to influences from policy challengers. Coalitions or interest groups can help work toward their collective cause by way of looking out for suitable policy venues to articulate their case. To varying degrees, MS, ACF and PE produce overlapping analyses of how individuals come together to produce (or prevent) policy change. The MS lack of accounting for collective action and the ACF lack of accounting for entrepreneurial strategies are not at odds with each other. Rather, they shed complementary light on the process (Mintrom and Vergari 1996; Schlager 1999).

Policy change

All three theoretical lenses refer chiefly to major policy change in contrasting periods of policy stasis. Only ACF makes a distinction between major and minor change. In accounting for major policy change, they consider macropolitical forces as influential because they can interrupt the course of everyday policy making. Such events, like dramatic deeds or governmental turnovers, make issues appear on the policy agenda, but are not in themselves sufficient to lead to major policy change.

ACF and PE argue that what has happened around an issue for a very long period determines its chances of reaching the policy agenda. When an issue appears on the policy agenda, this is often because a series of happenings and activities have occurred, which have led to shifts in policy ideas and/or advocacy coalition turnover. MS does not concern itself with long time spans, but would not in principal refute the ACF and PE contention. Repeated occurrence of events in the problem stream increases the likelihood of agenda attainment, for instance.

None of the theories is able to predict whether or not an issue that has emerged on the policy agenda will lead to policy change. The same dynamics that determine if an issue makes it to the policy agenda also determine if policy change will occur. In that sense, the theoretical lenses are analogous to the field of evolutionary biology rather than to the realms of experimental physics (John 1998: 169–88). With hindsight it is possible to give reasons for change or nonchange. One key element in their after-the-fact explanations is the extent to which actors have discovered and capitalised on opportunities for change.

The most obvious difference between MS, ACF and PE is that they aim at explaining different outcomes at the macro level of analysis: policy agenda attainment (MS), learning across coalitions and advocacy coalition turnovers (ACF), and public agenda shifts (PE). Only at an overarching level are the indirect outcomes supposed to relate to policy change or stability.

The discussions so far, as crystallised in Table 7.1, reveal that the three theories ascribe importance to similar and/or different drivers for policy change and stability. These are not mutually exclusive. Simplified, policy entrepreneurs and advocacy coalitions can be seen as

Table 7.1. *Multiple streams, advocacy coalition framework and punctuated equilibrium in comparison*

	Model of the individual	Collective action and institutional settings	Policy change
Multiple Streams	Satisficer	Entrepreneur-driven, where institutions provide more or less favourable accession points.	Policy agenda attainment leads to major change, depending on entrepreneurial skills.
Advocacy Coalition Framework	Belief-er	Driven by coalition's belief systems. Institutions are more or less susceptible to one coalition's beliefs.	Policy-oriented learning or coalition turnovers lead to minor or major change respectively, depending on actors' ability to capitalise on chances.
Punctuated Equilibrium	Selective attender	Driven by entrepreneurs, interest groups and public opinion. Institutions hinder collective action in negative feedback and facilitators in positive feedback.	Public agenda shifts lead to major change, depending on entrepreneurial skills to create a positive feedback process.
Comparative Status	MS and PE overlap. To some extent, also ACF	MS complements ACF on collective action, where PE overlaps in both ends. MS overlaps with ACF on institutional settings, where PE complements.	MS, ACF and PE overlap on preconditions for agenda attainment. MS and ACF overlap on mechanisms conducive to policy change, where PE complements.

Key
MS: Multiple Streams
ACF: Advocacy Coalition Framework
PE: Punctuated Equilibrium

independent variables that both explain the collective action formation necessary for change or stability. In a case-to-case comparison, their relative strength may differ. However, if we ask ourselves why ACF does not account for policy entrepreneurs, focus shifts to processes rather than factors. The theories thereby exhibit two distinct logics: one belief-based (ACF) and the other attention-based (PE and MS). The belief-based logic suggests the following proposition to explain processes of policy stability:

Crises are unlikely to alter policy core beliefs and do not therefore challenge belief-based coalition structures.

The attention-based logic instead suggests the following proposition:

Crises are likely to induce entrepreneurial efforts to promote policy change, but a policy monopoly and its status quo biases will work to promote negative feedback processes.

The extent to which these propositions explain the stability of Swedish counterterrorism policy in the decade following the embassy drama is probed below.

Understanding the stability of counterterrorism policy

Belief-based logic: decomposed coalitions, beliefs intact

The embassy drama stands out as the most frightening experience of terrorism on Swedish soil. According to Gösta Welander, the head of the Justice Ministry's police unit, only the embassy drama became salient at the Justice Ministry in terms of reflecting upon counterterrorism preparedness during his tenure, 1972–1984 (Welander 2003). We have seen also that the drama caused both the Stockholm police and the National Police Board to promote policy options intended to better meet the threat of terrorism. However, the embassy drama did not fundamentally alter ingrained ideas or beliefs about counterterrorism policy making – at least not during the course of the first decade after the siege.

The National Police Board and the Stockholm police formed an advocacy coalition to try and influence counterterrorism policies. For players outside the police, counterterrorism policy-making was to a large extent a matter of taking sides with or against the police. Thereby the police were left on their own to promote policy innovations that they found pertinent to counterterrorism. To some extent Carl Persson himself was the glue for this coalition. There were many reports of what an extraordinary and charismatic leader he was, as well as an efficient and skillful manager (Falkenstam 1983; Vinge 1988; Frånstedt 2003; Welander 2003; Axman 2004; Montgomery 2004; Munck 2004; Nygren 2004).

We have already established that the police were not overly successful in convincing wider circles of the virtues of a powerful antiterrorist police force. We have seen how the initial Stockholm police initiative was passed on to the government, which in turn forwarded the issue to the ongoing 1975 Police Commission. All of this happened between the embassy drama and the 1976 government turnover. The question is: why were the police not successful in mobilising support for their policy innovation?

It is quite unclear what support the police potentially had regarding their initiative to increase their striking capacity. The journey that the policy suggestion made does not show any evidence of venue shopping to mobilise support. Instead, the proposition was cultivated internally until it landed on the desk of the government in January 1976. The social democratic government included sceptics of the National Police Board, in particular Justice Minister Lennart Geijer. It is possible that the policy initiative by the government was seen as a new effort to centralise police power in Stockholm and, therefore, the initiative was received with limited enthusiasm. A policy core belief shared by the elite of the Social Democratic Labour Party and not least by local and regional police commissioners was that police power needed to be transferred from Stockholm to the local and regional police authorities. In any case, a natural forum to pass the policy initiative to was the ongoing Police Commission. Such a move was also fairly safe in terms of containing the understanding of the problem. The government had appointed the commission and the deputy justice minister chaired it. In that respect, it is not surprising that the commission decided not to touch upon organisational issues when preparing the partial study of the Stockholm police Special Response Units (Ds 1977, Vol. 2).

When the nonsocialist government took power in the fall of 1976, a policy window opened for breaking the deadlock on police policies.

It had been natural for the government to give the 1975 Police Commission supplementary directives. But that did not happen. In this regard, it is highly relevant that nonpoliticians with no police experience occupied the posts of justice minister and deputy. They did not have a police policy agenda (Welander 2003).

In addition, the conservative chair of the Parliament justice committee, Astrid Kristensson, became a fierce opponent of the nonsocialist government's justice politics, making it hard to find coalition compromises (Montgomery 2004). Allegedly the discontent was a result of her being passed over by Sven Romanus for the post of justice minister (Welander 2003). The Moderate Party's leader, Gösta Bohman, had, according to Kristensson, nursed an overconfidence in lawyers and wanted the justice minister to be a court lawyer, hence excluding Kristensson (Falkenstam 1983: 254–5). Besides, the People's Party's MPs (liberal) were not too keen on having Kristensson as justice minister (Falkenstam 1983: 254–5). Hence, one of Carl Persson's closest political allies did not get more political room to manoeuvre after the 1976 elections.

Even if the most conspicuous problems between the National Police Board and the Justice Ministry evaporated when Lennart Geijer left the ministry, tensions still prevailed. Deputy Justice Minister (1976–79) Henry Montgomery took over the chairmanship of the 1975 Police Commission and was also the person at the ministry who had most contact with Director General Carl Persson. Montgomery (2004) revealed that: 'When Carl Persson resigned, I saw that as a big relief'. He seldom opposed the policy suggestions that Carl Persson advocated but had considerable concerns regarding the way he played the political game (Montgomery 2004).

The police in charge of law and order were deeply troubled at not having the capability to meet critical incidents. But their efforts to come to terms with this deficiency failed to result in a better trained and equipped police, even during periods of nonsocialist governments. Social democratic MP Arne Nygren (2004) maintains that 'An antiterrorism police unit was just completely inconceivable in the 70s', in a view that neatly captures the opinions of the political-administrative justice establishment of that time. Similar views were conveyed by Johan Munck (2004), Håkan Winberg (2004), Gösta Welander (2003), Henry Montgomery (2004) and Ingvar Gullnäs (2004). Prime Minister

Olof Palme's comment only hours after the embassy drama, insinuating that only a police state could eliminate the risk of terrorism assaults (SVT 25/4/1975), clearly set the tone for future debate.

The explanation for policy stability provided by belief-based assumptions, reveals that preparedness to effectively meet terrorism was not necessarily a main concern for the actors involved – at least not for the majority coalition. Instead, policy-making was guided by scepticism about the intents of the National Police Board, in combination with an ambition to decentralise police power. These policy core beliefs survived the embassy drama, as well as initiatives promoted by the police and governmental turnovers. Interestingly, the embassy drama brought salience to the issue of terrorism, but it did not affect beliefs about the police and therefore did not change views on counterterrorism.

Attention-based logic: entrepreneurial efforts in adverse conditions

In the fall of 1975 an event unfolded that had nothing to do with terrorism yet called into question Säpo's operative methods. In October it was revealed that a person had been employed by a hospital in Gothenburg to map out extreme leftists at the hospital on behalf of Säpo. Subsequently, a plausible suggestion emerged that defence intelligence was behind the initiative. At the time, however, Säpo became the scapegoat (SOU 2002 Vol. 87: 546–50) and its public image was damaged.

Säpo had received signals about the embassy intrusion beforehand but lacked the means to act properly on them. The head of Säpo, Hans Holmér, commented that 'A reasonable increase of Säpo can have a reasonable effect' (Aftonbladet 13 May 1975). But Säpo did not get additional resources. Instead, the hospital spy affair acted to its detriment. In Parliament, especially after the socialist defeat in 1976, MPs from the Left Party Communists and Social Democratic Labour Party cast suspicion on Säpo. The criticism was based on reservations about Säpo's implementation of the Terrorist Act. As a reaction to rumours of infringements that had circulated in the media and in the Parliament over the years, both the communists and a faction of the Social Democratic Labour Party suggested to the government in 1979, that a parliamentary commission be set up to scrutinise Säpo (Motions 1979/80 No. 802 and 803). The Parliament's justice committee declined these requests, not least since the National Police Board in 1978, on their own initiative, had started to patch up Säpo (Ju 1979/80 No. 3). Despite these self-regulatory efforts, Säpo as an organisation was contested by leftist quarters. Understanding the sceptical debate about Säpo sheds light on the preemptive counterterrorism policy process of this decade, and also the image of the police in general.

In April 1977, Säpo busted a terrorist league that planned to kidnap the former minister Anna-Greta Leijon for her involvement in the embassy drama. Svensk Polis (National Police Board's peer journal) published an account of the action. Moreover, an editorial of Dagens Nyheter (Stockholm daily) was cited wholly, since it had attracted much attention within the police. The editorial, entitled 'The victory of self-control over great risks', had a punch line:

So far we have been spared one thing more than other people who have been battlegrounds and bases for capricious guerrilla warfare across borders: We have been spared having our own defence powers against outrage transformed into a tool for systematic excesses and harassment of citizens. (Svensk Polis 1977 No. 4: 2)

The article exposed and articulated the fear that many felt was consistent with creating an effective counterterrorism police capacity. Except for the expressions of the will of the Stockholm and the National Police Board, it is difficult to find any support for a police capacity capable of tackling terrorism or other severe incidents. Only the conservative chair of the Parliament's justice committee, Astrid Kristensson, speaking at two consecutive parliamentary discussions on the Terrorist Act (Protocol 1975 No. 78 § 6; Protocol 1975/76 No. 44 § 10) cautiously aired the prospect of considering a re-evaluation of the matter.

I think that we from a Swedish point of view can be happy that the police do their work in a good way, even if it is possible that we need to reconsider the issue of some kind of special education and maybe improved organisation to be able to act more effectively domestically in case we are hit by another act of terrorism. (Protocol 1975/76 No. 44 § 10)

The unfavourable public image of the police seems to have occasioned the non-socialist parties to abstain from taking any initiatives once they gained governmental power. The former Moderate Party Justice

Minister (1979–81) Håkan Winberg reflected upon the nonsocialist passivity between 1976 and 1982:

When we won the 1976 elections, the social democrats and the labour union started a scaremongering, stating that the entire social welfare system would be dismantled. Sick people would be left alone without medical attention. In a climate like that, we were cautious to propose anything that could cause loud disapproval. (Winberg 2004)

When incumbent, socialists did not openly contest Säpo or the National Police Board in the Parliament. The front against the police-sceptic Left Party Communists was unified. After the 1976 defeat, however, social democrats joined the chorus of Säpo critics. Likewise, whenever reorganisation of the Stockholm police Special Response Units became topical, Social Democrats openly aired their despondency. When they came back to governmental power in 1982, it is understandable that the issue of the Stockholm police Special Response Units was not pursued. Parliament had become an unpredictable venue for carrying through such policy suggestions. Counterterrorism policing was not a likely future winner for the new Social Democratic justice minister, and it had been far from a safe bet for his nonsocialist predecessors.

The counterterrorism policy stability can hence be explained as political abstention to capitalise on the Stockholm embassy seizure due to insufficient *expected* constituencies. The entrepreneurial efforts of the National Police Board and the Stockholm police resulted in processes of negative feedback because the image of the police, including Säpo, had become marred with problems of legitimacy.

Conclusion

The 1975 drama at the West German embassy certainly provoked the Swedish counterterrorism policy community. However, the changes that took place were quite modest. In this chapter, we have shed a number of different explanatory lights on the policy process, with the aim of coming closer to an understanding of the relationship between crises and patterns of policy change. In this concluding section, we will discuss the complementary nature of the two logics derived from the main theories discussed.

The belief-based explanation for policy stability tells us in this case that policy core beliefs concerning the police organisation (rather than police capabilities) were crucial, and that the seizure of the West German embassy did not affect these beliefs. The attention-based explanation, on the other hand, tells us that entrepreneurs within the police did indeed capitalise on the crisis. However, the public image of the police did not make it a worthwhile option for political investment. As a result, the entrepreneurial efforts were counterproductive. The police were not part of the solution, but rather of the problem. Both logics arrive at that conclusion and complement one another.

The empirical evidence in this study proves divergences from both the belief-based and the attention-based assumptions. The belief-based suppositions, essentially derived from ACF, certainly anticipated that prevailing beliefs would survive the crisis on the assumption that coalition interaction and cohesion be preserved. But government turnovers and reshuffles within the criminal justice bureaucracy do not seem to have provided advantageous conditions for the policy stability observed here. The inability to reach coalition compromises prevented beliefs being articulated on the issue of repressive counterterrorism policies.

The attention-based assumptions explain policy change or stability as effects of *intentional* entrepreneurial strategies. In this case it is evident that the police failed in their attempts to launch the idea of an antiterrorist police. Indeed, their entrepreneurial efforts were counterproductive, since the ambitions of the National Police Board became subject to considerable questioning in wider political circles. The outcomes of the entrepreneurial efforts were arguably *unintentional*. This finding implies that policy entrepreneurship cannot, in an unqualified way, be attributed to explain instances of policy change. To understand the role of policy entrepreneurship, instances of both success and failure require further analysis.

The case exhibits scant evidence of either policy-oriented learning, or accountability on behalf of elite policy makers. They are intertwined here, although our primary focus in this chapter is policy stasis and change. The police's entrepreneurial strategy can be seen as an effort to hold the political establishment to task for not having prioritised counterterrorism. In this sense, the handling of the issue can be interpreted as elite escape, whilst the outcome cannot even be characterised as fine tuning of existing policies (see Chapter 1 of this volume). Broadly speaking, even though the embassy drama was an elite challenge, none of the outcomes – elite reinvigoration, damage or escape – apply to the case. The crisis took place in the middle of an electoral term of office and in any case, counterterrorism in Sweden has never been an issue important enough to determine electoral outcomes. If at all, elite escape can be attributed to the nonsocialist governments that held office between 1976 and 1982, on whom the police more avidly put their hopes.

The upshot of this study is that dominant beliefs (among a broader constituency than elite politicians) are decisive in terms of the prospect of policy change and stability. If a crisis is to work as a change agent, policy entrepreneurs (elite policy makers or not) need to succeed in establishing a dominant frame in terms of the crisis (i.e. causes, consequences and lessons to be learned). Timing vis-à-vis other events then becomes a more crucial contextual factor compared with the proximity to electoral campaigns. To fully understand postcrisis policy dynamics, it is paramount to include in the analysis the broader array of players that have a stake in the issue, as well as a wider time horizon than the immediate aftermath or the next elections. As an ironic epilogue it is worth mentioning that the Swedish police eventually got their antiterrorist force, but as a direct consequence of the 1986 Palme murder – a crisis that was not terrorism-related as far as we know (Hansén 2006). But that is a different story.

References

Aftonbladet. 1975. Säpo förstärks för att 'stoppa terrorister'. 13 May.

Axman, F. 2004. Chief Inspector, Säpo. Interview with Dan Hansén.

Baumgartner, F. R., and Jones, B. D. 1993. Agendas and instability in American politics. Chicago: University of Chicago Press.

Baumgartner, F. R., and Jones, B. D. (eds.) 2002. Policy dynamics. Chicago: University of Chicago Press.

Ds, J. 1977. Vol. 2: Piketverksamheten i Stockholms polisdistrikt.

Falkenstam, C. 1983. Polisernas krig: Kampen om ordningsmakten under den viktigaste, mest dramatiska och konfliktladdade epoken i svensk polishistoria. Stockholm: Askild & Kärnekull.

Flyghed, J. 2000. Nationella insatsstyrkan mot terrorism. In Flyghed, J. (ed.) Brottsbekämpning – mellan effektivitet och integritet: kriminologiska perspektiv på polismetoder och personlig integritet. Stockholm: Studentlitteratur.

Frånstedt, O. 2003. Deputy Director, Säpo. Interview with Dan Hansén.

Gullnäs, I. 2004. Permanent Secretary of State, Justice Department. Interview with Dan Hansén.

Hansén, D., and Nordqvist, J. 2005. Kommando holger meins: Dramat på västtyska ambassaden och Operation Leo. Stockholm: Ordfront.

Hansén, D. 2006. Crisis and perspectives on policy change: Swedish counterterrorism policy making, Stockholm/Utrecht: doctoral dissertation.

John, P. 1998. Analysing public policy. London: Continuum.

Jones, B. D., 1994. Reconceiving decision-making in democratic politics: attention, choice, and public policy. Chicago: University of Chicago Press.

Jones, B. D., and Baumgartner, F.R. 2005. The politics of attention: how government prioritizes problems. Chicago: University of Chicago Press.

Ju U. 1979/80 No. 3. Justitieutskottets betänkande med anledning av motioner om den polisiära säkerhetstjänsten.

Kingdon, J. 1984. Agendas, alternatives, and public policies. London: HarperCollins.

Kingdon, J. 2003. Agendas, alternatives, and public policies, 2nd edn. New York: Longman.

Kuipers, S. 2004. Cast in concrete? The institutional dynamics of Belgian and Dutch social policy reform. Amsterdam: Eburon Academic Publishers.

Leijon, A. G. 1991. Alla rosor ska inte tuktas! Stockholm: Tiden.

Meijerink, S. 2005. Understanding policy stability and change. The interplay of advocacy coalitions and epistemic communities, windows of opportunity, and Dutch coastal flooding policy 1945–2003. Journal of European Public Policy 12(6): 1060–77.

Mintrom, M., and Vergari, S. 1996. Advocacy coalitions, policy entrepreneurs, and policy change. Policy Studies Journal 24(3): 420–34.

Montgomery, H. 2004. Deputy Justice Minister 1976–1979. Interview with Dan Hansén.

Motion. 1979/80, No. 802. Av Maj Britt Theorin m.fl. om en fristående parlamentarisk styrelse för säkerhetspolisen.

Motion. 1979/80, No. 803. Av Lars Werner m.fl. om säkerhetspolisens verksamhet.

Munck, J. 2004. Expert, Justice Department. Interview with Dan Hansén.

Nygren, A. 2004. Social Democratic MP 1970–1985. Interview with Dan Hansén.

Nylén, L. 2004. Police Chief, Tierp (nuclear power plant municipality). Interview with Dan Hansén.

Parsons, W. 1995. Public policy: An introduction to the theory and practice of policy analysis. Cheltenham, UK: Edward Elgar.

Persson, C., in collaboration with Sundelin, A. 1990. Utan omsvep. Stockholm: Norstedts.

206   *Dan Hansén*

Peterson, T. 2002. Olof Palme som jag minns honom. Stockholm: Albert Bonniers Förlag.

Pierson, P. 2000. Increasing returns, path dependence, and the study of politics. American Political Science Review 94(2):251–67.

Proposition 1977/78, No. 100, Appendix 5. Budgetpropositionen. Justitiedepartementet, Polisväsendet.

Proposition 1980/81, No. 13. Om polisens uppgifter, utbildning och organisation m.m.

Proposition 1980/81, No. 100, Appendix 5, Budgetpropositionen. Justitiedepartementet, Polisväsendet.

Proposition 1982/83, No. 100, Appendix 4. Budgetpropositionen. Justitiedepartementet, Polisväsendet.

Protocol 1975, No. 78, §6. Fortsatt giltighet av den s.k. terroristlagen.

Protocol 1975/76, No. 44, §10. Ändring i utlänningslagen.

Protocol 1978/79 No. 57 § 13. Om den planerade omorganisationen av Stockholmspolisen.

Rose, R., and Davies, P. 1994. Inheritance in public policy: change without choice in Britain. New Haven, CT: Yale University Press.

RPS, 1982. Polisiär beredskap vid vissa allvarliga brottsliga angrepp. Stockholm: National Police Board.

Sabatier, P. A., and Jenkins-Smith, H. C. (eds.) 1993. Policy change and learning: an advocacy coalition approach. Boulder, CO: Westview Press.

Sabatier P. A. 1999. Theories of the policy process: theoretical lenses on public policy. Boulder, CO: Westview Press.

Schlager, E. 1999. A comparison of frameworks, theories, and models of policy processes. In Sabatier, P. (ed.) Theories of the policy process: theoretical lenses on public policy. Boulder, CO: Westview Press, pp. 233–60.

SOU 1979, Vol. 6. Polisen.

SOU 2002, Vol. 87. Rikets säkerhet och den personliga integriteten: De svenska säkerhetstjänsternas författningsskyddande verksamhet sedan år 1945.

Stockholm police. 1975a. Polisens förundersökningsprotokoll rörande terroristöverfallet mot Förbundsrepubliken Tysklands ambassad.

Stockholm police. 1975b. Angående viss ändrad organisation för polisdistriktets ordningsavdelning samt behov av ytterligare utrustning. 16 September, Dnr AA 124–421/74.

Svensk Polis. 1977 No. 4. Framgången; Så här gick det till; Ledare i DN: Besinningens seger över stora risker. Stockholm: National Police Board peer journal.

Svensk Polis 1980 No. 5. Polisstyrka flygs in vid terroristangrepp mot kärnkraftverk. Stockholm: National Police Board peer journal.

SVT. Extrarapport 1975. Stockholm: Swedish Television 25 April.

Tophoven, R. 1984. GSG 9: Kommando gegen Terrorismus. Koblenz: Bernard & Graefe Verlag.

True, J., Jones, B. and Baumgartner, F. 1999. Punctuated-equilibrium theory: explaining stability and change in American policymaking. In Sabatier, P. (ed.) Theories of the policy process: theoretical lenses on public policy. Boulder, CO: Westview Press, pp. 97–115.

Vinge, P. G. 1988. Säpochef 1962–70. Stockholm: Wahlström & Widstrand.

Welander, G. 2003. Head, Justice Ministry's police unit 1972–1984. Interview with Dan Hansén.

Winberg, Håkan 2004. Justice Minister 1979–1981. Interview with Dan Hansén.

Zahariadis, N. 1999. Ambiguity, time, and multiple streams. In Sabatier, P. (ed.) Theories of the policy process: theoretical lenses on public policy. Boulder, CO: Westview Press, pp. 73–93.

8 | The Walkerton water tragedy and the Jerusalem banquet hall collapse: regulatory failure and policy change[1]

ROBERT SCHWARTZ AND ALLAN McCONNELL

Introduction: a puzzle emerging from tragedy

Risk regulation is a key feature of modern, complex, industrial and postindustrial societies. Reasons for the growth of such regimes are contested (see, e.g. Douglas and Wildavsky 1983; Beck 1999; Jordana and Levi-Faur 2004), but their 'formal' roles in systems of governance are clear. As Hood et al. (2001: 3) suggest, risk regulation is 'governmental interference with market or social processes to control potential adverse consequences to health'. Arguably therefore, the greatest blow to a regulatory policy regime is being implicated as a causal factor in crisis or disaster. With policy legitimacy damaged and operational regulatory matters proving insufficient for the task, it would be logical to assume that liberal democratic processes of inquiry and accountability in the aftermath of crisis/disaster would lead to mature lesson-drawing processes and culminate in regulatory reforms. Indeed, with such high salience and prominence given to the protection of public health, it may be difficult to imagine a regulatory regime which does not engage in policy reforms aimed at restoring operational efficacy and reputational legitimacy of regulators and policy overseers alike.

Herein lies the 'puzzle' addressed by this chapter. We tackle two cases of regulatory failure identified as significant causal factors in tragedies, yet vastly different policy outcomes were produced as a result of investigation and lesson drawing. Canada's Walkerton water tragedy (2000) – where drinking water was contaminated with *Escherichia coli*, 7 people died and over 2300 fell ill – produced long-term and significant *policy reform* (the fundamental adaption of policy principles and institutional values as per Chapter 1 of this volume) in the area of environmental

---

[1] We would like to thank Arjen Boin, Paul 't Hart and Dave Marsh for their helpful comments on an early draft of this chapter.

regulation. By contrast, Israel's Versailles Banquet Hall collapse (2001), led to 23 deaths and over 400 injuries yet produced virtually no *policy reform* or even *fine tuning* (instrumental adaption of policy and procedures) in policy surrounding building codes. Indeed, the outcome was closer to what Rose and Davies (1994: 41–2) describe as 'symbolic gestures' with no particular commitment to reform.

Drawing on sources such as commission reports, interviews with stakeholder representatives, documents provided by interviewees and secondary sources, we explore why two broadly similar 'regulatory failure crises' produced substantively different patterns of policy change. Our goal, therefore, is case-oriented, viewing the Canadian and Israeli experiences through the lenses of literatures on risk regulation and crisis management. Our comparative approach is broadly a 'most similar' one (George and Bennett 2004) in which we seek to explain why two separate political and policy systems with shared policy and political characteristics, produced substantially different crisis-induced policy outcomes. Our 'small *n*', discursive approach does not provide a controlled comparison where the influence of a single independent variable is subject to rigorous testing (Peters 1998). However, we have the corresponding advantage of thick description and country specificity.

In this context, we can identify broad commonalities in terms of the nature of the tragedy, media coverage, institutional procedures for investigation and the findings of the respective inquiries. Both crises involved breakdowns in systems upon which the public relies for basic daily needs – water and shelter. Both had a high profile in their respective countries with significant international media coverage. The institutional contexts of the subsequent investigations were also broadly similar. The two countries are liberal democracies and parliamentary systems, with established liberal-democratic processes for independent and quasi-independent postcrisis investigations. In addition, respected commissioners in both countries blamed the crises largely on regulatory systems and their operations.

To tackle our 'puzzle', this chapter is divided into four substantive sections. First, we suggest the importance of viewing risk regulation as a dynamic political activity rather than an objective scientific exercise. We use this as a basis to argue that crises that spring from regulatory failures do not necessarily lead to regulatory learning and change. Risk regulation is an inherently political activity, whose course and outcomes are determined by political actors and processes more than by technical ones. This is particularly clear when the occurrence of a disaster compromises the regulatory status quo, as in the two cases presented here. Postdisaster politics takes over from professional inquiry and technical learning. Depending on contextual and other factors, the politics of inquiry may stimulate or impede regulatory change. Second, we provide a straightforward descriptive outline of our two cases utilising the typologies of postcrisis policy change based upon the three-layer categorisation of policy change detailed by the editors in Chapter 1. Third, we develop an analytical framework which allows us to capture the significant contextual social factors related to each risk, the political backdrop, process of investigation and stakeholder influence. We then apply this framework to each of our cases. Finally, we draw out wider implications for regulatory policies that are subject to scrutiny and delegitimation in the wake of tragedy.

The politics of risk regulation

The functional rationale for regulatory systems is one of 'treating risks' (Drennan and McConnell 2007) in a preemptive way in order to ensure that information gathering, institutional standards and actor behaviour are subject to 'minimum' standards (Hood et al. 2001). The logic is that if standards are set at appropriate and attainable levels, then society is protected from the adverse and potentially disastrous consequences which might otherwise ensue.

Our two cases alone illustrate that such logic does not always unfold to guide processes of investigation and reform in the wake of regulatory failure. As a starting point for our analysis, we need to highlight the differences between our approach and one which sees risk regulation as science. The latter view is not uncommon in risk management texts. At the very least there is a veneer of science as a result of the use of risk matrices and coding systems (see, e.g. Bannister 1997; Fone and Young 2005). In reality, however, risk regulation is not a 'scientific' activity. Assessing both the levels of risk involved and which (if any) control measures need to be put in place is not a simple matter of applying regulatory policies which are proportional and appropriate to the risk involved. Risk assessments involve judgements, imperfect information, and acceptance that elimination of all risk is impossible and hence some level of risk needs to be tolerated. Furthemore, assessing risks typically takes place in the context of budgetary constraints and dominant political values – rendering some regulatory options less or more feasible than others (Leiss and Powell 1997; Slovic 2000; Hood et al. 2001; Weale 2002; Drennan and McConnell 2007).

Such contingencies and the role of subjectivity indicate that the regulation of risks is not simply a functional activity to regulate risks. The matter of which particular risks should be dealt with (and by what means) has ramifications elsewhere in the political systems and indeed in society as a whole. Therefore risk regulation, like any other policy regime, is the product of a combination of sociopolitical pressures, involving (among other things) trade-offs, dilemmas, inequalities and political ideologies that underpin the desirability or otherwise of government intervention. Identifying the factors shaping public policy lies at the very heart of debates in political science. We cannot hope to resolve perennial debates here, but what we can do is draw out some features of risk regulation regimes, indicating that they serve a role beyond the 'scientific' regulation of risks.

Risk regulation regimes perform a political-symbolic role. They help create the impression that political leaders and public regimes take public health and safety seriously, and that the public can rely on this commitment. Regulatory regimes might also provide a benefit to key stakeholders because of the precise form, or the limited nature, of that regulation. Risk regulation also legitimises the power of key stakeholders (for example in public utilities/infrastructures such as water, electricity, rail and gas) by ensuring that their productive capacities are subject to 'socially responsible' constraints. Similarly, risk regulation regimes are a means of allocating risk protection rights to certain societal groups, who might otherwise be badly affected if risks were not regulated. Furthermore, risk regulation regimes are vehicles for the maintenance of social order, both in an operational sense (for example, preventing the breakdown of critical infrastructures) and in a political-symbolic sense (demonstrating that government is capable of acting on knowable risks).

Risk regulation regimes, therefore, are *dynamic* and subject to both internal and external pressures, as well as contestation. Normally, however, the routines of politics predominate and policy change is incremental. Yet, as Chapter 1 demonstrates, 'crisis' is one of the few phenomena capable of punctuating policy regimes. Operational failings are there for all to see (often involving illness, loss of life and infrastructure damage), which in turn pose political-symbolic challenges for leaders as they try to straddle the line between offering reassurance that the system is essentially robust, and a commitment to change in order to reduce vulnerabilities for the future (Boin and 't Hart 2003; Boin et al. 2005; Drennan and McConnell 2007). Therefore, if risk regulation is indeed 'governmental interference with market or social processes to control potential adverse consequences to health' (Hood et al. 2001: 3), then failure opens up this regime to 'meaning-making' scrutiny. Why did control measures not work? Were they inappropriate in the first place (e.g. too lax or too complex to be practical)? Or were the measures appropriate but incorrectly implemented (e.g. as a result of corruption, neglect or incompetence)?

In line with the argument of the editors in Chapter 1, crisis can undermine risk regulation regimes and open windows of opportunity for reform (Birkland 1995, 2006; Kingdon 2003), but regulatory change is far from inevitable. Failures that are believed to result from misjudgements, errors and laxity, for example, are not likely to reveal a need for policy change in systems. They are more likely to result in the punishment of those individuals held responsible (Birkland and Nath 2000; Stone 2002). Furthermore, agenda-setting theory suggests that a crisis will in all likelihood focus public attention on an issue. However, unless there are coherent advocacy coalitions (Sabatier and Jenkins-Smith 1993; Wilson 2000), perceived viable solutions, or favourable political climates, the likelihood of policy change is low (Birkland 1997; Kingdon 2003).

We now turn to the cases to explore these ideas. First we describe the disaster events and the inquiries they engendered. Then we analyse why they produced such markedly different regulatory outcomes.

Two regulatory failures

Walkerton water contamination

Walkerton is a rural town of some 4800 residents in southern Ontario, Canada. In May 2000, Walkerton's drinking water became infected with *E. coli* (*Eshericha coli* 0157:H7.1) when a heavy rainstorm washed manure from the fields of a neighbouring farm into the water sources. Inadequate chlorination and monitoring allowed the deadly bacteria to pass through the town's rudimentary water production facilities, resulting in the deaths of seven people. More than 2300 became ill, many with long-lasting effects. News of the tragedy caused widespread panic about the quality of drinking water across Ontario (see Burke 2001; Perkel 2002).

The Ministry of Environment (MOE), with the full backing of the government of Ontario, acted quickly in a concerted effort to assure residents of Ontario that their water would be safe to drink. Within a short time, all municipalities were required to have an external engineer review their systems and report to the MOE. The government appointed a commission of inquiry headed by well-respected Associate Chief Justice Dennis O'Connor. Amongst the factual findings of the commission were that (1) managers and operators of the water system were incompetent; (2) lab results indicating infection were not reported to the proper authorities; and (3) the MOE had done nothing to remedy serious problems that it had known about for years (O'Connor 2002a).

While the O'Connor Commission found that some culpability lay with the individuals who operated Walkerton's water facility,[2] it placed blame for the Walkerton crisis squarely on the shoulders of the MOE regulators. An important context was dominant regulatory values in Ontario stemming from the election in 1995 of Premier Mike Harris and his neoliberal 'Common Sense Revolution' of large public expenditure cuts across a range of social programs, empowering business and redesigning systems of regulation and governance in order to increase productivity and growth (Keil 2002; McKenzie 2004). Under the Harris regime, MOE staffing was cut by 50 percent and departmental budgets were cut by 48.4 percent in the 3-year period after Harris came to power. The cuts were accompanied by the closure of all public water testing labs (water testing was privatised) and substantial reductions in the number of inspections of water treatment facilities (O'Connor 2002a: 404; Snider 2004: 271–2).

---

[2] The commission found that the Koebel brothers, who operated Walkerton's water facility, had acted improperly and had not complied with Ministry of Environment rules. The Koebels routinely labeled water samples taken from taps in their offices as if they had been taken at wells and also underchlorinated the water. Moreover, they were responsible for operating one water well with no chlorinator at all and for lying to the Ministry of Environment. Eventually, one brother was sentenced to a 1-year jail term and the other to 9 months of house arrest. Nevertheless, the commission's in-depth investigation revealed that the underlying cause of the tragedy rested with regulatory failure on the part of the Ministry of Environment. See Perkel (2002) and Mullen et al. (2006).

According to the O'Connor Report, the Ministry of Environment had known for years that Walkerton's water treatment facilities were poorly operated, microbiological sampling was inadequate and chlorination levels were too low. However:

The MOE took no action to legally enforce the treatment and monitoring requirements that were being ignored [...] I am satisfied that if the MOE had adequately fulfilled its regulatory and over-sight role, the tragedy in Walkerton would have been prevented (by the installation of continuous monitors) or at least significantly reduced in scope. (O'Connor 2002a: 27–30)

The report also revealed flaws in regulatory ethics connected with the budgetary cutbacks that restricted the MOE's ability to fulfil its role in protecting the safety of Ontario's drinking water. Budget cuts also resulted in significant curtailment of inspection and follow-up capacity. Taking an ethical stand, senior ministry officials warned that the cutbacks increased risks to unacceptable levels. However, these same officials said nothing when the ministry published a business plan stating explicitly that the cutbacks would not affect risk levels (O'Connor 2002a). Nor did they go public when a heavy workload considerably reduced the ability of inspectors to conduct inspections and follow up on the correction of deficiencies. The Walkerton Inquiry found, for example, that the MOE did not follow up on findings from its 1998 inspection of the Walkerton water system to ensure correction of monitoring and chlorination problems. The Inquiry Report makes this quite clear: 'With the proper follow-up, these proactive measures would likely have resulted in the PUC's adoption of chlorination and monitoring practices that would in turn very likely have substantially reduced the scope of the outbreak in May 2000' (O'Connor 2002a: 407).

The subsequent changes can be divided with relative ease into the *policy reform* and *fine-tuning* categories as outlined in Chapter 1. *Policy reform* came about via legislation and regulations to set standards that were previously only broad objectives, so that guidelines became standards. Ontario became a world leader for the stringency of its drinking water regulation. These became enshrined in three pieces of legislation and one set of detailed regulations: the Safe Drinking Water Act (2002); the Sustainable Water and Sewage Systems Act (2002); the Nutrient Management Act (2002) and the Drinking Water Systems

Regulation (2003). Included in these stipulations were requirements pertaining to sampling and analysis, chlorination, chemical and physical standards and other indicators of adverse water quality. In addition, new accountability and transparency rules required owners of waterworks to:

- Post a warning when the water production facility did not comply with the sampling and analysis requirements for microbiological parameters, or when corrective actions as outlined in the regulations had not been taken (s. 10)
- Make all information regarding the waterworks and the analytical results of all required samples available for the public to inspect (s. 11)
- Prepare a quarterly written report to the Ministry of Environment and to consumers of drinking water summarising analytical results and describing the measures taken to comply with the regulation and the ODWS (s. 12)
- Submit an independent engineer's report according to the schedule contained in the regulation and submit triennial reports thereafter (s. 13)
- Notify both the Medical Officer of Health and the MOE of adverse water quality

Fine tuning occurred in two main ways: systems for information gathering were upgraded and the new regulatory regime included mandatory annual inspections for all drinking water systems. These inspections were carried out over several days, depending on the size and complexity of each facility. Additional information was gathered from new requirements governing minimum sampling, analysis and reporting. *Fine tuning* also came about via a behavioural change in terms of inspectors. Prior to Walkerton, there was little enforcement. The relationship between inspectors and operators was collegial and advisory – the least effective form of regulation practices in ensuring compliance (May 2005). However, in the aftermath of Walkerton, the ministry instituted a 'zero tolerance policy' under which any infraction of standards was cited, followed up and referred to the enforcement branch if not corrected within a stipulated time frame. The zero-tolerance policy was applied to administrative as well as operational infractions (e.g. imposing fines for deficiencies in not having certificates properly posted). Within a short period, therefore, the regulatory system had shifted to a traditional, mandatory approach – the opposite end of the regulatory continuum (May 2005).

Jerusalem banquet hall collapse

The collapse on 24 May 2001 of the Versailles Banquet Hall in Jerusalem's industrial Talpiot neighbourhood captured worldwide attention by virtue of spectacular video shots of the dance floor caving in. The disaster left 23 people dead and over 400 wounded. It was by far the worst non-war-related disaster in the history of Israel.

Initial investigations by engineers revealed a number of deficiencies: (1) the building was originally designed for industrial use, not to sustain static and dynamic 'loads' of commercial/recreational activity; (2) a new floor was added; (3) a supporting column was partially removed during ground-floor renovations; and (4) the new floor was constructed using the prohibited Pal-Kal method. Pal-Kal is a method for constructing ceilings that considerably reduces the need for supporting columns by using steel plate boxes. This method was developed in Israel and has no known parallels elsewhere. Since the early 1980s, thousands of buildings had been constructed with Pal-Kal, including a number of buildings that housed government offices and several hospital wards.

Prime Minister Ariel Sharon spoke of a 'national tragedy', and a five-member commission was established under the chairmanship of Jerusalem's District Court President Vardi Zeiler. Its terms of reference covered building safety standards in general (its title was State Commission of Inquiry into the Safety of Buildings and Public Facilities), rather than merely the collapse itself (as many families had wanted).

In the course of the commission's investigations, explanations offered by city engineers for disregarding their legal duty to check building plans revealed that local authorities allocated sparse resources to engineering units, reducing the number and quality of engineers to conduct professional checks on building plans (Commission on New Building Methods 2001: 39; Knesset 2001b: 23). In Jerusalem, for example, only 18 out of 33 inspector positions were filled at the time of the Versailles collapse. Moreover, local authorities had financial interests in getting buildings up and running as sources of municipal tax income. In a Knesset (Israeli Parliament) Interior Committee meeting, the Jerusalem city engineer was reminded that there were almost 50,000 illegal buildings for which the municipality received municipal taxes

(Knesset 2001a: 18). Testifying before the Knesset Interior Committee, Jerusalem's city engineer admitted that the Versailles Hall had never received an 'approval for occupation' or a business license (Knesset 2001a). Legal proceedings to close the hall failed and the municipality did not issue an administrative closing order. Moreover, the engineer explained that, because the municipality did not check construction details in building plans, it was not aware that the ceiling had been constructed by the prohibited Pal-Kal method.

In the course of investigations, Pal-Kal became the subject of intense scrutiny, and it became apparent that numerous 'warning signs' existed. In 1987, for example, the head of the Station for Construction Research in the Technion, Israel's prominent engineering university, had issued a letter to the Ministry of Construction stating that the method was inappropriate. In the mid-1990s, the chief inspector in the Ministry of Labor, responsible for investigating work accidents, argued that there was 'a very high probability' that the Pal-Kal method had contributed to three incidents of roof collapses during the years 1994 and 1995, resulting in two deaths and numerous injuries. Similarly, in 1996, a potential disaster was avoided when a crack was found in the Pal-Kal ceiling of a shopping mall in the city of Rehovot.

The Pal-Kal incidents of the mid-1990s led to the ostensible tightening of existing legal accountability mechanisms. The Ministry of Interior issued a circular in 1996 to all local authorities stating that the Pal-Kal method was dangerous and did not comply with basic engineering principles. The circular requested that local authorities stop giving building permits for Pal-Kal construction and should not give approval for buildings already constructed in this way. In the same year, conclusive findings from tests conducted by the Israel Standards Institute led to an amendment of the standard governing roof construction to clarify that Pal-Kal roofs did not comply with the standard. In 1998, the Ministry of Interior issued a second circular, instructing local authorities to conduct 'visual inspections' of all buildings that had been constructed with the Pal-Kal method. In the same year, the Association of Contractors in Israel recommended that its members not use the Pal-Kal method.

These measures *appeared* to provide an effective means of preventing further Pal-Kal construction and dealing with existing Pal-Kal buildings, but the banquet hall collapse indicated that local authority overseers had failed to prevent the construction of dangerous buildings or to identify existing Pal-Kal structures in order to take appropriate safety steps. While Ministry of Interior directives to local authorities seemed to tighten existing legal accountability mechanisms, in practice they were largely ignored. It seemed that municipal budgetary constraints prevented allocation of resources to comply with these directives from both local authorities and the Ministry of Interior.

When the Zeiler Commission reported some 2 1/2 years after the disaster in December 2003, it found serious inadequacies in the entire regime for regulating the safety of building and construction. The commission recommended a major revamp of standards and the establishment of a new national authority for regulating the construction industry. Judge Zeiler stated on launching the report that: 'it will be a miracle if there isn't a second Pal-Kal affair' (*Jerusalem Post* 26 December 2003). The *Jerusalem Post* (26 December 2003) described the report as: 'nothing less than a searing indictment of the whole building industry . . . the entire system of construction in Israel is flawed to its core'.

The posttragedy policy stasis was foreshadowed when Judge Zeiler stated during the early months of the committee's deliberations that he did not expect the government to implement the findings of the committee. Based on past experience, he argued, the role of the committee was much more about raising public awareness (*Jerusalem Post* 3 September 2001). This is, in effect, what happened. If we consider our three postcrisis policy change categories, even *fine-tuning* reforms are virtually nonexistent. A separate government body established to deal with the Pal-Kal issue produced almost no results, and the Zeiler Commission was unable to investigate the reasons because of its own shortage of funds and time.

To date, therefore, there has been no action on the major restructuring recommended by the commission. The Ministry of Interior has taken only small steps to improve the state of business licensing. Local authorities, the fire commissioner and officials of relevant government ministries were instructed to take action to enforce the business licensing law; seminars were held for about 1,000 officials; and meetings were held to promote coordination amongst agencies connected with business licensing. These changes barely fit into the *fine-tuning* category. The certainly do not constitute a deeper *policy reform*, involving legislation, new building standards or a new government agency to regulate the fragmented systems of standards and their enforcement. Perhaps the biggest repercussions have been the convictions for negligence of Avraham Adi and Efraim Adviv, the coowners of the banquet hall; as well as Eli Ron, the Pal-Kal inventor; and three engineers.

A framework for explaining different policy trajectories in the wake of regulatory failure

The longer-term policy responses to our two cases could scarcely have been more different. The Walkerton water tragedy led to a radical swing of the regulatory pendulum towards stringent standards, comprehensive routine monitoring and a zero-tolerance enforcement strategy. By contrast, the Versailles Banquet Hall collapse had virtually no effect on regulatory policy or practice.

The existing literature on regulatory regimes takes us only so far towards explaining these divergent crisis-induced policy outcomes. We do know that differential postfailure outcomes can occur. For example, Lodge and Hood (2002) identify three mediating institutional factors. The most reformist is exploitation of the 'windows of opportunity' in order to promote preexisting reformist policy preferences. By contrast, a system maintenance approach is characterised by a defence of the status quo, while a 'partial reengineering' is more pragmatic in accepting the pressures for change but filtering out the more difficult and demanding aspects. A broader study by Hood et al. (2001) of nine risk regulation regimes focuses more on understanding the nature of each regime rather than on reasons for regulatory change. It offers three main explanations for risk regime content (market failure, popular opinion and interest pressures) but supplements these with factors such as organisational micropolitics and greater pressures for openness and transparency. It does recognise that sudden regulatory reform may be a response to tragedy, although it focuses simply on how effective such potentially 'knee jerk' changes can be. The study concludes with a plea for alternative ways to capture differences in risk regulation regimes.

In this spirit, we build on the work of Hood et al. by introducing 'crisis' themes from Chapter 1 of this volume. Accordingly, we offer four general propositions, covering the nature of the risks, the political context, the inquiry process and stakeholder pressure.

1. *Nature of the Risk*: The greater the risk, coupled with a greater challenge to public sector and civic values, the greater the likelihood of reform after a crisis.

Table 8.1. *Strength of factors conducive to regulatory change in Walkerton and Jerusalem*

	Walkerton	Jerusalem
Nature of the risk and its challenge to public values	Medium/high	Medium/high
Political context	Medium/high	Low
Inquiry process	Medium/high	Low/medium
Stakeholder pressure	Medium	Low

2. *Political Context*: The more a government is under political pressures for reform (e.g. through the media, public opinion), it is vulnerable in its capacity to govern (e.g. in relation to the timing of elections cycles, or opinion polls), and reform does not challenge dominant governing values, it is comparatively more likely that policy reform will occur in the wake of crisis.

3. *Inquiry Process*: The stronger the resources, mandate, leadership and framing capabilities of an inquiry, the greater will be its influence in producing regulatory change.

4. *Stakeholder Pressure*: The more powerful the stakeholders lobbying for change, the more likely it is that regulatory policy change will occur.

As we apply each of these broad propositions to our two cases, the analysis will also confirm our earlier contention that risk regulation is at heart a political activity, not just a 'scientific' regulation of risks involving an optimal system of risk regulation being matched with assessable and predictable risks. Our analysis is summarised in Table 8.1.

Walkerton: a regulatory regime backfires

The *nature of the risk* at the heart of the Walkerton tragedy was the risk that drinking water may not only be unfit for human consumption but may in fact produce illness and even death. Water is vital for human survival, and safe drinking water has become one of the key symbols of a modern society (Shiva 2002), especially when compared to the situation in many developing countries, where water scarcity and contamination constitute a way of life. Failure on the part of public authorities in the western world to provide and guarantee safe drinking water typically amounts to an 'agenda setting crisis' (Boin et al. 2005) because it is a focusing event (Birkland 2006) that hits a nerve and connects with deeper concerns about the fragility of our environment and our capacity to harness and/or control it. The fact that the Walkerton tragedy was about water raised the stakes, so that something had to be done. Concern about risks to drinking water 'runs deep' in modern societies.

Such an argument certainly permeated much of the ensuing social anxiety and political inquiry. The report of the O'Connor Inquiry recognised that the scope of the issue went beyond the small town of Walkerton and caused serious concerns about the safety of drinking water throughout the province of Ontario for its population of over 12 million people. As the Concerned Walkerton Citizens (the citizen action group set up in the wake of the contamination crisis) stated in its final argument to the inquiry: 'Before May of 2000, most Canadians turned the tap on for a drink of water with full confidence that the water was clean and safe for consumption.... Now, however, that sense of confidence and trust in the safety and security of drinking water has disappeared' (Concerned Walkerton Citizens 2001: 5). Such were the ramifications of the risk in Ontario that almost every other province and territory in Canada began to upgrade its regulatory regime in terms of new legislation, enforcement procedures and staff training. The nature or the perceived risk in Ontario was clearly such that the provincial government needed to be seen to address an issue of public safety.

The *political context* of Walkerton was also broadly favourable to change. The Walkerton crisis received considerable media and public attention over the subsequent 5 years, in part because the inquiry lasted almost 2 years and in part because the trials of Walkerton public utility workers were prolonged until 2004. The media-savvy Concerned Citizens of Walkerton, represented by the Canadian Environmental Law Association (CELA), ensured that the need for reform maintained a long-term high profile. The Walkerton crisis also became a reference point in the media for other policy problems (or 'fiascoes'), such as the Aylmer meat scandal and the failed privatisation of Ontario's electricity transmission grid. The wider context of Canadian values perhaps also created capacity for change. The Walkerton crisis, along with similar policy change patterns in Canada's Human Resources Development Canada HRDC crisis,[3] suggests that Canada might have a particularly strong reaction to inattention on the part of public officials to processes and procedures for ensuring safety and financial probity. This would be in line with Glor and Greene's (2002) contention that Canada's political culture places a particularly high value on integrity.

Added to the pressures and contexts conducive to change, the Harris administration had been subject to considerable criticism from citizens and stakeholder groups in terms of the broad direction of its Common Sense revolution – including its neoliberal approach to regulation. The existence of a regulatory system (even a light-touch one) had helped legitimise the Harris agenda because the government could argue that regulatory 'standards' acted as a safety net. However, a backlash was already under way before Walkerton. The political cleavage opened further by the crisis acted as a galvanising force for a variety of counter-Harris interests among citizens, trade unions, environmental groups and educational/legal elites (Snider 2004). The failures at Walkerton seem also to have been a factor in Harris resigning from office in April 2002 and his successor Ernie Eves failing to get reelected in October 2003 (*Toronto Star* 3 October 2003).

An important qualification is needed in terms of political context. We should not be hasty in assuming that the Walkerton crisis produced intense pressures for action and a vulnerable conservative government simply caved in. Certainly, the Harris and Eves administrations may

---

[3] See Good (2003), Sutherland (2003) and Phillips and Levasseur (2004). In January 2000 the media, public figures and opposition MPs demanded the head of a government minister, the disbanding of an entire department and the termination of the Transitional/Canada Jobs Fund – a $125 million program to encourage the creation of sustainable jobs in areas of high unemployment. They charged the prime minister with abusing the program to promote job projects in his riding. They also accused the ruling political party of using the TJF/CJF as a, 'political slush-fund with no accountability at all'. Media sensationalism and political opportunism combined to make this what some termed Canada's 'biggest scandal ever'. In this case, the crisis (or manufactured crisis) is nothing but the failure of HRDC to properly oversee grants and contributions. HRDC had consciously loosened control over the administration of these funds in the framework of new public management reforms, dramatic cutbacks and internal reorganization. HRDC reacted to the media-generated crisis by immediately swinging the regulatory pendulum way back to the control side of the continuum. Within a short time, HRDC established a 'comprehensive and elaborate set of administrative checklists and forms' (Good 2003: 115).

have had little choice but to act if they wanted to be seen as competent and caring guardians of public safety, but it can be argued that
postcrisis changes were pragmatic *policy reforms* (as per Chapter 1)
rather than a fundamental paradigm shift involving a jettisoning of
neoliberal ideals. A study by McKenzie (2004) argues convincingly
that Walkerton did not mark the death knell for 'new public management' values and policies. She suggests that the Harris government
adopted a blame-game strategy against the Walkerton Public Utilities
Commission and its staff and was able, with some success, to frame
the Walkerton tragedy as epitomising the weakness of the traditional
public administration model in order to produce a new initiative for
the privatisation of the Ontario Hydro.

The *inquiry process* was also conducive to change. Justice O'Connor
was a highly respected judge in the Ontario Court of Appeal and
was elevated to associate chief justice of Ontario during the course
of the inquiry. Despite tough budgetary constraints, he was able to
put together a seven-strong Research Advisory Panel of leading academics and practitioners and he adopted an expansive interpretation
of the committee's terms of reference into the causes of the outbreak
and recommendations for ensuring the safety of Ontario's drinking
water. In a survey of news articles over the course of the inquiry, we
could not find a single criticism of O'Connor. His conduct of the investigation was sharp, fair and good humoured and involved a highly
streamlined approach to investigations which grouped witnesses into
coalitions and avoided party politicisation (Burke 2001: 197–200).
The inquiry also worked very closely with CELA, representing the
Concerned Walkerton Citizens. As one of the few books on the Walkerton crisis argues: 'In criticizing public inquiries as a cumbersome,
ineffective, and seemingly never-ending process, Premier Mike Harris
might have misjudged the man chosen to lead it, Dennis O'Connor'
(Perkel 2002: 201). The nature of the risks to the public involved, coupled with O'Connor's leadership, meant that the inquiry was able to
construct narratives around the twin bastions of modernism (science
and the law), creating a strong degree of 'apolitical' legitimacy, which
were, nevertheless, highly critical of the Harris regime and its cutbacks
at the MOE and privatisation of water laboratories (Snider 2004).
Therefore, the conduct of the inquiry under O'Connor was clearly a
force for change, although, once again, we should be cautious about
fully embracing of the idea that it was paradigm-shattering. As Snider

(2004: 282) argues: 'The Report ... is a liberal document, not a radical script'.

As regards *stakeholder interest*, our proposition was that the more powerful the stakeholders lobbying for change, the more likely it is that policy change will occur. In the case of Walkerton, the galvanising forces for change were a loose alliance of interests, led by the Concerned Walkerton Citizens and their representatives in CELA and encompassing various other environmental groups and public sector unions, such as the Canadian Union of Public Employees and Ontario Public Service Employee Union. This loose alliance was opposed by numerous agricultural groups who would be affected by stricter regulatory measures, particularly because the spread of manure was considered the primary cause of the contamination, but it was difficult for them to produce an effective counterframe. As Snider (2004: 282) argues: 'Science gave the Inquiry the stamp of "objective, apolitical truth" (Phillips, 1996: 145–6), legitimating claims that public interest groups, unions and environmentalists – demonized as "special interests" by the Conservative Government – had been making for years'.

Jerusalem: a regulatory failure lost in high politics

In Israel, the *nature of the risk* of building collapse was reasonably high, especially given that Pal-Kal had been implicated in previous incidents, although building codes and their enforcement do not have quite as strong a symbolic connection to modernism and civic values as does water. The banquet hall collapse also happened at a private function, where public services were not consumed directly but indirectly through the implicit assumption that the building was safe and somehow protected by appropriate government regulation and enforcement. Nevertheless, the wider implications of the discredited Pal-Kal method were that other buildings may be at risk and vulnerable to collapse. However, risks have contexts in which perceptions are important – not just perceptions of the extent of the risk but also of our capacity to minimise these risks.

In this regard, the *political context* of Israeli politics was crucial. There was certainly some initial momentum for change. The fact the event was recorded on video and shown on news networks throughout the world certainly heightened media and citizen interest, although the high level of salience that typically follows tragedy dissipated fairly quickly. The timing of the tragedy was such that Ariel Sharon was only 3 months into his directly elected term of office. In a country in which coalition governments are almost routinely vulnerable in a political system and a polity characterised by a highly proportional electoral system, a strong multiparty system and a highly fragmented society, Sharon won a landslide victory over Ehud Barak (Diskin and Hazan 2002). He was able to form a grand coalition forging a national unity coalition with a strong emphasis on security in the face of the second Palestinian uprising, which had begun in September 2000.

The context of Sharon's grand coalition and its security agenda is important for the aftermath of Versailles tragedy. The preoccupation with terrorist attacks during this period clearly contributed to the quickly diminished public salience of the banquet hall collapse. Table 8.2 provides a taste of the scale of terrorist attacks. Israel was on high terrorist alert during the month of the collapse. Amongst the events of that month, a suicide bomber killed 18 people in Tel Aviv, mortar shells were fired from Gaza, a baby was stoned and several settlers and soldiers were killed in a long series of separate incidents. Indeed, hearing the endless sirens following the banquet hall collapse, Jerusalemites' natural reaction was that yet another terrorist had exploded a bomb. As Kirschenbaum (2004: 113) notes in his study of disaster management in Israel, even before the escalation of violence in 2000 and 2001, almost one third of the urban population had been involved at some time in an emergency situation where someone was killed or injured. The banquet hall tragedy pales by comparison.

In essence, it can be argued that Israel's public policy agenda is overloaded with crises, generally related to issues of security and defence, rooted in complex and competing views about Israel as a Jewish state, greater (Eretz) Israel, democracy and peace (or at least the minimising of conflict) (Arian 1995). Dror (1988) claims that agenda overload causes accountability to be a nonissue in Israel. Even the shocks of domestic disasters and crises fail to receive sufficient attention from senior policy makers. Therefore Israel's building safety crisis was of relatively low salience and not linked with any particular political agenda, political party or politician. In this instance, the agenda-breaking potential of crisis struggled to compete with the securitisation issues and the increasingly high politics of the Israel–Palestine conflict. When we factor in the role of memory and politics, particularly the special place of bereavement in Israeli society (Weiss 2002; Lebel

Table 8.2. *Terrorism-related events in Israel during June 2001*

Date	Event
29/06	Young mother killed by terrorist
28/06	Multiple shootings in West Bank
25/06	Fatah leader blown up in Nablus
25/06	Hezbollah fires on IAF planes
24/06	Two soldiers killed in Gaza
22/06	Long range mortar from Gaza
21/06	Settler from Homesh murdered
17/06	IDF pull-back from West Bank and Gaza marred by PA violations
15/06	Underground Jewish group claims responsibility for Arab's murder
11/06	Three Bedouin women killed by tank fire
11/06	Fatah terror cell responsible for bombings arrested
11/06	Deliberations to postpone Maccabiah games due to terrorist surge
8/06	Six mortar shells fired in Gaza Strip
8/06	Three Israelis wounded in shooting near Ramallah
8/06	Shiloh baby fights to survive after stoning
7/06	Masses rally against (IDF) restraint
7/06	Terror alert continues
5/06	Separation: A loaded political decision
3/06	Eighteen dead, more than 90 wounded by suicide bomber (dolphinarium)
1/06	Fourth terror killing this week

2006), we have a tradition with a very strong 'debt' to victims of conflict. Overall, therefore, it can be argued that the maintenance of social order in Israel is predicated on insulating the country from external, as opposed to internal, threats.

The *inquiry process* into building codes in the aftermath of the banquet hall collapse seemed initially to hold promise as a driver for change. Judge Vardi Zeiler was certainly well respected and his four-member committee delved into the history of building codes since the development of the Israeli state, heard over 200 witnesses and looked at examples of international practice. Upon receiving conclusive evidence concerning the dangers of Pal-Kal, Justice Zeiler initiated an interim report with the intent of spurring quick action to prevent additional building collapses. The final report ran to twenty-nine chapters and over 200 hundred papers and was notable for its thoroughness and specific recommendations on how to correct system deficiencies.

However, the fact that the investigation was not into the collapse itself (despite the wishes of many victims' families) but into the wider issue of building codes diluted the galvanising potential of tragedy to prompt 'tombstone' reforms (Hood et al. 2001), which are symbolic of 'healing' and a debt owed to those who have suffered. Furthermore, as indicated, Judge Zeiler stated at a press conference that he did not expect the government to fully implement any recommendations, and that an important remit of the commission was simply to raise awareness (*Jerusalem Post* 3 September 2001). He may simply have been accepting political realities, but in doing so he also framed the work of the commission in such a way that acknowledged and perpetuated its weakness in terms of influence. This point illustrates that we cannot easily separate the inquiry process from its context. Nevertheless, our basic point remains. An inquiry that is portrayed by its chair simply as an awareness-raising exercise is not likely to act as a major catalyst for policy reform.

The absence of any significant *stakeholders* lobbying for a change in building codes and their enforcement also made policy stasis more likely. In fact, the constraints of Israeli politics context aside, there were many interests that benefited from the status quo. For example, Israel's local authorities suffered from chronic budgetary deficits, while the Ministry of Interior was charged with ensuring budget stringency. Neither side had an interest in increasing expenditures for professional scrutiny of building plans and completed structures.

Conclusion: still a 'puzzle' of postcrisis politics?

Our two cases challenge the conventional orthodoxy that there is a direct correspondence between the nature of a risk and the corresponding regime that evolves to regulate and control that risk. The implication of such orthodoxy is that, when regulatory failures lead to disaster, inquiry processes of accountability and learning lead to a corresponding policy change to plug the 'regulatory gap'. These cases challenge such conventional thinking because here, broadly similar crises (public health tragedies, regulatory failure as a causal factor, investigation through due process by investigative committees) produced very different long-term crisis-induced policy outcomes. The Walkerton case produced clear *policy reform* which swung the regulatory pendulum from deregulation to reregulation. By contrast, the Jerusalem case resulted in little or no *fine tuning* to a loose and largely unenforced regulatory regime.

By developing and applying a heuristic classifying regulatory change (nature of the risk, political context, inquiry process and stakeholder influence), we have been able to make sense of these divergent pathways. In effect, our original puzzle has now been 'solved'. We cannot identify the precise influence of each factor. Rather, their interaction is 'political', involving a complex mix of conflicts which are resolved through processes of deliberation and authoritative decision making.

In the case of Walkerton, an emergent risk with major public health implications and revolving around an issue (water) that touched deeper values of modernisation put a radical, yet politically vulnerable government on the back foot when its light-touch approach to regulation was implicated in failure. An astutely run inquiry, deriving particular legitimacy from its use of the law and science as arbitration factors, allowed counteralliances to coalesce, promoting a pragmatic change in regulatory policy without compromising deeper new public management policies and values.

The contrast with the banquet hall collapse in Jerusalem is clear. Emerging public health risks in terms of building safety were inherently quite high but did not have as strong a connection to deeper values of modernisation and struggled to break through the dominant security-focused agenda of Israeli politics, heightened particularly by a new prime minister elected on a 'security' platform at a time of increased conflict. Even the chair of a well-run inquiry recognised the limited likelihood of being able to produce regulatory change, and so it proved to be. Opportunities for policy change became lost in the ether of Israeli politics.

Our two cases combined indicate that 'context' matters when we attempt to open up the black box of postcrisis and postregulatory failure periods. It may be the case that context is the most important of all influences on regulatory systems. The ability of extraordinary and tragic events inevitably raises questions over the legitimacy of a regulatory regime and its role (if any) in precipitating the tragedy, but any longer-term changes in regulatory policies will be the product of a complex mix of conservative and reformist political factors, straddling the political arena and processes of inquiry and accountability. Risk regulation is not an exact science. It is an inherently political activity which needs to be located in particular geographic, policy sector and historical contexts. As such, we should not be too surprised – as with post-crisis periods, more generally – when broadly similar tragedies lead to very different policy outcomes.

References

Arian, A. 1995. Security threatened: surveying Israeli public opinion on peace and war. New York: Cambridge University Press.

Bannister, J. 1997. How to manage risk. 2nd edn. London: LLP.

Beck, U. 1999. World risk society. Cambridge, UK: Polity Press.

Birkland, T. A. 1997. After disaster: agenda setting, public policy, and focusing events. Washington, DC: Georgetown University Press.

Birkland, T. A. 2006. Lessons of disaster: policy change after catastrophic events. Washington, DC: Georgetown University Press.

Birkland, T. A., and Nath, R. 2000. Business and political dimensions in disaster management. Journal of Public Policy 20(3):275–303.

Boin, A., and 't Hart, P. 2003. Public leadership in times of crisis: mission impossible? Public Administration Review 63(5):544–53.

Boin, A., 't Hart, P., Stern, E. and Sundelius, B. 2005. The politics of crisis management: public leadership under pressure. Cambridge, UK: Cambridge University Press.

Burke, B. L. 2001. Don't drink the water: the Walkerton tragedy. Victoria, BC: Trafford Publishing.

Commission of Inquiry into Safety of Buildings and Public Places 2004. Justice V. Zeiler, Jerusalem chair.

Commission on New Building Methods 2001. Recommendations for institutionalizing procedures for checking and approving new building methods. Jerusalem: Ministry of Interior.

Concerned Walkerton Citizens. 2001. Walkerton inquiry, part 1A and 1B: Final argument on behalf of the Concerned Walkerton Citizens. http://www.cela.ca/publications/cardfile.shtml?x=1067.

Diskin, A., and Hazan, R. Y. 2002. The 2001 prime ministerial election in Israel. Electoral Studies 21(4):659–64.

Douglas, M., and Wildavsky, A. 1983. Risk and culture: an essay on the selection of technological and environmental dangers. Berkley, CA: University of California Press.

Drennan, L. T., and McConnell, A. 2007. Risk and crisis management in the public sector. Abingdon, UK: Routledge.

Dror, Y. 1988. Public administration in Israel. In Rowat, D. C. (ed.) Public administration in developed democracies: a comparative study. New York: Marcel Dekker.

Fone, M., and Young, P. C. 2005. Managing risk in public organisations. Leicester, UK: Perpetuity Press.

George, A. L., and Bennett, A. 2004. Case studies and theory development in the social sciences. Cambridge, MA: MIT Press.

Glor, E., and Greene, I. 2002. The government of Canada's approach to ethics: the evolution of ethical government. Public Integrity 5(1):39–66.

Good, D. A. 2003. The politics of public management. Toronto: Institute of Public Administration of Canada.

Hood, C., Rothstein, H. and Baldwin R. 2001. The government of risk: understanding risk regulation regimes. Oxford, UK: Oxford University Press.

Jordana, J., and Levi-Faur, D. (eds.) 2004. The politics of regulation: institutions and regulatory reforms for the age of governance. Cheltenham, UK: Edward Elgar.

Keil, R. 2002. 'Common-sense' neo-liberalism: progressive conservative urbanism in Toronto, Canada. Antipode 34(3):578–601.

Kingdon, J. 2003. Agendas, alternatives, and public policies. 2nd edn. New York: Longman.

Kirschenbaum, A. 2004. Chaos organization and disaster management. New York: Marcel Dekker.

Knesset (Israeli Parliament). 2001a. Protocol of the meeting of the committee for the interior and environment, 5 June.

Knesset (Israeli Parliament). 2001b. Protocol of the meeting of the committee for the interior and environment, 7 July.

Lebel, U. 2006. The creation of the Israeli 'political bereavement model' – security crises and their influence on the political behaviour of loss: a psycho-political approach to the study of politics. Israeli Affairs 12(2): 439–61.

Leiss, W., and Powell, D. 1997. Mad cows and mother's milk: the perils of poor risk communication. 2nd edn. Montreal: McGill-Queens University Press.

Lodge, M., and Hood, C. 2002. Pavlovian policy responses to media feeding frenzies? Dangerous dogs regulation in comparative perspective. Journal of Contingencies and Crisis Management 10(1):1–13.

May, P. 2005. Regulation and compliance motivations: examining different approaches. Public Administration Review 65(1):31–43.

McKenzie, J. I. 2004. Walkerton: Requiem for the new public management in Ontario? International Journal of Environment and Pollution 21(4):309–24.

O'Connor, D. (chair) 2002a. Part One – Report of the Walkerton inquiry: the events of May 2000 and related issues. 2002. Ontario: Ontario Ministry for the Attorney General, http://www.attorneygeneral.jus.gov.on.ca/english/about/pubs/walkerton/part1/

O'Connor, D. (chair) 2002b. Part Two – Report of the Walkerton inquiry: a strategy for safe drinking water. 2002. Ontario: Ontario Ministry for the Attorney General, http://www.attorneygeneral.jus.gov.on.ca/english/about/pubs/walkerton/part2/.

Perkel, C. N. 2002. Well of lies: The Walkerton water tragedy. Toronto: McLelland & Stewart.

Peters, G. 1998. Comparative politics: theory and methods. New York: New York University Press.

Phillips, S., and Levasseur, K. 2004. Snakes and ladders of accountability: contradictions between contracting and collaborating for Canada's voluntary sector. Canadian Public Administration 47(4):451–74.

Rose, R., and Davies, P. L. 1994. Inheritance in public policy: change without choice in Britain. New Haven, CT: Yale University Press.

Sabatier, P. A., and Jenkins-Smith, H. C. 1993. Policy change and learning: an advocacy coalition approach. Boulder, CO: Westview Press.

Shiva, V. 2002. Water wars: privatization, pollution, and profit. Cambridge, MA: South End Press.

Slovic, P. 2000. The perception of risk. London: Earthscan.

Snider, L. 2004. Resisting neo-liberalism: the poisoned water disaster in Walkerton, Ontario. Social & Legal Studies 13(2):265–89.

Stone, D. 2002. Policy paradox: the art of political decision making. 2nd ed. New York: Norton.

Sutherland, S. 2003. Biggest scandal in Canadian history: HRDC audit starts probity war. Critical Perspectives on Accounting 14:187–224.

Weale, A. (ed.) 2002. Risk, democratic citizenship and public policy. Oxford, UK: Oxford University Press.

Weiss, M. 2002. Bereavement, commemoration, and collective identity in contemporary Israeli society. Anthropological Quarterly 70(2):91–101.

Wilson, C. E. 2000. Policy regimes and policy change. Journal of Public Policy 20(3):247–74.

9 | Learning from crisis: NASA and the Challenger disaster

ARJEN BOIN

Introduction: did NASA learn from the *Challenger* disaster?[1]

On 1 February 2003, the *Columbia* Space Shuttle disintegrated during
the final stages of its return flight to earth. The drama unfolded live on
television: spectacular pictures of the doomed flight were punctuated
by reactions of devastation and loss. It was in some ways a familiar
drama. Seventeen years before (28 January 1986), Space Shuttle *Challenger* had exploded within 2 minutes of its launch. The *Challenger*
disaster was etched in the minds of an entire generation of American
schoolchildren, who watched the launch in their classes (the teacher
Christa McAuliffe was on board to teach elementary school students
from space).

Both disasters were studied by a presidential commission.[2] Both
commissions were scathingly critical of the National Aeronautics and
Space Agency (NASA). The Rogers Commission, which studied the
causes of the *Challenger* disaster, criticised the space organisation for
not responding adequately to internal warnings about the impending
disaster. The Columbia Accident Investigation Board (CAIB) found
that little had changed since the *Challenger* disaster: 'By the eve of
the *Columbia* accident, institutional practices that were in effect at
the time of the *Challenger* accident – such as inadequate concern over
deviations, a silent safety programme, and schedule pressure – had
returned to NASA' (CAIB 2003: 101). The inescapable conclusion
emerging from the CAIB report is that NASA failed to learn the obvious

[1] I wish to thank the following people for their helpful comments on earlier drafts
of this chapter: Chris Ansell, Paul 't Hart, Stephen Johnson, Todd LaPorte,
Allan McConnell, José Olmeda, Paul Schulman, and all the participants of the
ECPR workshop 'Crisis and Politics', held in Granada (14–19 April 2005).
[2] Both the *Challenger* and the *Columbia* disasters have been researched by a large
number of academics as well. Diane Vaughan (1996) has written the best study
on the *Challenger* disaster. See Starbuck and Farjoun (2005) for a collection of
essays on the *Columbia* disaster.

lessons flowing from the *Challenger* disaster, which caused the demise of *Columbia* (see, e.g. Vaughan 2005). The CAIB thus sketches a picture of a recalcitrant organisation that irresponsibly gambled with the lives of its astronauts.

This chapter investigates if and what NASA learned in the wake of the *Challenger* disaster and explores if and how the *Challenger* aftermath is related to the *Columbia* disaster. We begin by briefly outlining NASA's history of human space flight. The next section explains why seemingly 'hard' assumptions about causes, risks and organisational learning rarely hold up to scrutiny. We then revisit the *Challenger* disaster and its aftermath, offering a reappraisal of NASA's learning capacity while reexamining the relation with the *Columbia* disaster. The chapter concludes with more generic points about organisational learning after crisis, with a specific focus on the role of commissions.

A brief history of NASA's human space flight: from Apollo to Columbia

The explosion of Space Shuttle *Challenger*, 73 seconds into flight, undermined belief in America's space agency. Unaccustomed to the risk of disaster (it had been 19 years since the deadly *Apollo* fire of January 1967), politicians, journalists and the public at large anxiously watched the hearings held by the Rogers Commission. The Rogers Commission was deeply critical of NASA's safety practices. It attacked both the organisational risk paradigm (which determined how NASA officials viewed risk) and the organisational procedures to deal with potential problems. The Rogers Commission concluded that NASA's risk definition had become too wide and its practices too lenient. Before we consider if and how NASA learned the lessons offered by the Rogers Commission, we need to briefly describe the origins of NASA's safety culture.[3]

The Apollo race: reconciling risk, resources and schedules

In 1958, President Eisenhower merged various aerospace and engineering centres of excellence under the NASA banner. The Russians had

---

[3] There is an abundant literature on NASA's history. In addition to the sources cited in this chapter, the NASA website provides much helpful material.

launched *Sputnik* and the United States could not afford to lose the space race. In 1961, President Kennedy upped the ante by declaring that the United States would bring a man to the moon and back before the decade was over. NASA certainly had a challenge to meet. Three weeks before Kennedy made his promise to the nation, Alan Shepard had become the first astronaut in space (his flight in the *Mercury* aircraft lasted no longer than 15 minutes). Although NASA had caught up with the Russians, it was still a long way from landing astronauts on the moon *and* bringing them back safely. The Apollo project was constrained by three factors: knowledge (nobody had done this before), time (racing the Russians) and money (nobody knew how much it would cost and Congress routinely cut the NASA budget).

The *Apollo* project critically depended on the ability of NASA leaders to make the centres work together (McCurdy 1993). These centres were notoriously independent. The Langley Research Center (established in 1919) had a long history of aeronautics design and a very peculiar way of working – 'the Langley way' (Murray and Cox 1989: 27). Langley personnel played a large role in designing the *Apollo* spacecraft. The George C. Marshall Space Flight Center (MSFC) in Huntsville, Alabama, housed Wernher von Braun's rocket team. The Germans had pioneered long-range ballistic missiles during World War II: they built the V-1 and V-2 rockets that the Germans rained on England.[4] They brought to NASA state-of-the-art knowledge of rocket development. The MSFC designed the rockets (Saturn boosters) that launched the *Apollo* and her crew into space. The launch facilities were at Cape Canaveral, Florida. The Space Task Group oversaw the Apollo project from its center in Houston (flight control was based there as well). Jim Webb 'ran' NASA from his small Washington, DC, headquarters.[5]

It soon became apparent that the decentralised centres were hard to manage. NASA initially managed the centres 'by committee', which amounted to facilitating and hoping for the best. The culture was informal and communication was based on sound engineering arguments. This 'loose anarchistic approach to project management' became a

---

[4] See Adams and Balfour (2004) for a very critical discussion of the role played by von Braun's team during the war. The authors discuss the ethics of having these alleged war criminals developing the rockets that would bring Americans to the moon.

[5] Webb and his colleagues at headquarters also managed the other NASA centres.

problem when test failures and huge budget overruns threatened the success of the *Apollo* project (Johnson 2002: 102). NASA administrator Webb realised that the way of managing the *Apollo* project was in need of drastic change if NASA were to maintain political support and succeed in its lunar mission (Johnson 2002: 130–2). Webb brought in George Mueller as the new director of the Office of Manned Spaceflight (OMSF) in September 1963. Mueller would become known as the father of space flight.

Mueller turned NASA around 'from a loosely organised research team to a tightly run development organisation' (Johnson 2002: 142; cf. Murray and Cox 1989). He introduced two crucial concepts that continue to mark NASA's culture to this day. First, he imposed a management technique known as 'systems engineering'. Pioneered in the U.S. Air Force, a set of procedures and project management techniques was brought in to integrate the design processes of the various centres. The procedures served to codify good scientific, engineering and managerial practices that were developed in the separate centres. Building on the shared engineering background, the procedures helped to define and circumscribe the autonomy of the centres.

The second change was the imposition of the 'all-up testing' concept. Both the Langley and German engineers subscribed to a conventional engineering approach, which dictated endless tests of all parts and the interaction between the parts. They learned through failure: firing rockets, watching them explode, determining what went wrong, redesigning the rocket – until the rocket was perfect. This time-proven practice had two drawbacks. First, it would take a long time to do a sufficient number of tests to create a statistical base for risk assessment. Second, the test process could never completely resemble a space environment. Once you strap people on top of the rocket, it has to work the first time around.

The all-up testing principle marked the end of endless testing. The new mantra was an ultrarational version of engineering logic: 'design it right, fabricate it per print, and the component will work' (Murray and Cox 1989: 103). Since 'there was no way to make 0.999999 claims on the basis of statistical evidence unless the engineers tested the parts millions of times', there really was no alternative (Murray and Cox 1989: 101). The all-up testing did imply a very distinct risk philosophy, described by flight director Chris Kraft (immortalised in the movie *Apollo 13*):

We said to ourselves that we have now done everything we know to do. We feel comfortable with all of the unknowns that we went into this program with. We know there may be some unknown unknowns, but we don't know what else to do to make this thing risk-free, so it is time to go. (cited in Logsdon 1999: 23)

A philosophy of calculated risk: success and failure

NASA rejected the verisimilitude of quantitative risk analysis and accepted the hard risk that every space flight can end in disaster. This philosophy demanded an unwavering commitment to 'sound engineering'. The technique of systems engineering offered the procedures to maintain these high levels of engineering quality. The stunning success of the moon landing affirmed this philosophy, while failures reinforced the organisation's commitment to this way of working.

NASA's first tragedy arrived on 27 January 1967. Three astronauts (the original moon crew) died when a fire broke out in the *Apollo* capsule during a simulated test run at Cape Canaveral. The accident, with the astronauts dressed in their space suits, took place in the *Apollo* capsule on top of a Saturn rocket. A small spark caused an intense fire and killed the trapped astronauts within seconds (the capsule was filled with pure oxygen).

In the turmoil that followed, *Apollo* engineers were accused of incompetence and negligence. A memo from General Electric, which warned of this scenario, surfaced. In reacting, NASA placed more emphasis on procedures to control individual quirks: 'Never again would individuals be allowed to take so much responsibility onto themselves, to place so much faith in their own experience and judgment' (Murray and Cox 1989: 203).

The spectacular success of the 1969 moon landing proved to many within NASA that the introduction of systems engineering had been the correct strategy (Johnson 2002). The centres had been curtailed in their freedom to run endless design-test-redesign cycles, yet they had been left with enough freedom to design a spacecraft that worked very effectively. The detailed rules were grounded in best practices; the emerging philosophy therefore facilitated a surprisingly informal culture.

Just how effective and resourceful NASA culture had become was perhaps demonstrated during the near-disaster that occurred some time after the successful lunar mission, when *Apollo 13* experienced an explosion in space (Murray and Cox 1989; Kranz 2000). The adherence of procedures enabled the engineers to figure out what had happened and what was possible. Yet it was the capacity to be flexible and to *depart* from enshrined rules that gave rise to the level of improvisation that in the end saved the day (and the crew). The shared commitment to sound engineering and the institutionalised practice of open communication made it possible to solve this crisis in the nick of time.

Valued traditions vs. new disasters

After the Rogers Commission criticised NASA's traditional approach to safety, it took nearly 3 years before NASA would return to flight. An impressive string of successes followed: NASA safely flew eighty-seven shuttle flights, launched the Hubble telescope (and later repaired it in space), the *Mars Pathfinder*, the *Sojourner Rover* and the *Lunar Prospector* (McCurdy 2001). It aggressively cut costs through its ambitious 'Faster, Better, Cheaper' programme (McCurdy 2001). However, the many successes did not restore the prestige and admiration that NASA enjoyed during the *Apollo* and early shuttle years. By the end of the 1990s, NASA's safety practices were scrutinised after a series of spectacular failures – *Mars Climate Orbiter*, *Mars Polar Lander* and *Deep Space 2* rank among the most visible. Several critical reports described what Farjoun (2005) refers to as a period of 'safety drift'. Suffering from serial budget cuts, NASA had begun to erode its safety margins (SIAT 2000). After shuttle flight STS-93 experienced serious in-flight anomalies in July 1999, the entire fleet was grounded.

In reaction to the critical report of the Space Shuttle Independent Assessment Team (SIAT 2000), NASA administrator Dan Goldin declared a 'shuttle crisis' (Farjoun 2005). The ageing fleet had become vulnerable. Safety procedures and practices had been eroded as a result of labour shortage, and the SIAT report unearthed a worrying number of narrow misses. The agency had successfully brought down the costs of shuttle launches (partially in order to fund the expensive International Space Station), but the administrators now sensed that the cost cutting had gone too far. Goldin convinced the Clinton administration to increase the programme's funding, which allowed NASA to address a variety of safety concerns as identified by SIAT. After meeting the short-term concerns of SIAT, the shuttles resumed their flight schedules.

By 2001, NASA's political credibility had reached a low point as a result of 'failed investments and inadequate cost-control efforts'. Congress and the White House effectively 'put NASA on probation' (Blount et al. 2005: 130; CAIB 2003). The appointment of Sean O'Keefe (formerly deputy director of the White House Office of Management and Budget) as the new NASA administrator signalled that NASA's problems were viewed as managerial and financial at heart (Farjoun 2005; McDonald 2005). O'Keefe prioritised the International Space Station (ISS), which had to be completed before NASA could move on to other human flight projects. The completion of ISS would require a series of tightly scheduled shuttle flights.

The *Columbia* disaster (1 February 2003) thus came at the worst possible time for NASA, which was politically vulnerable. The *Columbia* disaster instantly jeopardised the future of NASA's human space programme. The subsequent findings of the Columbia Accident Investigation Board (CAIB) further eroded the agency's remaining legitimacy base (see also Klerkx 2004).[6] Politicians and media representatives seemed to increase their vocal concerns about whether NASA still had the 'right stuff' to fulfil its mission (Wolfe 2005).

The CAIB report wove two story lines into one blasting analysis. The first line recaptured the findings of recent reports, which described a severely eroded safety culture and an alleged susceptibility to comply with irresponsible deadlines. The second line detailed the similarities with the pre-*Challenger* period. The combined outlook suggested a highly irresponsible organisation that had gambled with the lives of astronauts in order to please the agency's stakeholders. NASA, in other words, had failed to learn from the *Challenger* disaster – it had, in fact, made things worse.

Learning from disaster

From an engineering perspective, learning from technological failure is a fairly straightforward affair. If a bridge collapses or a space shuttle

---

[6] Many critics doubted whether NASA should continue to fly the space shuttles at all. After the next flight was plagued yet again by the foam problem, the shuttle was officially kissed off (see President Bush's 2005 space plan). Additional problems – especially with President Bush's political appointees, who were accused of muzzling NASA's climate scientists – have further increased the criticism of NASA.

explodes, it simply means that the original design – the 'null hypothesis' – has been falsified (Petroski 1992). Learning, then, pertains to the activity of redesigning. Learning has been successful if the redesigned contraption functions according to plan. A shared belief in the laws of physics and engineering underpins this notion of learning, which is prevalent in many if not most organisations that deal with and depend upon technology. This is not meant to suggest that engineers cannot disagree. Quite on the contrary: the *Apollo* history is filled with deep controversies between and within the various centres (Murray and Cox 1989). However, it does mean that engineers tend to resolve such controversies on the basis of engineering logic and the laws of physics. Most engineers – certainly those at NASA – would have a hard time considering a different way of learning.

The introductory chapter of this book explains why crisis-induced learning tends to be of a less rational nature. The aftermath of a disaster is dominated by political processes, which affect learning practices. The outside world imposes itself – through congressional hearings, media inquiries and investigative committees – upon the organisation that has 'produced' the disaster. Political elites, citizen outcries, victims' relatives and media representatives create a climate in which organisational learning is subjugated, at least temporarily, to the lessons learned of an outside body (a special committee or a standing investigative body). Most of us may find it hard to trust the self-corrective potential of an organisation that has just caused a disaster (cf. Sagan 1993; Perrow 1994).

The dynamics of the crisis aftermath fundamentally alters the learning process in at least three ways. First, it creates two domains of learning, each with its own characteristics. Second, it substantially widens the scope and scale of potential lessons to be learned. Third, it fundamentally alters the evaluation of lessons learned. Let us briefly expand on these notions.

Endogenous vs. exogenous learning

In the postcrisis phase, the venue for learning typically shifts away from the responsible organisation or network. The accountability process, which overrides organisational learning routines, dictates an independent investigation. This does not negate intraorganisational learning processes that may have been triggered by the disaster. But the organisation that has 'produced' the disaster must patiently await the findings of this investigative body.

The postcrisis phase thus sees at least two separate domains of learning, each with its own rules, dynamics, interests and time horizons. There is a voluminous literature that explains why it is hard for organisations to learn from a crisis (Stern 1997; Boin et al. 2005: 117–22; see also Parker and Dekker, this volume).[7] Learning processes in public organisations are typically shaped in unpredictable ways by the prevailing mix of laws, rules, routines, core values, bureaucratic rivalry and leadership interests.

Investigative committees try to learn from the same disaster, but the context in which they attempt to do so is very different from the context in which public organisations operate. Committees operate under time pressure and must typically produce a report before a certain date. Moreover, investigative committees are often affected by accountability concerns: even if they want to avoid finger pointing altogether, their report will be perused to find the 'guilty' actors. Finally, we should note that committees formulate recommendations that they will not have to implement. This simple fact allows – and may even induce – committees to formulate sweeping recommendations ('become a learning organisation') without taking into account organisational realities.

These differences may be further intensified when the official lessons come to be perceived within the receiving organisation as a partisan product. The members of a committee may have less direct knowledge of the processes leading up to a crisis (they were not there when it happened and they do not always understand the organisation or the core processes of that organisation). Critics of an organisation may have recognised the investigative committee as a promising venue to push their aims and solutions. Ad hoc committees that are installed to investigate tightly knit policy sectors (such as the space industry) may prove especially vulnerable for inside biases. These commissions are made up of 'independent outsiders', but there may be few available experts without any preconceived notion about the organisation, its core processes and technologies, or the disaster itself. These experts often have a history with the organisation (if not, we may wonder

---

[7] There may be various domains of learning (think of congressional subcommittees, academic investigations, media inquiries and interest groups) in which the crisis at hand is being subjected to learning processes.

about their expertise). This may have serious effects on the lessons learned and their prospects for implementation.

This is not meant to imply that 'outside' learning can never get to the bottom of an organisational crisis, but it seems safe to predict that the lessons learned and the recommendations made in both venues will not be identical. This creates a source of potential friction between the external investigator and the investigated organisation. Political considerations force a public organisation to adopt – grudgingly or enthusiastically – the lessons and recommendations offered to them by the external committee. But if and how these lessons find their way into the rules and routines of the organization, depends on the size of the gap separating the imposed blueprint from the home-grown lessons.

Single-loop vs. double-loop learning

The potential of flunked crisis learning is heightened by the type of lessons learned in the different learning venues. Most organisations appear to be capable of 'single-loop' learning: organisational members try to fix what was broken while preserving the overall structure and the institutionalised ways of working. This type of learning fits the postcrisis mood. Hurt and traumatised by a disaster, organisational members tend to fall back on proven routines and shy away from wild experiments.

One may expect organisational leaders to formulate lessons that are known in the literature as 'double-loop learning' (Argyris and Schön 1978). These are lessons that address the wider context in which the single-loop lessons were allowed to occur. They may, for instance, target policy paradigms or institutional foundations, which few organisations can alter without entering a very different type of crisis. Organisational leaders vary in their willingness to adopt double-loop lessons. In the absence of hard evidence, we may hypothesise that long-incumbent leaders with a record to defend will prioritise preservation over reform (Boin and 't Hart 2000). Incoming leaders and those who aspire to move up the ladder are more likely to welcome crises as reform opportunities (if only to discredit successors or incumbents).

It appears that investigative committees have become increasingly inclined to formulate double-loop lessons. The members of these ad hoc committees tend to take a wider view, investigating both the immediate causes of a disaster and the organisational context in which the disaster has taken place. They put up for discussion the institutional paradigms to which organisation members subscribe. Unless the disaster has convinced the organisational members that their conceptual and managerial foundations no longer suffice – and this is rarely the case – the lessons learned in both venues may thus be of a fundamentally different nature.

The most ambitious form of learning is known in the literature as 'deuterolearning' – learning to learn (Argyris and Schön 1978). This is a typical academic prescription: it is theoretically sound, but never clear how it should be accomplished in the real and messy life of organisations. The class of so-called high-reliability organisations is often said to harbor this learning ability. However, investigative committees often couch 'learning to learn' type recommendations in vague and abstract language. Such recommendations are easy to make, especially without having to provide a manual.

Technical vs. political evaluation

From a purely technical perspective, the evaluation of lessons learned is a relatively simple exercise: if the disaster that gave rise to the lessons does not reoccur, the organisation has 'learned its lesson'. But crisis-induced learning is political, not technical, at heart. If the committee succeeds in delivering an authoritative report – its status being decided upon by media, politicians and public opinion – the crisis narrative, the lessons and the recommendations may come to be seen as a benchmark for organisational effectiveness.

Most committees produce single-loop recommendations that appear to be 'easy fixes'. After the *Herald of Free Enterprise* sunk in sight of Brugge's harbour (1987), the investigative committee recommended various ways to make sure this particular type of ferry would not take off with open doors. Investigations of prison riots routinely prescribe better hardware (such as improved riot gear, impenetrable fences and unbreakable glass). Even double-loop recommendations tend to appear deceptively simple: improve training, hire better people, change the culture – it all makes sense.

As a result, the organisation at the receiving end of such prescriptions will have to be able to show that it learned the lessons offered by the committee at any point in the distant future. Some recommendations are simply imposed on an organisation through legal changes, policy reformulations and budget amendments. Others must be implemented in and by (parts of) the organisation. Even if an organisation adopts the recommendations wholesale, it will have to make some accommodation with organisational characteristics – if not immediately, certainly in the future. But this is the ideal scenario. Most public organisations accept only part or none of the recommendations, even though they embrace them publicly and promise to uphold them. The complexity of implementation feeds the temptation of symbolic reform.

Symbolic adherence may shield the organisation from further outside interference, but in the long run the organisation cannot escape from it. As the crisis becomes a historic marker for the organisation, future assessments will take into account how the organisation dealt with the crisis. Future failures will evoke scrutiny of past behaviour. An organisation may thus be forced to adopt externally formulated lessons or face the consequences in the future. The report hangs as a sword of Damocles above the future of the organisation.

NASA and the *Challenger*: the politics of learning revisited

On 29 September 1988, NASA resumed its human space programme with the launch of space shuttle *Discovery*. Its safe return marked the beginning of a successful series of nearly one hundred shuttle flights, which tragically ended on 1 February 2003. This performance would seem to indicate that NASA learned the lessons from the *Challenger* disaster. However, the Columbia Accident Investigation Board (CAIB) reached a different conclusion. This section addresses the apparent tension between a successful flight record and the damaging CAIB findings.

Internal vs. external learning: NASA's responsive attitude

The Rogers Commission offered two types of findings: it detailed the technical causes (the faulty O-rings) and the organisational causes (the failure to detect the technical causes). NASA accepted, adopted and implemented all recommendations offered by the Rogers Commission. Nobody within NASA doubted that the O-rings had to be redesigned before the shuttles could fly again.

Much more light separated the findings of the Rogers Commission on NASA's organisational functioning and NASA's self-perception. The

Rogers Commission identified three types of organisational failure: NASA's safety *culture*, NASA's organisational *structure* and NASA's schedule *pressure* were at fault. The commission's findings thus directly attacked what were widely perceived within NASA as the organisation's cultural anchors and valued ways of operating.

Diane Vaughan's (1996) analysis of the *Challenger* disaster suggests that much of the Rogers Commission's findings were misinformed. It appears, for instance, that the commission misunderstood NASA's safety system, especially the way NASA engineers dealt with anomalies. Moreover, Vaughan demonstrates that the launch decision was a tragic misunderstanding rather than a gross management error. Vaughan shows that NASA routinely delayed flights if technical problems emerged, thus putting to rest the idea that NASA would prioritise launch schedules over shuttle safety. From her extensive interviews with NASA workers, it becomes clear that the Rogers findings did not resonate with the lessons learned within NASA. To be sure, Vaughan did not find NASA to be a perfect organisation. Her findings, however, lacked the 'clear-cut character' of the Rogers findings. Vaughan described a rather effective safety culture, rooted in NASA's lessons of the past, which had nevertheless allowed this disaster to occur.

The findings of the Rogers Commission never became a cultural issue within NASA, because the recommendations of the commission only addressed the *structural* features of the organisation (entirely bypassing the cultural problems). The commission recommended a more centralised management structure (moving the shuttle management to NASA headquarters), a deeper involvement of astronauts in the shuttle programme's management, the establishment of a Shuttle Safety Panel and the establishment of an Office of Safety, Reliability and Quality Assurance. It had very little to recommend with regard to NASA's safety culture (even though its findings identified cultural factors as the main culprits).

This explains why NASA, despite very different views on the organisational causes of the *Challenger* disaster, accepted and adopted the recommendations put forward by the Rogers Commission. In December 1990, the Augustine Committee (advising on the future of the U.S. space programme) not only commended NASA's responsive attitude in the wake of the *Challenger* disaster but also observed that NASA had been 'burdened by excessive layers of management that are the legacy of the development era and recovery from the *Challenger* accident'

(Augustine Committee 1990: 30). In 1995, the Space Shuttle Management Independent Review Team (the Kraft Commission) paid compliment to the 'remarkable performance' of the space shuttle programme and effectively prescribed that NASA roll back the changes adopted after the *Challenger* disaster. As the Kraft Commission described it:

The performance of the machine as a space transportation system has been remarkable given the difficult operating conditions and management environment. The preflight operational parts of the program are excellent in delivering, preparing, assembling, and readying the vehicle for flight. Optimal flight designs and plans are developed and executed for diverse and complex payload operations. Crew and flight controller readiness for both nominal and contingency operations are unmatched. Over the last several years, while performing seven to eight flights per year, the Shuttle Program has continued its successful performance while incrementally reducing operating costs by approximately 25 percent. (Kraft Commission 1995: 11)

Single-loop vs. double-loop learning: Rogers opens Pandora's box

The recommendations formulated in the Rogers report seem to reflect what academics refer to as 'single-loop learning': the commission prescribed shuttle design fixes, organisational reparations (centralisation, improved communication) and organisational fortifications (a few new offices, more ex-astronauts in managerial positions). The Rogers Commission did not recommend a complete overhaul of the way NASA prepares, launches, flies and returns its shuttles. The latter would be called 'double-loop' learning.

The *findings* of the Rogers Commission suggest that such double-loop learning would be in order. In its report, the commission was highly critical of the way NASA dealt with emerging risk: the organisation irresponsibly broadened its risk definitions and failed to act on clear warnings of impending danger. One of the commission members, Nobel laureate Richard Feynman, was especially critical, both in public appearances and in a personal appendix to the report. We can only guess why there was such a disconnect between double-loop lessons and single-loop recommendations. But even if the Rogers Commission did not affect the heart of NASA's safety system, it certainly did initiate a debate that would come back to haunt NASA years down the road.

The Rogers Commission, perhaps unintentionally, exposed the rather particular risk conception that had taken root in NASA's organisational culture and determined its safety system. In its infant years (1958–1963), NASA engineers sought to minimise risk by the familiar design-test-redesign cycle, which was to be run until risk could be all but ruled out. This time-honoured model of experimenting and testing was abandoned after President Kennedy imposed a firm deadline on the Apollo project. If NASA was to fly astronauts to the moon, the old model of endless testing clearly did not suffice.

In response to this looming Catch-22 situation, NASA revolutionised the management of human space projects by introducing a new testing philosophy (all-up testing) and a new management philosophy (systems management), which brought a heavy reliance on rules and procedures. The subsequent successes of the Apollo project anchored this approach into NASA's organisational culture.

This new approach entailed a new risk philosophy, a development that remained unnoticed or unappreciated outside NASA for a long time.[8] This philosophy dictated that once the NASA engineers – the best in the world – had applied their engineering logic to the design and fabrication of a rocket, only real-life tests could prove whether the rocket worked. This always entails a risk, because experimental technology and the unforgiving conditions of space can and will interact in unforeseen ways. One can only discover these ways by flying. If progress is to be made, risks have to be taken. After flying the contraption, anomalies are discovered and fixed – and it is flown again. The more it is flown, the safer it becomes. The reverse is also true in this conception: if it is not flown, nothing can be learned.

The Rogers Commission took issue with this institutionalised risk conception, noting that a safe shuttle flight does not 'prove' everything will work the next time. Whereas NASA worked on an experience basis (the O-rings did not burn through completely, so the design worked well), the Rogers Commission leaned towards a quantatively oriented risk conception (the O-rings clearly did not live up to the design requirements, which means NASA and its contractors should go back to the design table). Whereas NASA viewed its designs as hypotheses to be

---

[8] The dominance of this risk philosophy is probably described best by the key players themselves. For an in-depth conversation between key players, see Logsdon (1999).

tested (cf. Petroski 1992), the Rogers Commission demanded proof that the shuttle would be safe. The idea that anything could be proven before a shuttle flight violated NASA's risk conception (which was a pillar of NASA's safety system).

This clash between two 'risk schools' would resurface periodically in the years following the *Challenger* disaster. In 1995, the Kraft report declared that the shuttle had become more reliable as a result of more than thirty safe flights. This embrace of NASA's risk conception should come as no surprise: Chris Kraft was a key player during the Apollo years and a strong believer in this risk philosophy. In 1990, the Advisory Committee on the Future of the U.S. Space Programme (known as the Augustine Committee) presented a report that framed NASA's risk conception in historical terms:

The space program is analogous to the exploration and settlement of the New World. In this view, risk and sacrifice are seen to be constant features of the American experience. There is a national heritage of risk taking handed down from early explorers, immigrants, settlers, and adventurers. It is this element of our national character that is the wellspring of the U.S. space program. [. .] If people stop taking chances, nothing great will be accomplished.

The SIAT (2000) report, consisting of outsiders, echoed the findings of the Rogers Commission and roundly criticised NASA's risk perceptions. The CAIB (2003) built on the SIAT report and outright rejected NASA's risk conception.

It is one thing to recommend double-loop learning, but it another to offer an alternative that is both feasible and effective. Even if NASA's risk philosophy should be rejected as unacceptable, it is not clear what the alternative would be. This question becomes especially pressing in the light of new visionary plans (to the Moon, Mars and beyond) announced by President Bush in 2005. Human space flight remains inherently risky. As long as budget and time constraints exist, it is not clear how NASA's philosophy should be amended.

Technical vs. political assessment: follow the trail

In its analysis of the *Columbia* disaster, the CAIB drew a straight line between the findings of the Rogers Commission (17 years old by then) and its own findings. The CAIB reported finding the same conditions that had caused the *Challenger* explosion still present in NASA. The implication was obvious and damaging: NASA had failed to learn from the most deadly disaster in its history. This 'finding' is at odds with the findings of other commissions, which assessed NASA and the shuttle programme in the years following *Challenger*. Before NASA was allowed to 'return to flight' in 1988, both the shuttle and the organisation were scrutinised. After all, the whole nation was watching as the *Discovery* resumed the shuttle programme.

In 1990, the Augustine Committee reported its findings. It remarked that NASA had suffered much criticism in recent years, but that the organisation now had its house in order.[9] After reiterating that NASA 'has the critical responsibility of doing everything it can to minimize the human risk involved in meeting the nation's space goals' the committee stated 'that we believe [NASA] has now firmly embraced [this responsibility]'. The committee concluded that NASA had made 'an intense effort' to redress the organisational vulnerabilities outlined by the Rogers Commission. It observed that 'a process appears to be in place which surfaces concerns [with regard to launch safety] and resolves them'. The committee hinted that NASA might have learned *too much* from *Challenger*. It found that 'the Shuttle launch operation has evolved into a relatively slow and deliberate process'. Agreeing that the 'ultimate goal should be a safe operation', the committee cautioned that NASA should not be 'burdened by excessive layers of management that are the legacy of the [. . .] recovery from the *Challenger* accident'.

In 1995, the Space Shuttle Management Independent Review Team produced its findings in what has become known as the Kraft report. The team lamented the safety bureaucracy ('duplicative and expensive') that had sprung up in response to the *Challenger* disaster (Kraft Commission 1995: 16), concluding that the shuttle had become 'a mature and reliable system – about as safe as today's technology will provide' (Kraft Commission 1995: 1). Kraft found that 'too many discrepancies result in detailed analysis and testing' (Kraft Commission 1995: 13). The report went as far to suggest that the post-*Challenger* reforms had made the shuttle *less* safe: 'indeed, the system used today may make the vehicle less safe because of the lack of individual responsibility it brings about' (Kraft Commission 1995: 17).

---

[9] The committee remarked that 'some parts of the media [. . .] by this time had turned "NASA bashing" into a journalistic art'.

The Kraft report prescribed 'a change to a new mode of management with considerably less NASA oversight'.[10] NASA should no longer treat the shuttle as a developmental programme (which made the shuttle much too expensive to operate) and should outsource shuttle operations to external contractors. NASA would then be able concentrate on developing new space programmes. All in all, this report had a great impact: a consortium of space contractors took over parts of the space programme.

In 1999, the Space Shuttle Independent Assessment Team (SIAT) scrutinised the shuttle programme after flight STS-93 had experienced two serious in-flight anomalies. NASA grounded the fleet and waited for the SIAT to produce what would turn out to be a very critical report. Its findings fall within two categories. The bulk of the findings relate to the erosion of safety practices, which were the apparent result of the 'routinising' and outsourcing that had fundamentally altered NASA following the Kraft report. In addition, the SIAT criticised NASA's risk perception, essentially reopening the debate initiated (but never really pursued) by the Rogers Commission.

The SIAT report makes clear that NASA's altered shuttle programme was suffering safety lapses. SIAT observed that the programme 'had undergone a massive change in structure in the last few years with the transition to a slimmed down, contractor-run operation [...] This has been accomplished with significant cost savings and without a major incident' (SIAT 2000: 1) SIAT also concluded that the safety programme had been eroded, making a disaster increasingly likely. Moreover, the report concluded that the shuttles were increasingly suffering age-related problems. It prescribed more resources and reinstating the safety and quality elements removed in response to Kraft. It also proposed an overhaul of the 'primary risk management strategy: more consideration should be given to risk understanding, minimization, and avoidance'.

NASA accepted the SIAT report. In response, the Clinton administration increased NASA's resources (the 'safety upgrades initiative'). The incoming Bush administration, however, imposed a 34 percent reduction on this programme (Blount et al. 2005: 136; McDonald 2005).

---

[10] More specifically, the Kraft Commission wanted to roll back the 'independent SR&QA element', which had been instituted in response to the Rogers recommendations.

The CAIB report (2003) is a combination of two reports: the SIAT report and the Rogers report.[11] It recaps the story of recent erosions as documented by SIAT. The cause of the *Columbia* disaster, however, had little to do with these safety erosions. The 'foam problem' had been one of the oldest problems in the shuttle catalogue. The analogy with *Challenger* seemed clear: why had NASA never solved the problem? The integrated story line – 'a broken safety culture' and unacceptable risk taking – created an image of a highly irresponsible organisation.

Conclusion: learning and the long shadow of the *Challenger* disaster

Did NASA learn from the *Challenger* disaster? This chapter demonstrates that the answer to such a seemingly straightforward question depends on whom you ask and when. From the outset, we expected postcrisis learning to be affected by the politics and dynamics of the crisis aftermath. It turns out that the postcrisis phase lasts much longer than imagined. The shadow cast by the *Challenger* disaster extends well into the next century (cf. 't Hart and Boin 2001; Rosenthal et al. 2001).

During the first few years after the *Challenger* disaster, several external bodies found that NASA had adopted the recommendations prescribed by the Rogers Commission. These recommendations represented single-loop lessons: relatively easy fixes that did not require NASA to change its institutionalised way of operating. NASA did not adopt the double-loop lessons that could have been derived from the Rogers report. Crucially, the Rogers Commission failed to translate its double-loop findings into double-loop recommendations. We may speculate that within NASA, very little enthusiasm existed to address the institutional core of the organisation. The *Challenger* disaster, as Vaughan (1996) shows, was not viewed as a result of lapses in NASA's safety system. On the contrary: it was viewed as a 'normal accident' (cf. Perrow 1999) – a dramatic yet inevitable hump on the road towards a more reliable space vehicle. The disaster did not shake the belief in the safety system that had served NASA so well in its proud history.

---

[11] This analogy with the *Challenger* findings appears to have been furthered by the influential role of Diane Vaughan as an advisor to the committee. See Vaughan (2006) for her reflections on her time with CAIB. Moreover, astronaut Sally Ride served on both the Rogers Commission and the CAIB. On the dangers of historical analogies, see Brändström et al. (2004).

This is not an indicator of 'organisational arrogance', as the Rogers Commission and CAIB wrote. It is the strong belief in a risk philosophy for which no feasible alternatives are thought to exist.

It is this deeply entrenched risk philosophy that would serve as a lighting rod for future commissions. NASA had never changed it since *Challenger*; and several external committees had confirmed it since. Nearly two decades after *Challenger*, CAIB framed its conclusions around this philosophy and blasted NASA for not learning its lessons. Ironically, the CAIB does not translate its double-loop findings into double-loop lessons, which evokes, once again, the question whether a feasible alternative exists. It does nevertheless provide us with a clear lesson: however responsive an organisation may be in the aftermath of a crisis, it does not negate the crisis itself. A disaster marks the history of an organisation, providing benchmarks for future evaluation.

There is something inherently unfair about this finding. NASA confronts the incredibly hard challenge of using experimental technology to ferry humans back and forth to the most unforgiving environment known. It does so with limited (and often shrinking) budgets. Political and societal scrutiny is harsh. Expectations are high, while successful performance is met with a yawn. Accidents are simply unacceptable. In such an environment, perfect safety is an illusion. Perhaps the real double-loop lesson is that space ambitions and the risk society do not mix well.[12] We simply cannot have our cake and eat it.

The findings of this chapter caution against embracing the outcomes of postcrisis reports without scrutinising the particular ways in which lessons were reached and recommendations were formulated. Commissions may authoritatively push intuitively acceptable findings, couching them in selected social science findings. They may take on board academics and experts who may be tempted to push their (own) favorite theory. The findings and recommendations may thus incur damaging deficits that can only be revealed by close scrutiny and expert discussion. In the rush towards political closure, there is not always room for such debate.

The results of such a rush to judgement are rather serious for the organisations and sectors involved. Long after the committees have

---

[12] The Augustine Commission (1990) noted and accepted that space flight is inherently risky; it predicted (on statistical grounds) another disaster within thirty flights or so. The CAIB report pays lip service to the notion of inherent risk in space adventures, but subsequently demands that NASA ask for 'proof' that it is safe to fly.

been dissolved, organisations must work with their heritage. The findings typically become enshrined as the sole accurate account of the crisis and its roots. The recommendations that build on the findings may become symbolic markers to measure progress in organisational compliance. The room for organisational adaptation informed by organisational experts may be limited. When external committees impose their learning trajectory upon the crisis-affected organisation, the end result may be less optimal than we like to believe.

References

Adams, G., and Balfour, D. 2004. Unmasking administrative evil. 2nd edn. New York: Sharpe.

Argyris, C., and Schön, D. A. 1978. Organizational learning: a theory of action perspective. Amsterdam: Addison-Wesley.

Augustine Committee. 1990. Report of the advisory committee on the future of the U.S. Space Program. http://history.nasa.gov/augustine/racfup1.htm.

Blount, S., Waller, M. J. and Leroy, S. 2005. Coping with temporal uncertainty: when rigid, ambitious deadlines don't make sense. In Starbuck, W. and Farjoun, M. (eds.) Organization at the limit: lessons from the Columbia disaster. Oxford, UK: Blackwell, pp. 122–39.

Boin, A., and 't Hart, P. 2000. Institutional crises in policy sectors: an exploration of characteristics, conditions and consequences. In Wagenaar, H. (ed.) Government institutions: effects, changes and normative foundations. Dordrecht: Kluwer Press, pp. 9–31.

Boin, A., 't Hart, P., Stern, E. K. and Sundelius, B. 2005. The politics of crisis management: public leadership under pressure. Cambridge, UK: Cambridge University Press.

Brändström, A., Bynander, F. and 't Hart, P. 2004. Governing by looking back: historical analogies and crisis management. Public Administration 82(1):191–210.

Columbia Accident Investigation Board. 2003. Columbia accident investigation report. Burlington, Ontario: Apogee Books.

Farjoun, M. 2005. Organizational learning and action in the midst of safety drift: revisiting the space shuttle program's recent history. In Starbuck, W. and Farjoun M. (eds.) Organization at the limit: lessons from the Columbia accident. Oxford, UK: Blackwell, pp. 60–80.

't Hart, P., and Boin, A. 2001. Between crisis and normalcy: the long shadow of post-crisis politics. In Rosenthal, U., Boin, A. and Comfort, L. K. (eds.) Managing crises: threats, dilemmas, opportunities. Springfield, IL: Charles C. Thomas, pp. 28–46.

Johnson, S. B. 2002. The secret of Apollo: systems management in American and European space programs. Baltimore, MD: Johns Hopkins University Press.

Klerkx, G. 2004. Lost in space: the fall of NASA and the dream of a new space age. New York: Pantheon Books.

Kraft Commission. 1995. Report of the space shuttle management independent review team. www.fas.org/spp/kraft.htm.

Kranz., G. 2000. Failure is not an option: mission control from Mercury to Apollo 13 and beyond. New York: Simon & Schuster.

Logsdon, J. M. (moderator). 1999. Managing the moon program: lessons learned from project Apollo. Proceedings of an oral history workshop, conducted July 21, 1999. Monographs in Aerospace History, Number 14. Washington, DC: NASA.

McCurdy, H. E. 1993. Inside NASA: High technology and organizational change in the U.S. space program. Baltimore, MD: Johns Hopkins University Press.

McCurdy, H. E. 2001. Faster, better, cheaper: low-cost innovation in the U.S. space program. Baltimore, MD: Johns Hopkins University Press.

McDonald, H. 2005. Observations on the Columbia accident. In Starbuck, W., and Farjoun, M. (eds.) Organization at the limit: lessons from the Columbia disaster. Oxford, UK: Blackwell, pp. 336–46.

Murray, C., and Cox, C. B. 1989. Apollo: The race to the moon. New York: Simon and Schuster.

Perrow, C. 1994. The limits of safety: the enhancement of a theory of accidents. Journal of Contingencies and Crisis Management 2(4):212–20.

Perrow, C. 1999. Normal accidents: living with high-risk technologies. Princeton, NJ: Princeton University Press.

Petroski, H. 1992. To engineer is human: the role of failure in successful design. New York: Vintage Books.

Presidential Commission on the Space Shuttle Challenger Accident. 1986. Report to the president by the presidential commission on the space shuttle Challenger accident. Washington, DC: Government Printing Office.

Rosenthal, U., Boin, A. and Bos, C. J. 2001. Shifting identities: the reconstructive mode of the Bijlmer plane crash. In Rosenthal, U., Boin, A. and Comfort L. K. (eds.) Managing crises: threats, dilemmas, opportunities. Springfield, IL: Charles C. Thomas, pp. 200–215.

Sagan, S. D. 1993. The limits of safety: organizations, accidents, and nuclear weapons. Princeton, NJ: Princeton University Press.

Space Shuttle Independent Assessment Team (SIAT). 2000. Report to associate administrator. Washington, DC: NASA.

Starbuck, W., and Farjoun, M. (eds.) 2005. Organization at the limit: lessons from the Columbia accident. Oxford, UK: Blackwell.

Stern, E. K. 1997. Crisis and learning: a balance sheet. Journal of Contingencies and Crisis Management 5:69–86.

Vaughan, D. 1996. The Challenger launch decision: risky technology, culture and deviance at NASA. Chicago: University of Chicago Press.

Vaughan, D. 2005. System effects: on slippery slopes, repeating negative patterns, and learning from mistakes? In Starbuck, W., and Farjoun, M. (eds.). Organization at the limit: lessons from the Columbia disaster. Oxford, UK: Blackwell, pp. 41–59.

Vaughan, D. 2006. NASA revisited: theory, analogy and public sociology. American Journal of Sociology 112(2): 353–393.

Wolfe, T. 2005. The right stuff. New York: Black Dog and Leventhal Publishers.

10 | September 11 and postcrisis investigation: exploring the role and impact of the 9/11 Commission

CHARLES F. PARKER AND SANDER DEKKER

Postcrisis politics and reform: the remarkable role of the 9/11 Commission[1]

Launching an official investigation almost seems a Pavlovian response to crises in western democracies. Well-known examples include the Roberts Commission after Pearl Harbor (1941), the Warren Commission after the assassination of John F. Kennedy (1963), the Ervin Committee after Watergate (1972), the Widgery and Saville Inquiries after Bloody Sunday (1972), the Scarman Inquiry after the Brixton riots in London (1981), the *Challenger* and *Columbia* commissions (1986/2003), the Dutch NIOD Inquiry after the fall of the Bosnian Muslim enclave of Srebrenica (1995), the Dutroux inquiry (Staelraeve and 't Hart, this volume), the Swiss Independent Expert Commission on the role of Swiss banks during World War II (1996) and the Spanish Parliamentary Inquiry after the terrorist attacks in Madrid (2004).

Whereas the establishment of postcrisis inquiries is a recurring pattern, their political impact varies significantly. Some commission reports set off substantive policy changes; others end up in the dustbin. In fact, when it comes to enacting meaningful reform, the latter outcome (the dustbin) appears to be the norm. Postcrisis commissions rarely result in dramatic change or substantial reform (March and Olsen 1983; Olsen and Peters 1996; Zegart 2005). The persistence of formal postcrisis inquiries, despite a seeming record of desultory results, raises two key questions: what motivates such efforts and why do some commissions have a major impact on policies, while others pass into oblivion?

---

[1] Although all dates in this volume are in the format 'day, month, year', the disastrous events which are the subject of this chapter are referred to as September 11. This format has come to symbolise a tragic day in American history.

The 9/11 Commission offers an important opportunity to probe questions concerning the role, functioning and consequences of postcrisis inquiries. In the wake of the attacks, an official investigation into the exact details of what had happened, what went wrong and how to fix the identified problems seemed a certainty. The exact form of the inquiry, its scope and its ultimate impact, however, were far from inevitable. In fact, the creation of an independent panel with sweeping authority – what became the National Commission on the Terrorist Attacks Upon the United States, better known as the 9/11 Commission – almost did not happen. Aware of the possible political jeopardy posed by an independent inquiry, the Bush administration and Republican leaders in Congress initially opposed the creation of an independent commission and only begrudgingly established one in the face of an effective campaign mounted by the families of the victims.

Despite being 'set up to fail',[2] as its chairman, Thomas Kean, former Republican governor of New Jersey, put it, the 9/11 Commission found innovative and effective ways to draw attention to its work and garnish support for its recommendations. In contrast to the typical fate of most commissions and reform efforts, the 9/11 Commission's final report had an enormous public impact and turned out to be 'a catalyst for the landmark legislation to reform the U.S. intelligence community' (Falkenrath 2004/05: 188). In December 2004, President George W. Bush signed the Intelligence Reform and Terrorism Prevention Act into law.

This chapter aims to explain how and why this commission succeeded whereas so many others did not. To shed light on the 9/11 Commission's origins, goals, limitations, failings, accomplishments and consequences, we apply three distinct analytical prisms: (1) the learning imperative, (2) the logic of realpolitik and (3) the symbolic perspective.

We set out by addressing the 9/11 Commission's impact. In the following three sections, we delve deeper into postcrisis inquiries in general and the 9/11 Commission in particular through the prisms of our three perspectives – learning, realpolitik and symbolic meaning making. The chapter's concluding section contains final reflections and considers whether any general insights into the nature of postcrisis politics and reform efforts can be drawn from our analysis.

---

[2] Kean's quote is taken from May (2005: 30).

The impact of the 9/11 Commission

Directly after the 9/11 attacks, calls for an independent board of inquiry were initially muted. But as time passed, the 'rally around the flag' effect faded. Leaders, journalists, citizens and, perhaps, most critically, the families of the 9/11 victims demanded to know why the United States did not foresee and do more to forestall the September 11 attacks.

On 27 September 2001, just over 2 weeks after the attacks, U.S. Senator Robert Torricelli called for a board of inquiry, patterned after the post–Pearl Harbor board of inquiry, into what he termed a 'stunning failure' of U.S. intelligence.[3] In February of 2002, the House and Senate intelligence committees announced a joint investigation of the intelligence failures that led to September 11. However, the narrow focus of this inquiry did not satisfy the families of the victims of 9/11. They demanded a broader investigation conducted by an independent commission that would include the role of all relevant agencies, the Congress, and the executive branch. In November 2002 the Congress and the Bush administration agreed to establish an independent commission. On 27 November 2002 President Bush signed into law an act that established the 9/11 Commission.[4]

The impact of a postcrisis commission can be judged according to a variety of criteria. To what extent did its account achieve widespread public recognition and acceptance? Did its findings and recommendations spark public debate? Was accountability established and were the responsible parties sanctioned? Did the recommendations spur substantive policy change?

In fulfilling its fact-finding mission and producing a history of September 11, the 9/11 Commission and its eighty-member staff did a prodigious amount of work and their efforts provide a gold mine of material and information on this epoch in U.S. history. The commission produced seventeen staff statements and two monographs; on 22 July 2004, it issued its final report. The 567-page final report, which included 116 pages of meticulously documented footnotes, devoted 11 of its 13 chapters to the history of 9/11 and concluded with 2 chapters of recommendations. The commission examined more than

---

[3] CNN online, 27 September 2001 and 'For a 'Pearl Harbor' Inquiry,' R. Torricelli, Washington Post, 17 February 2002: B07.
[4] Intelligence Authorization Act for Fiscal Year 2003, Public Law 107–306, title VI, 107th Cong., 2d sess. 27 November 2002.

2.5 million documents and interviewed more than 1,200 individuals in ten countries.[5] Taking advantage of a deep documentary base of classified material and full access to senior policy makers, the 9/11 Commission produced a historical document that was comprehensive and credible: a symbolic and scholarly success. As Charles Perrow (2005: 99) wrote in his review of the final report: 'The staff was incredible; this is top-notch research'.

The report found that vital intelligence information available within different parts of the U.S. government – primarily the FBI, CIA and NSA – was not properly distributed or shared. Furthermore, the report demonstrates that despite repeated warnings by elements of the intelligence community that Al-Qaeda had both the capacity and the desire to threaten thousands of American lives and that it wanted to pull off a spectacular attack *within* the United States, no coordinated and empowered domestic focus for the problem of catastrophic terrorism was established. The few officials that did take the threat of terrorism seriously, such as Richard Clarke, had a difficult time establishing a universal awareness and acceptance of radical Islamic terrorism in general and Al-Qaeda and Bin Laden in particular as top-tier threats to U.S. security.[6]

The panel's final report also determined that the analytical methods developed after Pearl Harbor to institutionalise the practice of imagination and avoid surprise attacks had not been adapted and had fallen into disuse. As a result, the intelligence community and the responsible authorities were insensitive to the warnings that were produced and were unable to systematically process and interpret the direction successive terrorist incidents were taking (9/11 Commission 2004: 346). The staff and commissioners could not explain to themselves 'why options that seemed obvious on the afternoon of 9/11', such as taking aggressive military action on Bin Laden's terrorist training camps and planning for terrorist attacks using airplanes as weapons, had not been the subject of serious staff work, planning or policy in either the Clinton or Bush administrations (May and Zelikow 2005: 209). This

---

[5] 9/11 Commission 2004: xv. Full transcripts of the testimony given under oath, along with the submitted statements and testimony, from the 160 witnesses that appeared before the commission in its public hearings are available on the commission's website.

[6] 9/11 Commission 2004: 339–350.

led to the report's 'diagnostic finding' that the government had suffered a failure of imagination (May and Zelikow 2005: 209).

In its goal to bring the country together and gain broad-based public support for its account of what happened, the 9/11 Commission clearly succeeded. A survey conducted in July 2004, just prior to the release of the final report, showed that by more than a two-to-one margin, 61 to 24 percent, the American people – Democrats (62 percent) and Republicans (61 percent) alike – approved of the job that the commission had done.[7]

The report immediately stimulated debate and inspired Congress to take the unusual step of holding hearings on its recommendations during its August recess. The report was released as the presidential campaign was heating up and both candidates, Democratic challenger John Kerry and Republican George W. Bush, lauded the report and publicly endorsed the commission's recommendations.

The 'holy-writ status' achieved by the 9/11 report, the 9/11 commissioners' high profile and vocal support for reform, the lobbying by several 9/11 victims' family groups, fallout from the intelligence failures regarding Iraq's WMD programs and the intense media coverage of the 9/11 panel's report[8] generated momentum for overhauling the intelligence community (Posner 2005: 57; Zegart 2005: 109). This groundswell of support for reform culminated with the successful passage of the Intelligence Reform and Terrorism Prevention Act, which President Bush signed into law in December 2004.[9] In light of the Pentagon's fierce opposition and the White House's ambivalence towards the bill,[10] the intelligence reform act would have likely been derailed and defeated if not for the strong backing of the 9/11 Commission and several 9/11 victims' family groups. This historic achievement

---

[7] The Pew Research Center. Survey report: http://people-press.org/ reports/display.php3?ReportID=219.
[8] Zegart's (2005: 109) analysis of media coverage found that the 9/11 Commission received greater national television news coverage than the war in Iraq between July and the passage of the Intelligence Reform and Terrorist Prevention Act in December 2004.
[9] The act created a Director of National Intelligence (DNI) to head the entire intelligence community and a national counterterrorism center. As the first DNI, it is up to John D. Negroponte to establish how this new system will work in practice.
[10] 'Republicans in charge: A steamroller that may lose its steam,' T. Purdum, New York Times, 28 November 2004: section 4, p. 1.

is especially impressive when one considers the multitude of previous efforts to reorganise the intelligence community that had come to naught since it was established by the National Security Act of 1947.[11] In the time that elapsed from the end of the Cold War to the September 11 attacks, six bipartisan blue-ribbon commissions, three government reviews and three think tank task forces recommended extensive intelligence reform with almost no effect (Zegart 2005: 85–6; Fessenden 2005: 107).

Making sense of the 9/11 commission: three perspectives

If one was to examine the public rhetoric and the legislative language that established the commission, one might conclude that the 9/11 Commission was simply a rational response to the need to learn lessons from the tragic events of that day. The 9/11 Commission's explicit purpose closely corresponds to what a *learning perspective* would predict: the provision of a comprehensive account of what went wrong in order to avoid future terrorist attacks. Politicians and government officials often emphasise the role of commissions in drawing lessons from dramatic events. Public statements, founding legislation and commission mission statements invariably make explicit the goal of learning.

A contrasting and far more cynical interpretation of what motivates the establishment of postcrisis inquiries is found in the *realpolitik perspective*. It stresses how commissions can be used to postpone difficult decisions on urgent issues or serve as mechanisms to provide cover for (deflect blame) or to attack (pin blame on) responsible officials and current power holders (cf. Platt 1971; Lipsky and Olsen 1977; Boin et al. 2005: 99–105).

A third view of postcrisis commissions – the *symbolic perspective* – focuses on the need for the appearance of a fair and rational procedure. After a traumatic episode there is a need to demonstrate that problems can be diagnosed, responsibility can be assigned and wisdom can be gained. A neutral, dispassionate interpretive authority, in the form of a commission made up of objective experts and wise men, provides a ritualised and recognised course of action to accomplish these goals (Boin et al. 2005: 86 and 109–110). We now consider the impact of the 9/11 Commission with the aid of each of our perspectives.

---

[11] For a history of intelligence reorganization proposals from 1949 to 2004, see Best (2004).

Commissions as fact-finding mechanisms and learning devices

Once the acute phase of a crisis subsides it is common that a shroud of uncertainty remains: What went wrong? How could it happen? How well did the responsible officials cope? And what should we do to prevent this from happening in the future? The creation of ad hoc commissions provides a means for answering these questions. In principle, commissions allow policy makers access to knowledge and expertise that may not be available in their own bureaucracies. They offer an alternative, and seemingly objective (as they are not hindered by prior organisational biases and constraints), mechanism for exposing problems and suggesting reforms. By providing an impartial appraisal of what happened and converting specific knowledge and expertise into recommendations to improve governmental performance, they hold the promise of creating 'usable knowledge' and enhancing the government's problem-solving capacity (Wheare 1955; Wraith and Lamb 1971; Lindblom and Cohen 1979; Stone 1994).[12]

The notion of commissions as 'learning devices' concentrates on their ability to generate suitable solutions to social problems through the use of a positivist and functionalist methodology and process. It is generally the most overt and manifest purpose of commissions, and much advocated in the literature that holds a predominantly technocratic view of government (Clokie and Robinson 1937). Driven by the idea that generating new knowledge provides a way to improve society, this perspective promotes a rather optimistic view of the capabilities of government (Bovens and 't Hart 1996).

Seen from this perspective, the work of commissions entails two important activities. First, they contribute to the collection of information about the causes of a crisis, a process that we may refer to as fact finding. Second, they engage in lesson drawing (Daft and Weick 1984; Huber 1991; Crossan et al. 1999). Whereas fact finding is merely descriptive, lesson drawing involves deriving inferences from those descriptive facts. The essence of lesson drawing ultimately lies in the diagnosis and explanation of those descriptive patterns, which ideally results in the development of a conceptual scheme concerning the causes of problems (cause–effect explanations) and possible ways to solve them (means–ends explanations). These 'lessons' are not options

---

[12] This view on the role of commissions is closely related to the concept of organizational learning (Cangelosi and Dill 1965, Fiol and Lyles 1985, Levitt and March 1988; Argyris and Schön 1996; Crossan et al. 1999).

to be decided in political terms but rather straightforward 'recommendations' for taking immediate action.

The 9/11 commission as a learning device

In the aftermath of the 9/11 terrorist acts, politicians publicly displayed their indignation and expressed severe criticism of the government's performance. Both Republicans and Democrats denounced intelligence and security agencies for their part in failing to secure the country, even though, at that time, no one understood precisely what had gone wrong.

The goal of learning is prominent and explicit in the legal mandate and official purpose of the 9/11 Commission. The act that established the commission required it to 'identify, review, and evaluate the lessons learned from the terrorist attacks of September 11 2001, regarding the structure, coordination, management policies, and procedures of the Federal Government ... '.[13] The commission's official remit was sweeping. The act directed it to look into 'any relevant legislation, Executive order, regulation, plan, policy, practice, or procedure' including those relating to intelligence agencies, law enforcement agencies, immigration and border control, the flow of assets to terrorist organisations, commercial aviation, the role of congressional oversight and resource allocation, and all other areas deemed relevant by the commission for its inquiry.[14] This meant that, in contrast to the Congressional Joint Inquiry, which limited its investigation to the intelligence community, both the Congress and the White House would fall within the scope of the 9/11 Commission's work. Furthermore, the commission was given robust powers to pursue these goals. It was afforded subpoena power to compel testimony, documents and evidence and was authorised to secure needed information directly from federal agencies, including the executive branch.[15]

In a nightly news interview, Vice-Chairman Lee Hamilton provided a succinct summary of how the 9/11 commissioners saw their mission: 'the mandate is to get all the information we can, which will help us do our job, to tell the story of 9/11 and to make recommendations to the

[13] Intelligence Authorization Act for Fiscal Year 2003, Public Law 107–306, title VI, 107th Cong., 2d sess. 27 November 2002, 116 Stat. 2410.
[14] Ibid., 116 Stat. 2409.
[15] Ibid., 116 Stat. 2410–2411.

American people so that they're safer'.[16] Thus, the 9/11 Commission publicly defined its work and framed its efforts as fact finding in the pursuit of drawing lessons. In their fidelity to learning, they eschewed the assignment of individual blame as a distraction to this objective (9/11 Commission 2004: xvi).

Bush reiterated the learning theme and his support of the panel's work in a radio address delivered at a time when the commission was in the process of holding a series of highly dramatic public hearings: 'For the past year, the 11 September Commission has met to examine the facts surrounding the terrorist attack on our nation. I look forward to the commission's report, and I expect it to contain important recommendations for preventing future attacks'.[17]

Bush's remarks reflect the standard justification that we often see when ad hoc bodies of inquiry are set up in the wake of a crisis. Yet there are more than a few reasons to doubt that leaders are always motivated by or committed to the noble ambitions they publicly profess or that these ambitions will actually be fulfilled. The history of postcrisis commissions reminds us that the rhetoric of learning rarely translates into the corrective courses of action envisioned in this learning perspective.

To explain the impact of the 9/11 Commission, therefore, we need additional explanations. This becomes even more apparent when we realise that the 'lessons learned' were not the best received part of the report. Whereas the report was hailed for its 'uncommonly lucid' historical sections (Posner 2004) and its 'dispassionate marshaling of the facts' (Drew 2004), the commission's analysis and advice were not as universally well received. Some have questioned the extent to which it actually learned the right lessons (Falkenrath 2004–05; Posner 2005). The final report's recommendations can be subjected to at least three types of criticism.

First, the recommendations are not always grounded in the empirical findings (Posner 2005: 12). According to Falkenrath, the 'commission makes no real effort to marshal the empirical evidence so laboriously assembled in the body of its report to support its case for reorganizing

---

[16] The NewsHour, 11 February 2004 (NewsHour transcript, available at: www.pbs.org/newshour/bb/terrorism/jan-june04/commission_02-11.html).

[17] President's Radio Address, Office of the Press Secretary, 17 April 2004 (available at: www.whitehouse.gov/news/releases/2004/04/20040417.html).

the intelligence community'. Second, some of the proposals, especially those dealing with 'strategy', are rather vague and amount to little more than empty bromides.[18] Third, even if one accepts the commission's diagnosis that the organisational fragmentation and maladapted organisational structure of the U.S. security apparatus were to blame for the problems in cooperation, coordination and policy attainment the report documents, it does not necessarily follow that their proposal for greater centralisation of the government's intelligence activities is the best solution for the security challenges facing the US.[19] A centralised, hierarchical intelligence system entails costs to diversity and competition. A structure that is unable to provide a menu of diverse opinions or voices of dissent runs the risk of 'groupthink' intelligence failures.[20] Moreover, as a number of commentators (see for example Bracken 2001: 181–4; Betts 2001: 155; Kam 1988) have warned, hasty wholesale reforms often create new problems while failing to adequately redress past deficiencies.

In his critique of the 9/11 Commission's policy recommendations, Posner questions the wisdom of even trying to draw lessons from the report's investigative findings. According to Posner (2005: 6):

To combine an investigation of the attacks (the causes, the missed opportunities, and the responses) with recommendations for preventing future attacks is the same mistake as combining intelligence and policy. The means believed available for solving a problem influence how the problem is understood and described. The commission's belief that the intelligence structure should be revamped predisposed it to find that the structure bore responsibility for failing to prevent the 9/11 attacks, whether it did or not.

---

[18] Consider, for example, the recommendation on identifying terrorist sanctuaries: 'We should reach out, listen to, and work with other countries that can help' (9/11 Commission 2004: 367). Or the recommendation to engage the struggle of ideas: 'The U.S. government must define what the message is, what it stands for. We should offer an example of moral leadership in the world, committed to treat people humanely, abide by the rule of law, and be generous and caring to our neighbors' (9/11 Commission 2004: 367).

[19] Cordesman (2004: 5) makes a similar remark as he criticises the recommended establishment of an intelligence czar: 'the 9/11 Commission fails to explain why a series of complex collection and analytic processes are going to be better simply by changing the top of the organizational chart'.

[20] The intelligence failure regarding Iraq's WMD programs, for example, exhibits elements of the problem of groupthink and an absence of meaningful dissent (cf. 't Hart 1994). The new more centralised US intelligence structure may in fact exacerbate rather than alleviate this type of problem.

The logic of realpolitik: the contested nature of postcrisis inquiries

Learning and reform are often seen as golden concepts that, at least in principle, everyone can support (Seidman 1980: 126; Wildavsky 1984: 245). The realpolitik perspective brings to mind that others may take a less sanguine view of the situation. Some participants may be leery of a postcrisis commission; they may be frightened of the negative consequences and political downside of such an effort and see it as a threat to cherished interests. As a result, the postcrisis process can entail issues of extreme political contestation.

The realpolitik approach takes seriously the fact that government is not a monolith. It takes into account the variety of political players and societal stakeholders that are involved in the postcrisis process and holds that these various participants act according to their own interpretations and interests. It recognises that the large number of organisations and often competitively interacting individuals that make up the government have a profound impact on policy. From this perspective, crisis outcomes are seen as the end result of competing individual, institutional and bureaucratic interests and preferences (Allison 1971; Halperin 1974; March and Olsen 1983; Stern and Verbeek 1998; Allison and Zelikow 1999; Parker and Stern 2002; Zegart 2005).

For presidents, legislators, specific agencies, individual bureaucrats and groups outside of government – all with their own interests and preferences – inquiry commissions become venues in which they can pursue their own agendas in the postcrisis political process. As arenas of opportunity, postcrisis inquiries can become garbage-can collections of difficult issues, competing combinations of political players, proponents and opponents of change, problems and solutions, and policy choices (Cohen et al. 1972; March and Olsen 1983: 286).

This perspective predicts that the investigatory machinery used in the postcrisis phase will become an object of contestation and the method selected will be infused with political implications and issues of control. With regards to congressional investigations, the party in power enjoys enormous prerogatives regarding whether or not to launch an investigation and over issues such as the form and focus of an inquiry. Presidents are unlikely to establish commissions to investigate crises that they will be implicated as being responsible for or empower a commission to investigate the presidency itself.

In contrast to presidential commissions and congressional inquiries, truly independent, bipartisan commissions – while by no means immune from partisan bias or battles – are less susceptible to political manipulation or partisan influence. From a realpolitik point of view, it is also clear that regardless of the form an inquiry takes, the executive branch is likely to resist investigations that target it.

The struggle over the 9/11 commission

The realpolitik perspective helps us see that the impact of the 9/11 Commission was anything but self-evident. It best explains the battle over its creation and the subsequent battles fought by the commission on various fronts after it was formed. Moreover, it suggests that the impact of this commission could easily have been modest, relegating its report to dusty library shelves.

The 9/11 Commission was established only after a drawn out political struggle. It was not until 14 months after the attacks on the Twin Towers and the Pentagon that an independent panel was created. The Bush administration, in particular, opposed the formation of an independent commission. It argued that a congressional joint inquiry into the attacks was more than adequate and that an independent blue-ribbon commission was an unnecessary distraction from the war on terror (Whitney 2004: xxi; Falkenrath 2004–05: 170).

On 14 February 2002, as an alternative to Senators Joseph Lieberman (D-CT) and John McCain's (R-AZ) December 2001 legislation for an independent commission, Senator Bob Graham (D-FL) and Congressman Porter Goss (R-FL) announced a joint inquiry by the Senate and House Select Committees on Intelligence. Their inquiry would focus specifically on the role of the intelligence agencies. The Bush administration took the position that this investigation would be sufficient.

The families of victims insisted that a broader inquiry was needed. Public pressure and an effective lobbying campaign persuaded enough House Republicans to join Democrats and produce a majority vote on 25 July 2002 to set up an independent commission. Still the White House continued to resist. The families were unrelenting, however, and the need for a thorough review gained momentum as the joint inquiry's investigation produced embarrassing revelations about missed warning signals and coordination failures by government agencies. On

20 September 2002, the Bush administration finally yielded to the idea of allowing a bipartisan independent inquiry. It took another 2 months of intense negotiations before the White House reached an agreement with Congress on the conditions under which the investigation would be conducted.

Congressional and administration negotiators agreed that a ten-member commission would be equally divided between five Republican appointees and five Democratic appointees. The president would name the chairman and the Democratic congressional leadership would pick the vice-chairman. Thomas H. Kean was appointed as the commission's chair, after Bush's first choice, Henry A. Kissinger, resigned as he refused to unveil a potential conflict of interest and make public the clients in his consulting firm.[21]

The new chairman was under no illusions that his would be an easy task. According to Kean: 'If you want something to fail you take a controversial topic and appoint five people from each party. You make sure they are appointed by the most partisan people from each party – the leaders of the party. And, just to make sure, let's ask the commission to finish the report during the most partisan period of time – the presidential election season'.[22]

Indeed, the 9/11 Commission was forced to fight a series of bruising, time-consuming battles with the White House and other federal departments and agencies on a variety of fronts. Kean and his lieutenant Hamilton did not shrink from the fight and proved skilled in the arts of realpolitik. They adeptly brandished the power resources at their disposal – the threat of their subpoena power, issuing subpoenas when needed, deploying the families of the victims, and the media – in the furtherance of the commission's mission (Kean and Hamilton 2006: 57–102). Although they did not win every battle and compromised on a number of issues, their ability to achieve the panel's aims in the face of opposition contributed mightily to the 9/11 Commission's ultimate impact.

Among the challenging conditions faced by the commission was the lack of sufficient time or financial resources to carry out its work. The

[21] Former Senator George Mitchell, the original vice chairman, citing the same reason as Kissinger, also withdrew. He was replaced by Lee Hamilton.
[22] Kean's quote is taken from Ernest May's 'memoir of the 9/11 Commission' (2005: 30). May served the commission as a senior adviser.

administration initially wanted the commission to publish its findings within a year, as to prevent the report from interfering with Bush's 2004 reelection campaign (Whitney 2004: xxii). In the negotiations over the legislation that set up the investigation, the deadline was stretched to a mere 18 months. As the commission went about its work, it became clear that more time would be required. However, when the commission asked for a 60-day extension in January 2004 – 'to make sure our work is credible and thorough' – the President and House Speaker Dennis Hastert (R-IL) turned down the request.[23] Following a public outcry, however, first Bush and then the even more reluctant Hastert reversed their position and provided an extension until July 2004.[24]

The commission's initial budget, a paltry $3 million, was inadequate and extremely poor compared with past commissions. This shoestring funding can be contrasted with the lavish funding received by other full-blown investigations, such as those into the explosion of the *Columbia* space shuttle and the Clintons' Whitewater affair, each of which had budgets that reached up to $50 million. Unsurprisingly, 4 months down the road, Kean had to call for an additional $11 million. After the White House resentfully agreed to an additional $9 million, Congress eventually upped this sum and the commission was granted $12 million in added funding.[25]

The struggle with the Bush administration over access to sensitive documents was particularly intense. Although the commission was authorised to receive such information, the administration initially blocked access to the Presidential Daily Briefs (PDBs). Alberto Gonzales, the White House counsel, felt the demand to see the PDBs infringed on executive privilege and feared that the commission would leak information to embarrass the president (Kean and Hamilton 2006: 93). After the commission threatened to subpoena the White House, a complicated compromise was eventually worked out. The compromise

---

[23] '9/11 Panel unlikely to get later deadline', D. Eggen, Washington Post, 19 January 2004: A09.

[24] 'Bush in reversal, supports more time for 9/11 inquiry', P. Shenon, New York Times, 5 February 2004: A21; 'Hastert, in reversal, backs extension for 9/11 panel, P. Shenon and C. Hulse, 28 February 2004: A8.

[25] '9/11 Panel to receive more money', D. Eggen, Washington Post, 29 March 2003: A4.

allowed Executive Director Philip Zelikow (R), Commissioner Jamie Gorelick (D), Kean and Hamilton to review the full run of PDBs (9/11 Commission 2004: 533; May 2005: 32).[26]

The commission's desire to interview Bush's closest advisors was another source of contention (Kean and Hamilton 2006: 105–06). The White House asserted that it would not allow serving presidential advisors to give sworn public testimony. Claming executive privilege, it initially refused to allow National Security Advisor Condoleezza Rice to publicly testify but finally had to bow to public pressure.[27] It was under questioning during Rice's testimony that the title of the damning PDB, 'Bin Laden Determined to Strike in U.S.', given to Bush on 6 August 2001, while he was vacationing at his ranch, was made public.

The president also tried to place strict limits on his own interview with the commission. The White House demanded that Bush not be forced to testify under oath and be allowed to appear together with Vice President Cheney. Bush and Cheney finally agreed to a private interview, but they did not testify under oath, nor were tape recorders allowed.

The commission encountered resistance from other quarters as well. As predicted by the realpolitik model, a potential agent for change, like the 9/11 Commission, will attract opposition by threatened status quo interests and groups that will fight for their own protection. The Pentagon, the Federal Aviation Administration (FAA) and the North American Aerospace Defense Command (NORAD) were especially uncooperative. To counter FAA and NORAD foot dragging over requested material, subpoenas had to be handed out (Kean and Hamilton 2006: 84–8).

The 9/11 Commission lost the battle with the CIA over access to Al-Qaeda detainees. CIA Director George Tenet refused to let the commission directly question key detainees involved in the September 11 plot, including, most significantly, the plot's mastermind Khalid Sheikh

---

[26] Although the commission had asked to look at 360 PDBs, dating back to 1998, at first the White House only permitted them to see 24 of them. It later produced a summary of the PDBs from the Clinton and Bush administration related to Al-Qaeda. Eventually, Zelikow, Gorelick, Kean and Hamilton were allowed to review the 'full run of PDBs' (May 2005: 32).

[27] 'Bush allows Rice to testify on 9/11 in a public session', P. Shenon and E. Bumiller, New York Times, 31 March 2004: A1.

Mohammed. Helping the 9/11 Commission simply was not a top priority for the CIA; it had its own turf and interests to protect.[28]

The commission had to ward off attacks on its integrity mounted by congressional Republicans. House Majority Leader Tom DeLay (R-TX) denounced the panel in April of 2004 saying that 'the politicization of the commission undermines the war effort and endangers our troops' (quoted in Fessenden 2005: 110). Congressman Jack Kingston (R-GA) questioned the panel's motives and tried to discredit it as a 'reunion of political has-beens who haven't had face time since *Seinfeld* was a weekly show' (Fessenden 2005: 110). One of the most serious attacks came in the form of an attempt to force commissioner Gorelick, a democratic commissioner and former deputy attorney general during the Clinton administration, to step down and 'testify on her alleged role in building the 'wall' between intelligence and law enforcement in the mid-1990s' (Fessenden 2005: 110). Attorney General John Ashcroft took the opportunity to level these charges and impugn Gorelick during his public testimony before the commission.[29] This gambit failed and the commission's final report debunked the charges.[30]

Partisan battles broke out concerning the charges made against the Bush administration by former top counterterrorism official Richard Clarke in his public testimony and his book, *Against All Enemies*. The fact that Clarke had blasted Bush for neglecting to prioritise terrorism on a popular television program just 3 days prior to his public appearance before the panel made his testimony particularly dramatic. The questioning of Clarke during his public hearing broke down along partisan lines.[31] The White House mounted a concerted campaign to discredit him. In fact, the need to publicly rebut Clarke was one of the factors that led the administration to reverse its position and allow Rice to testify publicly before the panel.

In sum, while Bush told the public that he wished the commission would learn important lessons and hailed its work as 'important for

---

[28] It has been speculated that the CIA did not want the commissioners to see the conditions in which the detainees were being held or find out about the interrogation methods being used – methods that reportedly included controversial coercive techniques, such as 'waterboarding', which in many eyes are tantamount to torture (Drew 2004: 6).

[29] John Ashcroft testimony, Tenth Public Hearing, Tuesday, 13 April 2004.

[30] 9/11 Commission 2004: 539.

[31] Richard A. Clarke testimony, Eighth Public Hearing, Wednesday, 24 March 2004.

future administrations',[32] his administration repeatedly tried to stall and impede the investigation. Although the stated reasons for establishing the 9/11 Commission reflect noble ambitions, the actions of a variety of actors, including the president's own administration, suggest other interests and priorities were at play for many participants. This perspective, in short, helps us understand just how remarkable the impact of the 9/11 Commission really was. The next perspective illuminates the main source of this success.

The symbolic dimension of meaning making: postcrisis commissions as interpretive authorities

This perspective highlights the symbolic aspects of postcrisis commissions and their role as interpretive authorities (cf. Ashforth 1990; Stone 1994). It suggests that the impact of postcrisis commissions is related to their capacity to reassure the public and to help restore or maintain confidence in public institutions (Lasswell 1935; Edelman 1985; Dye 1987; Edelman 1988). In this perspective, postcrisis inquiries serve a deeper purpose than formulating lessons or functioning as a device for damage control. They play a vital role in the 'meaning-making process', which helps the members of a stricken polity come to terms with the adversity encountered. This process, in turn, facilitates the return of a sense of order.

In this perspective, a crisis is defined as a 'breakdown of familiar symbolic frameworks legitimating the pre-existing socio-political order' ('t Hart 1993: 39). After a traumatic crisis or acute policy failure, governments may experience sharp declines in legitimacy. As a result of poor performances – sudden and dramatic failures of policy, negligence, or incompetence – large segments of society may begin to question the past, present and future performance of public officials and institutions. If the public's confidence goes into free fall, the government's ability to govern or stay in power is jeopardised (Boin and 't Hart 2000; Alink et al. 2001). If people suddenly realise that the government cannot be relied upon to secure their safety or provide for their well-being, the authority and functioning of public institutions will be gravely damaged.

[32] 'President Signs 911 Commission Bill', Office of the Press Secretary, 27 November 2002 (available at: www.whitehouse.gov/news/releases/2002/11/20021127-1.html).

Commissions can play an important role in relegitimating public institutions and avoiding a collapse in public confidence or, if necessary, restoring confidence in government. They do so in two key ways. First, the very act of establishing a commission and the public spectacle of an investigative commission carrying out its work are potent symbols of a functioning government. Second, in their role as interpretive authorities, commissions provide an accepted ritualised procedure for making sense of traumatic events, assigning responsibility,[33] discussing policy matters and proposing corrective solutions in a way that contributes to the development of meaning. This meaning-making process sustains and validates society's core values and institutions.

The formation of a public inquiry can thus be an important symbolic act in itself (Sheriff 1983). In the wake of a crisis, paralysis and admissions of impotence are unacceptable; as March and Olsen (1983: 290) put it, 'leaders are expected to act'. The creation of a postcrisis commission is an excellent way to symbolise meaningful action. Commissions of inquiry structure and consolidate varying opinions into one dominant and legitimate interpretation of the problem, a task that can have legitimising effects and possibly contribute to social harmony. Those directly affected by a crisis may find comfort in an authoritative and satisfying reconstruction of the 'facts' that brings closure to the crisis. As a result, the process of investigation and consultation can represent a form of catharsis for those directly involved in a crisis (cf. Peay 1996).

In their capacity as interpretive authorities, commissions provide a time-honoured way to deal with painful societal episodes and specify a way in which policy matters can be properly discussed (Ashforth 1990). They do so through the creation and deployment of symbols and language (Edelman 1988). Official inquiry reports are mainly written for public consumption and shape official discourse (Burton and Carlen 1979). Hence, their main contribution is directed at 'reaching understanding in a social context' and reducing the sense of crisis (de Haven-Smith 1988: 85). By providing an authoritative interpretation of events and corrective recommendations, the circumstances

---

[33] The restoration of confidence can also be initiated through accountability procedures in which commissions may play a pivotal role. They can be appointed to find out what happened, why and, more importantly, who should be held responsible (Fortune and Peters 1995; Elliott and McGuinness 2002).

surrounding the crisis are demystified and the public and government can move on with optimism about doing better in the future (Lipsky and Olsen 1977: 444; Stone 1994).

The Bush administration's symbolic needs and motives

From the realpolitik perspective, the White House's repeated expressions of public support for the 9/11 Commission, its willingness to grant unprecedented access to materials it did not see as encroaching on executive privilege,[34] and its public endorsement of the 9/11 panel's conclusions and recommendations seem puzzling. Of course, this behaviour could be painted simply as a tactical response to cut the losses of a losing political hand. However, such an explanation, which sees Bush's actions solely as cynical attempts to dupe the public and fool voters, is incomplete (cf. March and Olsen 1983: 290). It fails to recognise how the Bush administration's symbolic needs both placed limits on the extent it could move to obstruct the 9/11 Commission while at the same time created rewards for offering support.

For example, to publicly oppose and block the creation of an independent commission would have made the White House part of the problem of resolving questions about what went wrong on September 11. Doing so would have been associated with inaction and obstructionism, while publicly endorsing the commission was emblematic of leadership and the possibility of resolution and renewal.

Moreover, by publicly embracing the 9/11 Commission, Bush could accomplish a number of important symbolic ends. He could express concern and sympathy for the victims of 9/11. He could show that he and the victims' families were working together rather than at cross purposes. He could demonstrate that he was once again taking decisive action to reduce U.S. vulnerabilities. He could portray his support of the commission as the latest of the many initiatives he had already taken to make the country more secure, such as creating the Department of Homeland Security. Finally, he could express hope and confidence for doing better in the future. In short, regardless of the purity of

---

[34] According to May (2005: 32), with the notable exception of the dispute over access to the PDBs, 'the White House was much more helpful to the commission than the media perceived' and, as far as he could determine, 'we were allowed to see every document the White House staff could turn up'.

his motives, symbolic requirements compelled Bush to provide both rhetorical and substantive support for the 9/11 Commission.

The 9/11 commission: achieving the status of a trusted interpretive authority

To avoid the obscurity and irrelevance that typically meet the work of most commissions, the 9/11 Commission knew it would need to be seen as fair, transparent, comprehensive and above politics. The commission actively sought creative ways to enhance public recognition of its work. To that end, the commission held 19 days of hearings and took public testimony from 160 witnesses.

The 9/11 Commission embraced its role as an interpretive authority both as a virtue and a strategy. It sought to create a shared understanding and make sense of the events prior to, during and shortly after the attacks on the Twin Towers and the Pentagon. Senior advisor Ernest May (2005: 31), who could be described as the panel's house historian, writes that Kean, Hamilton and Executive Director Philip Zelikow made a conscious decision to produce a 'professional-quality narrative history' to tell the story of 9/11. In Kean's words, what the panel wanted was 'a report that our grandchildren can take off the shelf in fifty years and say, "This is what happened"' (quoted in May 2005:31).

Hamilton was less devoted to writing history for history's sake. For him the commission's recommendations were of paramount importance. He thought that producing an agreed history was a sound means to his ends. According to May (2005: 31), Hamilton 'saw at once that couching the report as a history might at least delay a partisan split within the commission, for the commissioners could begin by debating the facts of the story rather than their conclusions or recommendations'. May's account of the panel's work provides great insight to how it approached the final report and shows that it took its role as an interpretive authority seriously. As May sees it, 'the report was dedicated to the idea that a genuine concern for communicating an accurate picture of our reality to future generations may allow us to transcend the passions of the moment' (May 2005: 31).

May's quote also speaks to another important symbolic dimension of the 9/11 Commission's role: the need to appear neutral and eschew politics (Seidman 1980: 10–11; March and Olsen 1983: 290). If the panel's investigation was perceived as either a whitewash or a witch-hunt, it findings would be of little value. For the 9/11 Commission to succeed, it would need to rise above the poisonous partisan political atmosphere that presently characterise American politics. To that end, the 9/11 Commission made a concerted, vigorous and largely success-ful attempt to transcend partisanship. Although partisan behaviour seeped out at times, especially at some points during the public hear-ings in the form of confrontational exchanges between witnesses and commissioners (Whitney 2004; Drew 2004), the commissioners con-stantly preached the gospel of bipartisanship and, for the most part, backed it up in deed. The end result was a unanimously endorsed final report.

This did entail costs. Unanimity probably could not have been achieved without muting the interpretation of some sensitive topics and avoiding the direct apportioning of individual blame, especially con-cerning Clinton and Bush (Drew 2004; Posner 2004, May 2005; May and Zelikow 2005). One of the commissioners, Richard Ben-Veniste, explained that the commission was very aware of the necessity to reach agreement: 'There are folks out there who wanted to see this commis-sion devolve into a partisan food fight, but we were determined not to have that happen'.[35]

The commission's strategy of communication was designed to max-imise its credibility and gain support for its findings. The staging of public hearings generated massive media attention and enhanced the perception that the commission was honouring its stated intention to be as transparent as possible. These hearings functioned as a form of civic education, symbolically providing access to the inner workings of the government and producing crucial information that helped shape public opinion (cf. March and Olsen 1983: 288). The commission-ers also commented on their work in the media while the commission was still deliberating, a practice that further enhanced the panel's pub-lic visibility. Especially unusual for investigations of this kind was the commission's decision to publish staff reports in advance of the hear-ings. A total of seventeen staff statements – covering subjects such as aviation security, counterterrorism, threat warnings and responses, the

[35] 'The chairman; Unifier of partisan commission members', P. Shenon, New York Times, 22 July 2004: A19.

performance of the intelligence community and homeland defense – were released prior to the final report.[36] These statements, which contained genuine revelations, received widespread media coverage and sparked discussion and debate. Moreover, the staff statements helped contribute to the development of a common commission voice and, since they had to be cleared in advance for public release, 'the process also helped measurably to induce the White House, the CIA, and others to allow publication of the final report without prolonged battles over classification issues' (May 2005: 33).

The final report also was designed for maximum public impact. By producing a well-written report that targeted a mass audience and using a commercial publisher to make it immediately and widely accessible, the *9/11 Commission Report* became a publishing sensation and bestseller. The report presented an 'uncommonly lucid, even riveting, narrative [. . .] free from bureaucratese' (Posner 2004). Although the commission admittedly did not uncover every detail and included several compromises, its findings were remarkably forthright. By delivering an authoritative and vivid tableau of the events leading up to and through September 11, the commission provided the public with a virtual first-hand experience of what had occurred (cf. Brown 2000) and earned widespread acclaim and praise for its work. Publications such as *The Economist, Time, The New Republic* and *The New Yorker*, among others, sang encomiums, hailing the report as a 'masterpiece' and its account as 'novelistically intense'. The report was nominated for a National Book Award and 8 months after its release some 2 million copies had been sold and 6.9 million copies had been downloaded from the commission's website (May 2005: 35).

Finally, by showing a continuing commitment to its cause *after* the publication of the final report, the 9/11 Commission enhanced its credibility even further. Instead of merely 'going public', commissioners were literally 'going to the public' in order to spread the word. Thomas Kean made very clear that he would not allow the report to be ignored:

Our charter expires and we go out of business as a commission. We do not go out of business as people. And all ten of us have decided to keep in touch, to work to implement these recommendations, do everything we can, whether it's testimony or lobbying or speaking or whatever's necessary,

[36] The staff statements are available at www.9-11commission.gov/staff_statements/index.htm#statements.

to let the American people know about these recommendations, know how important they are, our belief that they can save lives, and continue to work as a group long after our charter goes out of existence. And we agreed to meet in a year to determine our progress.[37]

After the 9/11 Commission formally disbanded, the ten commissioners came together to form the '9/11 Public Discourse Project'. The project aimed to 'educate the public on the issue of terrorism and what can be done to make the country safer'.[38] Through the project, the 9/11 Commission lived on as a symbolic public watchdog. In this role it monitored the government's progress with respect to the forty-one recommendations that the 9/11 Commission had made in its final report. As its last act, the project issued a final report that graded the government's performance on all forty-one recommendations as of December 2005. The grades ranged from an 'A-' on terrorist financing efforts, a 'B' for the creation of a Director of National Intelligence, to an 'F' on air passenger prescreening.[39]

A key factor in explaining the commission's impact was its conscious avoidance of making judgements regarding individual responsibility. Rather than singling specific individuals out for blame (no one lost their job over mistakes or failures related to 9/11), the commission zeroed in on institutional, structural and procedural failures particularly in the FBI and CIA.

Critics, such as Falkenrath (2005: 211), have blasted the report for perpetuating a 'no fault' view of governance that sends future officials and those who train them 'exactly the wrong message'. But had the commission attempted to pin blame and make value judgements on exactly which officials were most responsible, it is highly unlikely that all ten commissioners would have signed off and endorsed the final report. Unanimity was key for the commission's two main desiderata: a comprehensive account that would be widely perceived as legitimate and the acceptance of its recommendations. The policy impact of a contested and divided final report likely would have been nil. As May and Zelikow (2005: 208) have noted, 'The fact that five Republicans

---

[37] National Public Radio (transcript), 22 July 2004.
[38] The 9/11 Public Discourse Project, www.9-11pdp.org/.
[39] 'Final Report on 9/11 commission recommendations', 9/11 Public Discourse Project, December 5, 2005, www.9-11pdp.org/press/2005-12-05_report.pdf. In total the ten former commissioners handed out five F's, twelve D's, nine C's, twelve B's, one A-, and two incompletes.

and five Democrats endorsed such a long and complex report without dissent about a single line is important'. In addition to being important, it was symbolically powerful and the commissioners skilfully wielded this power as they pursued the enactment of their recommendations.

Conclusion

With the benefit of hindsight we, can see that past boards of inquiry into national traumas, such as the Pearl Harbor fiasco and the Kennedy assassination, were the beginning – not the end – of the public's, policy makers' and analysts' struggle to understand how such traumatic events could come to pass (e.g. Wohlstetter 1962; Janis 1982; Levite 1987). The wealth of information produced by the 9/11 Commission gives us much to consider and, coupled with probable future revelations, ensures that the 9/11 Commission's report is unlikely to be the last word on the meaning of September 11. However, in contrast to the investigations into Pearl Harbor and Kennedy's death, which were greeted with scepticism by the American public and failed to produce findings that were widely accepted or even legitimate, the 9/11 Commission succeeded in producing a report that was widely seen as authoritative, legitimate and fair. Proponents of intelligence reorganisation, the families of the 9/11 victims and the 9/11 commissioners themselves used the symbolic and political clout generated by the public's favourable reception of the commission's work to help push through a major reform package.

Our analysis of the 9/11 Commission has helped shed light on how and why this unusual outcome came to pass. All three perspectives used here have valuable insights to offer. However, it is the symbolic meaning making dimension of postcrisis commissions, which is often neglected in favour of instrumental accounts that emphasise learning or the political struggle among contending interests, that best helps us understand why the creation of postcrisis inquiries endures as a social practice. Postcrisis commissions have become ritualised and persist because of the key role dispassionate bodies can play in restoring faith in the enterprise of government. Moreover, it this perspective that provides the greatest analytical leverage for understanding the dynamics that allow reform efforts and policy change to trump the forces of realpolitik that tend to stymie dramatic change. If a vivid, indisputable image of a broken system achieves widespread acceptance, and if the proposed solutions are able to capture a high degree of support, it is the *symbolic* imperative to take action that can overcome the inertia and interest groups that typically work against drastic change. The unique status achieved by the 9/11 Commission, its success in capturing the public's imagination and its emblematic standing as a competent, honest broker in an extremely bitter partisan political atmosphere all contributed to its rare political impact.

References

9/11 Commission (National Commission on Terrorist Attacks upon the United States 2004). The 9/11 Commission Report. New York: Norton.

Alink, F., Boin, A. and 't Hart, P. 2001. Institutional crises and reforms in policy sectors: the case of asylum policy in Europe. Journal of European Public Policy 8(2):286–306.

Allison, G. 1971. Essence of decision: explaining the Cuban missile crisis. Boston: Little, Brown.

Allison, G., and Zelikow, P. 1999. Essence of decision: explaining the Cuban missile crisis, 2nd edn. New York: Longman.

Argyris, C., and Schön, D. A. 1996. Organizational learning II: theory, method, and practice. Reading, PA: Addison-Wesley.

Ashforth, A. 1990. Reckoning schemes of legitimation: on commissions of inquiry as power/knowledge forms. Journal of Historical Sociology 3(1):1–22.

Best, R. A. Jr. 2004. Proposals for intelligence reorganization, 1949–2004. Washington, DC: Congressional Research Service (CRS Report RL 32500).

Betts, R. K. 2001. Intelligence test: the limits of prevention. In How did this happen? Terrorism and the new war. Hodge, J. F. Jr. and Rose, G. (eds.). New York: Public Affairs, pp. 145–61.

Boin, A., and 't Hart, P. 2000. Institutional crises and reforms in policy sectors. In Wagenaar, H. C. Government institutions: effects, changes and normative foundations. Boston: Kluwer.

Boin, A., 't Hart, P., Stern, E. and Sundelius, B. 2005. The politics of crisis management: public leadership under pressure. Cambridge, UK: Cambridge University Press.

Bovens, M., and 't Hart, P. 1996. Understanding policy fiascoes. New Brunswick, NJ: Transaction.

Bracken, P. 2001. Rethinking the unthinkable: new priorities for new national security. In Talbott, S. and Chanda, N. (eds.) The age of terror: America and the world after September 11. New York: Basic Books, pp. 171–91.

Brown, A. D. 2000. Making sense of inquiry sensemaking. Journal of Management Studies 37(1):45–75.

Burton, F., and Carlen, P. 1979. Official discourse: on discourse analysis, government publications, ideology and the state. London: Routledge & Kegan Paul.

Cangelosi, V. E., and Dill, W. R. 1965. Organizational learning: observations toward a theory. Administrative Science Quarterly 10(2):175–203.

Clokie, H. M., and Robinson, J. W. 1937. Royal commissions of inquiry: the significance of investigations in British politics. Stanford, CA: Stanford University Press.

Cohen, M. D., March, J. G. and Olsen, J. P. 1972. A garbage can model of organization choice. Administrative Science Quarterly 17(1):1–25.

Cordesman, A. H. 2004. The 9/11 commission report: strengths and weaknesses. Washington, DC: CSIS.

Crossan, M. M., Lane, H. W. and White, R. E. 1999. An organizational learning framework: from intuition to institution. Academy of Management Review 24(3):522–37.

Daft, R. L., and Weick, K. E. 1984. Towards a model of organizations as interpretation systems. Academy of Management Review 9:284–95.

de Haven-Smith, L. 1988. Philosophical critiques of policy analysis: Lindblom, Habermas, and the great society. Gainesville, FL: University of Florida Press.

Drew, E. 2004. Pinning the blame. The New York Review of Books 51(14):6–12.

Dye, T. R. 1987. Understanding public policy. Englewood Cliffs, NJ: Prentice-Hall.

Edelman, M. 1985. Political language and political reality. Political Studies 18(1):10–19.

Edelman, M. 1988. Constructing the political spectacle. Chicago: University of Chicago Press.

Elliott, D., and McGuinness, M. 2002. Public inquiry: panacea or placebo. Journal of Contingencies and Crisis Management 10(1):14–25.

Falkenrath, R. A. 2004–2005. The 9/11 commission report. International Security 29(3):170–90.

Falkenrath, R. A. 2005. Sins of commission? Falkenrath and his critics: the author replies. International Security 29 (4):209–11.

Fessenden, H. 2005. The limits of intelligence reform. Foreign Affairs 84(6):106–20.

Fiol, C. M., and Lyles, M. A. 1985. Organizational learning. Academy of Management Review 10(4):803–13.

Fortune, J., and Peters, G. 1995. Learning from failure. Chichester, UK: John Wiley & Sons.

Halperin, M. H. 1974. Bureaucratic politics and foreign policy. Washington, DC: Brookings.

't Hart, P. 1993. Symbols, rituals and power: the lost dimension of crisis management. Journal of Contingencies and Crisis Management 1(1):36–50.

't Hart, P. 1994. Groupthink in government: a study of small groups and government failure. Baltimore, MD: Johns Hopkins University Press.

Huber, G. P. 1991. Organizational learning: the contributing processes and the literatures. Organization Science 2(1):88–115.

Janis, I. L. 1982. Groupthink: psychological studies of policy decisions and fiascoes, 2nd edn. Boston: Houghton-Mifflin.

Kam, E. 1988. Surprise attack: the victim's perspective. Cambridge, MA: Harvard University Press.

Kean, T. H., and Hamilton, L. H. 2006. Without precedent: the inside story of the 9/11 Commission. New York: Knopf.

Lasswell, H. D. 1935. World politics and personal insecurity. New York: Whittlesey House.

Levite, A. 1987. Intelligence and strategic surprise. New York: Columbia University Press.

Levitt, B., and March, J. G. 1988. Organizational learning. Annual Review of Sociology 14:319–40.

Lindblom, C. E., and Cohen, D. K. 1979. Usable knowledge: social science and social problem solving. New Haven, CT: Yale University Press.

Lipsky, M., and Olsen, D. J. 1977. Commission politics: the processing of racial crisis in America. New Brunswick, NJ: Transaction.

March, J. G., and Olsen, J. P. 1983. Organizing political life: what administrative reorganization tells us about government. The American Political Science Review 77(2):281–96.

May, E. R., and Zelikow, P. D. 2005. Sins of commission? Falkenrath and his critics. International Security 29(4):208–09.

May, E. R. 2005, When government writes history: a memoir of the 9/11 commission. The New Republic (May) 30–5.

Olsen, J. P., and Peters, B. G. (eds.) 1996. Lessons from experience: experiential learning in administrative reforms in eight democracies. Oslo: Scandinavian University Press.

Parker, C. F., and Stern, E. K. 2002. Blindsided? September 11 and the origins of strategic surprise. Political Psychology 23(3):601–30.

Parker, C. F., and Stern, E. K. 2005. Bolt from the blue or avoidable failure? Revisiting September 11 and the origins of strategic surprise. Foreign Policy Analysis 1(3):301–31.

Peay, J. 1996. Inquiries after homicide. London: Duckworth.

Perrow, C. 2005. Organizational or executive failures. Contemporary Sociology 34(2):99–107.

Platt, A. 1971. The politics of riot commissions, 1917–1970: an overview. In Platt, A. (ed.) The politics of riot commissions, 1917–1970: a collection of official reports and critical essays. New York: Macmillan.

Posner, R. A. 2004. The 9/11 report: a dissent. The New York Times Book Review.

Posner, R. A. 2005. Preventing surprise attacks: intelligence reform in the wake of 9/11. Lanham, UK: Rowman & Littlefield.

Seidman, H. 1980. Politics, position and power: the dynamics of federal organization, 3rd edn. New York: Oxford University Press.

Sheriff, P. E. 1983. State theory, social science, and governmental commissions. American Behavioral Scientist 26(5):669–80.

Stern, E., and Verbeek, B. (eds.) 1998. Whither the study of governmental politics in foreign policymaking: a symposium. Mershon International Studies Review 42:205–55.

Stone, B. 1994. Success in public inquiries: an analysis and a case study. In Weller, P. (ed.) Royal commissions and the making of public policy. Melbourne: Macmillan.

Wheare, K. C. 1955. Government by committee. Oxford, UK: Oxford University Press.

Whitney, C. R. 2004. Introduction. In Strasser, S. (ed.) The 9/11 investigations. New York: Public Affairs.

Wildavsky, A. B. 1984. Speaking truth to power: the art and craft of policy analysis. New Brunswick, NJ: Transaction.

Wohlstetter, R. 1962. Pearl Harbor: warning and decision. Stanford, CA: Stanford University Press.

Wraith, R. E., and Lamb, G. B. 1971. Public inquiries as an instrument of government. London: Allen & Unwin.

Zegart, A. B. 2005. September 11 and the adaptation failure of the U.S. intelligence agencies. International Security 29(4):78–111.

Conclusion

11 | Conclusions: the politics of crisis exploitation

ARJEN BOIN, PAUL 't HART
AND ALLAN McCONNELL

Crisis aftermaths as framing contests

Crises cast shadows on the polities in which they occur. The sense of threat and uncertainty that pervades them shatters people's understanding of the world around them. Scholars have argued that the very occurrence of a crisis or the widespread use of the 'crisis' label to denote a particular state of affairs or development implies a 'dislocation' of hitherto dominant social, political or administrative discourses (Wagner-Pacifici 1986, 1994; Howarth et al. 2000). This dislocation can delegitimise the power and authority relationships that these discourses underpin, and may pose grave challenges to the position of incumbent officeholders and institutions or to established policies and organisations. At the same time, crisis opens up semantic and political space for actors to redefine issues, propose new policies, foster public reflection, or simply to gain popularity and strike at opponents. Typically, such opportunism rides on the wave of crisis-induced processes of accountability and learning.

Edelman was right in pointing out that incumbent elites are not necessarily threatened by crises. Some disturbances or emergencies may fit their purposes quite neatly. They may actively seek to 'create' crises in order to gain authority. He observes with characteristic succinctness: 'Any regime that prides itself on crisis management is sure to find crises to manage' (Edelman 1977: 47). But the same goes for the other end of the political power spectrum: parliamentary opposition figures, interest group leaders and self-appointed public voices may actively work to 'discover' and inflate crises. This accords with the 'garbage can' model of policy processes where policy entrepreneurs look for 'problems' in order to promote their own preferred 'solutions': in this case ranging from prompting a particular policy option to the removal from office of a political opponent (Cohen et al. 1972; Kingdon 2003).

Hence incumbent leaders as well as their critics and challengers engage in the kind of 'meaning making' that the collective stress generated by crisis evokes and requires (Edelman 1971; Boin et al. 2005). Crises can thus be understood as 'contests' between frames and counterframes. These contestations concern the nature and depth (severity) of a crisis, its causes (agency), the assignment of blame for its occurrence or escalation (responsibility), and implications for the future (learning and reform) put forward by actors with different interests and perspectives in relation to the status quo ante ('t Hart 1993; Tarrow 1994; Brändström et al., this volume; Olmeda, this volume). The bottom line of this process is that each of the actors involved seeks to exploit the disruption of 'governance as usual' that crises entail: to defend and strengthen their positions and authority, to attract or deflect public attention, to get rid of old policies or sow the seeds of new ones.

Given the multitude of stakeholders, the temporary absence of fixed rules for proceeding and the volatility of public passions, the outcomes of these crisis exploitation games are unpredictable. They unfold with differing speeds and intensities at different levels. The political fortunes of key players, policies and institutions may settle or change drastically over the course of a few days, as illustrated by the Spanish and German cases in this volume. But they may also be in limbo for several months if not years during and following the painstaking work of investigation committees, as highlighted by the saga of NASA following the Space Shuttle *Challenger* explosion (see Boin, this volume; Jarman and Kouzmin 1991). Some actors will initially be cast on the defensive, but may come to find that the crisis aftermath also throws up opportunities for them. George W. Bush, for example, unsuccessfully tried at first to prevent the 9/11 Commission inquiry, but subsequently embraced it and used it to his own political advantage (Parker and Dekker, this volume).

Others might experience the opposite. Federal Emergency Management Agency director Michael Brown was forced to resign after the Hurricane Katrina disaster and was vilified in a congressional hearing. When the House committee presented its final report in February 2006, it argued forcefully that Brown had by no means been the only public leader to fail prior to and following the disaster. In fact, the report spoke of nothing less than a 'national failure' – at all levels of the community, within and beyond government. This way of framing issues of causation and responsibility may have been bad news for national self-respect and, perhaps, the American public's trust in its government and public institutions, but paradoxically it was probably a relief for any individual agency or policy maker who had feared the committee's axe might have come down on them in particular.

This volume has examined up close the collision of frames and the evolving game of crisis exploitation that takes place as societies work through crisis-induced processes of accountability and learning. As the case chapters have demonstrated, these contests take place in different public forums – the mass media, official investigation committees, parliament and the courts. They have shown that despite government leaders being in a privileged position in the political game of 'normal' times, they are all but 'in control' of the thickening of activities and intensive communication in forums characteristic of crisis 'processing' in the public domain. Government leaders and top officials may try to regain such control in order to impose their frames upon the public understanding of the crisis and its wider implications, but as becomes apparent from the various chapters, their success at doing so is not to be taken for granted.

One question that looms large in any study of crisis-induced politics and public leadership is: under which conditions can incumbent elites (re)impose their control over the terms of the public debate, the rhythms of the political process and the content of policy and organisational agendas – all of which are shattered or at least disturbed by the crisis? In reflecting upon this question in this chapter, we will learn something about the conditions under which crises provide the proverbial 'windows of opportunity' (Keeler 1993; Kingdon 2003) for other actors to advance their ideas and interests, for organisations to survive and even prosper, and for public policies and institutions to endure or be changed. In short, when we capture the factors that shape the course and outcomes of crisis-induced framing contests, we will enhance our understanding of the reasons why some crises generate particular 'lessons' and 'reforms' and others do not. From an agency perspective on political analysis, we may then also be able to articulate a theory of *crisis exploitation*. By this we mean *the purposeful utilisation by actors of the institutional 'dislocation' generated by crisis, to significantly affect political processes of sense making, judgement and choice*.

Ours is intended as a modest step towards this aim. The cases assembled in this volume were not selected to enable regularised, systemic, national or sectoral comparisons. The case studies in Part I focused primarily on questions relating to the effects of crises on the (electoral) fortunes and accountability of political leaders. Those in Part II were designed to look primarily at the 'learning' process and its effects on policies and organisations. Moreover, the case study authors were free to articulate and employ their own analytical frameworks. This autonomy produced a variety of distinct but largely complementary theoretical angles: crisis leadership style (Preston), elite blame management strategies (Brändström et al.), crisis impact on government popularity (Bytzek, Olmeda), crisis commission politics (Staelraeve and 't Hart, Parker and Dekker), crisis-induced organisational learning (Boin), crises and policy stability and change (Hansén, Schwartz and McConnell). Hence it is impossible to treat these cases as a patterned sample allowing systematic comparison and external generalisation. We can, however, use the loosely structured variety of cases and insights gathered here for heuristic purposes: to advance inductive generalisations about various manifestations of the phenomenon that tie all these papers together: the course and outcomes of crisis-induced politics and governance.

We first reflect on the bottom-line outcomes of crisis: the impact on the fates of leaders, policies and organisations. In addressing these issues, we return to our typologies of leadership and policy and organisational outcomes outlined in Chapter 1. We look at one cluster of factors that shapes these outcomes: the behavior of public policy makers. In particular, we examine what the cases teach us about the ways in which elites handle the public accountability process that is part and parcel of crisis aftermaths. For example, are leaders who engage in blame avoidance and deflection likely to fare better or worse than those who accept responsibility for what have come to be publicly understood as errors and omissions? Next, we look at the dynamics and impact of a key arena where the framing contests of crisis-induced politics take shape: crisis inquiries. This section draws on the case findings to put forward ideas about how crisis inquiries may affect crisis outcomes; what members of crisis inquiries can do to make sure their work makes a difference; and what incumbent policy makers can do to make these inquiries work for and not against them. Finally, we examine the chances and limitations that crises offer for those seeking to exploit crises by forging learning and reform.

Shadows cast by crises

We begin by examining the course and outcomes of the crisis-induced trajectories presented in this book. The nature of this study dictated that so-called 'fast-burning' crises ('t Hart and Boin 2001), critical episodes whose political shadows fade quickly when the operational action is over, were few and far between. In a sense, the German floods were of this kind: intensely reported and debated for 3 weeks, and then their political significance declined sharply after the election (whose outcomes they helped shape). Obviously there were major debates about reconstruction issues as well as about the lessons for water management and crisis preparedness, but there were no politically critical issues concerning responsibility and blame.

The other cases all belonged to the category of 'long-shadow crises' (Boin et al. 2005): there was no immediate closure of the political crisis mood following the termination of the operational crisis response activities. Still, there were significant differences in the nature, duration and intensity of the sociopolitical tensions generated by the various crises. Following Boin et al. (2005), we distinguish between three types of long-shadow crises. Each generates a particular political agenda for the crisis aftermath.

'Incomprehensible' crises are highly unexpected events that surpass and defy existing political–bureaucratic repertoires of crisis prevention and response. These are crises that few people (if any) can even fathom let alone plan for: instances of strategic military surprise; major public disorders or collective disruption in otherwise highly peaceful and 'clean' societies. The 9/11 attacks represent a near-perfect example of this category. The Dutroux crisis in Belgium, although on a completely different scale, had a comparable traumatising impact. Incomprehensible crises come as a complete surprise to both the general public and political elites, and cause bewilderment and dismay. A nagging question tends to follow: 'why did we not see this coming?' Almost invariably, postmortem activities bring to light the existence of multiple, albeit scattered and sometimes ambiguous hunches, signals and warnings about growing vulnerabilities and threats along the lines of the scenario that actually transpired. These were evidently not acted upon effectively, and much of the political controversy in the aftermath of 'incomprehensible' crises focuses on the question of why no

action was taken. As Barry Turner (Turner and Pidgeon 1997), Willem Wagenaar (1986) and other scholars have argued, some crises occur *precisely because* people in charge appear to have been unaware of the very possibility that a crisis might be looming, or because they have chosen not to act on warnings. Politically, the difference between these two scenarios is highly salient. Debates about responsibility, blame and liability take a different turn depending upon which causal story about the genesis of the crisis comes to prevail: that of top-level policy makers not being informed about any looming vulnerabilities and threats (in which case blame goes down the hierarchy); or that of top brass unwilling to address the growing risk brought to their attention (in which case postcrisis politics can easily escalate into a full-blown political crisis). The 9/11 Commission steered a middle course when it ascribed the tragedy to 'a failure of imagination', and then demonstrated that this failure had deep-rooted institutional causes.

'*Mismanaged*' *crises* and their postcrisis controversies concern not the causes of crisis, but official crisis management responses. When the response to a particular incident or development is widely perceived as being slow, disorganised or insensitive to the needs of the stricken community, the image of institutional failure continues to fuel the crisis. Of the cases in this volume, the Scandinavian governments' tsunami responses and the U.S. federal response to the Katrina floods in Louisiana come closest to this ideal type. The main thrust of postcrisis politics is distinctly different from that of the 'incomprehensible' crisis, because it zooms in on crisis-coping capacity. Debates concerning accountability and blame put the spotlight mostly on officials and agencies tasked with contingency planning, civic preparedness and governmental emergency management. This is exactly what transpired in the tsunami and Katrina cases. In the United States, both the Federal Emergency Management Agency and the White House took a terrible public beating: not so much because they had failed to prevent the floods (although the federal government was certainly blamed by state and local authorities for long having neglected the poor state of flood defences in the region) but because the disaster presented an image of total disarray at the very heart of the government's much vaunted post-9/11 crisis management machinery. In Sweden, the tsunami investigation revealed clear evidence that the need to build and maintain crisis response capacity at cabinet level had not been given the priority it deserved. Moreover, the clumsy attempts by both the prime minister and the foreign minister to deflect blame for the slow response clearly compounded their problems. Not only did they fail to instigate quick and effective crisis operations, their limited grasp of the symbolic dimensions of the tsunami predicament was painfully exposed.

'*Agenda-setting*' *crises* hit at the heart of existing policy domains, exposing deficiencies in regulatory or service delivery arrangements. As a consequence, such crises provide a major opportunity for issue advocates to raise the salience of the issue domain and reshape its hitherto dominant problem definitions and policy mixes. The Three Mile Island near-accident with a nuclear reactor had this effect on U.S. energy policy, and the Chernobyl reactor fire focused attention on the special ramifications of the problem in (central and eastern) Europe. Among the cases in this volume, the Walkerton water crisis exemplifies this category, as does the dioxin contamination case in Belgium and the German embassy drama in Stockholm. From the point of view of government leaders, the crisis-induced politics of agenda-setting crises lends itself more readily to 'compartmentalisation' through expert committees making recommendations for policy reform and organisational renewal within the confines of the policy community at hand. This compartmentalisation will often serve to depoliticise the issues and remove them from the front stage of mainstream politics. To be sure, the policy aftermath of agenda-setting crises may at times throw up perplexing political questions – about the future of nuclear power plants, for example – but it is less likely to put into question the competence and legitimacy of the (centre of) government and its crisis management capacities.

Fates of leaders, institutions and policies

Each of these types of long-shadow crises is capable of generating a range of possible outcomes in terms of the fate of leaders, institutions and policies. What, however, actually transpired in our cases? We shall give some overall impressions here, before going more deeply into each of these domains (personal and policy/institutional effects) in separate sections to follow. In doing so, we return to the typologies of leadership fates and levels of learning as detailed in Chapter 1.

Table 11.1 shows that most but not all of the core political and executive leaders whose role and performance were scrutinised in the wake of crisis tended to survive this scrutiny. However, survival comes in

Table 11.1. Crisis outcomes: an overview

Case	Effects on key political officeholders	Category and strength of leadership outcomes	Effects on policies/ institutions	Levels of learning/ policy change
Spain – 3/11 attacks	Election loss, prime minister's party	Elite damage***	Withdrawal of Spanish troops from Iraq (precrisis electoral commitment by then opposition party)	Policy reform and paradigm shift
Germany – Elbe floods	Election win, governing coalition/chancellor	Elite reinvigoration**	National civil protection agency founded	Fine tuning
Sweden – tsunami	Reputation loss, prime minister and foreign minister	Elite damage**	Major upgrade of central government crisis coping capacities	Policy reform and fine tuning
Finland – tsunami	PM admission of 'government shortcomings'	Elite escape	No major institutional effects	Fine tuning
Norway – tsunami	Foreign minister and PM admission of errors	Elite escape	Government proposes major overhaul of crisis response system	Policy reform and fine tuning
U.S. – 9/11 attacks	Surge in presidential and mayoral popularity	Elite reinvigoration***	Major security policy and institutional reform	Policy reform and paradigm shift
Belgium – Dutroux	Large drop in government's public support; massive public marches nationwide; two ministerial resignations	Elite damage***	Major police reform	Policy reform and possibly paradigm shift

Belgium – dioxin	Ministerial resignations; election loss, government parties	Elite damage*	Agenda setting; minor policy adjustments	Fine tuning
U.S. – Katrina	Large drop in presidential support (recovering in longer term), resignation of agency chief executive	Elite damage**	Overhaul of policy and practices across sectors such as health, employment and emergency planning	Policy reform and fine tuning across multiple policy sectors, with possible paradigm shift in the longer term
U.S. – *Challenger* crash	Removal of key NASA administrators	Elite damage*	Major overhaul of Space Shuttle Program management and safety practices	Fine tuning
U.S. – *Columbia* crash	Some reorganisation of staff	Elite escape	Space shuttle is to be officially retired in the near future	Fine tuning
Sweden – embassy seizure	None	Elite escape	Agenda setting; no immediate policy change	Fine tuning – close to nil
Canada – Walkerton water	Some damage to premier and his neoliberal reform agenda	Elite damage*	Major changes in water management legislation and regulatory oversight practices	Policy reform and fine tuning
Israel – hall collapse	None	Elite escape	No policy change despite commission report urging major restructuring	Nil

Note: The number of asterisks denotes the strength of the phenomenon in each category: low (*), medium (**) and high (***).

different guises. *Elite reinvigoration* is certainly the most sought after outcome for those in positions of authority. Some elites benefited clearly and decisively from intensive media reporting of the statesman-like postures they adopted in dealing with major emergencies, reinforced by generic public solidarity at times of deep social trauma, and even genuine appreciation of their crisis performance. In our cases, the most compelling example is New York Mayor Rudy Giuliani: written off by all prior to 9/11, but a New York and national hero in its wake. Also, despite his dubious role in the subsequent inquiry (highlighted in the Parker and Dekker chapter), George W. Bush saw his popularity soar to unprecedented and long-enduring heights on the wings of the same crisis. Another beneficiary, although on a more modest scale, was German Chancellor Gerhard Schröder after the Elbe floods. Responsibility for operational crisis management was largely decentralised (to the states). This aspect of public administration created space for quite successful strategies of symbolic reassurance that national leaders were doing what they could to sort out the chaos that was being dealt with (as well as partly caused and escalated) by other levels of the governmental system.

Elite damage, by contrast, befell several key figures in our case studies. Some were relatively minor (such as NASA administrators, and Ontario Premier Mike Harris after the Walkerton tragedy). Others were more significant, with a few political careers, aspirations and reputations taking a sharp downturn (outgoing Prime Minister Aznar in Spain; chancellor candidate Stoiber in Germany; Belgian Prime Minister Dehaene). In others, the damage was temporary: their public standing and political strength was compromised considerably in the short term as they struggled with the 'crisis after the crisis' ('t Hart et al. 2001). As time elapsed, however, political agendas changed and the leaders in question could recuperate from the damage sustained. Tsunami-damaged Swedish Prime Minister Göran Persson was a case in point.

This recovery highlights the political fact that more often than not, the sharp and immediate edge of challenges to legitimacy posed by crises will blur over time, as they mingle with public judgements on the merits of new proposals, the advent of new issues and the media's inevitable quest for new political stories. Such features are the essence of *elite escape* postcrisis outcomes. This was certainly the case in the Norwegian and Finish tsunami responses, Swedish embassy seizure,

Columbia crash and the Israeli banquet hall collapse. There are no discernable patterns in these cases as to why 'escape' was possible (for example, the banquet hall collapse was dwarfed by security and defence issues in Israel, and pressure was eased on Finnish leaders because of early admission that mistakes had been made). Perhaps the only common theme is leadership judgement that political flak would diminish if a particular course of action (or inaction) was taken. As we will see shortly, however, such elite manoeuvring is a risky game with no guarantee of success.

As far as the effects of crises on public policies and institutions are concerned, the majority of cases in this book confirm the idea that crisis-induced learning processes can temporarily open sociopolitical windows for reform (Birkland 1997; Kingdon 2003). When change-oriented government critics and policy entrepreneurs play their cards well, crises may enable them to bring about shifts in the balance of public sympathies and policy coalitions. There are, however, degrees of learning, and we can capture these (as per Chapter 1) in our three layers of learning: *fine tuning, policy reform* and *paradigm shift*.

With the exception of the Israeli banquet hall, all our cases exhibited some degree of *fine tuning*. In other words, there was some form of instrumental adaption to procedures and ways of working. Sometimes such minor reforms were the product of clear political promises (Elbe floods, Finland's tsunami response) while others were the result of policy reform not matching reform rhetoric (NASA). As a general rule, it would be surprising if some form of secondary learning did not take place after a crisis. The legitimacy of any organisation (and perhaps even its funding from its paymasters) is vulnerable if it does not show willingness to promote some form of adaption in its procedures.

Fine tuning seems to be the 'quickest fix' possible. In the game of crisis-induced politics, government leaders are usually (but not always, as we will see) cheerleaders for the existing institutional order in their respective portfolios. Other than common sense might lead us to expect, it turns out that even in the aftermath of serious crises, most government leaders consider it far more politically expedient to throw in their lot with existing institutions and policies, while leaving lesson drawing and reform to the margins. When inquiries manage to gain widespread support for penetrating criticism of existing practices, leaders who are reluctant to change can attempt to ride out the political mood of the moment by making some symbolic changes and paying lip service to 'learning the lessons' on the front stage of politics, whilst on the backstage they can use their procedural and informal powers to put their foot on the brake. For example, although forced to admit after the Stockholm embassy drama that remote and peaceful Sweden could not hope to be spared the spells of terrorism that were plaguing most of Europe at the time, the fact that the event was semiexogenous (German terrorists trying to pressure the German government, albeit on Swedish soil) made it possible for Swedish Prime Minister Olof Palme to sidetrack calls from within the police for a significant upgrading of its counter-terrorist capabilities. Therefore, the immediate reflex that 'something must be done' was quelled by a largely symbolic codification of already emergent enforcement and extradition practices (see Hansén, this volume).

Policy reform refers to key changes in entrenched policies and policy sectors, and was evident in just under half of our cases. Based on this small sample, our more generalised instinct is that *policy reform* tends to occur when *fine tuning* alone is politically unsustainable. It could, for example, be to appease public concerns and/or satisfy a powerful coalition of interests (Belgian police reform, Walkerton/Ontario water regulation, U.S. homeland security). Sometimes the 'policy' aspect was the most reformist aspect of change (Ontario's water regulation) and at other times, reform of particular policy sectors touched on *paradigmatic* societal issues (Spain's withdrawal of troops from Iraq, and the United States' sweeping anti-terror reform). Indeed, it can be difficult at times to tell where *policy reform* and *paradigm shift* begin and end. To take the latter example, the post 9/11 overhaul of homeland security in the U.S. constituted *policy reform* because it entailed a thorough-going reform in one particular policy sector (domestic security), but it was underpinned by discourse that tapped into deeper *paradigmatic* constitutional rights to free speech and privacy.

Importantly, most of the cases examined here betray a greater tendency among incumbent policy makers to respond to crisis by attempts to consolidate the status quo than to make sweeping commitments to *policy reform* and change in societal *paradigms*. Perhaps this is unsurprising (see Boin et al. 2005; Heyse et al. 2006). Crisis-induced politics entails a competition between tight and loosely coupled coalitions in favour of either securing or altering the various rights and rewards that stakeholders received in the precrisis context. Those individuals and groups with inherited political, economic and social powers – sustained

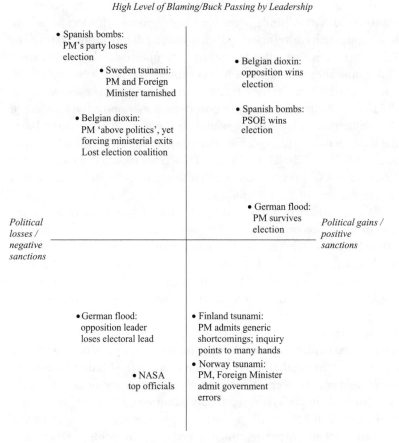

Figure 11.1. Does blame management work? Leader behaviour and leaders' postcrisis fates.

through institutional structures and path dependencies – do not easily submit to change in policies or entrenched societal values.

Crisis exploitation: elite manoeuvring

Table 11.1 shows that the fates of leaders vary greatly in the wake of crises. The issue we take up now is the extent to which these variations depend on leader behaviour in the crisis-induced aftermath. Figure 11.1 suggests that it is not easy to detect hard and fast 'winning strategies' for political leaders who are caught up in crisis-induced framing contests. It shows that virtually all government and opposition leaders for whose behaviour we have sufficient information to reliably score, resorted to 'blame game' style tactics in dealing with questions about the causes and significance of crises. Yet it also shows that there were roughly as many political beneficiaries as there were losers from these crises. Nor did these fall into the pattern of government vs. opposition (according the blame theory, the former would be the likely loser and the latter the likely beneficiary). Postcrisis election gains by the Spanish Socialists and the Belgian Liberal, Green and French Socialist parties stand next to incumbent Chancellor Schröder's hitherto unlikely electoral survival on the strength of the Elbe floods.

Blaming others is not a good predictor of these outcomes either. The most conspicuous losers – Spanish Prime Minister Aznar, Belgian Prime Minister Dehaene and German opposition chancellor candidate Stoiber, whose parties all lost elections in the immediate wake of crises – displayed different levels of blame management behaviour. Those who might argue that Stoiber lost precisely because he did not do what is expected of an opposition leader (blaming the government for the floods and criticising it for shortcomings in flood response) would have a hard time explaining why the Spanish socialist opposition candidate led his party to electoral success in the wake of the Madrid bombings, while deliberately keeping his own blaming rhetoric firmly in check. Also, incumbent leaders who publicly admitted government errors and took responsibility for them, such as the Norwegian foreign minister and the Finnish prime minister, ended up avoiding political flak much better than their Swedish counterparts who persisted with blame-avoidance strategies.

In short: there does not appear to be a self-evident pattern here. In part this is because the number of cases coded is low. In part it is simply in line with the results of voting behaviour studies that tend to show that the personality and behaviour of leaders matter a great deal less than commonly assumed (King 2004; McAllister 2006a, 2006b). Although often taken for granted (the 'rally effect' hypothesis; see Bytzek, this volume), electoral effects of crisis behaviour are actually difficult to prove and may in fact not be substantial.

There may also be a more fundamental reason why it is difficult to detect any straightforward pattern in the results of various crisis-induced blame management strategies. Perhaps the famous Miles' law assumption that underlies much of blame management theory – where you stand depends on where you sit – and which Graham Allison (1971) made so much of in his famous 'Model III' analysis of the Cuban missile crisis ('t Hart and Rosenthal 1998; Allison and Zelikov 1999) is too simple a guide to actor behaviour in postcrisis politics.

A 'Milesian' proposition concerning crisis-induced elite behavior would read as follows: ceteris paribus, government actors will (1) attribute crisis origins and response problems to exogenous circumstances, (2) seek to obstruct and constrain crisis inquiries and (3) resist taking responsibility. By contrast, nongovernment actors will (1) attribute crisis origins and response problems to endogenous factors (i.e. related to government actors and policies), (2) seek to promote, widen and deepen crisis inquiries and (3) insist on office-holders being held personally responsible for any faults and shortcomings noted by inquiries. To be sure, sometimes roles do seem unequivocally to induce postcrisis political stances: the Belgian opposition loudly advocated a wide-ranging parliamentary inquiry into the dioxin affair, but several weeks later some of the parties assumed government office and then made attempts to constrict the scope of the inquiry.

In the main, however, our cases provide much evidence to undercut 'Milesian' role-theoretical and implicit rational choice determinism. Government leaders do not always defend the government's record; opposition leaders do not invariably turn into moral crusaders whenever a crisis occurs; and the mass media do not always claim that government heads should roll.

Conceptualising crisis-induced politics in terms of framing contests must be tempered by the fact that the world is not infinitely malleable. The agency-based notion of 'crisis exploitation' should not blind us to the constraints upon the discourse and actions that policy makers and other stakeholders can feasibly engage in following a crisis.

Following our lead in Chapter 1, *situational* characteristics can play an autonomous role, particularly when events are so compelling that the scope for 'meaning making' is, or at least appears to be, rather limited. For example, it was obviously hard to deny that serious errors had been made when another NASA space shuttle exploded, or when it transpired that convicted child molester and rapist Marc Dutroux was not quickly and methodically investigated when children started disappearing. But it was not so obvious who was at fault when a bunch of fanatical and well-organised terrorists successfully used hitherto unprecedented methods to attack the U.S. mainland, or when a spate of bad weather upstream caused massive riverine flooding in Germany. To create a politically dominant view of those latter types of crises as a product of avoidable policy failures required a lot more 'framing work'. The evident role of exogenous forces – nature; foreign suicide bombers – constricted (at least initially) the scope of feasible opposition criticism of the government. The sheer gravity of the impact of both cases imposed on all actors a symbolic script emphasising national solidarity rather than political back biting. This offered the Bush administration and the Schröder government a different scope for defensive manoeuvres than enjoyed by NASA administrators and Belgian authorities. The Madrid bombings would have had the same type of impact had it not been for Spain's long experience with domestic terrorism and the preexisting intense controversies surrounding Basque separatists ETA. That alone served to immediately 'endogenise' and thus politicise a crisis that otherwise may have been experienced as an overwhelming, unique and exogenous tragedy.

There was, of course, another factor at play in Spain: it occurred a few days prior to national elections. This brings us to another set of factors (also outlined in Chapter 1) that limit the utility of a Model III-type analysis of postcrisis politics: *contextual* factors. Crises are discrete episodes in ongoing political and bureaucratic processes. Therefore, the timing of their occurrence matters greatly in relation to the ongoing rhythms of governance and organisational life. The contrast between the relatively intense yet ultimately politically inconsequential Swedish post-tsunami politics and the dramatic, immediate German and Spanish crisis-induced electoral reversals of fortune is illuminating in this regard. We can never know, of course, but would Göran Persson have survived the tsunami blame game had the crisis occurred in an election period rather than at midterm? The location of crises in political time provides different actors with particular incentives to inflate or deflate issues of responsibility and blame. On balance, the cases reported here suggest the following proposition about the timing of crisis in relation to elections: *ceteris paribus, the closer a crisis hits to the (anticipated) time of an election, the more likely that political actors will attempt to politicise an emergency/disturbance, and thus the longer the expected duration of the crisis aftermath, the greater the intensity of its blame games and the higher the likelihood that crisis investigations will produce political fatalities.*

The Miles law perspective assumes that the main predictor of elite behaviour in times of crisis is the big distinction between government and opposition. This overlooks the fact that crises occur at different points in the political careers of key protagonists. The cases show that long-time incumbent leaders are more likely to adopt defensive postures than newly incumbent leaders whose personal record is less likely to be at stake in postcrisis inquiries. Indeed they may in fact welcome crisis episodes as a way of putting distance between themselves and their predecessor's regime and policies. To be sure, doctrines of ministerial responsibility presuppose that the office-holder is held responsible even for the behaviour of his or her predecessors. However, in political practice, personal noninvolvement in crises or fiascoes is usually enough to get novice office-holders off the hook, particularly when they themselves champion the cause of far-reaching investigation and sweeping reform. Hence we can derive another contextual proposition: *the shorter an actor's occupancy of a position of influence on government/agency policy at the time of crisis occurrence, the more likely that that actor will forego defensive responses and escape political damage as a result of crisis-induced accountability proceedings.*

Finally, although most of the case studies in this book have not given systematic attention to crisis coverage by the mass media, we should not underestimate the importance of such coverage as a contextual 'backdrop' against which blame games take place. The chapter by Bytzek on German floods and Brändström et al. on the Scandinavian tsunami response, clearly indicate the relevance of such factors. Bytzek's analysis of the German case points to the importance of issue salience. In particular, media influence upon the political fortunes of key actors is greater for crises that receive continued intense media coverage, as opposed to those relegated to secondary importance once the operational crisis reporting has run its course. The content analysis of media coverage conducted by Brändström et al. provides some support for the idea that the selection and tone of media reporting also matter. Hence our third contextual proposition: *the more the media's crisis reporting and commentary emphasises exogenous interpretations of a crisis, the less likely that government actors will suffer negative political consequences in its aftermath; the more it emphasises endogenous ones, the more likely that they will.*

This proposition leads to a follow-up question: can we predict the emphasis ('bias') of media crisis reporting? Although the cases display too much variation in this regard to make any solid empirical statement, let us offer a speculative one: crises intensify but generally do not suddenly change the tone and content of media reporting about the chief actors involved (Wilkins 1987; Wilkins et al. 1989; Seeger et al. 2003). Hence our fourth proposition, posited with due awareness of its relative explanatory power: *the thrust of media reporting and opinion of an actor's behaviour in relation to crisis episodes correlates highly with its precrisis reporting and opinion about that actor, regardless of that actor's specific crisis communication behavior.* It is the media analogy of the so-called Matthew 'rule' – familiar to all scholars applying for research grants: he who has shall be given. And thus the already popular leaders (parties, governments) are more likely to emerge as the crisis heroes or will at least be spared from being publicly branded its villains.

This suggestion may be overly deterministic. It cannot be a coincidence that the bulk of contemporary crisis management textbooks are written from a communication perspective (cf. Coombs 1999; Seeger et al. 2003; Curtin et al. 2005). These books tell us that whilst public relations and media coverage in particular need to be 'managed' in normal times, the need to do so is even greater in times of crisis. And then they proceed in fine detail to describe what policy makers and managers can do to ensure their messages get heard and their personal and organisational reputations are spared (Henry 2000). Hence, as a counterweight to the former two propositions, we forward an additional one, more in line with the agency perspective of 'crisis exploitation', yet an equally well-refutable one: *the degree to which media reporting/commentary on crisis episodes aligns with the frames put forward by a particular political actor depends upon the quality (preparedness, timeliness, accuracy, understandability and 'symbolic intelligence') of that actor's crisis communication behavior.*

These heuristic comparisons of a limited number of like and unlike cases by no means allow us to draw firm conclusions about which factors determine the fortunes of political office-holders in the wake of major crises. The propositions formulated above are just a preliminary building block for the kind of rigorous, controlled, larger-N comparison that would be needed to gain more insight. Yet our limited effort does show very clearly that when a major crisis befalls the community, political leaders on both sides of the government-opposition fence have reason to be both fearful and hopeful. They may be fearful because crises can unleash public moods and political forces beyond their control, and appear to harbour strong incentives for many actors to start potentially damaging blame games. They can be hopeful because at the same time, and partly for the same reasons, quite a few political careers have actually been made or enhanced by smart and well-balanced crisis behaviour – in the operational arena, but even more so in the symbolic domain of public 'meaning making' in times of collective uncertainty and despair.

The politics of crisis commissions

Edelman (1977: 103) argued long ago that 'sceptical search for truth is bound before long to collide with established norms and authority'. One might expect crisis inquiries would lend ample illustration to this dictum. That is not the case for the crises studied in this book (see Table 11.2). Only the 9/11 Commission was confronted with overt and persistent attempts by President Bush and his staff to prevent, obstruct and 'shape' its work. In most of the other cases, the incumbent authorities may or may not have been tempted down an obstructionist path, but they were politically unable to do so. The Bush administration proved ultimately that resistance was not a politically viable option. Crises, it seems, tend to put so much public and political pressure on governments to open up and have the record examined, that little can be done to resist that push. Overt moves to do so would be politically counterproductive. Parker and Dekker (this volume) put it effectively when they observe: '... to publicly oppose and block the creation of an independent commission would have made the White House part of the problem of resolving questions about what went wrong on September 11. Doing so would have been associated with inaction and obstructionism, while publicly endorsing the commission was emblematic of leadership and the possibility of resolution and renewal'. We should note, however, that a public embracing of openness and investigation does not rule out more unobtrusive forms of resistance.

Most governments in our case studies probably did not cherish the prospect of an upcoming crisis inquiry but wisely chose default options: at least trying to prevent the inquiry from being run in the adversarial, politicised parliamentary arena (only the Belgian government had

Table 11.2. Crisis inquiries: a comparative overview

	Inquiry type and mandate	Politicisation of inquiry process	Govt attempt to obstruct/manipulate	Tone of inquiry report	Political and policy impact of inquiry
Belgium: Dutroux	Parliamentary; Case-based accountability assessment, as well as sweeping review of police/justice system	High: rationale, scope	No	Critical evaluation of police/justice system performance; advocates integration of rival police forces	Political: + Policy: + (in 2nd instance)
Belgium: dioxin	Parliamentary; Determine causes of contamination	Moderate: composition, scope	No	Broad sectoral analysis; reform proposals	Political: − Policy: −
Sweden: police reform	Expert commission led initially by politician and then by judge; sweeping review of entire police system; crisis component embedded in larger issues	Low	No	No specific crisis evaluation; broad programme of reform measures	Political: − Policy: −
USA: Challenger	Expert commission led by former secretary of state; determine causes of accident; recommend remedies	Low	No	Sweeping criticism of NASA risk management systems and practices	Political: − Policy: +
USA: Columbia	Expert commission led by former admiral; determine causes of accident; recommend remedies	Moderate	No	Sweeping criticism of NASA failure to learn lessons of the *Challenger* crisis/inquiry	Political: + Policy: ++
USA: 9/11	Independent blue-ribbon commission	High: Rationale, scope, composition, access	Yes	Highly critical analysis of U.S. homeland security architecture and practices; 'shopping list' of recommendations	Political: + Policy: +
Canada: water tragedy	Expert inquiry led by judge	Low	No	Across the board critique of all actors involved, particularly Ministry of Environment	Political: + Policy: ++
Israel: banquet hall	Expert inquiry led by judge	Low	No	Highly critical of building codes and the inaction on previous attempts to reform	Political: + Policy: −

to acquiesce to parliamentary investigations). The vast majority were conducted by blue-ribbon commissions or senior lawyers. Although such moves, as it turns out, are no guarantee that inquiry findings will be devoid of critical statements about the government's role in a crisis, there is at least a reasonable expectation that the inquiry will not become a political witch-hunt. Expert-driven inquiries tend to go for policy substance, not for 'political skulls'. This distinction is supported in our case studies. Whilst the tones of inquiries were grave, their focus was mostly on regulatory, managerial and cultural factors. Questions about political responsibility were usually hinted at but seldom addressed in an up-front manner – experts and lawyers predictably defer to parliaments to make those judgements. Hence, expert commissions are less likely to result in political fatalities.

It seems safe to assume that the relation between governmental leaders and postcrisis inquiries is affected by the perceived nature of the crisis at hand. A commission that investigates a crisis that directly threatens the heart of society (such as the 9/11 attacks) can count on more reticence or even active opposition from leaders. This contrasts with a commission investigating a crisis that falls in a government domain sufficiently far removed from central government (space shuttles/water crises) or within a domain that is characterised by indirect government responsibility (the Israeli banquet hall collapse). High politics during a crisis will translate into high commission politics.

When it comes to the fate of governmental leaders, much depends on the leadership of a postcrisis inquiry. It appears, paradoxically perhaps, that a high level of 'commission statesmanship' is least dangerous for the politicians and civil servants involved. Commission chairs who understand the importance of combining the symbolic function of their inquiry with the learning imperative, and who seek accordingly to separate back-stage politics from front-stage performance, also tend to understand that public mudslinging with the powers that be may erode the long-term legitimacy of the commission's efforts. If they want their report to 'make history' (i.e. be the authoritative guide to an important historical juncture that their grandchildren will read) (see Parker and Dekker, this volume) – commission leaders cannot afford to be seen as politically motivated finger pointers. It follows that public leaders who wish to avoid direct criticism are wise to appoint highly qualified, statesman-like commission chairs (or people known to harbour such ambitions).

Several chapters in this book help us understand that 'running' a commission of inquiry is no easy job. The leaders of these inquiries must somehow balance public performance – casting an image of sage, neutral, determined council to the nation – with a heavy administrative hand in order to coordinate the efforts of many researchers, manage limited resources and meet looming deadlines. Overt sympathy for the victims may undermine the commission's authority (see the 'spaghetti incident' in the Dutroux chapter, Staelraeve and 't Hart, this volume). By contrast too much emphasis on research technicalities may undermine faith in the commission's commitment to the bigger picture of improving societal safety and security.

The chapters also show that crisis commissions tend to work in rapidly evolving environments. The initiation of an inquiry creates a new venue that all actors in the postcrisis phase will seek to exploit (Jones and Baumgartner 2005). Some will seek to further escalate the crisis. For instance, the White Marches in Belgium (Staelraeve and 't Hart, this volume) deepened the crisis mood, as the victims' families demonstrated that they could count on the support of the Belgian public. Others sought to boost or transform their image by embracing the investigation and its outcomes. President Bush felt forced to change strategy midcourse to protect his image as the protector of American security (Parker and Dekker, this volume). After Hurricane Katrina, the Democrats distanced themselves from the House investigation (anticipating a Republican whitewash), only to welcome the findings when the Republicans eventually published a report that fiercely criticised the president and his administration (Preston, this volume).

Some chairmen (very few commissions are chaired by women) turn out to be remarkably well versed in the public choreography of inquiry dynamics. They use public hearings and partial reports to create a comprehensible storyline, preparing all involved for what then appears a 'logical' end result. They write a readable report, which leads the reader from a distant point in the past on the path toward disaster. They graciously distribute blame, but always emphasise the necessity of improving the system so this crisis will never happen again. They understand how the media works and try to accommodate their needs by equally dividing 'exclusives' and by providing sufficient background information that helps reporters understand what the commission is trying to achieve.

These chairmen understand that style cannot mask a lack of substance. A good report contains a narrative that is comprehensive and indisputable (the last thing a chairman wants is to argue about facts). It carefully separates analysis from recommendations. To become perceived as a fair judge, the analysis will have to pay attention to the interplay between various levels, actors and interests. It will have to take context (such as limited resources or impossible objectives) into account. It will have to carefully weigh avoidable errors against gross negligence. Finally, it will have to formulate recommendations that are both reasonable and feasible.

Several chapters in this book cast doubt on the quality of postcrisis inquiries and the reports they produce. The 9/11 report, for instance, was widely heralded for its literary qualities and its outstanding narrative, but the analysis and recommendations met with some persistent critics. The reports on the NASA shuttle failures hardly encountered any criticism, but a quick read will demonstrate the lack of specificity and feasibility surrounding some of the most powerful recommendations ('become a learning organisation'). Perhaps the perfect report simply does not exist.

At least some of this imperfection can be attributed to the role of experts in commissions. These ad hoc groups are forced to do what many academics have found impossible in practice: engage in interdisciplinary research. It is hard enough to get an engineer or a scientist to understand a psychologist or political scientist (the other way around may be even harder, we hasten to add), but to get experts with different theoretical backgrounds to *agree* on something is a truly monumental task. To do this within a limited time period and under media pressure is bound to incur some major compromises. As a coping measure, commissions will be tempted to adopt the non-intervention principle: technical experts study technological issues, psychologists study human error and political scientists study all remaining issues. This seemingly logical division of labour is helpful to a degree but may disguise the elementary differences that separate the disciplines. These divisions may subtly undermine the validity of the commission's findings (we will have more to say about this in the following section).

From an analytical point of view, it appears necessary to approach commissions and their effects from different angles. For further research, we suggest a distinction between three different lenses that shape expectations and interpretations of committees (similar, but not identical, to Parker and Dekker, this volume). These lenses help formulate hypotheses with regard to the degree of independence of the commissions. Taken singly, each of these hypotheses is obviously of limited explanatory value; but used in combination they form a useful, dialectic analytical tool kit.

The *just world* lens suggests that a good, analytically sharp and fair-minded committee will command public authority, which in turn enables it to make dominant judgements about causes, responsibilities and implications of the crisis. This perspective suggests a straightforward relation between the degree of independence (in terms of the authority of members, the width of terms of reference, resources and staffing, time limits and access to all relevant information) of a crisis inquiry and its accountability impact. Therefore, an operating hypothesis would be as follows: *the higher a crisis commission's degree of independence, the higher its political and policy impact.* Moreover: *the higher a crisis commission's degree of independence, the more likely its report is critical of key government policies, organisations and figures.*

The *garbage can* paradigm reminds us that crisis committees and their reports are just one among the many disparate forces operating in the crisis-induced framing contest, whose contributions interact in complex and impenetrable ways. The procedural and professional quality of a committee may not necessarily augment its potential impact. In postcrisis politics, anything can happen. The garbage can null hypothesis is thus obvious: *there is no correlation between the degree of independence of crisis commissions and the level of criticality of inquiry reports towards governments; nor is there any correlation with policy impact.*

The *perverse effects* paradigm views crisis-induced politics as such a tough and mean game that it devours crisis committees trying to operate on the basis of detached expert inquiry. In the absence of sweeping mandates and extensive powers to create political faits accomplis, crisis inquiries and the political discussions that follow their inquiry reports are, obviously, focal points not only for supporters for typically reformist policy recommendations, but also for veto players and lobbyists bent on shielding existing policies and institutions from any crisis-induced 'knee-jerk' responses (Hood and Lodge 2002). At worst, they are susceptible to manipulation and abuse by the most astute and unscrupulous actors in the game – inside and outside government.

The key underlying hypothesis, therefore, is: *the higher a crisis com-mission's degree of independence, the lower its political and policy impact.*

Political crisis exploitation by 'learning' and 'reform'

In the wake of devastation and sorrow, we expect more from govern-ment than restoring a sense of order. We expect government to study the causes and initiate actions that ensure this crisis will never hap-pen again. The chapters in this book explain why this expectation is unlikely to be met: the politics of the postcrisis phase create dynamics that make learning a difficult enterprise.

To be sure, it appears relatively easy to establish the direct cause of a crisis – especially those involving technology: experts locate the mal-functioning part, identify the operator who last touched it and describe how this first-order factor triggered the crisis. They often puzzle the crisis trajectory together within a very short period of time. These first-order causes are usually easy to fix (e.g. redesign the part, fire the operator). If crisis learning was confined to first-order causes and quick fixes, there would be little room for crisis dynamics to impede this process.

In recent decades, this simple, linear model of crisis causation has come to be seen as inadequate and incomplete. We no longer accept that a crisis is caused by a broken part or an erring operator. As a result, or so it seems, contemporary crisis investigations have begun to pay much more attention to the conditions under which these first-order factors cause a crisis. The investigations concentrate on second-dimension factors such as ergonomics, group dynamics, organisational rules and cultures, interagency warfare, budget cuts and risk regimes (Van Duin 1992). This common wisdom may be viewed as a victory for social science research: notably the insights of academics such as Barry Turner (Turner and Pidgeon 1997) who emphasised the importance of the incubation periods that precede crises.

This work is often used to support the common misperception that crises leave a trail of early warning signals. The crisis is perceived in this line of thinking as an ontological entity, something 'out there'. It is envisioned to produce 'signals' that announce its impending arrival. If only public organisations would pay attention! Looking back at a crisis, there are plenty of signals. The question is whether these signals really matter, for they tend to be ubiquitous in most organisations or policy fields (many of which do not suffer from a crisis).

The search for second-order causalities thus is not as simple as it may seem (Perrow 1994). With the benefit of hindsight, it is fairly easy to construct a narrative that combines various levels of causality with the immediate agreed-upon trigger. Yet although such a narrative may seem convincing, it really is only a hypothesis. The existing theories simply do not 'provide proof' as lay persons are wont to think. They provide *possible explanations* that require much more work before they can be accepted as 'truths'. But commissions are not in the business of theory testing; they must construct a convincing storyline under severe time pressure. The weakness of second-order causations is often revealed by the accompanying recommendations. Second-order causalities require reform, but when we consider the reform proposals in the various reports, it is rarely self-evident how these proposed changes will remedy the observed cause of the crisis.

The investigation of second- and third-order dimensions of crisis is not only a mission impossible (at least from a truth-finding perspective), it renders the investigation vulnerable to the forces of postcrisis politics. By considering 'all possible factors' and 'leaving no stone unturned' – the typical remit of today's commissions – the investigation leaves the domain of exact science and detective work, and enters a new domain of imprecise concepts, abstract theories, multiple perspectives and alternate futures. In short, investigations enter the world of contestable and competing frames. The increased vagueness opens the door for intense and often politically inspired discussions that cannot be resolved on the basis of agreed-upon criteria. The laws of physics do not apply to second-order causalities.

In other respects, the use of experts does help justify any call for reform that the commission may agree upon. If commission members are convinced that failed intelligence lay at the heart of the crisis, there are plenty of experts and theories that will allow for a convincing underlying analysis. However, in the absence of hard and undisputable proof, opponents of the proposed reform can easily formulate equally convincing alternatives or counternarratives. Learning and reform can thus rapidly become subject to the forces of politicisation. And rightly so: in the absence of hard proof of their effectiveness, learning and reform are political at heart.

The political nature of postcrisis lessons and reform proposals is, of course, not lost on those who have to implement them (Boin and Otten 1996). In the most optimistic scenario, the organisations that bear the brunt of reform will seek a subtle accommodation between organisational routines that work, and first-order causalities that must be fixed. But the more politically inspired reforms become reified as the one and only path towards a safer future, the harder it will be for organisations to honour them in practice without compromising long-standing routines and structures that had nothing to do with the crisis.

For those who adhere to the 'learning imperative' (akin to the 'just world' perspective outlined earlier), the solution is easy. The remit of postcrisis commissions should be limited to identifying key errors and design failures, which can be resolved – not necessarily quickly or easily – without changing all parameters (changing the parameters may, after all, introduce new failure paths). Identifying second-order causes should probably be left to academic researchers and those working in the organisations. The commission could organise follow-up audits by experts and colleagues to gauge the level of improvement. The same process could apply to policy change.

From the 'garbage can' and 'perverse effects' perspectives presented above, such a solution is naïve at best and perhaps misleading. If there is no exact science of reform, then reform should be considered either as some sort of non-linear process and/or as a highly political issue to be addressed and resolved through the pulling and hauling of the political process. In this sense, an investigation committee provides a temporary venue to deal with the crisis. It can also be done through existing venues, but the initiation of a crisis inquiry helps to remedy the legitimacy problems incurred as a result of the crisis. Whether this venue manages to articulate an authoritative diagnosis and produce widely supported 'lessons' and 'reforms' is another matter.

One way of bridging the gap between these perspectives is an a priori debate with regard to the preventable nature of a crisis. Very few inquiries begin to ask whether and to which extent the crisis at hand is the result of preventable factors (of the first or second order) or should be considered the unfortunate materialisation of a risk taken. Can terrorist attacks such as 9/11 really be prevented (and at which costs)? If we operate dangerous technology, should we not expect an occasional major accident – and thus debate whether we are willing to run that risk (Perrow 1984)? Such debates would help define the boundaries of inquiry, limiting (but not prohibiting) room for crisis-induced learning and reform.

All this suggests that postcrisis inquiries may help to restore order to a tumultuous period by performing two types of activities. First, these committees should establish direct causes in an authoritative way. They should help people understand what happened before, during and immediately after a crisis. Second, they should set the stage for a political and perhaps societal debate on the necessity of reform. Rather than aiming to 'close' the crisis by presenting a firm set of reforms, they should leave the political dimension of crisis to the political arena.

This may sound like a throwback to the artificial separation between politics and administration, a fiction that has long informed normative debates in public administration and political science. It is, however, quite the opposite. It recognises that the postcrisis phase is intensely political and suggests that the politics of crisis management should take place in the arenas designed for such activities. It moves politics from the back stage to the front stage. In a period when society debates future options and directions, that is exactly where it should be.

Coda: crisis management and the transformation of governance

Ulrich Beck was prophetic when he argued 20 years ago that issues of 'risk' would become the dominant mobilising force in western societies and polities (Beck 1992). The first 5 years of the twenty-first century have borne out his prediction. We live in a world where many social issues and entire domains of public policy have become 'securitised' (Buzan et al. 1997) and where 'threat politics' (Eriksson 2001) has become well and truly institutionalised, pervading public debates, election campaigns and government policy making on issues as widely divergent as education, border control, food chain management, privacy, water management and freedom of religion.

In polities where the discovery, framing and management of threats are the stuff of the main political game in town, crises are no longer marginal phenomena. From occasional disturbances in a political system that is otherwise preoccupied by issues of economic management and welfare provision, crises of various kinds (past and future ones, local and far away ones, natural, technological and antagonistic ones),

have risen to unprecedented prominence on public and political agendas. This heightened salience has occurred partly because, as Beck and
others have shown, the reflexivity of modern technologies of production and social control has increased the scope for truly catastrophic
damage on a transnational scale to human life, property and ecosys-
tems. At the same time, a relative convergence in dominant party ideologies, in contrast to the more adversary divisions that dominated
most of the twentieth century, has created a void to be filled by other
logics of political mobilisation. Finally, the current prominence of
threat, risk and crisis in political discourse and public policy making has also been a by-product of the increasing importance of mass
media in public life (the media thrives on the kinds of ominous stories
and pictures that crises tend to provide). To the extent that the media's
reporting choices shape public attention, politicians cannot but follow
suit in taking these things seriously.

It follows that 'crisis management' – once an esoteric, unprestigious
activity pursued by small bands of expert practitioners and scholars
alike – has now become a highly topical subject. While it is surely an
exaggeration to say, as U.S. Secretary of Defense McNamara is said to
have remarked after the Cuban missile crisis, that 'there is no longer
such a thing as strategy, only crisis management', there is no denying
that today's politicians and officials cannot afford to ignore its imperatives. Crisis management has gone beyond the essentially low-level,
technocratic sphere it was once confined to in all but the foreign and
defence policy domains. It has also become considerably more complex than the mere deployment of 'fixers', 'spin doctors' and 'lightning
rods' as coping mechanisms vis-á-vis scandal-hungry journalists. In the
post-9/11 era we have seen crisis management become professionalised
and institutionalised in many different ways – both in 'politics' and in
'administration'.

To understand what this means, for the way in which we are being
governed and the future of democracy, should be a central imperative of political scientists. It is time for crisis management research to
come out of its academic ghetto and blend in with the mainstay of
research on governance and democracy. Likewise, it is time for mainstream scholars – from those involved in voting studies, policy analysis
and leadership studies to name but a few – to examine much more
systematically, how the 'punctuations' that crises cause in political life
may transform it in fundamental and enduring ways. If this volume

helps convince some of them that it might be worthwhile to make that intellectual leap, it will have served its purpose.

References

Allison, G. T. 1971. Essence of decision: explaining the Cuban missile crisis. Boston: Little Brown.

Allison, G. T., and Zelikov, P. 1999. Essence of decision: explaining the Cuban missile crisis. 2nd edn. New York: Longman.

Beck, U. 1992. Risk society: towards a new modernity. London: Sage. [Translated from first German publication in 1986].

Birkland, T. A. 1997. After disaster: agenda setting, public policy, and focusing events. Washington, DC: Georgetown University Press.

Boin, A., 't Hart, P., Stern, E. and Sundelius, B. 2005. The politics of crisis management: public leadership under pressure. Cambridge, UK: Cambridge University Press.

Boin, R. A., and Otten, M. H. P. 1996. Beyond the crisis window for reform: some ramifications for implementation. Journal of Contingencies and Crisis Management 4(3):149–61.

Buzan, B., Wver, O. and de Wilde, J. 1997. Security: a new framework for analysis. Boulder, CO: Lynne Reinner.

Cohen, M. D., March, J. G. and Olsen, J. P. 1972. A garbage can model of organizational choice. Administrative Science Quarterly 17(1):1–25.

Coombs, W. T. 1999. Ongoing crisis communication: planning, managing and responding. Thousand Oaks, CA: Sage.

Curtin, T., Hayman, D. and Husein, N. 2005. Managing a crisis: a practical guide. Houndmills, UK: Palgrave Macmillan.

Edelman, M., 1971. Politics as symbolic action: mass arousal and quiescence. Chicago: Markham.

Edelman, M., 1977. Political language: words that succeed and policies that fail. New York: Academic Press.

Eriksson, J., (ed.) 2001. Threat politics: new perspectives on security, risk and crisis management. Aldershot, UK: Ashgate.

't Hart, P., 1993. Symbols, rituals and power: the lost dimension in crisis management. Journal of Contingencies and Crisis Management 1(1): 36–50.

't Hart, P., and Rosenthal, U. 1998. Reappraising bureaucratic politics. Mershon International Studies Review 41(2): 233–40.

't Hart, P., and Boin, A. 2001. Between crisis and normalcy: the long shadow of post-crisis politics. In Rosenthal, U., Boin, A. and Comfort, L. K. (eds.) Managing crises: threats, dilemmas and opportunities. Springfield, IL: Charles C. Thomas, pp. 28–46.

't Hart, P., Hesyse, L. and Boin, A. 2001. New trends in crisis management practice and research: setting the agenda. Journal of Contingencies and Crisis Management 9(4):181–88.

Henry, R. A. 2000. You'd better have a hose if you want to put out the fire. Windsor, UK: Gollywobbler Productions.

Heyse, L., Resodihardjo, S. L., Lantink, T. and Lettinga, B. (eds.) 2006. Reform in Europe: breaking the barriers in government. Aldershot, UK: Ashgate.

Hood, C., and Lodge, M. 2002. Pavlovian policy responses to media feeding frenzies? Dangerous dogs regulation in comparative perspective. Journal of Contingencies and Crisis Management 10(1):1–13.

Howarth, D., Norval, A. J. and Stavrakakis, Y. (eds.) 2000. Discourse theory and political analysis: identities, hegemonies and social change. Manchester, UK: Manchester University Press.

Jarman, A., and Kouzmin, A. 1991. Decision pathways from crisis: a contingency-theory simulation heuristic for the Challenger shuttle disaster (1983–1988). In Rosenthal, U., and Pijnenberg, B. (eds.) Crisis management and decision making: simulation oriented scenarios. Dordrecht: Kluwer, pp. 123–57.

Jones, B. D., and Baumgartner, F. R. 2005. The politics of attention: how government prioritizes problems. Chicago: University of Chicago Press.

Keeler, J. 1993. Opening the window for reform: mandates, crises, and extraordinary policy-making. Comparative Political Studies 25(1):433–86.

King, A. (ed.) 2004. Leaders' personalities and the outcomes of democratic elections. Oxford, UK: Oxford University Press.

Kingdon, J. 2003. Agendas, alternatives and public policies. 2nd edn. New York: Longman.

McAllister, I. 2006a. The personalization of politics. In Dalton, R. J., and Klingemann, H.-D. (eds.) Oxford handbook of political behavior. Oxford, UK: Oxford University Press.

McAllister, I. 2006b. Political leaders in Westminster systems. In Aarts, K., Blais, A. and Schmitt, H. (eds.) Political leaders and democratic elections. Oxford, UK: Oxford University Press.

Perrow, C. 1984. Normal accidents: living with high-risk technologies. New York: Basic Books.

Perrow, C. 1994. The limits of safety: the enhancement of a theory of accidents. Journal of Contingencies and Crisis Management 2(4):212–20.

Seeger, M. W., Sellnow, T. L. and Ulmer, R. R. 2003. Communication and organizational crisis. Westport, CT: Praeger.

Tarrow, S. 1994. Power in movement. Cambridge, UK: Cambridge University Press.

Turner, B. A., and Pidgeon, N. 1997. Man-made disasters. 2nd edn. London: Butterworth Heinemann.

Van Duin, M. J. 1992. Van rampen leren: Vergelijkend onderzoek naar de lessen uit spoorwegongevallen, hotelbranden en industriële ongelukken. Den Haag: Haagse Drukkerij en Uitgeverij.

Wagenaar, W. A. 1986. De oorzaak van onmogelijke ongelukken, Deventer: Van Loghum Slaterus.

Wagner-Pacifici, R. 1986. The Moro morality play: terrorism as social drama. Chicago: University of Chicago Press.

Wagner-Pacifici, R. 1994. Discourse and destruction: the city of Philadelphia versus MOVE. Chicago: University of Chicago Press.

Wilkins, L. 1987. Shared vulnerability: the media and American perceptions of the Bhopal disaster. New York: Greenwood Press.

Wilkins, L., Walters, T. and Walters, L. M. (eds.) 1989. Bad tidings: communication and catastrophe. New York: Lawrence Erlbaum Associates.

Index

accountability
  acknowledgement of, 55, 144
  content analysis, 134
  defined, 9
  pre-existing accountability episodes, 35
  processes, 11
  situational contexts and, 18
  trends impacting, 11–13
advisory systems
  Bush administration, 43–44
  open versus closed, 40–41
advocacy coalition framework, 189–197
  collective action and, 193–195
  policy change and, 195
agenda-setting crises, 19, 291
  dioxin contamination, 164
Al-Qaeda, 70–71
Asian tsunami
  blame management, 123, 140, 143–144
  as incomprehensible crisis, 121
  responses compared by country, 124
attention-based logic
  counter-terrorism policy, 197–200
  versus belief-based logic, 197
Aznar, José María. See also Madrid bombings (Spain)
  lame duck, 81
  latent vulnerability, 66–68
  leadership style, 68, 81–82

Belgium. See also dioxin contamination; Dutroux crisis (Belgium)
  parliamentary investigations, 157–158
  political system, 151–152
belief-based logic

counter-terrorism policy, 197–200
  versus attention-based logic, 197
blame avoidance
  contestability and, 46–47
  tactics, 52–56
  versus blame management, 117–118
blame games, 11, 17–18
  centralisation of executive power, 143–144
  control needs and, 37
  crises types and avoidance of, 41
  defined, 116
  dueling divergent perceptions and, 45–46
  Hurricane Katrina, 55
  loci of blame, 120
  Madrid bombings, 62–83
  outcomes, 120
  pre-existing, 35
  sensitivity to context, 39
blame management
  Asian tsunami, 114
  strategies, 116–121
  versus blame avoidance, 117–118
blaming tree, 120–121
Brown, Michael, 52–55, 286
bureau-political conflict
  Bush administration, 43
  control needs and, 36–37
Bush, George W. See also Hurricane Katrina (US); September 11 (9/11) attacks;
  closed advisory system, 43–44
  elite damage, 34, 57
  explaining behavior of ignorance, 49
  leadership style, 43–44
  meaning making, 47–50
  political crisis, 34
  political learning and, 15–16

cathartic crises, 41–42
Challenger space shuttle disaster,
    232–233, 243–245,
    252
collective action, 193–195
Columbia space shuttle disaster,
    232–233
commissions. *See also* specific
    commission
    analytical perspectives, 260
    independence, 308–309
    politics of, 303–309
communication of public information,
    8, 64
complexity scores, 38–39
constructing agency, 118–119
    Asian tsunami, 130
    content analysis, 131
    defined, 116
constructing responsibility,
    119–120
    Asian tsunami, 133
    content analysis, 137
    defined, 116
constructing severity, 117–118
    Asian tsunami, 123–130
    content analysis, 128
    defined, 116
contextual factors, 20–21,
    300–302
control needs
    bureau-political conflict and,
        36–37
    crisis management and, 36–37
counter-framing, 65
    Madrid bombings, 70–71, 74
    public opinion and, 73
counter-terrorism policy, stability,
    197–200
credibility, framing and, 64
crises
    academic study of, 5–6
    agenda setting, 19
    as framing contests, 286
    as tipping points, 65–66
    defined, 3
    incomprehensible, 19
    meaning-making stage, 47
    mismanaged, 19
    triggers, types of, 3

types of, 19, 41
    dimensions for determining, 41
    dueling divergent perceptions on,
        45–46
    leadership style and, 41–43
crisis analysis, operational versus
    strategic, 7–8
crisis exploitation, 287, 297–303
crisis management
    challenges, 8–9
    control needs and, 36–37
    domains of, 90
    governance and, 312–314
    historic record and, 19–20
    Hurricane Katrina, 51–56
    leadership style, impact of, 35–44
    personality, impact of, 35
    political careers and, 4–5, 76, 88–89,
        138–139, 156, 161, 294–295
    research on, 6
    sensitivity to context and, 37–40
    voting behaviour and, 88–93
crisis politics, 4–5. *See also*
    accountability; learning
    defined, 17
    processes, 18
cronyism, 52

debate framing, strategies for, 18
decision-making, sensitivity to context
    and, 37–40
'definition of the situation,' 5–6, 41,
    47, 91–92
deuterolearning, 14
dioxin contamination, 148–149,
    155–157
    agenda-setting crisis, 164
    blame management, 150–151, 155
    contextual factors, 169–170
    investigation, 164–168, 170–171,
        176
double-loop learning, versus
    single-loop, 241–242, 245–247
drama, 95, 97, 105
    government popularity and, 106
    statistics, 113
dueling divergent perceptions, 45–46
Dutroux crisis (Belgium), 148,
    152–155
    accountability, 163

blame management, 150–151, 154
contextual factors, 169–170
incomprehensible crisis, 159
investigation, 154, 158–164,
    170–171, 176
  reform proposals, 162–163
  stakeholders, 161–162
reforms, 163–164

E. coli contamination. *See* Walkerton
    water contamination (Canada)
Elbe flood (Germany)
  crisis management chronology, 89
  fast-burning crises, 87
  framing analysis, 100
  media analysis, 93–107
  political outcome, 85–89, 108
elite damage, 13, 294
  Bush, George W., 34, 57
elite escape, 13, 294–295
elite manoeuvering, 297–303
elite reinvigoration, 13, 294
  Schröder, Gerhard, 85–108
emergency response, ineffective, 33
endogenous learning, versus
    exogenous, 239–241, 243–245
Euskadi Ta Askatasuna (ETA)
  Madrid bombings blamed on, 63,
    68–70
  modus operandi, 69, 72
exogenous learning, versus
    endogenous, 239–241, 243–245
explaining behavior of ignorance, 49

fallout of crises, 8–9
fast-burning crises, 41
  Elbe flood, 87, 289
  leadership style and, 41, 43
fear, discourse of, 12
Federal Emergency Management
    Agency (FEMA), 52–55
fine tuning, 16, 215–216, 295–296
framing
  content analysis, 135
  contests, 72, 286
  counter-framing, 65
  credibility and, 64
  defined, 64
  Madrid bombings, 62–70, 83
  mass media and, 33–34, 73–76, 92

perceptual, contestability of, 46–47
political hurdles to, 65
pre-existing political context and,
    44–45
public demonstrations and, 72–74,
    78
rally-'round-the-flag effect and, 82
reversal of fortune and, 63–66
rigidification, 77
statistics, 113
strategies, 18, 116–121
framing tree, 120–121

'garbage can'
  commission independence, 308
  policy reform and, 311
government popularity
  drama and, 106
  mass media and, 86, 93–107
  statistics, 111
  variables, 102

high-reliability organisations (HROs),
    learning in, 14
historic record, crisis management and,
    19–20, 142
Hurricane Katrina (US), 51–56. *See
    also* Bush, George W.
  accountability, 33–35, 57
  blame games, 33–57
  ineffective emergency response to,
    33
  meaning making stage, 47–50
  as policy fiasco, 33–34

incomprehensible crises, 19, 289–290
  Asian tsunami, 121
  Dutroux crisis, 159
information needs
  complexity scores, 38–39
  decision-making and, 37–38
inquiry and investigation. *See also*
    commissions
  analytical perspectives, 256
  comparative overview, 304
  controlled versus independent,
    51–52
  crisis exploitation and, 309–312
  Hurricane Katrina, 51–56
  lack of cooperation with, 56

inquiry and investigation (*cont.*)
  learning through, 14–15
  political context, 150–151
  process, 223–224, 226–227
  process management, 151
  timing of, 144
Iraqi war, 66–68

Janssens, Charles, 165
Jerusalem banquet hall collapse (Israel)
  investigation, 216–217
  policy reform, 224–227
  policy stasis, 218–219
  regulatory failure, 216–219
journalists. *See* mass media
'just world'
  commission independence, 308
  policy reform and, 311

lame ducks, 81
latent vulnerability, 66–68
leadership style
  Aznar, José María, 68, 81–82
  Bush, George W., 43–44
  impact on crisis management,
    35–44
  public opinion influenced by, 35,
    37
  types of crises and, 41–43
learning
  defined, 9
  endogenous versus exogenous,
    239–241, 243–245
  examples of, 14–15
  impediments to, 15
  organisational, 14, 232–252
  single-loop versus double-loop,
    241–242, 245–247
  situational contexts and, 18
  technical versus political evaluation,
    242–243, 247–250
learning perspective, 260, 262–265
'lessons learned', Hurricane Katrina,
    55–56
'lightning rods', 13, 33–34
  defined, 52–53
  Hurricane Katrina, 53–55
long-shadow crises, 41, 289–291
  Hurricane Katrina, 47
  leadership style and, 41, 43

Madrid bombings (Spain)
  blame game, 62–83
  counterframing, 70–71, 74
  framing, 62–78, 83
    contest, 71–73
  Iraqi war and, 66–68
  political outcome, 62
  public demonstrations, 72–74
  public opinion and, 66–67
  reversal of fortune in, 62–83
mass media
  accountability and, 12
  as contextual factor, 21
  blame and, 45, 52
  framing and, 33–34, 72–76, 92
  government popularity and, 86, 93
  Hurricane Katrina, 33–34, 52
  micro media, 66
  middle media, 66
  new media, 66
  political outcome and, 301–302
  tipping points and, 65–66
  voting behaviour and, 90
meaning-making stage, 47
media analysis
  Asian tsunami, 122–124
  Elbe flood, 93–107
  micro media, 66
  middle media, 66
Miles' law, 298–299
mismanaged crises, 19, 290–291
modus operandi
  Al-Qaeda, 71
  Euskadi Ta Askatasuna, 69, 72
multiple streams theory, 189–197
  collective action and, 193–195
  policy change and, 195

National Aeronautics and Space
    Administration (NASA)
  Apollo project, 233–236
  calculated risk, 236–237
  Challenger space shuttle disaster,
    232–233, 243–245, 252
  Columbia space shuttle disaster,
    232–233
  human space flight history and,
    233–238
  nature of the risk, 220–221, 224
  new media, framing and, 66, 78–80

New Orleans. *See also* Hurricane
  Katrina (U.S.)
  levy system failure, 33
operational level of crisis response,
  7–8, 90–91, 97, 112
organisational learning, 14

paradigm shift, 17, 296–297
personality of political leaders, public
  opinion influenced by, 35
Persson, Göran
  Asian tsunami, 132–133, 138–139,
    142–143
  historic record, 142
'perverse effects'
  commission independence, 308–309
  policy reform and, 311
policy fiasco, Hurricane Katrina as,
  33–34
policy reform, 16–17, 296–297
  commission independence and, 311
  crisis exploitation and, 310–311
  factors impacting, 219–224, 227
  impediments to, 15
  rhetoric of, 16
  Walkerton water contamination,
    214–215
policy stasis
  Jerusalem banquet hall collapse,
    218–219
  Stockholm embassy seizure, 183
political careers. *See also* specific leader
  impact of crises on, 4–5, 13, 20, 34,
    62, 76
political context, 221–226
political decisions, past, blame
  vulnerability and, 45
politicisation of crises. *See* crisis
  politics
pre-existing political context
  framing and, 44–45
  Hurricane Katrina and, 35
priming effects, 90, 100–102
public demonstrations, framing and,
  72–74, 78
public information, communication of,
  8
public institutions, impact of crises on,
  16–17, 295–297

public opinion
  contestability of, 46–47
  counter-framing and, 73
  leadership style and, 35, 37
  Madrid bombings and, 66–67
  mass media and, 12, 34
  personality and, 35
public policy
  fine tuning of, 16
  impact of crises on, 16–17
  paradigm shift in, 17
  punctuated equilibrium theory,
    189–197
  collective action and, 193–195
  policy change and, 195

rally-'round-the-flag effect, 62–65,
  82
realpolitik perspective, 260,
  266–271
regulatory failures
  Jerusalem banquet hall collapse,
    216–219
  Walkerton water contamination,
    212–216
reports, learning through, 14–15
responsibility. *See* accountability;
  blame
reversal of fortune
  Elbe flood, 85–108
  Madrid bombings and, 62–83
rhetoric of reform, 16
rigidification, framing and, 77
risk regulation, 208, 210–212
rituals, 91
  defined, 91
  of solidarity, 81
Rogers Commission, 243–245

Scandinavia, response to Asian
  tsunami, 114, 123, 140,
  145
scapegoats, constructing responsibility,
  119–120
Schröder, Gerhard. *See also* Elbe flood
  (Germany)
  crisis management, 88–89
  elite reinvigoration, 85–108
security policies, impact of 9/11
  attacks on, 5

sensitivity to context
  blame games and, 39
  complexity scores, 38–39
  crisis management and, 37–40
September 11 (9/11) attacks
  crisis research funding prompted by,
    5–6
  impact on public institutions, 5
  impact on security policies, 5
  investigation, 255–261
  learning and, 15
  political outcomes of, 4
September 11 (9/11) Commission
  analytical perspectives, 262–271,
    277–278
  Bush administration support of,
    273–274
  impact, 257–261
  interpretive authority, 277–278
single-loop learning, versus
    double-loop, 241–242, 245–247
situational factors, 18–20, 299–300
slow-burning crises, 41
  leadership style and, 42
social catharsis, mechanisms of, 9
space shuttle disasters. *See* National
    Aeronautics and Space
    Administration (NASA)
stakeholder interest, 224, 227
Stockholm embassy seizure (Sweden)
  counter-terrorism policy, 197–202
  police response, 183, 184–185
  investigation, 186–187
  proposed reforms, 185–188

policy stasis, 183, 189–197
political outcome, 188–189
strategic level of crisis response, 8
symbolic level of crisis response,
    91–92, 97
  government popularity and,
    93
  speed of response, 91
  statistics, 112
symbolic perspective, 260,
    277–278

terrorist attacks, 226. *See also* specific
    attack or group
timing of crises, 20–21, 300–301
tipping points
  crises as, 65–66
  mass media and, 65–66
tsunami. *See* Asian tsunami

Vanhanen, Matti, 133–136
Verwilghen, Marc, 160–161
victims, accountability and, 12–13
voting behaviour
  impact on crisis management,
    88–93
  mass media and, 90

Walkerton water contamination
    (Canada)
  blaming, 213
  fine tuning, 215–216
  policy reform, 214–215, 220–224
  regulatory failure, 212–216